Culture, Ideology and Social Process

The Open University

'Popular Culture' Course Team

Authors

Tony Bennett *(Chairman)*
Tony Aldgate
Geoffrey Bourne
David Cardiff
Alan Clarke
Noel Coley
James Donald
Dave Elliott
Ruth Finnegan
Francis Frascina
John Golby
Stuart Hall
Graham Martin
Colin Mercer
Richard Middleton
Dave Morley
John Muncie
Gill Perry
Bill Purdue
Carrie Roberts
Paddy Scannell
Grahame Thompson
Ken Thompson
Bernard Waites
Paul Willis
Janet Woollacott

Other Members

Jane Bailey — *Course Manager*
Susan Boyd-Bowman — *BBC Producer*
Kate Clements — *Editor*
John Greenwood — *Liaison Librarian*
Liz Lane — *Editor*
Vic Lockwood — *BBC Producer*
Robert Nicodemus — *Representative from the Institute of Educational Technology*
Lesley Passey — *Designer*
Mike Philps — *BBC Producer*
Sarah Shepherd — *Editor*

Culture, Ideology and Social Process

A Reader

edited by Tony Bennett, Graham Martin,
Colin Mercer and Janet Woollacott
at the Open University

B.T. Batsford Ltd
in association with
The Open University Press

First published 1981
Reprinted 1983, 1985, 1986, 1987

Typeset by Typewise Limited, Wembley
and printed in Great Britain by
Billing & Sons Ltd, Worcester
for the publishers
B.T. Batsford Ltd
4 Fitzhardinge Street
London W1H 0AH

British Library Cataloguing in Publication Data
Culture, ideology and social process
1. Sociology
I. Bennett, Tony
301 HM51
ISBN 0-7134-4314-6 Pbk

Contents

Acknowledgements

Grateful acknowledgement is made to the following sources for permission to reproduce material used in this Reader:
Hall, Stuart (1980) 'Cultural Studies: two paradigms', *Media, Culture and Society*, Vol 2, No 1, copyright © 1980 by Academic Press Inc (London) Limited; Williams, Raymond (1961) *The Long Revolution*, Chatto and Windus Ltd, copyright © 1961 Raymond Williams; Clarke, J. et al (1976) 'Subcultures, cultures and class' in Hall, S. and Jefferson, T. (eds.) *Resistance through Rituals: Youth Subcultures in Post-War Britain*, Hutchinson, copyright © Centre for Contemporary Cultural Studies, University of Birmingham; Willis, P. (1977) *Learning to Labour: How Working Class Kids get Working Class Jobs*, Saxon House; McRobbie, A. (1980) 'Settling Accounts with Subcultures: a feminist critique', *Screen Education*, No 34; Culler, J. (1976) *Saussure*, Fontana, copyright © Jonathan Culler; Volosinov, V. N. (1973) *Marxism and the Philosophy of Language*, Academic Press Inc, New York, copyright © 1973 Seminar Press; Coward, R. and Ellis, J. (1977) 'Structuralism and the Subject: a critique' in *Language and Materialism*, Routledge and Kegan Paul Ltd; Barthes, Roland (1977) *Image/Music/Text* trans Stephen Heath, Fontana, first published in French by du Seuil, Paris, 1977, copyright © 1977 Roland Barthes, translation copyright © 1977 Stephen Heath; Gramsci, Antonio (1971) extracts from Hoare, Q. and Nowell-Smith, G. (trans. and eds.) *Selections from the Prison Notebooks of Antonio Gramsci*, Lawrence and Wishart, copyright © 1971, Geoffrey Nowell-Smith and Quintin Hoare; Mouffe, C. (1979) 'Hegemony and Ideology in Gramsci' in Mouffe, C. (ed) *Gramsci and Marxist Theory*, Routledge and Kegan Paul Ltd; Gray, Robert (1977) 'Bourgeois Hegemony in Victorian Britain' in Bloomfield, J. (ed.) *Class, Hegemony, Party*, Lawrence and Wishart Ltd; Davies, T. (1978) 'Education, Ideology and Literature', *Red Letters*, No 7; Roberts, K. (1978) *Contemporary Society and the Growth of Leisure*, Longman; Tagg, J. (1980) 'Power and Photography – A Means of Surveillance: The Photograph as Evidence in Law', *Screen Education*, No 36.

The photographs reproduced following p. 308 appear by kind permission of the following:
Fig. 1, West Midlands Police; Fig. 2, Stockport Metropolitan Borough, Library of Local Studies; Fig. 3, Royal Society of Medicine; Fig. 4, Public Record Office, ref. 2/CASE 4/1, Crown copyright material reproduced by permission of the Controller of Her Majesty's Stationery Office; Figs. 5 and 6, Dr Barnardo's Homes; Figs. 7 and 8, Mansell Collection; Fig. 9, The Master and Fellows of Trinity College, Cambridge.

Editors' Introduction

This collection of readings has been prepared with a view to assembling, in one volume, representative statements of the different theoretical traditions that have most influenced the development of cultural studies over the last two decades and which, today, comprise the main contending lines of approach to both teaching and research in this rapidly expanding area of inquiry. Conceived with the needs of students taking the Open University course *Popular Culture* uppermost in mind, the Reader aims to make the somewhat complicated and often abstract debates which have characterized this area of study accessible to the uninitiated in a way that should be of value to both teachers and students more generally.

The shape of the Reader can perhaps best be explained by way of a commentary on the intellectual biography of Raymond Williams. Writing in 1958, Williams, surveying the work of such Marxist cultural critics of the 1930s as Christopher Caudwell, indicated that the debate as to whether or not Caudwell's work could be regarded as authentically Marxist was 'a quarrel which one who is not a Marxist will not attempt to resolve' (Williams, 1963, p.269). More generally, throughout *Culture and Society* – and especially in the chapter on 'Marxism and Culture' – Williams is careful to distance himself from Marxism; a valued tradition, yes, but not one within which Williams was willing to locate his own work. By contrast, in the introduction to *Marxism and Literature,* first published in 1977, Williams forcefully states that the thesis of cultural materialism developed in that book 'is, in my view, a Marxist theory, and indeed that in its specific fields it is, in spite of and even because of the relative unfamiliarity of some of its elements, part of what I at least see as the central thinking of Marxism' (Williams, 1977, pp. 5-6).

This was clearly a significant shift in self-location on Williams's part, the first time that he had been willing publicly to nail his colours firmly to the Marxist tradition. In truth, however, the shift is explicable less with regard to changes in Williams's own concerns and theoretical orientations – these have exhibited a remarkable constancy from the fifties through to the eighties – than to changes in the internal composition and structure of Marxism. The Marxism from which Williams was anxious to dissociate himself in the fifties was one which, so far as questions of culture were concerned, was characterized by an extreme form of economic reductionism. Culture, within the topography of Marx's and Engels's unfortunate metaphor, was merely the 'superstructure' erected upon, determined by and, seemingly, having little impact on the economic 'base' of society. During the intervening period, however, the region of Marxist theory concerned specifically with questions of culture and ideology has been so intensively re-worked as to be virtually unrecognizable. Extreme reductionist formulations of the relationships between culture, ideology and the economy have been deeply, and hopefully lastingly buried with the result that, today, the central questions concern not *whether* culture and ideology should be regarded as 'relatively autonomous' in relation to economic and political processes; rather, contemporary debates focus much more closely on the *precise ways* in which this relative autonomy might be conceived and accounted for. The stress that had previously been placed on the *determination* of culture has been displaced, with the emphasis now more clearly falling on the *action* of culture, on the view of culture as a *practice* which relates *interactively* with economic and political processes, shaping and conditioning these as well as being shaped and conditioned by them.

Raymond Williams has, of course, played a central part in these developments. Indeed, together with the historical studies of E.P. Thompson, Williams's early writings provided the basis for that view of culture – subsequently significantly extended and modified in the work that has emerged from the Centre for Contemporary Cultural Studies at the University of Birmingham – as the set of practices through which men and women actively respond to the conditions of their social existence, creatively fashioning experienced social relationships into diverse and structured patterns of living, thinking and feeling. The emphasis, within this account, is placed on the notion of human agency. It is this that provides the crucial mediation between the determined conditions of a given cultural practice and the outcome of that practice, connecting and yet at the same time separating the two. The transition between the conditions of cultural practice and its outcome is never automatic, never guaranteed in advance; how the one is translated into the other depends on how the gap between them is filled by the operations of human agency.

In short, within this tradition – known, by convention, as 'culturalism' – the stress is placed on the *making* of culture rather than on its determined conditions. This perspective, developed initially as a distinctively British contribution to Marxist cultural debate, was complemented in the late sixties by the translation of a body of continental Marxist literary theory – especially the works of Georg Lukács and Lucien Goldmann – which, although in a language that owed as much to Hegel as it did to Marx, offered related ways of accounting for the relative autonomy of culture. Cutting against both of these traditions, however, the influence of structuralism has, over the same period, suggested alternative and, indeed, in some respects, radically opposing ways of conceiving and accounting for the relative autonomy of culture and ideology. (One of the difficulties involved in disentangling the often complicated relationships between culturalism and structuralism is that, whereas 'culture' is a central concept within the former, it is almost entirely absent from the latter where, as Stuart Hall argues in the introductory essay to this volume, the term 'ideology' – operating a related but not entirely symmetrical range of meanings – has been preferred). The term 'structuralism' of course, is used here merely as a convenient label. There are certainly real and important differences between the various bodies of theory to which it has conventionally been applied and nearly all of the thinkers who have been grouped together under this heading – Lévi-Strauss in anthropology, Roland Barthes in literary criticism, Jacques Lacan in psychoanalysis, Michel Foucault in the history of the sciences – have, at one time or the other, vigorously repudiated the label. Nonetheless, the term has a value if used, in a qualified way, to refer to a broadly based and, in some respects, radically heterogeneous intellectual tradition which derives its 'complex unity' from the degree to which the different strands within it owe a shared indebtedness to the pioneering work of Ferdinand de Saussure in the field of linguistics.

According to structuralist accounts, the relative autonomy of culture and ideology in relation to economic and political processes is secured not by an insistence on the mediating role of human agency. Rather, the stress is placed on the specific nature of those supposedly irreducible formal properties which characterize the structure of different types of signifying practice and distinguish them one from another. In structuralist parlance, the phrase 'relative autonomy' does not convey the sense, implied by its usage within culturalist writings, that culture and ideology constitute the spheres within which human agency asserts itself in ways that are, to a degree, untrammeled by prior determinations of whatever kinds – economic, social or political. Rather, it registers the claim that the spheres of culture and ideology themselves consist of sets of *relatively autonomous determinations*, of *structures* – the structures of language, of myth, of literature – which mould and condition the forms of human symbolic exchange in ways that are, again to a degree, independent of the immediate context of prevailing economic, social and political relationships. It is this emphasis on the determining properties of the structural regularities exhibited by different forms of signifying practice that most clearly distinguishes structuralist from culturalist approaches. Whereas, within the latter, cultural forms are viewed as the objectifications of the socially shaped, lived experiences of different subjects – whether these be conceived as individuals or as social groups, the 'collective subjects' of Goldmann's world-view analysis – structuralists have contended that cultural forms are not the products but the producers of experience. Structuralism views experience not as the ground of culture but as its effect, the product of the ways in which individuals are transformed into thinking, feeling and perceiving subjects of different kinds in the context of differently structured relations of symbolic exchange. In extreme structuralist formulations, the orders of culture – of language, cinema, painting, literature, television – have been conceived as so many 'machines' for producing and regulating the orders of subjectivity; determinations of the imaginary orders which regulate the consciousness of human subjects. The mediating role which culturalism accords to the category of human agency is necessarily called into question by such a view. For the structuralist, the diverse forms of human agency – the forms in which men and women think, feel and act out their lives – are the product of cultural determinations, not the other way round.

The formation of cultural studies as a distinctively interdisciplinary body of theoretical and empirical work concerned with the connections between culture, ideology and social process has been paced and conditioned by the tension between the contending perspectives of culturalism and structuralism. In cultural studies, as Stuart Hall argues, 'theirs are the "names of the game"'. But not the only names. In particular, mention must also be made of Antonio Gramsci, not least because the concept of hegemony associated with his writings has suggested ways in which the oppositions between culturalism and structuralism might be by-passed to yield a way of posing questions concerning the relations between cultural and economic and political processes which, whilst retaining elements of both, would also correct their polemical and one-sided excesses. If, as Stuart Hall intimates, cultural studies is currently poised to enter into a post-culturalist, post-structuralist phase, recasting the terms of the debate by integrating both perspectives within a new synthesis, it is likely that Gramsci's work will provide the meeting place at which that synthesis will be forged.

The readings collected in this volume are intended as a condensation of this history. In 'Cultural studies: two paradigms', Stuart Hall offers an overview of both culturalist and structuralist paradigms and of the complex ways in which these have interacted with and influenced one another within the development of cultural studies in Britain since the late fifties. It is a commanding essay which takes due account of both the weaknesses and strengths of each position and which outlines the ways in which they have, between them, clearly dislocated cultural studies from its roots, in the late fifties, in the radical offshoots of Leavisism. Tracing the various stages of its development from its beginnings in the early works of Raymond Williams and Richard Hoggart, through to the subsequent influence of such structuralist theorists as Louis Althusser and Jacques Lacan, Hall claims that the result has been the formation of a radically new problematic concerned with the active role played by cultural and ideological practices in the processes whereby existing social formations are reproduced or, more exceptionally, transformed. Although careful to stress the respects in which culturalist and structuralist perspectives have developed complementary insights within a project that has been, in many respects, a shared one, Hall is equally careful not to minimize the differences between them. 'In their sustained and mutually reinforcing antagonisms,' he concludes, 'they hold out no promise of an easy synthesis. But, between them, they define where, if at all, is the space, and what are the limits, within which such a synthesis might be constituted.'

The second and third sections of this Reader reflect the balanced spirit of this conclusion. They are intended to introduce the reader to both the strengths and weaknesses of the structuralist and culturalist perspectives, as well as to the ways in which these have influenced one another. We have accordingly aimed, in both of these sections, to include exemplary statements of the founding assumptions of the two approaches together with examples of the ways in which these have been applied and, as a result, modified, in the context of empirical work. Each section also includes contributions which question the founding assumptions of the two approaches. (The relationships between the various readings are outlined in greater detail in the relevant Section Introductions). In the third section of the Reader, a selection of those passages from Gramsci's translated writings which bear most directly on questions of culture and ideology is complemented by Chantal Mouffe's extrapolation of the significance of Gramsci's concept of hegemony for the development of a non-reductionist theory of ideology. The contributions of Robert Gray and Tony Davies illustrate the ways in which Gramsci's work has influenced contemporary debates in both historical and literary scholarship.

In a recent survey of the development of cultural studies, Richard Johnson has argued that 'many of the most important questions in the theory and sociology of culture are now posed not between Marxist and other accounts, but *within Marxism itself*'. A key element in 'this very odd state of affairs', he continues, 'is the absence of an emergent rival system capable of thinking about culture as a whole (rather than some special, class-bound and form-bound part of it)' (Johnson, 1979, p.67). This is, indeed, a significant development. In the 1930s, Williams has argued, the English Marxist critics not only lost in their contest with T.S. Eliot, Leavis and the *Scrutiny* group; they *deserved* to lose, so reductive were their formulations (see Williams, 1971). The ascendancy of Marxist cultural theory since the sixties has, likewise, been a *deserved* ascendancy in the respect that the capacity it has developed to 'think' the connections between culture and society non-reductively has given it an edge over such indigenous traditions as that exemplified by Leavis as well as over the implanted traditions of American and European sociology. It is not, however, an uncontested ascendancy; the centre of debate may well be *within* Marxism, but there are still important and unresolved debates *between* Marxism and other approaches. The final section of the Reader offers instances – albeit two very different ones – of such debates. Whereas Ken Roberts outlines the case against Marxist cultural theory from a liberal-pluralist perspective, John Tagg's article offers a useful summary and application of the central themes embodied in the work of Michel Foucault, an enigmatic figure who, in his constant refusal to be labelled, resists easy classification and who, in questioning traditional Marxist conceptions of the nature of power and of the way in which it is exercised, has seemed constantly to threaten to upset not this or that aspect of Marxism but the whole apple-cart. In spite of this, or perhaps because of it, Foucault's work has come to occupy a central position within contemporary Marxist theoretical debate. For some, his radical refusal of any form of reductionism is regarded as a vital and necessary antidote to the legacy of the base-superstructure metaphor. For others (Stuart Hall, for example) the refusal is too radical, embodying 'so thoroughgoing a scepticism about any determinacy or relationship between practices' that it becomes impossible to specify how culture and ideology interact with economic, social and political processes in any other than an *ad hoc*, contingent way.

This book is largely the result of the collective effort of a number of people involved in preparing the Open University course *Popular Culture*. The editors would therefore like to thank all members of the course team for the part they played in the discussions which gave birth to the shape of this Reader. In particular, our thanks to Geoffrey Bourne, James Donald, Ruth Finnegan, John Muncie and Bernard Waites for their help both in suggesting articles for inclusion in the Reader and indicating how best they might be edited. Thanks also to Jane Bailey, whose assistance in coordinating the activities of the editors has been invaluable, and to Deirdre Smith – a secretary valued as much for her unfailing good humour as for her remarkable efficiency. We are also indebted to John Taylor of the Publishing Division at the Open University for the assistance he has rendered the course team in all stages of the production of this Reader. Finally, we are grateful to all of the contributors to this volume for allowing us to publish their work in an abbreviated form.

References

JOHNSON, R., 'Culture and the historians', in Clarke, J., Critcher, C., and Johnson, R., *Working Class Culture: Studies in history and theory,* (London: Hutchinson, 1979).

WILLIAMS, R., *Culture and Society 1780-1950* (Harmondsworth: Penguin, 1963).

WILLIAMS, R., 'Literature and Sociology: in memory of Lucien Goldmann' *New Left Review*, no. 67, 1971.

WILLIAMS, R., *Marxism and Literature* (Oxford: Oxford University Press, 1977).

SECTION 1

Overview

1 Cultural studies: two paradigms

Stuart Hall

In serious, critical intellectual work, there are no 'absolute beginnings' and few unbroken continuities.... What we find, instead, is an untidy but characteristic unevenness of development. What is important are the significant *breaks* – where old lines of thought are disrupted, older constellations displaced, and elements, old and new, are regrouped around a different set of premises and themes. ... Such shifts in perspective reflect, not only the results of an internal intellectual labour, but the manner in which real historical developments and transformations are appropriated in thought, and provide Thought, not with its guarantee of 'correctness' but with its fundamental orientations, its conditions of existence. It is because of this complex articulation between thinking and historical reality, reflected in the social categories of thought, and the continuous dialectic between 'knowledge' and 'power,' that the breaks are worth recording.

Cultural Studies, as a distinctive problematic, emerges from one such moment, in the mid-1950s. It was certainly not the first time that its characteristic questions had been put on the table. Quite the contrary. The two books which helped to stake out the new terrain – Hoggart's *Uses of Literacy* and Williams's *Culture and Society* – were both, in different ways, works (in part) of recovery. Hoggart's book took its reference from the 'cultural debate,' long sustained in the arguments around 'mass society' and in the tradition of work identified with Leavis and *Scrutiny*. *Culture and Society* reconstructed a long tradition which Williams defined as consisting, in sum, of 'a record of a number of important and continuing reactions to... changes in our social, economic and political life' and offering 'a special kind of map by means of which the nature of the changes can be explored' (Williams, 1963, p. 16). The books looked, at first, simply like an updating of these earlier concerns, with reference to the post-war world. Retrospectively, their 'breaks' with the

Source: *Media, Culture and Society*, No. 2, 1980, pp. 57-72.

traditions of thinking in which they were situated seems as important, if not more so, than their continuity with them. The *Uses of Literacy* did set out – much in the spirit of 'practical criticism' – to 'read' working class culture for the values and meanings embodied in its patterns and arrangements: as if they were certain kinds of 'texts'. But the application of this method to a living culture, and the rejection of the terms of the 'cultural debate' (polarized around the high/low culture distinction) was a thorough-going departure. *Culture and Society* – in one and the same movement – constituted a tradition (*the* 'culture-and-society' tradition), defined its 'unity' (not in terms of common positions but in its characteristic concerns and the idiom of its inquiry), itself made a distinctive modern contribution to it – *and* wrote its epitaph. The Williams book which succeeded it – *The Long Revolution* – clearly indicated that the 'culture-and-society' mode of reflection could only be completed and developed by moving somewhere else – to a significantly different kind of analysis. The very difficulty of some of the writing in *The Long Revolution* – with its attempt to 'theorize' on the back of a tradition resolutely empirical and particularist in its idiom of thought ... stems, in part, from this determination to *move on*. The 'good' and the 'bad' parts of *The Long Revolution* both arise from its status as a work 'of the break'. The same could be said of E. P. Thompson's *Making of the English Working Class,* which belongs decisively to this 'moment', even though, chronologically it appeared somewhat later. It, too, had been 'thought' within certain distinctive historical traditions: English marxist historiography, Economic and 'Labour' History. But in its foregrounding of the questions of culture, consciousness and experience, and its accent on agency, it also made a decisive break: with a certain kind of technological evolutionism, with a reductive economism, and an organizational determinism. Between them, these three books constituted the *caesura* out of which – among other things – 'Cultural Studies' emerged.

They were, of course, seminal and formative texts. They were not, however, in any sense 'text-books' for the founding of a new academic sub-discipline ... Whether historical or contemporary in focus, they were, themselves, focused *by*, organized through and constituted responses to, the immediate pressures of the time and society in which they were written. They not only took 'culture' seriously – as a dimension without which historical transformations, past and present, simply could not adequately be thought. They were, themselves, 'cultural' in the *Cultural and Society* sense. They forced on their readers' attention the proposition that 'concentrated in the word *culture* are questions directly raised by the great historical changes which the changes in industry, democracy and class, in their own way, represent, and to which the changes in art are a closely related response' (Williams, 1963, p. 16). This was a question for the 1960s and 70s, as well as the 1860s and 70s.

And this is perhaps the point to note that this line of thinking was roughly coterminous with what has been called the 'agenda' of the early New Left, to which these writers, in one sense or another, belonged, and whose texts these were. This connection placed the 'politics of intellectual work' squarely at the centre of Cultural Studies from the beginning – a concern from which, fortunately, it has never been, and can never be, freed. In a deep sense, the 'settling of accounts' in *Culture and Society*, the first part of *The Long Revolution*, Hoggart's densely particular, concrete study of some aspects of working-class culture and Thompson's historical reconstruction of the formation of a class culture and popular traditions in the 1790-1830 period formed, between them, the break, and defined the space from which a new area of study and practice opened....

'Culture' was the site of the convergence. But what definitions of this core concept emerged from this body of work? ... The fact is that no single, unproblematic definition of 'culture' is to be found here. The concept remains a complex one – a site of convergent interests, rather than a logically or conceptually clarified idea. This 'richness' is an area of continuing tension and difficulty in the field. It might be useful, therefore, briefly to resume the characteristic stresses and emphases through which the concept has arrived at its present state of (in)-determinacy....

Two rather different ways of conceptualizing 'culture' can be drawn out of the many suggestive formulations in Raymond Williams's *Long Revolution*. The first relates 'culture' to the sum of the available descriptions through which societies make sense of and reflect their common experiences. This definition takes up the earlier stress on 'ideas', but subjects it to a thorough reworking. The conception of 'culture' is itself democratized and socialized. It no longer consists of the sum of the 'best that has been thought and said', regarded as the summits of an achieved civilization – that ideal of perfection to which, in earlier usage, all aspired. Even 'art' – assigned in the earlier framework a privileged position, as touchstone of the highest values of civilization – is now redefined as only one, special, form of a general social process: the giving and taking of meanings, and the slow development of 'common' meanings – a common culture: 'culture', in this special sense, 'is ordinary' (to borrow the title of one of Williams's earliest attempts to make this general position more widely accessible – see Williams, 1958). If even the highest, most refined of descriptions offered in works of literature are also 'part of the general process which creates conventions and institutions, through which the meanings that are valued by the community are shared and made active' (Williams, 1965, p. 55), then there is no way in which this process can be hived off or distinguished or set apart from the other practices of the historical process ... Accordingly, there is no way in which the communication of descriptions, understood in this way, can be set aside and compared externally with other things. 'If the art is part of society, there is no solid whole, outside it, to which, by the form of our question, we concede priority. The art is there, as an activity, with the production, the trading, the politics, the raising of families. To study the relations adequately we must study them actively, seeing all activities as particular and contemporary forms of human energy' (*ibid*, p. 61).

If this first emphasis takes up and re-works the connotation of the term 'culture' with the domain of 'ideas', the second emphasis is more deliberately anthropological, and emphasizes that aspect of 'culture' which refers to social *practices*. It is from this second emphasis that the somewhat simplified definition – 'culture is a whole way of life' – has been rather too neatly abstracted. Williams did relate this aspect of the concept to the more 'documentary' – that is, descriptive, even ethnographic – usage of the term. But the earlier definition seems to me the more central one, into which 'way of life' is integrated. The important point in the argument rests on the active and indissoluble relationships between elements or social practices normally separated out. It is in *this* context that the 'theory of culture' is defined as 'the study of relationships between elements in a whole way of life'. 'Culture' is not *a* practice; nor is it simply the descriptive sum of the 'mores and folkways' of societies – as it tended to become in certain kinds of anthropology. It is threaded through *all* social practices, and is the sum of their inter-relationship. The question of what, then, is studied, and how, resolves itself. The 'culture' is those patterns of organization, those characteristic forms of human energy which can be discovered as revealing themselves – in 'unexpected identities and correspondences' as well as in 'discontinuities of an unexpected kind' (*ibid* p.63) – within or underlying *all* social practices. The analysis of culture is, then, 'the attempt to discover the nature of the organization which is the complex of these relationships'. It begins with 'the discovery of patterns of a characteristic kind'. One will discover them, not in the art, production, trading, politics, the raising of families, treated as separate activities, but through 'studying a general organisation in a particular example' (*ibid* p.61). Analytically, one must study 'the relationships between these patterns'. The purpose of the analysis is to grasp how the interactions between all these practices and patterns are lived and experienced as a whole, in any particular period. This is its 'structure of feeling'.

It is easier to see what Williams was getting at, and why he was pushed along this path, if we understand what were the problems he addressed, and what pitfalls he was trying to avoid. This is particularly necessary because *The Long Revolution* (like many of Williams's works) carries on a submerged, almost 'silent' dialogue with alternative positions, which are not always as clearly identified as one would wish. There is a clear engagement with the 'idealist' and 'civilizing' definitions of culture – both the equation of 'culture' with *ideas*, in the idealist tradition; and the assimilation of culture to an *ideal*, prevalent in the elitist terms of the 'cultural debate'. But there is also a more extended engagement with certain kinds of Marxism, against which Williams's definitions are consciously pitched. He is arguing against the literal operations of the base/superstructure metaphor, which in classical Marxism ascribed the domain of ideas and of meanings to the 'superstructures', themselves conceived as merely reflective of and determined in some simple fashion by 'the base'; without a social effectivity of their own. That is to say, his argument is constructed against a vulgar materialism and an economic determinism. He offers, instead, a radical interactionism: in effect, the interaction of all practices in and with one another, skirting the problem of determinacy. The distinction between practices is overcome by seeing them all as variant forms of *praxis* – of a general human activity and energy. The underlying patterns which distinguish the complex of practices in any specific society at any specific time are the characteristic 'forms of its organisation' which underlie them all, and which can therefore be traced in each.

There have been several, radical revisions of this early position: and each has contributed much to the redefinition of what Cultural Studies is and should be. We have acknowledged already the exemplary nature of Williams's project, in constantly rethinking and revising older arguments – in going on thinking. Nevertheless, one is struck by a marked line of continuity through these seminal revisions. One such moment is the occasion of his recognition of Lucien Goldmann's work, and through him, of the array of marxist thinkers who had given particular attention to superstructural forms and whose work began, for the first time, to appear in English translation in the mid-1960s. The contrast between the alternative marxist traditions which sustained writers like Goldmann and Lukács, as compared with Williams's isolated position and the impoverished marxist tradition he had to draw on, is sharply delineated. But the points of convergence – both what they are against, and what they are about – are identified in ways which are not altogether out of line with his earlier arguments. Here is the negative, which he sees as linking his work to Goldmann's: 'I came to believe that I had to give up, or at least to leave aside, what I knew as the Marxist tradition: to attempt to develop a theory of social totality; to see the study of culture as the study of relations between elements in a whole way of life; to find ways of studying structure... which could stay in touch with and illuminate particular art works and forms, but also forms and relations of more general social life; to replace the formula of base and superstructure with the more active idea of a field of mutually if also unevenly determining forces' (Williams, 1971, p.10). And here is the positive – the point where the convergence is marked between Williams's 'structure of feeling' and Goldmann's 'genetic structuralism': 'I found in my own work that I had to develop the idea of a structure of feeling... But then I found Goldmann beginning... from a concept of structure which contained, in itself, a relation between social and literary facts. This relation, he insisted, was not a matter of content, but of mental structures: "categories which simultaneously organize the empirical consciousness of a particular social group, and the imaginative world created by the writer". By definition, these structures are not individually but collectively created' (*ibid* p.12). The stress there on the interactivity of practices and on the underlying totalities, and the homologies between them, is characteristic and significant....

A second such 'moment' is the point where Williams really takes on board E.P. Thompson's critique of *The Long Revolution* (Thompson, 1962) that no 'whole way of life' is without its dimension of struggle and confrontation between opposed *ways* of life – and attempts to rethink the key issues of determination and domination via Gramsci's concept of 'hegemony'. This essay ('Base and Superstructure in Marxist Cultural Theory,' Williams, 1973) is a seminal one, especially in its elaboration of dominant, residual and emergent cultural practices, and its return to the problematic of determinacy as 'limits and pressures'. None the less, the earlier emphases recur, with force: 'we cannot separate literature and art from other kinds of social practice, in such a way as to make them subject to quite special and distinct laws'.... And this note is carried forward – indeed, it is radically accented – in Williams's most sustained and succinct recent statement of his position: the masterly condensations of *Marxism and Literature*. Against the structuralist emphasis on the specificity and 'autonomy' of practices, and their analytic separation of societies into their discrete instances, Williams's stress is on 'constitutive activity' in general, on 'sensuous human activity, as practice', from Marx's first 'thesis' on Feuerbach; on different practices conceived as a 'whole indissoluble practice'; on totality. 'Thus, contrary to one development in Marxism, it is not "the base" and "the superstructure" that need to be studied, but specific and indissoluble real processes, within which the decisive relationship, from a Marxist point of view, is that expressed by the complex idea of "determination"' (Williams, 1977, pp. 30-31, 82).

...The organizing terrain of Thompson's work – classes as relations, popular struggle, and historical forms of consciousness, class cultures in their historical particularity – is foreign to the more reflective and 'generalizing' mode in which Williams typically works.... Thompson also operates with a more 'classical' distinction than Williams, between 'social being' and 'social consciousness' (the terms he infinitely prefers, from Marx, to the more fashionable 'base and superstructure'). Thus, where Williams insists on the absorption of all practices into the totality of 'real, indissoluble practice', Thompson does deploy an older distinction between what is 'culture' and what is 'not culture'. 'Any theory of culture must include the concept of the dialectical interaction between culture and something that is *not* culture.' Yet the definition of culture is not, after all, so far removed from Williams's: 'We must suppose the raw material of life experience to be at one pole, and all the infinitely complex human disciplines and systems, articulate and inarticulate, formalised in institutions or dispersed in the least formal ways, which "handle", transmit or distort this raw material to be at the other'. Similarly, with respect to the commonality of 'practice' which underlies all the distinct practices: 'It is the active process – which is at the same time the process through which men make their history – that I am insisting upon' (Thompson 1961, p.33). And the two positions come close together around – again – certain distinctive negatives and positives. Negatively, against the 'base/superstructure' metaphor, and a reductionist or 'economistic' definition of determinacy:... 'The dialectical intercourse between social being and social consciousness – or between "culture" and "*not* culture" – is at the heart of any comprehension of the historical process within the Marxist tradition... The tradition inherits a dialectic that is right, but the particular mechanical metaphor through which it is expressed is wrong. This metaphor from constructional engineering... must in any case be inadequate to describe the flux of conflict, the dialectic of a changing social process... All the metaphors which are commonly offered have a tendency to lead the mind into schematic modes and away from the interaction of being-consciousness'.... And, more positively – a simple statement which may be taken as defining virtually the whole of Thompson's historical work, from *The Making* to *Whigs and Hunters, The Poverty of Theory* and beyond – 'capitalist society was founded upon forms of exploitation which are simultaneously economic, moral and cultural. Take up the essential defining productive relationship... and turn it round, and it reveals itself now in one aspect (wage-labour), now in another (an acquisitive ethos), and now in another (the alienation of such intellectual facilities as are not required by the worker in his productive role)' (Thompson, 1965, p.356).

Here, then, despite the many significant differences, is the outline of one significant line of thinking in Cultural Studies – some would say, *the* dominant paradigm.... In its different ways, it conceptualizes culture as interwoven with all social practices; and those practices, in turn, as a common form of human activity: sensuous human praxis, the activity through which men and women make history. It is opposed to the base-superstructure way of formulating the relationship between ideal and material forces, especially where the 'base' is defined as the determination by 'the economic' in any simple sense. It prefers the wider formulation – the dialectic between social being and social consciousness: neither separable into its distinct poles.... It defines 'culture' as *both* the meanings and values which arise amongst distinctive social groups and classes, on the basis of their given historical conditions and relationships, through which they 'handle' and respond to the conditions of existence; *and* as the lived traditions and practices through which those 'understandings' are expressed and in which they are embodied. Williams brings together these two aspects – definitions and ways of life – around the concept of 'culture' itself. Thompson brings together the two elements – consciousness and conditions – around the concept of 'experience'. Both positions entail certain difficult fluctuations around these key terms. Williams so totally absorbs 'definitions of experience' into our 'ways of living', and both into an indissoluble real material practice-in-general, as to obviate any distinction between 'culture' and 'not-culture'. Thompson sometimes uses 'experience' in the more usual sense of consciousness, as the collective ways in which men 'handle', transmit or 'distort' their given conditions, the raw materials of life; sometimes as the domain of the 'lived', the mid-term *between* 'conditions' and 'culture'; and sometimes as the objective conditions themselves – against which particular modes of consciousness are counterposed. But, whatever the terms, both positions tend to read structures of relations in terms of how they are 'lived' and 'experienced'.... This is a consequence of giving culture-consciousness and experience so pivotal a place in the analysis. The *experiential pull* in this paradigm, and the emphasis on the creative and on historical agency, constitute the two key elements in the *humanism* of the position outlined. Each, consequently accords 'experience' an authenticating position in any cultural analysis. It is, ultimately, where and how people experience their conditions of life, define them and respond to them, which, for Thompson defines why every mode of production is also a culture, and every struggle between classes is always also a struggle between cultural modalities; and which, for Williams, is what a 'cultural analysis', in the final instance, should deliver. In 'experience', all the different practices intersect; within 'culture' the different practices interact – even if on an uneven and mutually determining basis. This sense of cultural totality – of *the whole* historical process – over-rides any effort to keep the instances and elements distinct. Their real interconnection, under given historical conditions, must be matched by a totalizing movement 'in thought', in the analysis. It establishes for both the strongest protocols against any form of analytic abstraction which distinguishes practices, or which sets out to test the 'actual historical movement' in all its intertwined complexity and particularity by any more sustained logical or analytical operation.... In their tendency to reduce practices to *praxis* and to find common and homologous 'forms' underlying the most apparently differentiated areas, their movement is 'essentialising'. They have a particular way of understanding the totality – though it is with a small 't', concrete and historically determinate, uneven in its correspondences. They understand it 'expressively'. And since they constantly inflect the more traditional analysis towards the experiential level, or read the other structures and relations downwards from the vantage point of how they are 'lived', they are properly (even if not adequately or fully) characterized as 'culturalist' in their emphasis: even when all the caveats and qualifications against a too rapid 'dichotomous theorizing' have been entered....

The 'culturalist' strand in Cultural Studies was interrupted by the arrival on the intellectual scene of the 'structuralisms'. These, possibly more varied than the 'culturalisms', nevertheless shared certain positions and orientations in common which makes their designation under a single title not altogether misleading. It has been remarked that whereas the 'culturalist' paradigm can be defined without requiring a conceptual reference to the term 'ideology' (the *word*, of course, does appear: but it is not a key concept), the 'structuralist' interventions have been largely articulated around the concept of 'ideology': in keeping with its more impeccably Marxist lineage, 'culture' does not figure so prominently. Whilst this may be true of the Marxist structuralists, it is at best less than half the truth about the structuralist enterprise as such. But it is now a common error to condense the latter exclusively around the impact of Althusser and all that has followed in the wake of his interventions – where 'ideology' has played a seminal, but modulated rôle: and to omit the significance of Lévi-Strauss. Yet, in strict historical terms, it was Lévi-Strauss, and the early semiotics, which made the first break. And though the Marxist structuralisms have superseded the latter, they owed, and continued to owe, an immense theoretical debt ... to his work. It was Lévi-Strauss's structuralism which, in its appropriation of the linguistic paradigm, after Saussure, offered the promise to the 'human sciences of culture' of a paradigm capable of rendering them scientific and rigorous in a thoroughly new way. And when, in Althusser's work, the more classical Marxist themes were recovered, it remained the case that Marx was 'read' – and reconstituted – through the terms of the linguistic paradigm. In *Reading Capital*, for example, the case is made that the mode of production – to coin a phrase – could best be understood as if 'structured like a language' (through the selective combination of invariant elements). The a-historical and synchronic stress, against the historical emphasis of 'culturalism', derived from a similar source. So did a pre-occupation with 'the social, *sui generis*' – used not adjectivally but substantively: a usage Lévi-Strauss derived, not from Marx, but from Durkheim....

This structuralism shared with culturalism a radical break with the terms of the base/superstructure metaphor, as derived from the simpler parts of the *German Ideology*. And though 'It is to this theory of the superstructures, scarcely touched on by Marx' to which Lévi-Strauss aspired to contribute, his contribution was such as to break in a radical way with its whole terms of reference, as finally and irrevocably as the 'culturalists' did. Here – and we must include Althusser in this characterization – culturalists and structuralists alike ascribed to the domains hitherto defined as 'superstructural' a specificity and effectivity, a constitutive primacy, which pushed them beyond the terms of reference of 'base' and 'superstructure'. Lévi-Strauss and Althusser, too, were anti-reductionist and anti-economist in their very cast of thought, and critically attacked that transitive causality which, for so long, had passed itself off as 'classical Marxism'.

Lévi-Strauss worked consistently with the term 'culture'. He regarded 'ideologies' as of much lesser importance: mere 'secondary rationalizations'. Like Williams and Goldmann, he worked, not at the level of correspondences between the *content* of a practice, but at the level of their forms and structures. But the manner in which these were conceptualized were altogether at variance with either the 'culturalism' of Williams or Goldmann's 'genetic structuralism'. This divergence can be identified in three distinct ways. First, he conceptualized 'culture' as the categories and frameworks in thought and language through which different societies classified out their conditions of existence – above all (since Lévi-Strauss was an anthropologist), the relations between the human and the natural worlds. Second, he thought of the manner and practice through which these categories and mental frameworks were produced and transformed, largely on an analogy with the ways in which language itself – the principal medium of 'culture' – operated. He identified what was specific to them and their operation as the 'production of meaning': they were, above all, *signifying* practices. Third,... he largely gave up the question of the relation *between* signifying and non-signifying practices – between 'culture' and 'not-culture', to use other terms – for the sake of concentrating on the *internal* relations within signifying practices by means of which the categories of meaning were produced. This left the question of determinacy, of totality, largely in abeyance. The causal logic of determinacy was abandoned in favour of a structuralist causality – a logic of *arrangement*, of internal relations, of articulation of parts within a structure. Each of these aspects is also positively present in Althusser's work and that of the Marxist structuralists, even when the terms of reference had been regrounded in Marx's 'immense theoretical revolution'. We can see this in Althusser's seminal formulations about ideology – defined as the themes, concepts and representations through which men and women 'live', in an imaginary relation, their relation to their real conditions of existence (see Althusser, 1971).... 'Ideologies' are here being conceptualized, not as the contents and surface forms of ideas, but as the unconscious categories through which conditions are represented and lived. We have already commented on the active presence in Althusser's thinking of the linguistic paradigm – the second element identified above. And though, in the concept of 'over-determination' – one of his most seminal and fruitful contributions – Althusser did return to the problems of the relations *between* practices and the question of determinacy,... he did tend to reinforce the 'relative autonomy' of different practices, and their internal specificities, conditions and effects at the expense of an 'expressive' conception of the totality, with its typical homologies and correspondences.

Aside from the wholly distinct intellectual and conceptual universes within which these alternative paradigms developed, there were certain points where, despite their apparent overlaps, culturalism and structuralism were starkly counterposed. We can identify this counterposition at one of its sharpest points precisely around the concept of 'experience', and the rôle the term played in each perspective. Whereas, in 'culturalism', experience was the ground – the terrain of 'the lived' – where consciousness and conditions intersected, structuralism insisted that 'experience' could not, by definition, be the ground of anything, since one could only 'live' and experience one's conditions *in and through* the categories, classifications and frameworks of the culture. These categories, however, did not arise from or in experience: rather, experience was their 'effect'. The culturalists had defined the forms of consciousness and culture as collective. But they had stopped far short of the radical proposition that, in culture and in language, the subject was 'spoken by' the categories of culture in which he/she thought, rather than 'speaking them'. These categories were, however, not merely collective rather than individual productions: they were for the structuralists, *unconscious* structures. That is why, though Lévi-Strauss spoke only of 'Culture', his concept provided the basis for an easy translation, by Althusser, into the conceptual framework of ideology: 'Ideology is indeed a system of "representations", but in the majority of cases these representations have nothing to do with "consciousness":... it is above all as structures that they impose on the vast majority of men, not via their "consciousness"... it is within this ideological unconsciousness that men succeed in altering the "lived" relation between them and the world and acquiring that new form of specific unconsciousness called "consciousness"' (Althusser, 1969, p. 233). It was, in this sense, that 'experience' was conceived, not as an authenticating source but as an effect: not as a reflection of the real but as an 'imaginary relation'. It was only a short step... to the development of an account of how this 'imaginary relation' served, not simply the dominance of a ruling class over a dominated one, but (through the reproduction of the relations of production, and the constitution of labour-power in a form fit for capitalist exploitation) the expanded reproduction of the mode of production itself. Many of the other lines of divergence between the two paradigms flow from this point: the conception of 'men' as bearers of the structures that speak and place them, rather than as active agents in the making of their own history: the emphasis on a structural rather than a historical 'logic';... the recasting of history as a march of the structures:... the structuralist 'machine'...

There is no space in which to follow through the many ramifications which have followed from the development of one or other of these 'master paradigms' in Cultural Studies. Though they by no means account for all, or even nearly all, of the many strategies adopted, it is fair to say that, between them, they have defined the principal lines of development in the field. The seminal debates have been polarized around their thematics; some of the best concrete work has flowed from the efforts to set one or other of these paradigms to work on particular problems and materials. Characteristically,... the arguments and debates have most frequently been over-polarized into their extremes. At these extremities, they frequently appear only as mirror-reflections or inversions of one another. Here, the broad typologies we have been working with – for the sake of convenient exposition – become the prison-house of thought.

Without suggesting that there can be any easy synthesis between them, it might usefully be said at this point that neither 'culturalism' nor 'structuralism' is, in its present manifestation, adequate to the task of constructing the study of culture as a conceptually clarified and theoretically informed domain of study. Nevertheless, something fundamental to it emerges from a rough comparison of their respective strengths and limitations.

The great strength of the structuralisms is their stress on 'determinate conditions'. They remind us that, unless the dialectic really can be held, in any particular analysis, between both halves of the proposition – that 'men make history... on the basis of conditions which are not of their making' – the result will inevitably be a naïve humanism, with its necessary consequence: a voluntarist and populist political practice. The fact that 'men' can become conscious of their conditions, organize to struggle against them and in fact transform them – without which no active politics can even be conceived, let alone practised – must not be allowed to override the awareness of the fact that, in capitalist relations, men and women are placed and positioned in relations which constitute them as agents. 'Pessimism of the intellect, optimism of the will' is a better starting point than a simple heroic affirmation. Structuralism does enable us to begin to think – as Marx insisted – of the *relations* of a structure on the basis of something other than their reduction to relationships between 'people'. This was Marx's privileged level of abstraction: that which enabled him to break with the obvious but incorrect starting point of 'political economy' – bare individuals.

But this connects with a second strength: the recognition by structuralism not only of the necessity of abstraction as the instrument of thought through which 'real relations' are appropriated, but also of the presence, in Marx's work, of a continuous and complex movement *between different levels of abstraction.* It is, of course, the case – as 'culturalism' argues – that, in historical reality, practices do not appear neatly distinguished out into their respective instances. However, to think about or to analyse the complexity of the real, the act of practice of thinking is required; and this necessitates the use of the power of abstraction and analysis, the formation of concepts with which to cut into the complexity of the real, in order precisely to reveal and bring to light relationships and structures which cannot be visible to the naive naked eye, and which can neither present nor authenticate themselves.... Of course, structuralism has frequently taken this proposition to its extreme. Because thought is impossible without 'the power of abstraction', it has confused this with giving an absolute primacy to the level of the formation of concepts – and at the highest, most abstract level of abstraction only: Theory with a capital 'T' then becomes judge and jury. But this is precisely to lose the insight just won from Marx's own practice. For it is clear in, for example, *Capital,* that the *method* – whilst, of course, taking place 'in thought' (as Marx asked in the 1857 Introduction, where else?) – rests, not on the simple exercise of abstraction but on the movement and relations which the argument is constantly establishing between *different levels* of abstraction: at each, the premises in play must be distinguished from those which – for the sake of the argument – have to be held constant.... This method is adequately represented in *neither* the absolutism of Theoretical Practice, in structuralism, nor in the anti-abstraction (of E.P. Thompson's) 'Poverty Of Theory' position into which, in reaction, culturalism appears to have been driven or driven itself. Nevertheless it is intrinsically *theoretical,* and must be. Here, structuralism's insistence that thought does not reflect reality, but is articulated on and appropriates it, is a necessary starting point. An adequate *working through* of the consequences of this argument might begin to produce a method which takes us outside the permanent oscillations between abstraction/anti-abstraction and the false dichotomies of Theoreticism *vs.* Empiricism which have both marked and disfigured the structuralism/culturalism encounter to date.

Structuralism has another strength, in its conception of 'the whole'. There is a sense in which, though culturalism constantly insists on the radical particularity of its practices, its mode of conceptualizing the 'totality' has something of the complex simplicity of an expressive totality behind it.* Its complexity is constituted by the fluidity with which practices move into and out of one another: but this complexity is reducible, conceptually, to the 'simplicity' of praxis - human activity, as such - in which the same contradictions constantly appear, homologously reflected in each. Structuralism goes too far in erecting the machine of a 'Structure', with its self-generating propensities, ... equipped with its distinctive instances. Yet it represents an advance over culturalism in the conception it has of the necessary *complexity* of the unity of a structure.... Moreover, it has the conceptual ability to think of a unity which is constructed through the *differences* between, rather than the homology of, practices. Here, again, it has won a critical insight about Marx's method: one thinks of the complex passages of the 1857 Introduction to the *Grundrisse* where Marx demonstrates how it is possible to think of the 'unity' of a social formation as constructed, not out of identity but out of *difference*. Of course, the stress of difference can – and has – led the structuralisms into a fundamental conceptual heterogeneity, in which all sense of structure and totality is lost. Foucault and other post-Althussereans have taken this devious path into the absolute, not the relative, autonomy of practices, via their necessary heterogeneity and 'necessary non-correspondence'. But the emphasis on unity-in-difference, on complex unity – Marx's concrete as the 'unity of many determinations' – can be worked in another, and ultimately more fruitful direction: towards the problematic of relative autonomy and 'over-determination', and the study of *articulation*. Again, articulation contains the danger of a high formalism. But it also has the considerable advantage of enabling us to think of how specific practices (articulated around contradictions which do not all arise in the same way, at the same point, in the same moment), can nevertheless be thought *together*. The structuralist paradigm thus does – if properly developed – enable us to begin really to *conceptualize* the specificity of different practices (analytically distinguished, abstracted out), without losing its grip on the ensemble which they constitute. Culturalism constantly affirms the specificity of different practices – 'culture' must not be absorbed into 'the economic': but it lacks an adequate way of establishing this specificity theoretically.

The third strength which structuralism exhibits lies in its decentering of 'experience' and its seminal work in elaborating the neglected category of

*[The concept of 'expressive totality' was developed by Althusser in his critique of Hegelian forms of Marxism. According to these, the structure of the social whole is said to be determined by an essential or single contradiction – between the forces and the relations of production, for instance. Ideological and political contradictions are then viewed as the 'expressions' – that is, particular forms of the appearance – of this essential and determining contradiction.]

'ideology'. It is difficult to conceive of a Cultural Studies thought within a Marxist paradigm which is innocent of the category of 'ideology'. Of course, culturalism constantly makes reference to this concept: but it does not in fact lie at the centre of its conceptual universe. The authenticating power and reference of 'experience' imposes a barrier between culturalism and a proper conception of 'ideology'. Yet, without it, the effectivity of 'culture' for the reproduction of a particular mode of production cannot be grasped. It is true that there is a marked tendency in the more recent structuralist conceptualisations of 'ideology' to give it a functionalist reading – as the necessary cement of the social formation. From this position, it is indeed impossible – as culturalism would correctly argue – to conceive either of ideologies which are not, by definition, 'dominant': or of the concept of struggle (the latter's appearance in Althusser's famous ISA's article being – to coin yet another phrase – largely 'gestural'). Nevertheless, work is already being done which suggests ways in which the field of ideology may be adequately conceptualized as a terrain of struggle (through the work of Gramsci, and more recently, of Laclau – see Laclau, 1977), and these have structuralist rather than culturalist bearings.

Culturalism's strengths can almost be derived from the weaknesses of the structuralist position already noted, and from the latter's strategic absences and silences. It has insisted, correctly, on the affirmative moment of the development of conscious struggle and organization as a necessary element in the analysis of history, ideology and consciousness: against its persistent down-grading in the structuralist paradigm. Here, again, it is largely Gramsci who has provided us with a set of more refined terms through which to link the largely 'unconscious' and given cultural categories of 'common sense' with the formation of more active and organic ideologies, which have the capacity to intervene in the ground of common sense and popular traditions and, through such interventions, to organize masses of men and women. In this sense, culturalism *properly* restores the dialectic between the unconsciousness of cultural categories and the moment of conscious organization: even if, in its characteristic movement, it has tended to match structuralism's over-emphasis on 'conditions' with an altogether too-inclusive emphasis on 'consciousness'. It therefore not only recovers – as the necessary moment of any analysis – the process by means of which classes-in-themselves, defined primarily by the way in which economic relations position 'men' as agents – become active historical and political forces-for-themselves: it also – against its own anti-theoretical good sense – *requires* that, when properly developed, each moment must be understood in terms of the level of abstraction at which the analysis is operating. Again, Gramsci has begun to point a way through this false polarization in his discussion of 'the passage between the structure and the sphere of the complex superstructures', and its distinct forms and moments.

We have concentrated in this argument largely on a characterization of what seem to us to be the two seminal paradigms at work in Cultural Studies. Of course, they are by no means the only active ones. New developments and lines of thinking are by no means adequately netted with reference to them. Nevertheless, these paradigms can, in a sense, be deployed to measure what appear to us to be the radical weaknesses or inadequacies of those which offer themselves as alternative rallying-points. Here, briefly, we identify three.

The first is that which follows on from Lévi-Strauss, early semiotics and the terms of the linguistic paradigm, and the centering on 'signifying practices', moving by way of psychoanalytic concepts and Lacan to a radical recentering of virtually the whole terrain of Cultural Studies around the terms 'discourse' and 'the subject'. One way of understanding this line of thinking is to see it as an attempt to fill that empty space in early structuralism (of both the Marxist and non-Marxist varieties) where, in earlier discourses, 'the subject' and subjectivity might have been expected to appear but did not. This is, of course, precisely one of the key points where culturalism brings its pointed criticisms to bear on structuralism's 'process without a subject'. The difference is that, whereas culturalism would correct for the hyper-structuralism of earlier models by restoring the unified subject (collective or individual) of consciousness at the centre of 'the Structure', discourse theory, by way of the Freudian concepts of the unconscious and the Lacanian concepts of how subjects are constituted in language (through the entry into the Symbolic and the Law of Culture), restores the *decentered* subject, the contradictory subject, as a set of positions in language and knowledge, from which culture can appear to be enunciated. This approach clearly identifies a gap, not only in structuralism but in Marxism itself. The problem is that the manner in which this 'subject' of culture is conceptualized is of a trans-historical and 'universal' character: it addresses the subject-in-general, not historically-determinate social subjects, or socially determinate particular languages. Thus it is incapable, so far, of moving its in-general propositions to the level of concrete historical analysis. The second difficulty is that the processes of contradiction and struggle – lodged by early structuralism wholly at the level of 'the structure' – are now, by one of those persistent mirror-inversions, lodged exclusively at the level of the unconscious processes of the subject. It may be, as culturalism often argues, that the 'subjective' is a necessary moment of any such analysis. But this is a very different proposition from dismantling the whole of the social processes of particular modes of production and social formations, and reconstituting them exclusively at the level of unconscious psychoanalytic processes....

A second development is the attempt to return to the terms of a more classical 'political economy' of culture. This position argues that the concentration on the cultural and ideological aspects has been wildly overdone. It would restore the older terms of 'base/superstructure', finding, in the last-instance determination of the cultural-ideological by the economic, that hierarchy of determinations which both alternatives appear to lack. This position insists that the economic processes and structures of cultural production are more significant than their cultural-ideological aspect: and that these are quite adequately caught in the more classical terminology of profit, exploitation, surplus-value and the analysis of culture as commodity. It retains a notion of ideology as 'false consciousness'.

There is, of course, some strength to the claim that both structuralism and culturalism, in their different ways, have neglected the economic analysis of cultural and ideological production. All the same, with the return to this more 'classical' terrain, many of the problems which originally beset it also reappear. The specificity of the effect of the cultural and ideological dimension once more tends to disappear. It tends to conceive the economic level as not only a 'necessary' but a 'sufficient' explanation of cultural and ideological effects. Its focus on the analysis of the commodity form, similarly, blurs all the carefully established distinctions between different practices, since it is the most *generic* aspects of the commodity-form which attract attention. Its deductions are therefore, largely, confined to an epochal level of abstraction: the generalizations about the commodity-form hold true throughout the capitalist epoch as a whole. Very little by way of concrete and conjunctural analysis can be derived at this high-level 'logic of capital' form of abstraction. . . .

The third position is closely related to the structuralist enterprise, but has followed the path of 'difference' through into a radical heterogeneity. Foucault's work – currently enjoying another of those uncritical periods of discipleship through which British intellectuals reproduce today their dependency on yesterday's French ideas – has had an exceedingly positive effect: above all because – in suspending the nearly-insoluble problems of determination Foucault has made possible a welcome return to the concrete analysis of particular ideological and discursive formations, and the sites of their elaboration. Foucault and Gramsci between them account for much of the most productive work on *concrete analysis* now being undertaken in the field: thereby reinforcing and – paradoxically – supporting the sense of the concrete historical instance which has always been one of culturalism's principal strengths. But, again, Foucault's example is positive only if his general epistemological position is not swallowed whole. For in fact Foucault so resolutely suspends judgment, and adopts so thoroughgoing a scepticism about any determinacy or relationship between practices, other than the largely contingent, that we are entitled to see him, not as an agnostic on these questions, but as deeply committed to the necessary non-correspondence of all practices to one another. From such a position neither a social formation, nor the State, can be adequately thought. And indeed Foucault is constantly falling into the pit which he had dug for himself. For when – against his well-defended epistemological positions – he stumbles across certain 'correspondences' (for example, the simple fact that all the major moments of transition he has traced in each of his studies – on the prison, sexuality, medicine, the asylum, language and political economy – all appear to converge around exactly that point where industrial capitalism and the bourgeoisie make their fateful, historical rendezvous), he lapses into a vulgar reductionism, which thoroughly belies the sophisticated positions he has elsewhere advanced. He is quite capable of wheeling in through the back door the classes he recently expelled from the front.

I have said enough to indicate that, in my view, the line in Cultural Studies which has attempted to *think forwards* from the best elements in the structuralist and culturalist enterprises, by way of some of the concepts elaborated in Gramsci's work, comes closest to meeting the requirements of the field of study. And the reason for that should by now also be obvious. Though neither structuralism nor culturalism will do, as self-sufficient paradigms of study, they have a centrality to the field which all the other contenders lack because, between them (in their divergences as well as their convergences) they address what must be the *core problem* of Cultural Studies. They constantly return us to the terrain marked out by those strongly coupled but not mutually exclusive concepts culture/ideology. They pose, together, the problems consequent on trying to think *both* the specificity of different practices and the forms of the articulated unity they constitute. They make a constant, if flawed, return to the base/superstructure metaphor. They are correct in insisting that this question – which resumes all the problems of a non-reductive determinacy – is the heart of the matter: and that, on the solution of this problem will turn the capacity of Cultural Studies to supersede the endless oscillations between idealism and reductionism. They confront – even if in radically opposed ways – the dialectic between conditions and consciousness. At another level, they pose the question of the relation between the logic of thinking and the 'logic' of historical process. They continue to hold out the promise of a properly materialist theory of culture. In their sustained and mutually reinforcing antagonisms they hold out no promise of an easy synthesis. But, between them, they define where, if at all, is the space, and what are the limits within which such a synthesis might be constituted. In Cultural Studies, theirs are the 'names of the game'.

References

ALTHUSSER, L, *For Marx,* Allen Lane, 1969.

ALTHUSSER, L. 'Ideology and Ideological State Apparatuses' in *Lenin and Philosophy, and other Essays*, New Left Books, 1971.

ALTHUSSER, L and BALIBAR, E, *Reading Capital,* New Left Books, 1970.

HOGGART, R, *The Uses of Literacy*, Penguin, 1969.

LACLAU, E, *Politics and Ideology in Marxist Theory*, New Left Books, 1977.

MARX, K, and ENGELS, F, *The German Ideology*, Lawrence and Wishart, 1965.

MARX, K, *Grundrisse: Foundations of the Critique of Political Economy,* Penguin, 1973.

MARX, K, *Capital: A Critique of Political Economy,* 3 vols, Lawrence and Wishart, 1970.

THOMPSON, E.P., *The Making of the English Working Class,* Penguin, 1968.

THOMPSON, E.P., 'Peculiarities of the English', *Socialist Register,* 1965.

THOMPSON, E.P., Reviews of Raymond Williams's *The Long Revolution, New Left Review,* Nos. 9 and 10, 1961.

THOMPSON, E.P., *Whigs and Hunters,* Allen Lane, 1975.

THOMPSON, E.P., *The Poverty of Theory,* Merlin Press, 1978.

WILLIAMS, R, *Culture and Society, 1780-1950,* Penguin, 1963.

WILLIAMS, R, *The Long Revolution,* Penguin, 1965.

WILLIAMS, R, 'Culture is Ordinary', *Conviction, 1958.*

WILLIAMS, R, 'Literature and Sociology: in memory of Lucien Goldmann', *New Left Review,* No. 67, 1971.

WILLIAMS, R, 'Base and Superstructure in Marxist Cultural Theory', *New Left Review,* No. 82, 1973.

WILLIAMS, R, *Marxism and Literature,* Oxford University Press, 1977.

WILLIAMS, R, *The Country and the City,* Chatto and Windus, 1973.

SECTION 2

Culturalist Approaches

In 'The Analysis of Culture', originally a part of *The Long Revolution,* first published in 1961, Raymond Williams advances his famous definition of culture as 'a description of a particular way of life, which expresses certain meanings and values, not only in art and learning but also in institutions and ordinary behaviour' (p.43). The democratization of the concept of culture which Williams thus proposed was not an isolated development. Similar perspectives are to be found in Richard Hoggart's *The Uses of Literacy,* first published in 1957, and in E.P. Thompson's *The Making of the English Working Class,* published two years after *The Long Revolution.* Between them, these three studies constitute the founding texts to which, in its subsequent development, culturalism has constantly referred, grounding itself in these as a distinctively British tradition of cultural theory deriving its protocols and procedures from these identifiably indigenous roots. Although the perspectives introduced by Williams, Hoggart and Thompson have since been deployed across many areas of scholarship – history, sociology, literature – they have perhaps been most sustainedly and critically *developed* in the work that has emerged from the Centre for Contemporary Cultural Studies at the University of Birmingham, a centre established by Richard Hoggart in 1964 and subsequently directed by Stuart Hall between 1968 and 1979. Over this period, although the impetus of these initial, founding texts has never been lost sight of, culturalism has proved itself a dynamic tradition, capable of responding to new theoretical developments – sometimes incorporating these, sometimes warding them off – to yield, today, forms of analysis that are considerably more complex and sophisticated than those first made available by Williams, Hoggart and Thompson. The readings collected here encapsulate the various stages in this development of the culturalist perspective, indicating the ways in which it has been advanced, qualified and, in turn, subjected to critical correction in the light of perspectives afforded by rival traditions.

Williams's 'The Analysis of Culture' offers the classic, and most condensed statement of the basic protocols and procedures of culturalism. He views culture, in its widest definition, as consisting of the structurally patterned 'ways of living', identifiable in institutional forms and in everyday behavior as well as in such more recognizably cultural forms as art, literature and music, through which individuals and groups – or, more accurately, individuals *in* groups – characteristically respond to and make meaningful the circumstances in which they are placed by virtue of their positions in society and in history. The aim of analysis, given this definition, is that of reading through the documentary or textual forms which such cultures leave behind as their sedimented expressions, their records to posterity, in order to re-constitute, as closely as possible, the 'structure of feeling' – the patterned ways of thinking, feeling and living shared by individuals living in similar circumstances – which originally lay behind or supported such forms.

In 'Subcultures, Cultures and Class', John Clarke, Stuart Hall, Tony Jefferson and Brian Roberts define culture as 'the practice which realises or *objectivates* group life in meaningful shape and form.' 'The "culture" of a group or class', they go on to argue, 'is the peculiar and distinctive "way of life" of the group or class, the meanings, values and ideas embodied in institutions, in social relations, in systems of beliefs, in *mores* and customs, in the use of objects and material life. Culture is the distinctive shapes in which this material and social organization of life expresses itself' (p.53). The indebtedness of these formulations to Williams's work is clear enough. In the course of grappling with the problems posed by the study of the development of youth sub-cultures during the post-war period – and particularly with the problem as to how the relationship between youth sub-cultures and their 'parent' class cultures should be conceived – Clarke and his co-authors significantly modify these original formulations. Taking into account not only the development of the sociological study of sub-cultures in the 1960s but, more significantly, Gramsci's work and Althusser's writings on the subject of ideology, they finally suggest that sub-cultures should be regarded as forms within which 'imaginary' ways of resolving the real contradictions which different groups face, but which they are unable to resolve practically, are posed, lived and rehearsed.

A similar extension of and qualified departure from the founding canons of culturalism is discernible in Paul Willis's 'Class and institutional form of counter-school culture'. As is the case with the previous essay, this too is the product of work conducted at the Birmingham Centre: a study in the formation of cultures of resistance to the official ethos of secondary school institutions on the part of working class male adolescents, a study undertaken between 1972-5 and subsequently published by Willis under the title *Learning to Labour: How working class kids get working class jobs.*

A highly original and penetrating study, *Learning to Labour* analyzes the formation of highly elaborate and codified forms of resistance to schooling on the part of a group of imminent school leavers as a product of their contradictory insertion between, on the one hand, home and neighbourhood culture, and the resolutely middle-class culture of the school on the other. The extract reprinted here focuses particularly on these contradictory tensions, showing the ways in which such cultures of resistance are the product of complex rather than of simple determinations, moulded by the dynamic interaction between the resources of their parental working-class culture and the institutional relations of the school which defines the primary, daily tension for the majority of working-class youths during their final years at school. The sting in the tail, however, is in Willis's subtitle; in the suggestion that, in rejecting school culture and preferring the shop-floor culture of their parents, working-class youths are merely taking a realistic view of their employment prospects, acquiring – and rehearsing – attitudes and forms of behaviour that will subsequently facilitate their insertion in the labour market as unskilled and undifferentiated labour-power. The development of oppositional working-class culture within the school, Willis provocatively suggests, is an unintended consequence of the role of the school within state capitalism, but also a necessary one; necessary to the maintenance of the existing structure of society, to that reproductive process whereby working-class kids get working-class jobs – again and again, routinely, regularly, repeatedly and predictably.

In the final contribution to this section, Angela McRobbie – also associated with the Birmingham Centre as once a post-graduate student there – takes to task the study of youth cultures, as developed at Birmingham, for its exclusive concentration on *male* youth cultural forms. Whilst acknowledging their importance in other respects, her criticisms are made with particular reference to Paul Willis's work as well as to Dick Hebdige's equally influential *Subcultures: The Meaning of Style* (Methuen, 1979). McRobbie's intervention is pointed in two directions, however. On the one hand, she forcibly argues that working-class male youth cultures need to be inserted in the context of the home and the family as well as that of the school and the workplace if a fully *sexed* understanding of working-class culture is to be produced. On the other hand, she urges the development of the study of teenage girls' and women's subcultures as an important task for feminists. More than that, she argues that feminists have a positive role to play in contributing to the development of such subcultures as pre-figurative forms of social relations within which adolescent experience might be shaped in ways that, to a degree, might project and nurture alternatives to the ever-impending feminine career of marriage, home, children.

Although all sharing certain basic assumptions and orientations – a stress on creative agency, on the active making of culture rather than its passive reception – the readings collected in this section nonetheless exhibit a remarkable diversity of approach. Collectively, they attest to the liveliness and productiveness of the debate which has characterized the development of the culturalist perspective in cultural studies; to the fact that there is not one 'culturalism', but several.

1 The Analysis of Culture

Raymond Williams

There are three general categories in the definition of culture. There is, first, the 'ideal', in which culture is a state or process of human perfection, in terms of certain absolute or universal values. The analysis of culture, if such a definition is accepted, is essentially the discovery and description, in lives and works, of those values which can be seen to compose a timeless order, or to have permanent reference to the universal human condition. Then, second, there is the 'documentary', in which culture is the body of intellectual and imaginative work, in which, in a detailed way, human thought and experience are variously recorded. The analysis of culture, from such a definition, is the activity of criticism, by which the nature of the thought and experience, the details of the language, form and convention in which these are active, are described and valued. Such criticism can range from a process very similar to the 'ideal' analysis, the discovery of 'the best that has been thought and written in the world', through a process which, while interested in tradition, takes as its primary emphasis the particular work being studied (its clarification and valuation being the principal end in view) to a kind of historical criticism which, after analysis of particular works, seeks to relate them to the particular traditions and societies in which they appeared. Finally, third, there is the 'social' definition of culture, in which culture is a description of a particular way of life, which expresses certain meanings and values not only in art and learning but also in institutions and ordinary behaviour. The analysis of culture, from such a definition, is the clarification of the meanings and values implicit and explicit in a particular way of life, a particular culture. Such analysis will include the historical criticism already referred to, in which intellectual and imaginative works are analysed in relation to particular traditions and societies, but will also include analysis of elements in the way of life that to followers of the other definitions are not 'culture' at all: the

Source: Raymond Williams *The Long Revolution,* Chatto and Windus, 1961, Chapter 2.

organization of production, the structure of the family, the structure of institutions which express or govern social relationships, the characteristic forms through which members of the society communicate. Again, such analysis ranges from an 'ideal' emphasis, the discovery of certain absolute or universal, or at least higher and lower, meanings and values, through the 'documentary' emphasis, in which clarification of a particular way of life is the main end in view, to an emphasis which, from studying particular meanings and values, seeks not so much to compare these, as a way of establishing a scale, but by studying their modes of change to discover certain general 'laws' or 'trends', by which social and cultural development as a whole can be better understood.

It seems to me that there is value in each of these kinds of definition. For it certainly seems necessary to look for meanings and values, the record of creative human activity, not only in art and intellectual work, but also in institutions and forms of behaviour. At the same time, the degree to which we depend, in our knowledge of many past societies and past stages of our own, on the body of intellectual and imaginative work which has retained its major communicative power, makes the description of culture in these terms, if not complete, at least reasonable. It can indeed be argued that since we have 'society' for the broader description, we can properly restrict 'culture' to this more limited reference. Yet there are elements in the 'ideal' definition which also seem to me valuable, and which encourage the retention of the broad reference. I find it very difficult, after the many comparative studies now on record, to identify the process of human perfection with the discovery of 'absolute' values, as these have been ordinarily defined. I accept the criticism that these are normally an extension of the values of a particular tradition or society. Yet, if we call the process, not human perfection, which implies a known ideal towards which we can move, but human evolution, to mean a process of general growth of man as a kind, we are able to recognize areas of fact which the other definitions might exclude. For it seems to me to be true that meanings and values, discovered in particular societies and by particular individuals, and kept alive by social inheritance and by embodiment in particular kinds of work, have proved to be universal in the sense that when they are learned, in any particular situation, they can contribute radically to the growth of man's powers to enrich his life, to regulate his society, and to control his environment. We are most aware of these elements in the form of particular techniques, in medicine, production, and communications, but it is clear not only that these depend on more purely intellectual disciplines, which had to be wrought out in the creative handling of experience, but also that these disciplines in themselves, together with certain basic ethical assumptions and certain major art forms, have proved similarly capable of being gathered into a general tradition which seems to represent, through many variations and conflicts, a line of common growth. It seems reasonable to speak of this tradition as a general human culture, while adding that it can only become active within particular societies, being shaped, as it does so, by more local and temporary systems.

The variations of meaning and reference, in the use of culture as a term, must be seen, I am arguing, not simply as a disadvantage, which prevents any kind of neat and exclusive definition, but as a genuine complexity, corresponding to real elements in experience. There is a significant reference in each of the three main kinds of definition, and, if this is so, it is the relations between them that should claim our attention. It seems to me that any adequate theory of culture must include the three areas of fact to which the definitions point, and conversely that any particular definition, within any of the categories, which would exclude reference to the others, is inadequate. Thus an 'ideal' definition which attempts to abstract the process it describes from its detailed embodiment and shaping by particular societies – regarding man's ideal development as something separate from and even opposed to his 'animal nature' or the satisfaction of material needs – seems to me unacceptable. A 'documentary' definition which sees value only in the written and painted records, and marks this area off from the rest of man's life in society, is equally unacceptable. Again, a 'social' definition, which treats either the general process or the body of art and learning as a mere by-product, a passive reflection of the real interests of the society, seems to me equally wrong. However difficult it may be in practice, we have to try to see the process as a whole, and to relate our particular studies, if not explicitly at least by ultimate reference, to the actual and complex organization.

We can take one example, from analytic method, to illustrate this. If we take a particular work of art, say the *Antigone* of Sophocles, we can analyse it in ideal terms – the discovery of certain absolute values, or in documentary terms – the communication of certain values by certain artistic means. Much will be gained from either analysis, for the first will point to the absolute value of reverence for the dead; the second will point to the expression of certain basic human tensions through the particular dramatic form of chorus and double *kommos,* and the specific intensity of the verse. Yet it is clear that neither analysis is complete. The reference, as an absolute value, is limited in the play by the terms of a particular kinship system and its conventional obligations – Antigone would do this for a brother but not for a husband. Similarly, the dramatic form, the metres of the verse, not only have an artistic tradition behind them, the work of many men, but can be seen to have been shaped, not only by the demands of the experience, but by the particular social forms through which the dramatic tradition developed. We can accept such extensions of our original analysis, but we cannot go on to accept that, because of the extensions, the value of reverence, or the dramatic form and the specific verse, have meaning only in the contexts to which we have assigned them. The learning of reverence, through such intense examples, passes beyond its context into the general growth of human consciousness. The dramatic form passes beyond its context, and becomes an element in a major and general dramatic tradition, in quite different societies. The play itself, a specific communication, survives the society and the religion which helped to shape it, and can be re-created to speak directly to unimagined audiences. Thus, while we could not abstract the ideal value or the specific document, neither could we reduce these to explanation within the local terms of a particular culture. If we study real relations, in any actual analysis, we reach the point where we see that we are studying a general organization in a particular example, and in this general organization there is no element that we can abstract and separate from the rest. It was certainly an error to suppose that values or art-works could be adequately studied without reference to the particular society within which they were expressed, but it is equally an error to suppose that the social explanation is determining, or that the values and works are mere by-products. We have got into the habit, since we realized how deeply works or values could be determined by the whole situation in which they are expressed, of asking about these relationships in a standard form: 'what is the relation of this art to this society?' But 'society', in this question, is a specious whole. If the art is part of the society, there is no solid whole, outside it, to which, by the form of our question, we concede priority. The art is there, as an activity, with the production, the trading, the politics, the raising of families. To study the relations adequately we must study them actively, seeing all the activities as particular and contemporary forms of human energy. If we take any one of these activities, we can see how many of the others are reflected in it, in various ways according to the nature of the whole organization. It seems likely, also, that the very fact that we can distinguish any particular activity, as serving certain specific ends, suggests that without this activity the whole of the human organization at that place and time could not have been realized. Thus art, while clearly related to the other activities, can be seen as expressing certain elements in the organization which, within that organization's terms, could only have been expressed in this way. It is then not a question of relating the art to the society, but of studying all the activities and their interrelations, without any concession of priority to any one of them we may choose to abstract. If we find, as often, that a particular activity came radically to change the whole organization, we can still not say that it is to this activity that all the others must be related; we can only study the varying ways in which, within the changing organization, the particular activities and their interrelations were affected. Further, since the particular activities will be serving varying and sometimes conflicting ends, the sort of change we must look for will rarely be of a simple kind: elements of persistence, adjustment, unconscious assimilation, active resistance, alternative effort, will all normally be present, in particular activities and in the whole organization.

The analysis of culture, in the documentary sense, is of great importance because it can yield specific evidence about the whole organization within which it was expressed. We cannot say that we know a particular form or period of society, and that we will see how its art and theory relate to it, for until we know these, we cannot really claim to know the society. This is a problem of method, and is mentioned here because a good deal of history has in fact been written on the assumption that the bases of the society, its political, economic, and 'social' arrangements, form the central core of facts, after which the art and theory can be adduced, for marginal illustration or 'correlation'. There has been a neat reversal of this procedure in the histories of literature, art, science, and philosophy, when these are described as developing by their own laws, and then something called the 'background' (what in general history was the central core) is sketched in. Obviously it is necessary, in exposition, to select certain activities for emphasis, and it is entirely reasonable to trace particular lines of development in temporary isolation. But the history of a culture, slowly built up from such particular work, can only be written when the active relations are restored, and the activities seen in a genuine parity. Cultural history must be more than the sum of the particular histories, for it is with the relations between them, the particular forms of the whole organization, that it is especially concerned. I would then define the theory of culture as the study of relationships between elements in a whole way of life. The analysis of culture is the attempt to discover the nature of the organization which is the complex of these relationships. Analysis of particular works or institutions is, in this context, analysis of their essential kind of organization, the relationships which works or institutions embody as parts of the organization as a whole. A key-word, in such analysis, is pattern: it is with the discovery of patterns of a characteristic kind that any useful cultural analysis begins, and it is with the relationships between these patterns, which sometimes reveal unexpected identities and correspondences in hitherto separately considered activities, sometimes again reveal discontinuities of an unexpected kind, that general cultural analysis is concerned.

It is only in our own time and place that we can expect to know, in any substantial way, the general organization. We can learn a great deal of the life of other places and times, but certain elements, it seems to me, will always be irrecoverable. Even those that can be recovered are recovered in abstraction, and this is of crucial importance. We learn each element as a precipitate, but in the living experience of the time every element was in solution, an inseparable part of a complex whole. The most difficult thing to get hold of, in studying any past period, is this felt sense of the quality of life at a particular place and time: a sense of the ways in which the particular activities combined into a way of thinking and living. We can go some way in restoring the outlines of a particular organization of life; we can even recover what Fromm calls the 'social character' or Benedict the 'pattern of culture'. The social character – a valued system of behaviour and attitudes – is taught formally and informally; it is both an ideal and a mode. The 'pattern of culture' is a selection and configuration of interests and activities, and a particular valuation of them, producing a distinct organization, a 'way of life'. Yet even these, as we recover them, are usually abstract. Possibly, however, we can gain the sense of a further common element, which is neither the character nor the pattern, but as it were the actual experience through which these were lived. This is potentially of very great importance, and I think the fact is that we are most conscious of such contact in the arts of a period. It can happen that when we have measured these against the external characteristics of the period, and then allowed for individual variations, there is still some important common element that we cannot easily place. I think we can best understand this if we think of any similar analysis of a way of life that we ourselves share. For we find here a particular sense of life, a particular community of experience hardly needing expression, through which the characteristics of our way of life that an external analyst could describe are in some way passed, giving them a particular and characteristic colour. We are usually most aware of this when we notice the contrasts between generations, who never talk quite 'the same language', or when we read an account of our lives by someone from outside the community, or watch the small differences in style, of speech or behaviour, in someone who has learned our ways yet was not bred in them. Almost any formal description would be too crude to express this nevertheless quite distinct sense of a particular and native style. And if this is so, in a way of life we know intimately, it will surely be so when we ourselves are in the position of the visitor, the learner, the guest from a different generation; the position, in fact, that we are all in, when we study any past period. Though it can be turned to trivial account, the fact of such a characteristic is neither trivial nor marginal; it feels quite central.

The term I would suggest to describe it is *structure of feeling:* it is as firm and definite as 'structure' suggests, yet it operates in the most delicate and least tangible parts of our activity. In one sense, this structure of feeling is the culture of a period: it is the particular living result of all the elements in the general organization. And it is in this respect that the arts of a period, taking these to include characteristic approaches and tones in argument, are of major importance. For here, if anywhere, this characteristic is likely to be expressed; often not consciously, but by the fact that here, in the only examples we have of recorded communication that outlives its bearers, the actual living sense, the deep community that makes the communication possible, is naturally drawn upon. I do not mean that the structure of feeling, any more than the social character, is possessed in the same way by the many individuals in the community. But I think it is a very deep and very wide possession, in all actual communities, precisely because it is on it that communication depends. And what is particularly interesting is that it does not seem to be, in any formal sense, learned. One generation may train its successor, with reasonable success, in the social character or the general cultural pattern, but the new generation will have its own structure of feeling, which will not appear to have come 'from' anywhere. For here, most distinctly, the changing organization is enacted in the organism: the new generation responds in its own ways to the unique world it is inheriting, taking up many continuities, that can be traced, and reproducing many aspects of the organization, which can be separately described, yet feeling its whole life in certain ways differently, and shaping its creative response into a new structure of feeling.

Once the carriers of such a structure die, the nearest we can get to this vital element is in the documentary culture, from poems to buildings and dress-fashions, and it is this relation that gives significance to the definition of culture in documentary terms. This in no way means that the documents are autonomous. It is simply that, as previously argued, the significance of an activity must be sought in terms of the whole organization, which is more than the sum of its separable parts. What we are looking for, always, is the actual life that the whole organization is there to express. The significance of documentary culture is that, more clearly than anything else, it expresses that life to us in direct terms, when the living witnesses are silent. At the same time, if we reflect on the nature of a structure of feeling, and see how it can fail to be fully understood even by living people in close contact with it, with ample material at their disposal, including the contemporary arts, we shall not suppose that we can ever do more than make an approach, an approximation, using any channels.

We need to distinguish three levels of culture, even in its most general definition. There is the lived culture of a particular time and place, only fully accessible to those living in that time and place. There is the recorded culture, of every kind, from art to the most everyday facts: the culture of a period. There is also, as the factor connecting lived culture and period cultures, the culture of the selective tradition.

When it is no longer being lived, but in a narrower way survives in its records, the culture of a period can be very carefully studied, until we feel that we have reasonably clear ideas of its cultural work, its social character, its general patterns of activity and value, and in part of its structure of feeling. Yet the survival is governed, not by the period itself, but by new periods, which gradually compose a tradition. Even most specialists in a period know only a part of even its records. One can say with confidence, for example, that nobody really knows the nineteenth-century novel; nobody has read, or could have read, all its examples, over the whole range from printed volumes to penny serials. The real specialist may know some hundreds; the ordinary specialist somewhat less; educated readers a decreasing number: though all will have clear ideas on the subject. A selective process, of a quite drastic kind, is at once evident, and this is true of every field of activity. Equally, of course, no nineteenth-century reader would have read all the novels; no individual in the society would have known more than a selection of its facts. But everyone living in the period would have had something which, I have argued, no later individual can wholly recover: that sense of the life within which the novels were written, and which we now approach through our selection. Theoretically, a period is recorded; in practice, this record is absorbed into a selective tradition: and both are different from the culture as lived.

It is very important to try to understand the operation of a selective tradition. To some extent, the selection begins within the period itself; from the whole body of activities, certain things are selected for value and emphasis. In general this selection will reflect the organization of the period as a whole, though this does not mean that the values and emphases will later be confirmed. We see this clearly enough in the case of past periods, but we never really believe it about our own. We can take an example from the novels of the last decade. Nobody has read all the English novels of the nineteen-fifties; the fastest reader, giving twenty hours a day to this activity alone, could not do it. Yet it is clear, in print and in education, not only that certain general characteristics of the novel in this period have been set down, but also that a reasonably agreed short list has been made, of what seem to be the best and most relevant works. If we take the list as containing perhaps thirty titles (already a very drastic selection indeed) we may suppose that in fifty years the specialist in the novel of the 1950s will know these thirty, and the general reader will know perhaps five or six. Yet we can surely be quite certain that, once the 1950s have passed, another selective process will be begun. As well as reducing the number of works, this new process will also alter, in some cases drastically, the expressed valuations. It is true that when fifty years have passed it is likely that reasonably permanent valuations will have been arrived at, though these may continue to fluctuate. Yet to any of us who had lived this long process through, it would remain true that elements important to us had been neglected. We would say, in a vulnerable elderly way, 'I don't understand why these young people don't read X any more', but also, more firmly, 'No, that isn't really what it was like; it is your version'. Since any period includes at least three generations, we are always seeing examples of this, and one complicating factor is that none of us stay still, even in our most significant period: many of the adjustments we should not protest against, many of the omissions, distortions and reinterpretations we should accept or not even notice, because we had been part of the change which brought them about. But then, when living witnesses had gone, a further change would occur. The lived culture would not only have been fined down to selected documents; it would be used, in its reduced form, partly as a contribution (inevitably quite small) to the general line of human growth; partly for historical reconstruction; partly, again, as a way of having done with us, of naming and placing a particular stage of the past. The selective tradition thus creates, at one level, a general human culture; at another level, the historical record of a particular society; at a third level, most difficult to accept and assess, a rejection of considerable areas of what was once a living culture.

Within a given society, selection will be governed by many kinds of special interest, including class interests. Just as the actual social situation will largely govern contemporary selection, so the development of the society, the process of historical change, will largely determine the selective tradition. The traditional culture of a society will always tend to correspond to its *contemporary* system of interests and values, for it is not an absolute body of work but a continual selection and interpretation. In theory, and to a limited extent in practice, those institutions which are formally concerned with keeping the tradition alive (in particular the institutions of education and scholarship) are committed to the tradition as a whole, and not to some selection from it according to contemporary interests. The importance of this commitment is very great, because we see again and again, in the workings of a selective tradition, reversals and re-discoveries, returns to work apparently abandoned as dead, and clearly this is only possible if there are institutions whose business it is to keep large areas of past culture, if not alive, at least available. It is natural and inevitable that the selective tradition should follow the lines of growth of a society, but because such growth is complex and continuous, the relevance of past work, in any future situation, is unforseeable. There is a natural pressure on academic institutions to follow the lines of growth of a society, but a wise society, while ensuring this kind of relevance, will encourage the institutions to give sufficient resources to the ordinary work of preservation, and to resist the criticism, which any particular period may make with great confidence, that much of this activity is irrelevant and useless. It is often an obstacle to the growth of a society that so many academic institutions are, to an important extent, self-perpetuating and resistant to change. The changes have to be made, in new institutions if necessary, but if we properly understand the process of the selective tradition and look at it over a sufficiently long period to get a real sense of historical change and fluctuation, the corresponding value of such perpetuation will be appreciated.

In a society as a whole, and in all its particular activities, the cultural tradition can be seen as a continual selection and re-selection of ancestors. Particular lines will be drawn, often for as long as a century, and then suddenly with some new stage in growth these will be cancelled or weakened, and new lines drawn. In the analysis of contemporary culture, the existing state of the selective tradition is of vital importance, for it is often true that some change in this tradition – establishing new lines with the past, breaking or re-drawing existing lines – is a radical kind of *contemporary* change. We tend to underestimate the extent to which the cultural tradition is not only a selection but also an interpretation. We see most past work through our own experience, without even making the effort to see it in something like its original terms. What analysis can do is not so much to reverse this, returning a work to its period, as to make the interpretation conscious, by showing historical alternatives; to relate the interpretation to the particular contemporary values on which it rests; and, by exploring the real patterns of the work, confront us with the real nature of the choices we are making. We shall find, in some cases, that we are keeping the work alive because it is a genuine contribution to cultural growth. We shall find, in other cases, that we are using the work in a particular way for our own reasons, and it is better to know this than to surrender to the mysticism of the 'great valuer, Time'. To put on to Time, the abstraction, the responsibility for our own active choices is to suppress a central part of our experience. The more actively all cultural work can be related, either to the whole organization within which it was expressed, or to the contemporary organization within which it is used, the more clearly shall we see its true values. Thus 'documentary' analysis will lead out to 'social' analysis, whether in a lived culture, a past period, or in the selective tradition which is itself a social organization. And the discovery of permanent contributions will lead to the same kind of general analysis, if we accept the process at this level, not as human perfection (a movement towards determined values), but as a part of man's general evolution, to which many individuals and groups contribute. Every element that we analyse will be in this sense active: that it will be seen in certain real relations, at many different levels. In describing these relations, the real cultural process will emerge.

2 Sub Cultures, Cultures and Class

John Clarke
Stuart Hall
Tony Jefferson
Brian Roberts

Our subject in this essay is Youth Cultures: our object, to explain them as a phenomenon, and their appearance in the post-war period. The subject has, of course, been massively treated, above all in the mass media. Yet, many of these surveys and analyses seem mainly to have multiplied the confusions and extended the mythologies surrounding the topic.... First, then, we must clear the ground, try to get behind the myths and explanations which cover up, rather than clarify, the problem....

A. Some definitions

We begin with some minimal definitions. The term, 'Youth Culture', directs us to the 'cultural' aspects of youth. We understand the word 'culture' to refer to that level at which social groups develop distinct patterns of life, and give *expressive form* to their social and material life-experience. Culture is the way, the forms, in which groups 'handle' the raw material of their social and material existence;... it is the practice which realises or *objectivates* group-life in meaningful shape and form.... The 'culture' of a group or class is the peculiar and distinctive 'way of life' of the group or class, the meanings, values and ideas embodied in institutions, in social relations, in systems of beliefs, in *mores* and customs, in the uses of objects and material life. Culture is the distinctive shapes in which this material and social organisation of life expresses itself. A culture includes the 'maps of meaning' which make things intelligible to its members. These 'maps of meaning' are not simply carried around in the head: they are objectivated in the patterns of social organisation and relationship through which the individual becomes a 'social individual'. Culture is the way the social relations of a group are structured and shaped: but it is also the way those shapes are experienced, understood and interpreted.

Source: Stuart Hall and Tony Jefferson (eds.) *Resistance through Rituals: youth sub cultures in post-war Britain,* Hutchinson, 1976, pp. 9-69.

A social individual, born into a particular set of institutions and relations, is at the same moment born into a peculiar configuration of meanings, which give her access to and locate her within 'a culture'. The 'law of society' and the 'law of culture' (the symbolic ordering of social life) are one and the same. These structures – of social relationship and of meaning – shape the on-going collective existence of groups. But they also limit, modify and *constrain* how groups live and reproduce their social existence. Men and women are, thus, formed, and form themselves through society, culture and history. So the existing cultural patterns form a sort of historical reservoir – a pre-constituted 'field of the possibles' – which groups take up, transform, develop. Each group makes something of its starting conditions – and through this 'making', through this practice, culture is reproduced and transmitted. But this practice only takes place within the given field of possibilities and constraints (See Sartre, 1963). 'Men make their own history, but they do not make it just as they please; they do not make it under circumstances chosen by themselves, but under circumstances directly encountered, given and transmitted from the past' (Marx, 1951; p. 225). Culture, then, embodies the trajectory of group life through history: always under conditions and with 'raw materials' which cannot wholly be of its own making.

Groups which exist within the same society and share some of the same material and historical conditions no doubt also understand, and to a certain extent share each others' 'culture'. But just as different groups and classes are unequally ranked in relation to one another, in terms of their productive relations, wealth and power, so *cultures* are differently ranked, and stand in opposition to one another, in relations of domination and subordination, along the scale of 'cultural power'. The definitions of the world, the 'maps of meaning' which express the life situation of those groups which hold the monopoly of power in society, command the greatest weight and influence, secrete the greatest legitimacy.... This does not mean that there is only *one* set of ideas or cultural forms in a society. There will be more than one tendency at work within the dominant ideas of a society. Groups or classes which do not stand at the apex of power, nevertheless find ways of expressing and realising in their culture their subordinate position and experiences. In so far as there is more than one fundamental class in a society (and capitalism is essentially the bringing together, around production, of two fundamentally *different* classes – capital and labour) there will be more than one major cultural configuration in play at a particular historical moment. But the structures and meanings which most adequately reflect the position and interests of the most powerful class – however complex it is internally – will stand, in relation to all the others, as a *dominant* social-cultural order. The dominant culture represents itself as *the* culture. It tries to define and contain all other cultures within its inclusive range.... Other cultural configurations will not only be subordinate to this dominant order: they will enter into struggle with it, seek to modify, negotiate, resist or even overthrow its reign – its *hegemony*.... We might want, here, to make a distinction between 'culture' and 'ideology'. Dominant and subordinate classes will each have distinct cultures. But when one culture gains ascendancy over the other, and when the subordinate culture *experiences* itself in terms prescribed by the dominant culture, then the dominant culture has also become the basis of a dominant ideology.

The dominant culture of a complex society is never a homogeneous structure. It is layered, reflecting different interests within the dominant class (e.g. an aristocratic versus a bourgeois outlook), containing different traces from the past (e.g. religious ideas within a largely secular culture), as well as emergent elements in the present. Subordinate cultures will not always be in open conflict with it. They may, for long periods, coexist with it, negotiate the spaces and gaps in it, make inroads into it, 'warrenning it from within' (Thompson, 1965). However, though the nature of this struggle over culture can never be reduced to a simple opposition, it is crucial to replace the notion of 'culture' with the more concrete, historical concept of 'cultures'; a redefinition which brings out more clearly the fact that cultures always stand in relations of domination – and subordination – to one another, are always, in some sense, in struggle with one another. The singular term, 'culture', can only indicate, in the most general and abstract way, the large cultural configurations at play in a society at any historical moment. We must move at once to the determining relationships of domination and subordination in which these configurations stand; to the processes of incorporation and resistance which define the cultural dialectic between them; and to the institutions which transmit and reproduce 'the culture' (i.e. the dominant culture) in its dominant or 'hegemonic' form.

In modern societies, the most fundamental groups are the social classes, and the major cultural configurations will be, in a fundamental though often mediated way, 'class cultures'. Relative to these cultural-class configurations, *sub*-cultures are sub-sets – smaller, more localised and differentiated structures, within one or other of the larger cultural networks. We must, first, see sub-cultures in terms of their relation to the wider class-cultural networks of which they form a distinctive part. When we examine this relationship between a sub-culture and the 'culture' of which it is a part, we call the latter the 'parent' culture. This must not be confused with the particular relationship between 'youth' and their 'parents'.... What we mean is that a sub-culture, though differing in important ways – in its 'focal concerns', its peculiar shapes and activities – from the culture from which it derives, will also share some things in common with that 'parent' culture.... Sub-cultures, then, must first be related to the 'parent cultures' of which they are a sub-set. But, sub-cultures must *also* be analysed in terms of their relation to the dominant culture - the overall disposition of cultural power in the society as a whole. Thus, we may distinguish respectable, 'rough', delinquent and the criminal sub-cultures *within* working-class culture: but we may also say that, though they differ amongst themselves, they *all* derive in the first instance from a 'working-class parent culture': hence, they are all subordinate sub-cultures, in relation to the dominant middle-class or bourgeois culture....

Sub-cultures, therefore, take shape around the distinctive activities and 'focal concerns' of groups. They can be loosely or tightly bounded. Some sub-cultures are merely loosely-defined strands or 'milieux' within the parent culture: they possess no distinctive 'world' of their own. Others develop a clear, coherent identity and structure. Generally, we deal in this essay *only* with 'sub-cultures' (whether drawn from a middle or working class 'parent culture') which have reasonably tight boundaries, distinctive shapes, which have cohered around particular activities, focal concerns and territorial spaces. When these tightly-defined groups are also distinguished by age and generation, we call them 'youth sub-cultures'.

'Youth sub-cultures' form up on the terrain of social and cultural life. Some youth sub-cultures are regular and persistent features of the 'parent' class-culture: the ill-famed 'culture of delinquency' of the working-class adolescent male, for example. But some sub-cultures appear only at particular historical moments: they become visible, are identified and labelled (either by themselves or by others): they command the stage of public attention for a time: then they fade, disappear or are so widely diffused that they lose their distinctiveness. It is the *latter* kind of sub-cultural formation which primarily concerns us here. The peculiar dress, style, focal concerns, milieux, etc. of the Teddy Boy, the Mod, the Rocker or the Skinhead set them off, as distinctive groupings, both from the broad patterns of working-class culture as a whole, and also from the more diffused patterns exhibited by 'ordinary' working-class boys (and, to a more limited extent, girls). Yet, despite these differences, it is important to stress that, as sub-cultures, they continue to exist within, and coexist with, the more inclusive culture of the class from which they spring. Members of a sub-culture may walk, talk, act, look 'different' from their parents and from some of their peers: but they belong to the same families, go to the same schools, work at much the same jobs, live down the same 'mean streets' as their peers and parents. In certain crucial respects, they share the same position (vis-a-vis the dominant culture), the same fundamental and determining life-experiences, as the 'parent' culture from which they derive. Through dress, activities, leisure pursuits and life-style, they may project a different cultural response or 'solution' to the problems posed for them by their material and social class position and experience. But the membership of a sub-culture cannot protect them from the determining matrix of experiences and conditions which shape the life of their class as a whole....

In what follows, we shall try to show why this *double articulation* of youth sub-cultures – first, to their 'parent' culture (e.g. working-class culture), second, to the dominant culture – is a necessary way of staging the analysis. For our purposes, sub-cultures represent a necessary, 'relatively autonomous', but *inter-mediary* level of analysis. Any attempt to relate sub-cultures to the 'socio-cultural formation as a whole' must grasp its complex unity by way of these necessary differentiations....

B. Dominant and subordinate cultures

In this section, we discuss briefly some of the broad shifts in class relations over the post-war period as a whole, before coming to the specific question of the sub-cultures.

One determining level of change is the way production was reorganised and modernised in the post-war period, and the impact of this on the division of labour, on occupational cultures, on forms of working-class response, defence and resistance. The war and post-war situation accelerated changes already in train in the inter-war period. One general result was a widening of the gap between 'old' and 'new' sectors in the economy – old and new industries, old and new areas and regions. On the one hand, the 'new' industries, based on modern technical and electronic processes or tied to the consumer and export drives; on the other hand, the 'declining' industries, the legacy of the first industrial revolution. The impact of this partial and unplanned 'rationalisation', first on skills and the division of labour, secondly on the economic life of regions and areas, was profound but quite *'uneven'*. Some areas – the South-East especially – spurted ahead; others – sometimes whole industries and regions – were impelled into a long decline....

What matters here is not some general idea of 'social change and the working-class' but, rather, the particular social and cultural composition of those sectors of the working-class whose concrete situation is being restructured by quite specific economic forces. Here, changes in the economic mode of production register on a particular complex of trades, skills, workshops, a particular 'mix' of occupational cultures, the specific distribution of different class strata within them. The wider economic forces then *throw out of gear* a particular working-class complex: they dismantle a set of particular internal balances and stabilities. They reshape and restructure the productive basis, which forms the material and social conditions of life, the 'givens', around which a particular local working-class culture has developed. They disturb a particular historical network of defences and 'negotiations'....

These productive relations also form the basis of the everyday life and culture of the class. Changes in housing and in the ecology of the working-class neighbourhood are part of the same pattern; and the different facets of change react on and reverberate through each other. The impact of post-war redevelopment on traditional working-class neighbourhoods seems in general to go through three broad phases. First, the break-up of traditional housing patterns by post-war re-housing: the new housing estates and new towns. The areas left behind decay; they drift downwards towards the 'urban ghetto' or 'new slum' pattern, the prey of rack-renting, speculative landlordism and multiple occupation. The drift inwards of immigrant labour highlights and compounds the ghettoising process. Then some parts of the ghettoes are selectively redeveloped, through the combination of planning and speculative property development. The entry of middle class families 'up-classes' certain neighbourhoods, and 'planned development' ... redefines the area towards this more 'up-graded', middle-income pattern of life. Again, these are not simply forces working abstractly *on* an area. They graphically reconstruct the *real* material and social conditions in which working people live.

The forces restructuring the working-class neighbourhood and local economy also had a decisive impact on the structure of the family. Those pushed upwards and away in occupational terms were often also moving to estates and towns which prescribed, in their layout and design, a different, less extended, more 'nucleated' family pattern. Even estates rebuilt in or near the old areas have been constructed – more consistently, perhaps, than their pre-war counterparts – in the image of an 'ideal' family: that is, a more middle-class, 'nuclear' one. The working-class family did not 'disappear' under these conditions nor did working people actively subscribe to the new 'bourgeois' domestic ideal. But the family may have become more isolated; relations between children and parents, or between peers and siblings were altered, with special effect on younger family members and on women. What, in sum, was *unsettled* was the precise position and role of the working-class family within a defensive class culture. What was disturbed was a concrete set of relations, a network of knowledge, things, experiences – the *supports* of a class culture....

In the early post-war period, these changes in the intricate mechanisms and balances of working-class life and culture were overlaid by the spectacular ideology of 'affluence'. We know now what were the limits of its real impact, its uneven distribution – even in terms of wages and consumption – for most sections of the working-class. There was no 'qualitative leap'. Indeed, 'affluence' assumed the proportions of a full-blown ideology precisely because it was required to cover over the gaps between real inequalities and the promised Utopia of equality-for-all and ever-rising-consumption to come. By projecting this ideological scenario, the 'affluence' myth aimed to give the working-classes a stake in a future which had not yet arrived, and thus to bind and cement the class to the hegemonic order. Here, precisely, the ideology of affluence reconstructed the 'real relations' of post-war British society into an 'imaginary relation'. This is the function of social myths. The myth provided, for a time, the ideological basis of the political hegemony of the 1950s. 'Affluence' was, essentially, an ideology of the dominant culture *about* and *for* the working-class, directed *at* them (through the media, advertising, political speeches, etc). Few working-class people subscribed to a version of their own situation which so little squared with its real dimensions. What mattered, therefore, was *not* the passive re-making of the working class in one 'affluent' image, but the *dislocations* it produced – and the responses it provoked....

To locate youth sub-culture in this kind of analysis, we must first situate youth in the dialectic between a 'hegemonic' dominant culture and the subordinate working-class 'parent' culture, of which youth is a fraction. These terms – hegemonic/corporate, dominant/subordinate – are crucial for the analysis, but need further elaboration before the sub-cultural dimension can be introduced. Gramsci used the term 'hegemony' to refer to the moment when a ruling class is able, not only to *coerce* a subordinate class to conform to its interests, but to exert a 'hegemony' or 'total social authority' over subordinate classes. This involves the exercise of a special kind of power – the power to frame alternatives and contain opportunities, *to win and shape consent,* so that the granting of legitimacy to the dominant classes appears not only 'spontaneous' but natural and normal.... The terrain on which this hegemony is won or lost is the terrain of the superstructures; the institutions of civil society and the state – what Althusser (1971) and Poulantzas (1973), somewhat misleadingly, call 'ideological state apparatuses'. Conflicts of interest arise, fundamentally, from the difference in the structural position of the classes in the productive realm: but they 'have their effect' in social and political life. Politics, in the widest sense, frames the passage from the first level to the second. The terrain of civil and state institutions thus becomes essentially 'the stake, but also the site of class struggle' (Althusser, 1971). In part, these apparatuses work 'by ideology'. That is, the definitions of reality institutionalised within these apparatuses come to constitute a lived 'reality as such' for the subordinate classes – that, at least, is what hegemony attempts and secures.... A hegemonic cultural order tries to *frame* all competing definitions of the world within *its* range. It provides the horizon of thought and action within which conflicts are fought through, appropriated (i.e. experienced), obscured (i.e. concealed as a 'national interest' which should unite all conflicting parties) or contained (i.e. settled to the profit of the ruling class). A hegemonic order prescribes, not the specific content of ideas, but the *limits* within which ideas and conflicts move and are resolved. . . .

Hegemony works through ideology, but it does not consist of false ideas, perceptions, definitions. It works *primarily* by inserting the subordinate class into the key institutions and structures which support the power and social authority of the dominant order. It is, above all, in these structures and relations that a subordinate class *lives its subordination.* Often, this subordination is secured only because the dominant order succeeds in weakening, destroying, displacing or incorporating alternative institutions of defence and resistance thrown up by the subordinate class. Gramsci insists, quite correctly, that 'the thesis which asserts that men become conscious of fundamental conflicts on the level of ideology is not psychological or moralistic in character but *structural and epistemological.*' (Our italics; Gramsci, 1971; p. 164).

Hegemony can rarely be sustained by one, single class stratum. Almost always it requires an *alliance* of ruling-class fractions – a 'historical bloc'. The content of hegemony will be determined, in part, by precisely which class fractions compose such a 'hegemonic bloc', and thus what interests have to be taken into account within it. Hegemony is not simple 'class rule'. It requires to some degree the 'consent' of the subordinate class, which has, in turn, to be won and secured; thus, an ascendancy of social authority, not only in the state but in civil society as well, in culture and ideology. Hegemony prevails when ruling classes not only rule or 'direct' but *lead*. The state is a major educative force in this process. It educates through its regulation of the life of the subordinate classes. These apparatuses reproduce class relations, and thus class subordination (the family, the school, the church and cultural institutions, as well as the law, the police and the army, the courts).

The struggle against class hegemony also takes place within these institutions, as well as outside them – they become the 'site' of class struggle. . . .

So hegemony cannot be taken for granted – either by the state and the dominant classes, or, for that matter, by the analyst. The current use of the term, to suggest the unending and unproblematic exercise of class power by every ruling class, and its opposite – the permanent and finished incorporation of the subordinate class – is quite false to Gramsci's usage. It limits the historical specificity of the concept. To make that point concrete: we would argue that, though the dominant classes remained massively in command during the 1930s, it is difficult to define them as 'hegemonic'. Economic crisis and unemployment disciplined, rather than 'led', the working classes into subordination in this period. . . . By contrast, the 1950s seem to us a period of true 'hegemonic domination', it being precisely the role of 'affluence', as an ideology, to dismantle working-class resistance and deliver the 'spontaneous consent' of the class to the authority of the dominant classes. Increasingly, in the 1960s, and more openly in the 1970s, this 'leadership' has again been undermined. The society has polarised, conflict has reappeared on many levels. The dominant classes retain power, but their 'repertoire' of control is progressively challenged, weakened, exhausted. One of the most striking features of this later period is the shift in the exercise of control from the mechanisms of consent to those of coercion (e.g. the use of the law, the courts, the police and the army, of legal repression, conspiracy charges and of force to contain an escalating threat to the state and to 'law and order'). This marks a *crisis* in the hegemony of the ruling class.

Hegemony, then, is not universal and 'given' to the continuing rule of a particular class. It has to be *won*, worked for, reproduced, sustained. Hegemony is, as Gramsci said, a 'moving equilibrium', containing 'relations of forces favourable or unfavourable to this or that tendency'. It is a matter of the nature of the balance struck between contending classes: the compromises made to sustain it; the relations of force; the solutions adopted. Its character and content can only be established by looking at concrete situations, at concrete historical moments. The idea of 'permanent class hegemony', or of 'permanent incorporation' must be ditched.

In relation to the hegemony of a ruling class, the working-class is, by definition, a *subordinate* social and cultural formation. Capitalist production, Marx suggested, reproduces capital and labour in their ever-antagonistic forms. The role of hegemony is to ensure that, in the social relations between the classes, each class is continually *reproduced* in its existing dominant-or-subordinate form. Hegemony can never wholly and absolutely absorb the working-class *into* the dominant order. Society may seem to be, but cannot actually ever be, in the capitalist mode of production, 'one-dimensional'. Of course, at times, hegemony is strong and cohesive, and the subordinate class is weak, vulnerable and exposed. But it cannot, by definition, disappear. It remains, as a subordinate structure, often separate and impermeable, yet still contained by the overall rule and domination of the ruling class. The subordinate class has developed its own corporate culture, its own forms of social relationship, its characteristic institutions, values, modes of life. Class conflict never disappears. English working-class culture is a peculiarly strong, densely-impacted, cohesive and defensive structure of this corporate kind. Class conflict, then, is rooted and embodied in this culture: it cannot 'disappear' – contrary to the ideology of affluence – until the productive relations which produce and sustain it disappear. But it can be more or less open, more or less formal, more or less institutionalised, more or less autonomous. The period between the 1880s and the present shows, not a single thrust towards incorporation but a marked alternating rhythm. It is important to insist that, even when class conflict is most institutionalised, it remains as one of the fundamental base-rhythms of the society.

In old and developed industrial capitalist societies, like Britain, the culture is in fact *covered* by a network of what we might call 'institutional solutions', which structure how the dominant and subordinate cultures coexist, survive, but also struggle, with one another inside the same social formation. Many of these institutions *preserve* the corporate culture of the subordinate class, but also *negotiate* its relations with the dominant culture. These are the 'negotiated' aspects of a subordinate class culture....

Working-class culture has consistently 'won space' from the dominant culture. Many working-class institutions represent the different outcomes of this intense kind of 'negotiation' over long periods. At times, these institutions are adaptive; at other times, combative. Their class identity and position is never finally 'settled': the balance of forces within them remains open. They form the basis of what Parkin has called a 'negotiated version' of the dominant system ... dominant values are not so much rejected or opposed as modified by the subordinate class as a result of circumstances and restricted opportunities (Parkin, 1971; p. 92). Often, such 'negotiated solutions' prevail, not because the class is passive and deferential to ruling class ideas, but because its perspectives are bounded and contained by immediate practical concerns or limited to concrete situations. (This is the material basis and 'rational core' of working-class 'economism'.) From this arise the *situated solutions* to problems arising at a wider, more global, level, beyond the immediate class horizon. In situations where 'purely abstract evaluations are called for, the dominant value system will provide the moral frame of reference; but in concrete social situations involving choice and action, the negotiated version – or subordinate value system – will provide the moral framework' (Parkin, 1971; p. 93). Authority, enshrined in the major institutional order of society (e.g. the rule of the law) may be accepted at an abstract level, but much more ambivalently handled at the face-to-face level (e.g. attitudes to the police). English working-class culture is massively orchestrated around attitudes of 'Us' and 'Them', even when this structured difference does not lead directly to counter-hegemonic strategies by the working-class....

The working-class neighbourhood, which assumes its 'traditional' form in and after the 1880s, represents one, distinctive example of the outcome of negotiation between the classes. In it, the different strata of the working-class have won space for their own forms of life. The values of this corporate culture are registered everywhere, in material and social forms, in the shapes and uses of things, in patterns of recreation and leisure, in the relations between people and the character of communal spaces. These spaces are both physical (the networks of streets, houses, corner shops, pubs and parks) and social (the networks of kin, friendship, work and neighbourly relationships). Over such spaces, the class has come to exert those 'informal social controls' which redefine and reappropriate them for the groups which live in them: a web of rights and obligations, intimacies and distances, embodying in its real textures and structures 'the sense of solidarity . . . local loyalties and traditions' (Cohen, 1972). These are the 'rights', not of ownership or force, but of territorial and cultural possession, the customary occupation of the 'sitting tenant'. The institutions are, of course, cross-cut and penetrated by outside forces. The structure of work and workplace, near or far, link the local labour force to wider economic forces and movements. Not far away are the bustling commercial high streets, with their chain stores and supermarkets, linking the home to the wider economy through trade and consumption. Through these structures, the neighbourhood is socially and economically *bounded*. At one level – the horizontal – are all those ties which bind spaces and institutions to locality, neighbourhood, local culture and tradition. At another level – the vertical – are those structures which tie them to dominant institutions and cultures.

The local school is a classic instance of such 'double-binding' (Hall, 1974a; p. 49-55). It is the *local* school, next to houses, streets and shops where generations of working-class children have been 'schooled', and where ties of friendship, peer-group and marriage are forged and unmade. Yet, in terms of vertical relationships, the school has stood for kinds of learning, types of discipline and authority relations, affirmed experiences quite at variance with the local culture. Its selective mechanisms of streaming, 'tracking', eleven-plus, its knowledge boundaries, its intolerance of language and experience outside the range of formal education, link the urban working-class locality to the wider world of education and occupations in ways which are connective but also, crucially, *disconnective*. It remains a classic, negotiated, or mediated class institution. In this context, we can begin to look again and assess differently the varying strategies, options and 'solutions' which develop in relation to it: the 'scholarship' boy or girl; the 'ordinary, average-ability' kids; the 'trouble-makers'; truants and absentees; the educationally-and emotionally 'deprived'; the actively mis-educated (e.g. E.S.N.-ed black kids). . . .

Negotiation, resistance, struggle: the relations between a subordinate and a dominant culture, wherever they fall within this spectrum, are always intensely active, always oppositional, in a structural sense (even when this opposition is latent, or experienced simply as the normal state of affairs – what Gouldner called 'normalised repression'). Their outcome is not given but *made*. The subordinate class brings to this 'theatre of struggle' a repertoire of strategies and responses – ways of coping as well as of resisting. Each strategy in the repertoire mobilises certain real material and social elements: it constructs these into the supports for the different ways the class lives and resists its continuing subordination....

C. The subcultural response

We can return, now, to the question of 'sub-cultures'. Working-class sub-cultures, we suggested, take shape on the level of the social and cultural class-relations of the subordinate classes. In themselves, they are not simply 'ideological' constructs. They, too, *win space* for the young: cultural space in the neighbourhood and institutions, real time for leisure and recreation, actual room on the street or street-corner. They serve to mark out and appropriate 'territory' in the localities. They focus around key occasions of social interaction: the weekend, the disco, the bank-holiday trip, the night out in the 'centre', the 'standing-about-doing-nothing' of the weekday evening, the Saturday match. They cluster around particular locations. They develop specific rhythms of interchange, structured relations between members: younger to older, experienced to novice, stylish to square. They explore 'focal concerns' central to the inner life of the group: things always 'done' or 'never done', a set of social rituals which underpin their collective identity and define them as a 'group' instead of a mere collection of individuals. They adopt and adapt material objects – goods and possessions – and reorganise them into distinctive 'styles' which express the collectivity of their being-as-a-group. These concerns, activities, relationships, materials become embodied in rituals of relationship and occasion and movement. Sometimes, the world is marked out, linguistically, by names or an *argot* which classifies the social world exterior to them in terms meaningful only within their group perspective, and maintains its boundaries....

Though not 'ideological', sub-cultures have an ideological dimension: and, in the problematic situation of the post-war period, this ideological component became more prominent. In addressing the 'class problematic' of the particular strata from which they were drawn, the different sub-cultures provided for a section of working-class youth (mainly boys) *one* strategy for negotiating their collective existence. But their highly ritualised and stylised form suggests that they were also *attempts at a solution* to that problematic experience: a resolution which, because pitched largely at the symbolic level, was fated to fail. The problematic of a subordinate class experience can be 'lived through', negotiated or resisted; but it cannot be *resolved* at that level or by those means. There is no 'sub-cultural career' for the working-class lad, no 'solution' in the sub-cultural milieu, for problems posed by the key structuring experiences of the class.

There is no 'subcultural solution' to working-class youth unemployment, educational disadvantage, compulsory miseducation, dead-end jobs, the routinisation and specialisation of labour, low pay and the loss of skills. Sub-cultural strategies cannot match, meet or answer the structuring dimensions emerging in this period for the class as a whole. So, when the post-war sub-cultures address the problematics of their class experience, they often do so in ways which reproduce the gaps and discrepancies between real negotiations and symbolically displaced 'resolutions'. They 'solve', but in an imaginary way, problems which at the concrete material level remain unresolved. Thus the 'Teddy Boy' expropriation of an upper class style of dress 'covers' the gap between largely manual, unskilled, near lumpen real careers and life-chances, and the 'all-dressed-up-and-nowhere-to-go' experience of Saturday evening. Thus, in the expropriation and fetishisation of consumption and style itself, the 'Mods' cover for the gap between the never-ending-weekend and Monday's resumption of boring, dead-end work. Thus, in the resurrection of an archetypal and 'symbolic' (but, in fact, anachronistic) form of working-class dress, in the displaced focussing on the football match and the 'occupation' of the football 'ends', Skinheads reassert, but 'imaginarily', the values of a class, the essence of a style, a kind of 'fan-ship' to which few working-class adults any longer subscribe: they 're-present' a sense of territory and locality which the planners and speculators are rapidly destroying: they 'declare' as alive and well a game which is being commercialised, professionalised and spectacularised. 'Skins Rule, OK'. OK? But in ideology, men do indeed express, not the real relation between them and their conditions of existence, but *the way* they live the relation between them and the conditions of their existence; this presupposes both a real and an *'imaginary'*, *'lived'* relation....

Working-class sub-cultures are a response to a problematic which youth shares with other members of the 'parent' class culture. But class structures the adolescent's experience of that problematic in distinctive ways. First, it locates the young, at a formative stage of their development, in a particular material and cultural milieu, in distinctive relations and experiences. These provide the essential cultural frame-works through which that problematic is made sense of by the youth. This 'socialisation' of youth *into* a class identity and position operates particularly through two 'informal' agencies: family and neighbourhood. Family and neighbourhood are the specific structures which *form*, as well as frame, youth's early passage into a class. For example, the sex-typing roles and responsibilities characteristic of a class are reproduced, not only through language and talk in the family, but through daily interaction and example. In the neighbourhood, patterns of community sociality are embedded partly through the structure of interactions between older and younger kids.... These intimate contexts also refer the young to the larger world outside. Thus it is largely through friends and relations that the distant but increasingly imminent worlds of work or of face-to-face authority (the rent man, Council officials, social security, the police) are appropriated. Through these formative networks, relations, distances, interactions, orientations to the wider world and its social types are delineated and reproduced in the young.

Class also, broadly, structures the young individual's life-chances. It determines, in terms of statistical class probabilities, the distribution of 'achievement' and 'failure'. It establishes certain crucial orientations towards careers in education and work – it produces the notoriously 'realistic' expectations of working-class kids about future opportunities. It teaches ways of relating to and negotiating authority....

These are only some of the many ways in which the way youth is inserted within the culture of a class also serves to reproduce, within the young, the problematics of that class. But, over and above these shared class situations, there remains something privileged about the specifically *generational experience* of the young. Fundamentally, this is due to the fact that youth encounters the problematic of its class culture in *different sets of institutions and experiences* from those of its parents; and when youth encounters the same structures, it encounters them at *crucially different points* in its biographical careers.

We can identify these aspects of 'generational specificity' in relation to the three main life areas we pointed to earlier: education, work and leisure. Between the ages of five and sixteen, education is the institutional sphere which has the most sustained and intensive impact on the lives of the young. It is the 'paramount reality' imposing itself on experience, not least through the fact that it cannot (easily) be avoided. By contrast, the older members of the class encounter education in various *indirect* and distanced ways: through remembered experiences ('things have changed' nowadays); through special mediating occasions – parents' evenings, etc.; and through the interpretations the young give of their school experiences.

In the area of work, the difference is perhaps less obvious, in that both young and old alike are facing similar institutional arrangements, organisations and occupational situations. But within this crucial differences remain. The young face the problem of choosing and entering jobs, of learning both the formal and informal cultures of work – the whole difficult transition from school to work. We have already observed how the changing occupational structures of some areas and industries may dislocate the traditionally evolved 'family work – career structure' – thus making the transition even more difficult. For the older members of the class, work has become a relatively routine aspect of life; they have learnt occupational identities and the cultures of work, involving strategies for coping with the problems that work poses – methods of 'getting by'.

In the broader context, the young are likely to be more vulnerable to the consequence of increasing unemployment than are older workers: in the unemployment statistics of the late sixties, unskilled school leavers were twice as likely to be unemployed as were older, unskilled workers. In addition, the fact of unemployment is likely to be differentially *experienced* at different stages in the occupational 'career'.

Finally, leisure must be seen as a significant life-area for the class.... In working-class leisure, we see many of the results of that 'warrenning' of society by the working-class discussed above. Leisure and recreation seem to have provided a more negotiable space than the tightly-disciplined and controlled work situation. The working-class has imprinted itself indelibly on many areas of mass leisure and recreation. These form an important part of the corporate culture and are central to the experience and cultural identity of the whole class. Nevertheless, there are major differences in the ways working-class adults and young people experience and regard leisure. This difference became intensified in the 1950s and 1960s, with the growth of the 'teenage consumer' and the reorganisation of consumption and leisure provision (both commercial and non-commercial) in favour of a range of goods and services specifically designed to attract a youthful clientele. This widespread availability and high visibility of Youth Culture structured the leisure sphere in crucially different ways for the young. The equation of youth with consumption and leisure rearranged and *intensified* certain long-standing parent culture orientations; for example, towards the special and privileged meaning of 'freetime', and towards 'youth' as a period for 'having a good time while you can' – the 'last fling'. This reshaping of attitudes from within the class, in conjuction with pressures to rearrange and redistribute the patterns of leisure for the young from outside, served to highlight – indeed to *fetishise* – the meaning of leisure for the young. Thus, not only did youth encounter leisure in different characteristic institutions from their parents (caffs, discos, youth clubs, 'all nighters', etc.): these institutions powerfully presented themselves to the young as different from the past, partly because they were so uncompromisingly youthful.

Here we begin to see how forces, working right across a class, but differentially experienced as between the generations, may have formed the basis for generating an outlook – a kind of consciousness – specific to age position: a *generational consciousness.* We can also see exactly why this 'consciousness', though formed by class situation and the forces working in it, may nevertheless have taken the form of a consciousness apparently separate from, unrelated to, indeed, able to be set over against, its class content and context. Though we can see how and why this specific kind of 'generational consciousness' might arise, the problem is not resolved by simply reading it once again out of existence – that is, by re-assigning to youth a clear and simple class-based identity and consciousness. This would be simply to over-react against 'generational consciousness'. We have suggested that, though a fully-blown 'generational consciousness' served unwittingly to repress and obscure the class dimension, it did have a 'rational core' in the very experience of the working-class young in the period; the specificity of the institutions in which post-war changes were encountered, and above all, in the way this sphere was reshaped by changes in the leisure market....

'Generational consciousness' thus has roots in the real experience of working-class youth as a whole. But it took a peculiarly intense form in the post-war sub-cultures which were sharply demarcated – amongst other factors – by age and generation. Youth felt and experienced itself as 'different', especially when this difference was inscribed in activities and interests to which 'age', principally, provided the passport. This does not necessarily mean that a 'sense of class' was thereby obliterated. Skinheads, for example, are clearly both 'generationally' and 'class' conscious. As Cohen suggested, 'sub-culture is ... a compromise solution, between two contradictory needs: the need to create and express *autonomy and difference* from parents ... and the need to maintain ... the *parental identifications* which support them' (Cohen, 1972; p. 26). It is to the formation of these generationally distinct working-class sub-cultures that we next turn.

D. Sources of style

The question of style, indeed, of generational style, is pivotal to the post-war formation of these youth sub-cultures. .... What concerns us here is, first, how 'class' and 'generational' elements interact together in the production of distinctive group-styles; second, how the materials available to the group are constructed and appropriated in the form of a visibly organised cultural response.

Working-class youth inhabit, like their parents, a distinctive structural and cultural *milieu* defined by territory, objects and things, relations, institutional and social practices. In terms of kinship, friendship networks, the informal culture of the neighbourhood, and the practices articulated around them, the young are already located in and by the 'parent' culture. They also encounter the dominant culture, not in its distant, remote, powerful, abstract forms, but in the located forms and institutions which mediate the dominant culture to the subordinate culture, and thus permeate it. Here, for youth, the school, work (from Saturday jobs onwards), leisure are the key institutions. Of almost equal importance – for youth above all – are the institutions and agencies of public social control: the school serves this function, but alongside it, a range of institutions from the 'hard' coercive ones, like the police, to the 'softer' variants

– youth and social workers.

It is at the intersection between the located parent culture and the mediating institutions of the dominant culture that youth sub-cultures arise. Many forms of adaptation, negotiation and resistance, elaborated by the 'parent' culture in its encounter with the dominant culture, are borrowed and adapted by the young in *their* encounter with the mediating institutions of provision and control. In organising their response to these experiences, working-class youth sub-cultures take some things principally from the located 'parent' culture: but they apply and transform them to the situations and experiences characteristic of their own distinctive group-life and generational experience....

But there are also 'focal concerns' more immediate, conjunctural, specific to 'youth' and its situation and activities. On the whole, the literature on post-war sub-culture has neglected the first aspect (what is shared with the 'parent' culture) and over emphasised what is distinct (the 'focal concerns' of the youth groups). But, this second element – which is, again, generationally very specific – must be taken seriously in any account. It consists both of the materials available to the group for the construction of subcultural identities (dress, music, talk), and of their contexts (activities, exploits, places, caffs, dance halls, day-trips, evenings-out, football games, etc.)....

The various youth sub-cultures have customarily been identified by their possessions and objects: the boot-lace tie and velvet-collared drape jacket of the Ted, the close crop, parka coats and scooter of the Mod, the stained jeans, swastikas and ornamented motorcycles of the bike-boys, the bovver boots and skinned-head of the Skinhead, the Chicago suits or glitter costumes of the Bowieites, etc. Yet, despite their visibility, things simply appropriated and worn (or listened to) do not make a style. What makes a style is the activity of stylisation – the active organisation of objects with activities and outlooks, which produce an organised group-identity in the form and shape of a coherent and distinctive way of 'being-in-the-world'....

Working-class sub-cultures could not have existed without a real economic base: the growth in money wages in the 'affluent' period, but, more important, the fact that incomes grew more rapidly for teenagers than for adults in the working-class, and that much of this was 'disposable income' (income available for leisure and non-compulsory spending). But income, alone, does not make a style either. The sub-cultures could not have existed without the growth of a consumer market specifically geared to youth. The new youth industries provided the raw materials, the goods: but they did not, and when they tried failed to, produce many very authentic or sustained 'styles' in the deeper sense. The objects were there, available, but were *used* by the groups in the construction of distinctive styles. But this meant, not simply picking them up, but actively constructing a specific selection of things and goods *into* a style. And this frequently involved...subverting and transforming these things, from their given meaning and use, to other meanings and uses. All commodities have a social use and thus a cultural meaning; they are... cultural *signs*. They have already been invested, by the dominant culture, with meanings, associations, social connotations. Many of these meanings seem fixed and 'natural'. But this is only because the dominant culture has so fully appropriated them to its use, that the meanings which it attributes to the commodities have come to appear as the only meaning which they can express. In fact, in cultural systems, there is no 'natural' meaning as such. Objects and commodities do not mean any one thing. They 'mean' only because they have already been arranged, according to social use, into culture codes of meaning, which *assign meanings to them*.... It is possible to expropriate, as well as to appropriate, the social meanings which they seem 'naturally' to have: or, by combining them with something else,... to change or inflect their meaning. Because the meanings which commodities express are socially given – Marx called commodities 'social hieroglyphs' – their meaning can also be socially altered or reconstructed....

Working-class youth needed money to spend on expressive goods, objects and activities – the post-war consumer market had a clear economic infrastructure. But neither money nor the market could fully dictate what groups used these things to *say* or *signify* about themselves. This re-signification was achieved by many different means. One way was to inflect 'given' meanings by combining things borrowed from one system of meanings into a different code, generated by the sub-culture itself, and through sub-cultural use. Another way was to modify, by addition, things which had been produced or used by a different social group (e.g. the Teddy Boy modifications of Edwardian dress) .... Another was to intensify or exaggerate or isolate a given meaning and, so change it (the 'fetishising' of consumption and appearance by the Mods, ... or the elongation of the pointed winkle-picker shoes of the Italian style) .... Yet another way was to combine forms according to a 'secret' language or code, to which only members of the group possessed the key (e.g. the *argot* of many sub-cultural and deviant groups; the 'Rasta' language of black 'Rudies'). These are only *some* of the many ways in which the sub-cultures used the materials and commodities of the 'youth market' to construct meaningful styles and appearances for themselves.

Far more important were the aspects of group life which these appropriated objects and things were made to reflect, express and resonate. It is this reciprocal effect, between the things a group uses and the outlooks and activities which structure and define their use, which is the generative principle of stylistic creation in a sub-culture. This involves members of a group in the appropriation of particular objects which are, or can be made, 'homologous' with their focal concerns, activities, group structure and collective self-image – objects in which they can see their central values held and reflected. The adoption by skinheads of boots and short jeans and shaved hair was 'meaningful' in terms of the sub-culture only because these external manifestations resonated with and articulated Skinhead conceptions of masculinity, 'hardness' and 'working-classness'. This meant overcoming or negotiating or, even, taking over in a positive way many of the negative meanings which, in the dominant cultural code, attached to these things: the 'prison-crop' image of the shaved head, the work-image, the so-called 'outdated cloth-cap image', and so on. The new meanings emerge because the 'bits' which had been borrowed or revived were brought together into a new and distinctive stylistic *ensemble*: but also because the symbolic objects – dress, appearance, language, ritual occasions, styles of interaction, music – were made to form *a unity* with the group's relations, situation, experiences: the crystallisation in an expressive form, which then defines the group's public identity....

This registering of group identity, situation and trajectory in a visible style both consolidates the group from a loosely-focussed to a tightly-bounded entity: and sets the group off, distinctively, from other similar and dissimilar groups. Indeed, like all other kinds of cultural construction, the symbolic use of things to consolidate and express an internal coherence was, in the same moment, a kind of implied opposition to (where it was not an active and conscious contradition of) *other* groups *against* which its identity was defined. This process led, in our period, to the distinctive visibility of those groups which pressed the 'sub-cultural solution' to its limits along this stylistic path. It also had profound negative consequences for the labelling, stereotyping and stigmatisation, in turn, of those groups by society's guardians, moral entrepreneurs, public definers and the social control culture in general....

E. Rise of the counter-cultures

Up to this point, we have dealt exclusively with working-class youth sub-cultures. And there are some problems in deciding whether we can speak of *middle*-class sub-cultures in the same way and within the same sort of theoretical framework. Yet, not only has the period since the war witnessed the rise of quite distinctive kinds of 'expressive movements' among middle-class youth, different from the school or 'student' cultures of the pre-war period, but, as we get closer to the 1970s, these have attracted, if anything, *more* public attention – and reaction – than their working-class counterparts. We point, of course, not simply to the growing involvement of middle-class youth with the commercialised popular culture and leisure associated with 'Youth Culture', but the appearance of quite distinct 'sub-cultural' currents: the Hippie movement; the various 'deviant' drug, drop-out and gay sub-cultures; the elements of cultural revolt in the student protest movements, etc. Most significant is the widespread cultural disaffiliation of broad sectors of middle-class youth – the phenomenon of the Counter-Culture. This has, in turn, been linked with the general radicalisation and politicisation (and de-politicisation) of some middle-class youth strata.

We must note some clear structural differences in the response of the youth of the different classes. Working-class sub-cultures are clearly articulated, collective structures – often, 'near-' or 'quasi'-gangs. Middle-class counter-cultures are diffuse, less group-centred, more individualised. The latter precipitate, typically, not tight sub-cultures but a diffuse counter-culture *milieu*. Working-class sub-cultures reproduce a clear dichotomy between those aspects of group life still fully under the constraint of dominant or 'parent' institutions (family, home, school, work), and those focussed on non-work hours – leisure, peer-group association. Middle-class counter-culture *milieux* merge and blur the distinctions between 'necessary' and 'free' time and activities. Indeed, the latter are distinguished precisely by their attempt to explore 'alternative institutions' to the central institutions of the dominant culture: new patterns of living, of family-life, of work or even 'un-careers'. Middle class youth remains longer than their working-class peers 'in the transitional stage'. Typically, working-class youth appropriate the existing environment, they construct distinct leisure-time activities around the given working-class environment – street, neighbourhood, football ground, seaside town, dance-hall, cinema, bomb-site, pub, disco. Middle class youth tend to construct enclaves within the interstices of the dominant culture. Where the former represent an appropriation of the 'ghetto', the latter often make an exodus *to* the 'ghetto'. During the high point of the Counter-Culture, in the 1960s, the middle-class counter-cultures formed a whole embryo 'alternative society', providing the Counter-Culture with an underground, institutional base. Here, the youth of each class reproduces the position of the 'parent' classes to which they belong. Middle-class culture affords the space and opportunity for sections of it to 'drop out' of circulation. Working-class youth is persistently and consistently structured by the dominating alternative rhythm of Saturday Night and Monday Morning.

The objective oppositional content of working-class sub-cultures expresses itself socially. It is therefore often assimilated by the control culture to traditional forms of working-class 'delinquency', defined as Hooliganism or Vandalism. The counter-cultures take a more overtly ideological or political form. They make articulate their opposition to dominant values and institutions - even when, as frequently occurred, this does not take the form of *an overtly* political response. Even when working-class sub-cultures are aggressively class conscious, this dimension tends to be repressed by the control culture, which treats them as 'typical delinquents'. Even when the middle-class counter-cultures are explicitly anti-political, their objective tendency is treated as, potentially, political.

Middle-class counter-cultures are a feature of the mid-1960s and after, rather than of the 1950s. Only a handful of the more intellectual youth was involved in the English counter-part to the 'Beat Movement'. The post-Beat, 'on-the-road', style was prevalent in and around CND and the peace-movement in the late 1950s - the beatnik/peacenik period, associated with the folk revival and the music of Bob Dylan. The Hippies of the later 1960s were the most distinctive of the middle-class sub-cultures. Their cultural influence on this sector of youth was immense, and many counter-culture values must still be traced back to their Hippie roots. Hippies helped a whole quasi-bohemian sub-cultural *milieu* to come into existence, shaped styles, dress, attitudes, music and so on. The alternative institutions of the Underground emerged, basically, from this matrix. But Hippie culture quickly fragmented into different strands - heads, freaks, street people, etc. It fed both the 'drop-out' and the drug sub-cultures of the period. It permeated student and ex-student culture. It was then crosscut by influences stemming from the more political elements among middle-class youth - the student protest movement, radical social work, community action groups, the growth of the left sects and so on. All these tendencies came to a partial fusion in the period between 1967 and 1970 - the high point of the Counter-Culture. This formation, too, has fragmented in several directions. The two most distinctive strands flow, one way, via drugs, mysticism, the 'revolution in life-style' into a Utopian alternative culture; or, the other way, via community action, protest action and libertarian goals, into a more activist politics. What we have here, in short, is a host of variant strands, connections and divergencies within a broadly defined counter-culture *milieu*, rather than (with the exception of the drug and sexual sub-cultures) a sequence of tightly-defined, middle-class sub-cultures.

Both working-class sub-cultures and middle-class counter-cultures are seen, by moral guardians and the control culture, as marking a 'crisis in authority'. The 'delinquency' of the one and the 'disaffiliation' of the other index a weakening of the bonds of social attachment and of the formative institutions which manage how the former 'mature' into hard-working, law-abiding, respectable working-class citizens, or the latter into sober, career-minded, 'possessively-individual' bourgeois citizens. This is a break in, if not a break-down of, the reproduction of cultural-class relations and identities, as well as a loss of deference to 'betters and elders'. The difference is that where the first was a weakening of control over the youth of a subordinate class, the second was a crisis among the youth of the dominant class....

Middle-class counter-culture spearheaded a dissent from their own, dominant, 'parent' culture. Their disaffiliation was principally ideological and cultural. They directed their attack mainly against those institutions which reproduce the dominant cultural-ideological relations – the family, education, the media, marriage, the sexual division of labour. These are the very apparatuses which manufacture 'attachment' and internalise consent. 'Women, hippies, youth groups, students and school children all question the institutions which have formed them and try to erect their obverse ...' (Mitchell, 1971, p. 32). Certainly, some of these groups aimed for a systematic inversion, a symbolic upturning, of the whole bourgeois ethic. By pushing contradictory tendencies in the culture to extremes, they sought to subvert them, but from the inside, and *by a negation*....

Once again, this emergent movement among middle-class youth must be located, first, in the dynamic and contradictions peculiar, in this period, to its 'parent' middle-class culture. The middle classes have also been affected by the advancing division of labour under modern capitalist production. We have seen the growth of the intermediate white-collar and lower managerial strata, the rise of new professions alongside the old, a growth in the administrative and 'welfare-state' non-commercial middle classes, and new strata connected with the revolutions in communications, management and marketing. These are what Gramsci called 'the organic intelligentsia' of modern capitalism – groups marked out by their 'directive and technical capacity', their role as organisers, in the whole expanded sphere of production, of 'masses of men ... of the "confidence" of investors ... and of the customers for his product, etc.' (Gramsci, 1971, p. 5). Schools and universities are the instruments 'through which intellectuals of various levels are elaborated ... the more extensive the "area" covered by education and the more numerous the "vertical" levels of schooling, the more complex is the cultural world ...' (ibid.). The expansion in education was, thus, central to changes in the composition, character and problematic of this class. Hence, a crisis in the youth of this class expressed itself, specifically, as a crisis in the educational and ideological apparatuses.

The relation between intellectual strata and the world of production is '"mediated" by the whole fabric of society and by the complex of superstructures' (ibid.). The culture of 'bourgeois' man, with its intricate emotional restraints and repressions, its regulated tempo of restraint and release, its commitment to the protestant 'ethic' of work, career, competitive achievement and possessive individualism, to the ideology of family privacy and the ideal of domesticity, forms a rich and complex integument around the developing mode of production. But, as capitalism moved, after the war, into its more technically-advanced, corporate, consumer stage, this cultural integument was eroded. Critical rifts began to appear in this superstructural complex. The post-war reorganisation of the technical and productive life of the society, and the unsuccessful attempt to stabilise the mode of production at this more 'advanced' level, had an equally unsettling and 'uneven' impact on middle-class culture.

Many habits of thought and feeling, many settled patterns of relationship in middle-class culture, were disturbed by the cultural upheaval which accompanied this 'unfinished revolution'. This was not simply because the middle-classes – 'backbone of the nation' – were suddenly exposed to the controlled hedonism of the 'ideology of affluence'. It was, more fundamentally, because the shift in the way the mode of production was organised *required* and *provoked* a qualitative expansion in the forces of 'mental production', a revolution in the spheres of modern consciousness. The harnessing of Capital's productive power needed, not only new social and technical skills, new political structures, but a more repetitive cycle of consumption, and forms of consciousness, more attuned to the rhythms of consumption, and to the new productive and distributive capacities of the system.... A greater share of productive wealth thus went to the formation of consciousness itself: to the production of that type of social intelligence which Marx once predicted would 'regulate the reproduction and growth of wealth', as well as that type of false consciousness which found its apogee in the spectacular 'fetishism of commodities'.

This was an altogether different – puzzling, contradictory – world for the traditional middle classes, formed in and by an older, more 'protestant' ethic. Advanced capitalism now required not thrift but consumption; not sobriety but style; not postponed gratifications but immediate satisfaction of needs; not goods that last but things that are expendable: the 'swinging' rather than the sober life-style. The gospel of work was hardly apposite to a life increasingly focussed on consumption, pleasure and play. The sexual repressiveness and ideals of domesticity enshrined in the middle-class family could not easily survive the growth of 'permissiveness'. Naturally, the middle-classes took fright at this erosion of their whole way of life: and when the middle-classes take fright, they conjure demons from the air. Traditional middle-class life, they imagined, was being undermined by a conspiracy between progressive intellectuals, soft liberals, the pornographers and the counter-culture. The fact is that this traditional culture was first, and most profoundly, *unhinged,* not by enemies of the class outside, but by changes within and stemming directly from the needs of the productive system *itself*. Long before *OZ* began its campaign against a repressive sexual morality, that morality had been eroded and undermined by, for example, the language of mass advertising with its aggressively exploitative pseudo-sexuality. As 'modern woman' undertook her 'long march' from *Woman's Own* to *Nova* and *Cosmopolitan* she passed from respectable homebody to bejewelled good-time-girl, swinger of the ad-trade, without pausing for so much as a nod at Mrs. Whitehouse on the way. Naturally, the older ethic was challenged, not in the name of a fuller liberation, but only in the name of those needs which could be satisfied by commodities....

Gradually, a struggle has emerged between the traditional bourgeois – more accurately, 'petit-bourgeois' – strata and the more 'progressive' modern middle classes. But, in the first flush of affluence, the guardians of the middle-class ideal first encountered the break in the shape of 'youth': first, working-class, then its own. In the name of society, they resisted its hedonism, its narcissism, its permissiveness, its search for immediate gratifications, its anti-authoritarianism, its moral pluralism, its materialism: all defined as 'threats' to societal values springing from both aspirant working-class youth and mal-formed, badly-socialised middle-class youth. They misrecognised the crisis *within* the dominant culture as a conspiracy *against* the dominant culture. They failed (as many members of the counter-cultures also failed) to see the cultural 'break' as, in its own traumatic and disturbing way, *profoundly adaptive* to the system's productive base.

...The counter-cultures were born within this qualitative break inside the dominant culture: in the *caesura* between the old and the new variants of the dominant ethic. But for some time, youth appeared, phenomenally, as both its most aggressive and its most visible bearers. The response was, characteristically, two sided. Traditionalists bewailed the 'crisis in authority', the loss in the stable reference points of older class cultures. The progressive strata, however, boosted, incorporated and mercilessly exploited it, commercially. Youth Culture was thus the first 'phenomenal form' of the cultural crisis. Though the revolt of middle-class youth was not contained by this adaptive framework, its subsequent trajectory owes much to its ambivalent starting-position between the two 'moral worlds' of the system: that is, to its paradoxical position within capitalism's uneven and incomplete transition.

If we think of the 'middle-class revolt' in its purest, counter-cultural phase, though much of what it embodied was overtly antogonistic to sacred, traditional middle-class values, some of its goals were, objectively, profoundly adaptive for the system in a transitional moment... Alternative values, dysfunctional for the 'protestant ethic', may form the necessary, contested, contradictory bridge between older structures and the controlled de-sublimation of a post-protestant capitalism....

Some aspects of this cultural upheaval were, clearly, adaptive and incorporable. The counter-cultures performed an important task on behalf of the system by pioneering and experimenting with new social forms which ultimately gave it greater flexibility. In many aspects, the revolutions in 'life-style' were a pure, simple, raging, commercial success. In clothes, and styles, the counter-culture explored, in its small scale 'artisan' and vanguard capitalist forms of production and distribution, shifts in taste which the mass consumption chain-stores were too cumbersome, inflexible and over-capitalised to exploit. When the trends settled down, the big commercial battalions moved in and mopped up. Much the same could be said of the music and leisure business, despite the efforts here to create real, alternative, networks of distribution. 'Planned permissiveness', and organised outrage, on which sections of the alternative press survived for years, though outrageous to the moral guardians, did not bring the system to its knees. Instead, over-ground publications and movies became more permissive - *Playgirl* moved in where *OZ* had feared to tread. The mystical-Utopian and quasi-religious revivals were more double edged: but the former tended to make the counter-culture anti-scientific in a mindless way, and over-ideological – the idea that 'revolution is in the mind', for example; or that 'youth is a class'; or that Woodstock is 'a nation': or, in Jerry Rubin's immortal words, that 'people should do whatever the fuck they want' (Silber, 1970, p. 58).... The new individualism of 'Do your own thing', when taken to its logical extremes, seemed like nothing so much as a looney caricature of petit-bourgeois individualism of the most residual and traditional kind.

This does not, however, exhaust their oppositional content. At the simplest level their emergence marked the failure of the dominant culture to win over the attachment of a sector of its 'brightest and best'. The disaffiliation from the goals, structures and institutions of 'straight society' was far-reaching. Here, the counter-cultures provided, at the very least, that social and cultural breathing-space – a hiatus in the reproduction of cultural relations – in which a deeper disaffiliation was hatched. It cracked the mould of the dominant culture. 'Repressive desublimation' is a dangerous, two-sided phenomenon. When the codes of traditional culture are broken, and new social impulses are set free, they are impossible fully to contain. Open the door to 'permissiveness' and a more profound sexual liberation may follow. Raise the slogan of 'freedom', and some people will give it an unexpectedly revolutionary accent and content. Invest in the technical means for expanding consciousness, and consciousness may expand beyond predictable limits. Develop the means of communication, and people will gain access to print and audiences for which the web-offset litho press were never intended.... In fact, as soon as the counter-cultures began to take the new slogans at face value, the slogans were transformed into their opposite. Though the nature of this inversion remained, centrally, ideological and cultural – 'superstructural' in character –

the systematic up-turning of the traditional ethic gave the counter-cultures an objective oppositional thrust which was not wholly absorbable – and was not wholly absorbed. A sustained assault on the ideological structure of a society is a moment of high contradiction; especially if it occurs in societies which increasingly depend precisely on the institutions of consciousness-formation both for the engineering of consent and the social control of the productive process. This represents a *break* in society's 'higher nervous system' (Nairn, 1968, p. 156). This break not only 'brings the contradictions out into the open', converting private alienation into 'trouble in the streets'. It tends to – and did – unleash the 'powers of the coercive state violence that are always there as a background support' (Mitchell, 1971, p. 32). And repression – or rather, 'this relationship between the quietude of consensus and the brutality of coercion' hardens the line between the 'permissive' and the impermissible, creates solidarities, installs the counter-cultures as a semi-permanent free-zone, and pushes forwards the incipient tendency towards politicisation. In the period between 1968 and 1972, many sectors of the counter-culture fell into 'alternative' paths and Utopian solutions. But others went forwards into a harder, sharper, more intense and prolonged politics of protest, activism, community action, libertarian struggle and, finally, the search for a kind of convergence with working-class politics....

At one level, middle-class counter-cultures – like working-class sub-cultures – also attempted to work out or work through, but at an 'imaginary' level, a contradiction or problematic in their class situation. But, because they inhabit a dominant culture (albeit in a negative way) they are strategically placed (in ways which working-class sub-cultures are *not*) to generalise an internal contradiction for the society as a whole. The counter-cultures stemmed from changes in the 'real relations' of their class: they represented a rupture inside the dominant culture which then became linked with the crisis of hegemony, of civil society and ultimately of the state itself. It is in *this* sense that middle-class counter-cultures, beginning from a point *within* the dominant class culture, have become an emergent ruptural force for the whole society. Their thrust is no longer contained by their point of inception. Rather, by extending and developing their 'practical critique' of the dominant culture from a privileged position inside it, they have come to inhabit, embody and express many of the contradictions of the system itself. Naturally, society cannot be 'imaginarily' reconstructed from that point. But that does not exhaust their emergent potential. For they also prefigure, anticipate, foreshadow – though in truncated, diagrammatic and 'Utopian' forms – emergent social forms. These new forms are rooted in the productive base of the system itself, though when they arise at the level of the 'counter-culture' *only,* we are correct to estimate that their maturing within the womb of society is, as yet, incomplete. They prefigure, among other things, the increasingly *social* nature of modern production, and the outdated social, cultural, political and ideological forms in which this is confined. The counter-cultures come, at best, half-way on the road to making manifest this base contradiction. ...

References

ALTHUSSER, L., 'Ideology and Ideological State Apparatuses' in *Lenin and Philosophy, and Other Essays,* New Left Books, 1971.

COHEN, P., 'Sub-cultural conflict and working class community', *Working Papers in Cultural Studies,* No. 2, Spring, 1972.

GRAMSCI, A., *Selections from the Prison Notebooks,* Lawrence and Wishart, 1971.

HALL, S., 'Education and the Crisis of the Urban School' in Raynor, J. (ed) *Issues in Urban Education,* Open University Press, 1974.

MARX, K.H., 'The Eighteenth Brumaire of Louis Bonaparte' in *Marx – Engels, Selected Works,* Lawrence and Wishart, 1951.

MITCHELL, J., *Woman's Estate,* Penguin, 1971.

NAIRN, T. and QUATTROCCHI, A., *The Beginning of the End,* Panther, 1968.

PARKIN, F., *Class Inequality and Political Order,* McGibbon and Kee, 1971.

POULANTZAS, N., *Political Power and Social Classes,* New Left Books, 1973.

SARTRE, J.P., *The Question of Method,* Methuen, 1963.

SILBER, I., *The Cultural Revolution: A Marxist analysis,* Times-Change Press, 1970.

THOMPSON, E.P., 'The Peculiarities of the English', *The Socialist Register,* 1965.

3 Class and institutional form of counter-school culture

Paul Willis

[The essay which follows is an extract from Paul Willis's *Learning to Labour: How working class kids get working class jobs* – a study based on field research into the formation of a counter-school culture on the part of working class adolescents in a non-selective secondary school in a Midlands Town. The research was conducted during the period from 1972 to 1975. In the chapter from which this essay is taken, Willis's primary concern is to place the oppositional culture of 'the lads' in the context of both the wider working class culture which they share with their parents and of the institutional structure of the school, arguing that the characteristic forms of opposition within the school are shaped by the contradictory pressures to which these give rise. The transcripts have been reproduced here in accordance with the conventions originally used by Willis:
[ ] Background information
... Pause
(...) Material edited out
- Unidentified speaker
—Transcription from different discussion follows
*From field notes, not transcription]

Class form

... Counter-school culture has many profound similarities with the culture its members are mostly destined for – shopfloor culture. Though one must always take account of regional and occupational variations, the central thing about the working class culture of the shopfloor is that, despite harsh conditions and external direction, people do look for meaning and impose frameworks. They exercise their abilities and seek enjoyment in activity, even

Source: *Learning to Labour: How working class kids get working class jobs*, Saxon House, 1977, Chapter 3.

where most controlled by others. Paradoxically, they thread through the dead experience of work a living culture which is far from a simple reflex of defeat. This is the same fundamental taking hold of an alienating situation that one finds in counter-school culture and its attempt to weave a tapestry of interest and diversion through the dry institutional text. …

The credentials for entry into shopfloor culture proper, as into the counterschool culture, are far from being merely one of the defeated. They are credentials of skill, dexterity and confidence and, above all, a kind of presence which adds to, more than it subtracts from, a living social force. A force which is *on the move,* not supported, structured and organised by a formal named institution, to which one may apply by written application.

The masculinity and toughness of counter-school culture reflects one of the central locating themes of shopfloor culture – a form of masculine chauvinism. The pin-ups with their enormous soft breasts plastered over hard, oily machinery are examples of a direct sexism but the shopfloor is suffused with masculinity in more generalised and symbolic ways too. Here is a foundryman, Joey's father, talking at home about his work. In an inarticulate way, but perhaps all the more convincingly for that, he attests to that elemental, in our culture essentially masculine, self-esteem of doing a hard job well – and being known for it:

> I work in a foundry … you know, drop forging … do you know anything about it … no … well you have the factory down in Bethnal St with the noise … you can hear it in the street … I work there on the big hammer … it's a six tonner. I've worked there twenty-four years now. It's bloody noisy, but I've got used to it now … and it's hot … I don't get bored … there's always new lines coming and you have to work out the best way of doing it … You have to keep going … and it's heavy work, the managers couldn't do it, there's not many strong enough to keep lifting the metal … I earn eighty, ninety pounds a week, and that's not bad, is it? … It ain't easy like … you can definitely say that I earn every penny of it … you have to keep it up you know. And the managing director, I'd say 'hello' to him you know, and the progress manager … they'll come around and I'll go … 'Alright' [thumbs up] … and they know you, you know … a group standing there watching you … working … I like that … there's something there … watching you like … working … like that … you have to keep going to get enough out.

The distinctive complex of chauvinism, toughness and machismo on the shopfloor is not anachronistic, neither is it bound to die away as the pattern of industrial work changes. Rough, unpleasant, demanding jobs which such attitudes seem most to be associated with still exist in considerable numbers. .... The ubiquity and strength of such attitudes, however, is vastly out of proportion to the number of people actually involved in heavy work. Even in so-called light industries, or in highly mechanised factories where the awkwardness of the physical task has long since been reduced, the metaphoric figures of strength, masculinity and reputation still move beneath the more varied and visible forms of workplace culture. Despite the increasing numbers of women employed, the most fundamental ethos of the factory is still profoundly masculine.

Another main theme of shopfloor culture – at least as I observed and recorded it in the manufacturing industries of the Midlands – is the massive attempt to gain informal control of the work process. Limitation of output or 'systematic soldiering' and 'gold bricking' have been observed from the particular perspective of management from Taylor onwards* but there is evidence now of a much more concerted – though still informal – attempt to gain control. It sometimes happens now that the men themselves to all intents and purposes actually control at least manning and the speed of production. Again this is effectively mirrored for us by working class kids' attempts, with the aid of the resources of their culture, to take control of classes, substitute their own unofficial timetables, and control their own routines and life spaces....

Shopfloor culture also rests on the same fundamental organisational unit as counter-school culture. The informal group locates and makes possible all its other elements. It is the zone where strategies for wresting control of symbolic and real space from official authority are generated and disseminated. It is the massive presence of this informal organisation which most decisively marks off shopfloor culture from middle class cultures of work....

The informal group on the shopfloor also shows the same attitude to conformists and informers as do 'the lads'. 'Winning' things is as widespread on the shopfloor as theft is amongst the lads, and is similarly endorsed by implicit informal criteria. Ostracism is the punishment for not maintaining the integrity of the world in which this is possible against the persistent intrusions of the formal. Here is the father of another of 'the lads' on factory life:

> A foreman is like, you know what I mean, they're trying to get on, they're trying to get up. They'd cut everybody's throat to get there. You get people like this in the factory. Course these people cop it in the neck off the workers, they do all the tricks under the sun. You know what I mean, they

*[The reference here is to Frederick Taylor, the founder of the 'scientific management' movement in America in the late nineteenth century]

> don't like to seem anyone crawlin' (...) Course instead of taking one pair of glasses [from the stores] Jim had two, you see, and a couple of masks and about six pairs o'gloves. Course this Martin was watching and actually two days after we found out that he'd told the foreman see. Had 'im, Jim, in the office about it, the foreman did, and, (...) well I mean, his life hasn't been worth living has it? Eh, nobody speaks to him, they won't give him a light, nobody'll give him a light for his fag or nothin' ... Well, he won't do it again, he won't do it again. I mean he puts his kettle on, on the stove of a morning, so they knock it off, don't they, you know, tek all his water out, put sand in, all this kind of thing (...) if he cum to the gaffer, 'Somebody's knocked me water over',or, er, 'They put sand in me cup' and all this business, 'Who is it then?'. 'I don't know who it is'. He'll never find out who it is.

The distinctive form of language and highly developed intimidatory humour of the shopfloor is also very reminiscent of counter-school culture. Many verbal exchanges on the shopfloor are not serious or about work activities. They are jokes, or 'pisstakes', or 'kiddings' or 'windups'. There is a real skill in being able to use this language with fluency: to identify the points on which you are being 'kidded' and to have appropriate responses ready in order to avoid further baiting....

Associated with this concrete and expressive verbal humour is a well-developed physical humour: essentially the practical joke. These jokes are vigorous, sharp, sometimes cruel, and often hinged around prime tenets of the culture such as disruption of production or subversion of the boss's authority and status. Here is the man who works in a car engine factory:

> They play jokes on you, blokes knocking the clamps off the boxes, they put paste on the bottom of his hammer you know, soft little thing, puts his hammer down, picks it up, gets a handful of paste, you know, all this. So he comes up and gets a syringe and throws it in the big bucket of paste, and it's about that deep, and it goes right to the bottom, you have to put your hand in and get it out ... This is a filthy trick, but they do it (...) They asked, the gaffers asked X to make the tea. Well it's fifteen years he's been there and they say 'go and make the tea'. He goes up the toilet, he wets in the tea pot, then makes the tea. I mean, you know, this is the truth this is you know. He says, you know, 'I'll piss in it if I mek it, if they've asked me to mek it' (...) so he goes up, wees in the pot, then he puts the tea bag, then he puts the hot water in (...) Y was bad the next morning, one of the gaffers, 'My stomach isn't half upset this morning'. He told them after and they called him for everything. 'You ain't makin' our tea no more'. He says, 'I know I ain't not now'.

It is also interesting that, as in the counter-school culture, many of the jokes circle around the concept of authority itself and around its informal complement, 'grassing'. The same man:

> He [Johnny] says, 'Get a couple of pieces of bread pudding Tony [a new worker] we'll have them with our tea this afternoon see. The woman gi'd him some in a bag, he says, 'Now put them in your pocket, you won't have to pay for them when you go past, you know, the till' (...) Tony put 'em in his pocket didn't he and walked past with his dinner (...) When we come back out the canteen Johnny was telling everybody that he'd [i.e. Tony] pinched two pieces of bread pudding (...) he told Fred, one of the foremen see, 'cos Fred knows, I mean ... Johnny says, 'I've got to tell you Fred', he says, 'Tony pinched two pieces of bread pudding', I mean serious, the way they look you know (...) he called Johnny for everything, young Tony did. Fred said, 'I want to see you in my office in twenty minutes', straightfaced you know, serious. Oh I mean Johnny, he nearly cried (...) We said, 'It's serious like, you're in trouble, you'll get the sack', you know and all this (...) they never laugh. He says, 'What do you think's gonna happen?'. 'Well what can happen, you'll probably get your cards' (...) 'Oh what am I gonna do, bleeding Smith up there, he's really done me. I'll do him'. I says, 'Blimey, Tony', I says, 'It ain't right, if other people can't get away with it, why should you 'a' to get away with it'. 'Ooh'. Anyway Fred knocked the window, and he says, 'Tell Tony I want him'. He says, 'You've got the sack now Tony', you know. 'Hope I haven't', he says, 'I dunno what I'm gonna do' (...) After they cum out, laughing, I said, 'What did he say to you Tony'. He says, 'He asked me if I pinched two pieces of bread pudding', so I couldn't deny it, I said I had. He says, 'All I want to know is why you didn't bring me two pieces an' all'.

The rejection of school work by 'the lads' and the omnipresent feeling that they know better is also paralleled by a massive feeling on the shopfloor, and in the working class generally, that practice is more important than theory. As a big handwritten sign, borrowed from the back of a matchbox and put up by one of the workers, announces on one shopfloor: 'An ounce of keenness is worth a whole library of certificates'. The shopfloor abounds with apocryphal stories about the idiocy of purely theoretical knowledge. Practical ability always comes first and is a *condition* of other kinds of knowledge. Whereas in middle class culture knowledge and qualifications are seen as a way of shifting upwards the whole mode of practical alternatives open to an individual, in working class eyes theory is riveted to particular productive practices. If it cannot earn its keep there, it is to be rejected. This is Spanksy's father talking at home. The fable form underlines the centrality and routinisation of this cultural view of 'theory'.

> In Toll End Road there's a garage, and I used to work part-time there and ... there's an elderly fellow there, been a mechanic all his life, and he must have been seventy years of age then. He was an old Hammertown professional, been a professional boxer once, an elderly chap and he was a practical man, he was practical, right? ... and he told me this (...) I was talking to him, was talking about something like this, he says (...) 'This chap was all theory and he sends away for books about everything', and he says, 'Do you know', he says, 'he sent away for a book once and it came in a wooden box, and it's still in that box 'cos he can't open it'. Now that in't true, is it? But the point is true. That in't true, that didn't happen, but his point is right. He can't get at that box 'cos he don't know how to open the box! Now what's the good of that?

This can be seen as a clear and usually unremarked class function of knowledge. The working class view would be the rational one were it not located in class society, i.e. that theory is only useful insofar as it really does help to do things, to accomplish practical tasks and change nature. Theory is asked to be in a close dialectic with the material world. For the middle class, more aware of its position in a class society, however, theory is seen partly in its social guise of qualifications as the power to move up the social scale. In this sense theory is well worth having even if it is never applied to nature. It serves its purpose as the *means* to decide precisely which bit of nature one wants to apply it to, or even to choose not to apply it at all. Paradoxically, the working class distrust and rejection of theory comes partly from a kind of recognition, even in the moment that it oppresses, of the hollowness of theory in its social guise. ...

It is, of course, the larger class dimension which gives the working class counter-school culture its special edge and resonance in terms of style, its particular force of opposition and its importance as an experiential preparation for entry into working class jobs. Although all forms of institution are likely to breed their own informal accretions, and although all schools of whatever class always create oppositional cultures, it is the crucial conjunction of institutional opposition with a working class context and mode which gives the special character and significance to 'the lads' culture. Institutional opposition has a different meaning according to its class location and expression. The non-conformists in the high status grammar school, although sharing similar attitudes to school, know that they are different from the Hammertown lads. They cannot through institutional means alone transcend their class location. Ultimately, they have not only a different attitude to qualifications but also an inevitable sense of different social position. ...

Some of the non-conformist group in the grammar school are, in fact, from working class families*. Despite even their origins and anti-school attitude, the lack of a dominant working class ethos within their school culture profoundly separates their experience from 'the lads'. It can also lead to artificial attempts to demonstrate solidarity on the street and with street contacts. That the working class cultural forms of school opposition are creative, specific, borne and reproduced by particular individuals and groups from afresh and in particular contexts — though always within a class mode — is shown by the cultural awkwardness and separation of such lads. The lack of the collective school based and generated form of the class culture, even despite a working class background and an inclination to oppositional values, considerably weakens their working class identity:

> *John* Kids (...) have casually bracketed me as that [a snob] (...) I live near a school called The Links, and there's a lot of kids there, 'Oh he goes to grammar school. Oh'. Well, my attitude's been, I never want to be called anything like that, I think it's really horrible, so for a start, I've never tried to improve my language. I have these basic things of doing things daft, doing things daft. It's mainly just to make sure that everybody knows that I'm not a typical Percival Jones (...), he's got a really posh accent, 'Old chap', Lady Byron Lane type [indicating a middle class accent] of person, you know, not one of us kind, proud of the school and all that (...) I've said to kids who've really been getting on my nerves, you know, 'I know I'm better than you', you know, but these things when I muck about, that's trying to make sure that everybody knows I'm not.

It could be suggested that what non-conformists in middle class schools — no matter what their individual origins — are struggling for is some kind of conversion of their institutional opposition into a more resonant working class form. Insofar as they succeed, so does their future 'suffer'. Insofar as they fail, or insofar as, for instance, conformist working class boys in a working class school are insulated from working class culture, and become free from its processes, so they are likely to 'succeed'. Cultural location, especially in terms of shifts between patterns, is a much better model for explaining social mobility than is the mechanistic undialectical notion of 'intelligence'.

Institutional form

No matter how hard the creation, self-making and winning of counter-school

*[Willis refers here to his comparative study of working-class non-conformist pupils in the all-boys grammar school of the same Midland town.]

culture, it must, then, be placed within a larger pattern of working class culture. This should not lead us however, to think that this culture is all of a piece, undifferentiated or composed of standard clonal culture modules spontaneously reproducing themselves in an inevitable pattern.

Class cultures are created specifically, concretely in determinate conditions, and in particular oppositions. They arise through definite struggles over time with other groups, institutions and tendencies. Particular manifestations of the culture arise in particular circumstances with their own form of marshalling and developing of familiar themes. The themes are *shared* between particular manifestations because all locations at the same level in a class society share similar basic structural properties, and the working class people there face similar problems and are subject to similar ideological constructions. In addition, the class culture is supported by massive webs of informal groupings and countless overlappings of experience, so that central themes and ideas can develop and be influential in practical situations where their direct logic may not be the most appropriate. A pool of styles, meanings and possibilities are continuously reproduced and always available for those who turn in some way from the formalised and official accounts of their position and look for more realistic interpretations of, or relationship to, their domination. As these themes are taken up and recreated in concrete settings, they are reproduced and strengthened and made further available as resources for others in similar structural situations.

However, these processes of borrowing, regeneration and return in particular social regions are not often recognised by those concerned as class processes. Neither the institutionalised, customary and habitual forms in which domination is mediated from basic structural inequality, nor the regional forms in which they are broken out of, opposed and transformed, are recognised for what they are. This is partly because social regions and their institutional supports and relationships really do have a degree of autonomy and separateness from each other and the rest of the social system. They have their own procedures, rules and characteristic ideological balances. They have their own legitimising beliefs, their own particular circles of inversion and informality.

Despite their similarity, it is a mistake, therefore, to reduce particular social forms and regions too quickly to the obvious central class dynamics of domination and resistance. They have simultaneously both a local, or institutional, logic and a larger class logic. The larger class logic could not develop and be articulated without these regional instances of struggle, nor could, however, these instances be differentiated internally and structured systematically in relation to other instances and the reproduction of the whole without the larger logic.

The state school in advanced capitalism, and the most obvious manifestations of oppositional working class culture within it, provide us with a central case of mediated class conflict and of class reproduction in the capitalist order. It is especially significant in showing us a circle of unintended consequences which act finally to reproduce not only a regional culture but the class culture and also the structure of society itself.

Emergence of opposition

Even if there is some form of social division in the junior school, in the first years of the secondary school everyone, it seems, is an 'ear'ole'. Even the few who come to the school with a developed delinquent eye for the social landscape behave in a conformist way because of the lack of any visible support group:

[In a group discussion]

Spike In the first year... I could spot the ear'oles. I knew who the fucking high boys was, just looking at 'em walking around the playground — first day I was there (...) I was just quiet for the first two weeks, I just kept meself to meself like, not knowing anybody, it took me two years to get in with a few mates. But, er ... after that, the third year was a right fucking year, fights, having to go to teachers a lot....

In the second to fourth years, however, some individuals break from this pattern. From the point of view of the student this break is the outstanding landmark of his school life, and is remembered with clarity and zest. 'Coming out' as a 'lad' is a personal accomplishment:

[In an individual interview]

Joey And in the second year, I thought, 'This is a fucking dead loss', 'cos I'd got no real mates, I saw all the kids palling up with each other, and I thought, 'It's a fucking dead loss, you've got to have someone to knock about with'. So I cracked eyes on Noah and Benson, two kids who weren't in the group, fucking Benson, summat's happened to Benson, summat terrible, he's really turned fucking ear'ole now, but I still like him, he still makes me laff. He can't say his r's properly (...) but I clocked ... I seen these two, 'cos our mum used to be at work then, and our dad used to go out at night, so I grabbed them and I said, 'Do you want to come down to our fucking house tonight?', and skinheads just starting up then, and I think Benson and them had the first fucking levis and monkey boots. And I started knocking about with them, they came down the first night, and we drank a lot of whisky, and I pretended to be fucking drunk like, which we warn't, and it was from there on. We parted off from the rest (...) we always

> used to sit together, we used to start playing up wild, like, 'cos playing up in them days was fucking hitting each other with rulers, and talking, and it just stemmed from there. And Bill started to come with us, Fred and then Spike ... And from then on it just escalated, just came more and more separated. We used to go out of nights, and carrying on from hitting each other with rulers we used to fucking chuck bottles at each other, so the major occupation was roaming around the streets, looking for bottles to lam at each other. And from that came a bit of vandalism, here and there like....

'The lads' themselves very rarely identify any deep causes for the changes they describe so vividly. Apparently for them it really is a question of the need for friendship or even of *accidental* causality — sitting by so and so in class, meeting 'the lads' at night by chance or being 'called for' unexpectedly. Of course these accounts do testify to the importance of the group in the change.

Staff too notice these dramatic changes and are not short of explanations. Kids start 'lording it about' and develop 'wrong attitudes' because they become exposed to 'bad influences'. The 'bad influences' arise from behaviour attributed, in the first place, to individual pathology: 'He's made of rubber, there's nothing to him at all', 'If you want the truth, you just take the opposite of what he says,' 'He's a mixed up lad, no idea where he's going', 'He worries me stiff, his personality is deficient'. We have the classic model of a minority of 'troublemakers' being followed by the misguided majority:

> *Deputy head* Joey is the outstanding one as far as follow my leader is concerned (...) Spike being the barrack room lawyer would support him, and those two did the stirring (...) and Will is easily led.

It is interesting generally to note just how much teachers personalise, and base observations about kids — themselves lost in social and class processes — on what are taken to be concrete individual characteristics. Verbal comments start with 'I like' or 'I haven't much time for', and accounts are interrupted — in a way which is presented as illuminating — with '... a bloody good lad too', or '... a bad lot altogether, have you seen his dad?' Written school leaving and other reports clearly demonstrate notions of pathology in relation to a basic social model of the leaders and the led:

> [Joey] proved himself to be a young man of intelligence and ability who could have done well at most subjects, but decided that he did not want to work to develop this talent to the full and allowed not only his standard of work to deterioriate, except for English, but also attendance and behaviour (...) too often his qualities of leadership were misplaced and not used on behalf of the school....

Explanations involving random causality or pathology may or may not hold elements of truth. Certainly they are necessary explanations-in-use for teachers trying to run a school and make decisions in the contemporary situation; they will not do, however, as proper social explanations for the development of an anti-school culture.

Differentiation and the teaching paradigm

The particular process by which working class culture creatively manifests itself as a concrete form within, and separates itself from even as it is influenced by, the particular institution I shall call *differentiation*. *Differentiation* is the process whereby the typical exchanges expected in the formal institutional paradigm are reinterpreted, separated and discriminated with respect to working class interests, feelings and meanings. Its dynamic is opposition to the institution which is taken up and reverberated and given a form of reference to the larger themes and issues of the class culture. *Integration* is the opposite of *differentiation* and is the process whereby class oppositions and intentions are redefined, truncated and deposited within sets of apparently legitimate institutional relationships and exchanges. Where *differentiation* is the intrusion of the informal into the formal, *integration* is the progressive constitution of the informal into the formal or official paradigm. It may be suggested that all institutions hold a balance between *differentiation* and *integration*, and that *differentiation* is by no means synonymous with breakdown or failure in function. Indeed, as I will go on to argue, it is the aspects of *differentiation* in the make up of an institution, and its effects upon particular social regions, which allow it to play a successful, if mystifying, role in social reproduction. *Differentiation* is experienced by those concerned as, on the one hand, a collective process of learning whereby the self and its future are critically separated from the pre-given institutional definitions and, on the other hand, by institutional agents, as inexplicable breakdown, resistance and opposition. What is produced, on the one side, are working class themes and activities reworked and reproduced into particular institutional forms and, on the other, retrenchment, hardening, or softening — all variants of a response to loss of legitimacy — of the formal institutional paradigm. Within the institution of the school the essential official paradigm concerns a particular view of teaching and its *differentiation* produces forms of the counter-school culture.

There are a number of possible relationships between teacher and taught.... I want to outline the basic teaching paradigm which I suggest locates all others — even as they attempt to go beyond it — and which, I would argue, remains massively dominant in our schools. Whether modified or not, near to the surface or not, its structure is common to all the varied main forms of classroom teaching.

Teachers know quite well that teaching is essentially a relationship between potential contenders for supremacy. It makes sense to speak of, and it does feel like, 'winning and losing'.

> *Deputy head* It's a funny thing (...) you get a situation where you've got a class or a boy and you think, 'God, he's beaten me,' but the dividing line is so close, push a bit harder and you're over, and you're there (...) this is surprising about kids who are supposed to be dull. They will find a teacher's weakness as quickly as any lad.

Yet the teacher's actual power of direct coercion in modern society is very limited. The kids heavily outnumber the teachers and sanctions can be run through with frightening rapidity. The young teacher often wants a show of force to back him up; the experienced teacher knows that the big guns can only fire once:

> *Deputy head* You see we have very few sanctions and punishments we can apply. Very few indeed. So it's a question of spacing them out and according them as much gravity as you can. ... (...) You can't go throwing suspensions around all the time. Like the football referees today, I mean they're failing because they're reduced to the ultimate so quickly somehow (...) the yellow card comes out first of all, and once they've done that, they've either got to send the player off or ignore everything else he does in the game (...)...

The teacher's authority must therefore be won and maintained on moral not coercive grounds. There must be consent from the taught. However, the permanent battle to assert and legitimate a personal moral supremacy, especially with limited personal power, is tiring and not really a viable strategy for the long term. Sleight of hand is involved. It is this which marks off the 'experienced' teacher. It is the learning of the relative autonomy of the teaching paradigm: the recognition that the ideal of teaching is related only variably to particular individuals. It is the *idea* of the teacher, not the individual, which is legitimised and commands obedience.

This idea concerns teaching as a fair exchange — most basically of knowledge for respect, of guidance for control. Since knowledge is the rarer commodity this gives the teacher his moral superiority. This is the dominant educational paradigm which stands outside particular teachers but enables them to exert control legitimately upon the children. It is legitimated in general because it provides equivalents which can enter into other successive exchanges which are to the advantage of the individual. The most important chain of exchanges is, of course, that of knowledge for qualifications, qualified activity for high pay, and pay for goods and services. The educational is, therefore, the key to many other exchanges.

All of these exchanges are supported in structures which hold and help to define, as well as being themselves to some extent created and maintained by, the particular transaction. The educational exchange is held in a defining framework which establishes an axis of the superiority of the teacher in a particular way. Whilst the exchange and its 'fairness' is open to view and is the basis for consent, the framework which holds and defines the terms is both less explicit and in some ways more powerful. It must be considered as an integral part of our basic view of the teaching paradigm. The exchange spins, as it were, like a giro in this framework which it thus helps to stabilise and orientate. But the framework must be secured and ensured by other means as well. It must be capable both of enforcing definitions to some degree where the exchange itself cannot generate them (which is, of course, the case for such as 'the lads'), and to reinforce the exchange, where it is successful, by guaranteeing the equivalents, the concrete referents, external signs and visible supports.

This framework or axis is held by the school on the material basis of its buildings, organisation, timetable and hierarchy. It is sanctioned (in normal times) by dominant cultural and social values and backed up in the last analysis by larger state apparatuses. .... Within the school 'good teaching' is maintained only by the proper establishment and reproduction of this axis. Usually much short of any direct force the establishment of the often implicit structural axis necessary for the explicit teaching paradigm proceeds through the 'slow drip' and the suppression of other or private meanings which might tilt the axis, devalue the teacher's knowledge, or make responses other than politeness appropriate....

The school is the agency of face to face control *par excellence*. The stern look of the inquiring teacher; the relentless pursuit of 'the truth' set up as a value even above good behaviour; the common weapon of ridicule; the techniques learned over time whereby particular troublemakers can 'always be reduced to tears'; the stereotyped deputy head, body poised, head lowered, finger jabbing the culprit; the head unexpectedly bearing down on a group in the corridor — these are all tactics for exposing and destroying, or freezing, the private. What successful conventional teaching cannot tolerate is private reservation, and in the early forms in virtually any school it is plain to see that most kids yield that capacity willingly. The eager first form hands reaching and snapping to answer first are all seeking approval from an acknowledged superior in a very particular institutional form. And in the *individual* competition for approval the possibility of any private reservations becoming *shared* to form any oppositional definition of the situation is decisively controlled....

Discipline becomes a matter not of punishment for wrongs committed in the old testament sense, but of maintaining the institutional axis, of reproducing the social relationships of the school in general: of inducing respect for elemental frameworks in which other transactions can take place.

> *Deputy head* If you can catch them you do, and you make hay of it. But only to impress on them, of course, that you can't do as you please in this life, and you can't break rules (...) every time you bring home to them something that's gone wrong, then it does some good somewhere ...

It is the moral intensity of maintaining this axis and attempting to exclude or suppress the contradictory, murky cross-currents of normal life which can give to the school a cloying, claustrophobic feel of arrested adolescence. Everything ultimately turns on the fair exchange and the maintenance of the axis which makes it possible. In this sense the school is a kind of totalitarian regime. There is relatively little direct coercion or oppression, but an enormous constriction of the range of moral possibilities. Everything is neatly tied in, every story has the same ending, every analogy has the same analogue. The word 'co-operation' – the common-sense-in-use term for the exchange of 'equivalents' – creeps in everywhere. It is what has *not* happened when one is punished. It is what *has* happened when one is rewarded, ironically often by early release from the very system one has excelled in.

Perhaps the essence of the fair exchange, the quality of the axis which supports it, and the nature of the attempts to maintain it are best illustrated by programmatic statements made in what is still widely regarded as the ritual keystone of the institution of the school: morning assembly. This is the head talking to the school after his office has been broken into and human faeces deposited under his chair:

> I respect you, I respect your abilities. In some areas your abilities are greater than mine. I accept that (...) Last Friday I was feeling pretty low after I found out about this lot, I thought, there's not not much here to respect ... but then I went to football on Saturday, there were several lads and teachers there, playing their hearts out, or giving up their time just for the school, and then I thought, 'Perhaps it's not so bad after all' ... I do respect your talents and abilities ... but I expect you to respect my talents as a teacher, and accept what I say ... Here we're trying to do what's best for you, really help you, not give you the easy way out ...

It is of the utmost importance to appreciate that the exchange relationship in the educational paradigm is not primarily in terms of its own logic a relationship between social classes or in any sense at all a self-conscious attempt on the part of teachers to dominate or suppress either working class individuals or working class culture as such. The teachers, particularly the senior teachers of the Hammertown school, are dedicated, honest and forthright and by their own lights doing an exacting job with patience and humanity. Certainly it would be quite wrong to attribute to them any kind of sinister motive such as miseducating or oppressing working class kids. The teacher is given formal control of his pupils by the state, but he exerts his social control through an educational, not a class, paradigm.

It is important to realise just how far the teaching paradigm and especially the axis of control and definition which makes it possible are clearly bound up, supported and underwritten in countless small and in certain large, as it were, architectural ways by the material structure, organisation and practices of the school as we know it in our society.

In a simple physical sense school students, and their possible views of the pedagogic situation, are subordinated by the constricted and inferior space they occupy. Sitting in tight ranked desks in front of the larger teacher's desk; deprived of private space themselves but outside nervously knocking the forbidden staff room door or the headmaster's door with its foreign rolling country beyond; surrounded by locked up or out of bounds rooms, gyms and equipment cupboards; cleared out of school at break with no quarter given even in the unprivate toilets; told to walk at least two feet away from staff cars in the drive — all of these things help to determine a certain orientation to the physical environment and behind that to a certain kind of social organisation. They speak to the whole *position* of the student.

The social organisation of the school reinforces this relationship. The careful bell rung timetable; the elaborate rituals of patience and respect outside the staff room door and in the classroom where even cheeky comments are prefaced with 'sir'; compulsory attendance and visible staff hierarchies — all these things assert the superiority of staff and of their world. And, of course, finally it is the staff who are the controllers most basically and despite the advent of 'resources centres' of what is implied to be the scarce and valuable commodity of knowledge. The value of knowledge to be exchanged in the teaching paradigm derives not only from an external definition of its worth or importance for qualifications and mobility but also from its protected institutional role: its disposition is the prerogative of the powerful. Teachers distribute text books as if they owned them and behave like outraged, vandalised householders when they are lost, destroyed or defaced; teachers keep the keys and permissions for the cupboards, libraries and desks; they plan courses and initiate discussions, start and end the classes....

It is especially important to bear this material infrastructure of the school in mind when considering the extent to which what I have called the basic teaching paradigm can be and is modified in practice.... Leaving aside individualistic, stoic or heroic solutions there seem to be two main sets of (linked) variants of the basic paradigm identifiable in school: those from 'below' and those from 'above'. Essentially, I argue, both are responses to *differentiation,* or the fear of *differentiation,* whether or not this occurs in particular cases as a direct response to opposition or as an aspect of overall school policy. Neither modify the material basis and organisation of the school in any significant way. No matter what their internal ideologies or justifications, they are attempts, I argue, to *re-integrate* the same basic paradigm on a somewhat different and wider footing.

Many experienced teachers in working class schools sense a potential weakness in the hold of the basic paradigm on their 'less able', disinterested and disaffected students and seek to modify one of its terms in some way or another. Perhaps the classic move here, and one which is absolutely typical of the old secondary modern school and still widespread in working class comprehensives, is the revision from an objective to a moral basis of what is in the teacher's gift and is to be exchanged by him for obedience, politeness and respect from the students. This is the crucial shift and mystification in many forms of cultural and social exchange between unequal territories in late capitalist society; that the objective nature of the 'equivalents' are transmuted into the fog of moral commitment, humanism and social responsibility. A real exchange becomes an ideal exchange. The importance of all this is not, of course, that the values and stances involved might be admirable or execrable, correct or incorrect, or whatever. The point is a formal one: the moral term, unlike the objective one, is capable of infinite extension and assimilation because it has no real existence except in itself. The real world cannot act as a court of appeal. Moral definitions make their own momentum. So far as the basic teaching paradigm is concerned what it is worth the student striving for becomes, not knowledge and the promise of qualification, but somehow deference and politeness themselves — those things which are associated certainly with academic and other kinds of success but are only actually their cost and precondition. The shift implies that such qualities are desirable in their own right, detachable from the particular project and negotiable for themselves in the market place of jobs and social esteem.

The pivotal notion of 'attitudes' and particularly of 'right attitudes' makes its entry here. Its presence should always warn us of a mystificatory transmutation of basic exchange relationships into illusory, ideal ones. If one approaches school and its authority, it seems, with the 'right attitude' then employers and work will also be approached with the 'right attitude' in such a way indeed that real social and economic advances can be made — all without the help of academic achievement or success. Of course this crucial move renders the basic paradigm strictly circular and tautological since the same thing is being offered on both sides without any disjunctions or transformations occurring in the circle of the relationship. What the student gets all round is deference and subordination to authority. He could learn this for himself. The objective tautology which turns on that too little examined category, 'the right attitude' does not necessarily damage the basic paradigm so long as its nature remains concealed or mystified. Indeed insofar as it maintains the tempo of apparently fair exchange, reinforces the institutionally defined axis and restrains other tendencies this modification strengthens the basic paradigm. It keeps its giro spinning....

Another, so to speak, grass roots variant of the basic paradigm is also a product of long experience in the school. It concerns a revision of the other item in the expected exchange — respect, politeness and what is expected from the students. Quite simply not much is expected and there is no particular moral indignation when it does not come. Allied with this is often a non-programmatic interest in providing useful information where possible. Though this represents an unillusioned reduction of the teaching relationship, and provides the elements towards a realistic assessment of what is actually possible with disaffected kids, it still remains within the basic paradigm since institutional control remains the essential stake and no effort is made to change the material arrangements and organisation of the school. The yielding of some ground to the students and to their definitions and interests is made in the interests of ensuring a more basic control. The fundamental axis of the teaching relationship is maintained by accepting with good grace battles which are already lost — and making sure that the really important battles can never be fought. Such educational views are often associated with what might be called a pragmatic, not over-hopeful and poorly integrated solidarity with the working class — an uneasy but fatalistic sense of their basic oppression.

> *A senior teacher at the Hammertown school* I've never been one who thinks we are really teaching these lads (...) even if they are reacting away from the school, they're still experiencing, still growing up, and our job is to listen to them, be around, be there to be argued with (...) and we might get something in on the side, quickly (...) With the fifth [year] I reckon it's careful containment, we give them little bits you know, let them think they're big tough men getting their own way, but in all the important things they're doing what you want ... you know, don't confront them, let them think it's going their way.

The other basic set of variants of the teaching paradigm observable in schools come, so to speak, from 'above'. They enjoy a more public and influential provenance, but turn, I argue, on the same broadening and redefinition of the exchange relationship and acceptance of what is basically the same if somewhat modified material structure and organisation of the school. *In situ,* at least, it concerns *reintegration* of a *differentiated* or threatened teaching paradigm.

'Relevant' education proposes that the teacher of the non-academic working class child should start off from where the child is in terms of his/her own interests, rather than from the distanced interests of an academic subject. The local neighbourhood, work, tax matters and dealing with officials, and civics should be the curricula of the boys; home-making, family life and bringing up children those of the girls; and popular music, art and the mass media are to be studied by both. 'Progressivism' suggests that activities should not be imposed, but encouraged: approaches are 'child centred' rather than 'subject centred'; 'individual programmes' allow children to go at their own speed; and 'team teaching' opens up the widest resources possible to the children. In Britain these techniques have made the greatest inroads in the primary sector of education, and have been steadily spreading upwards....

These ideas and techniques have had a thorough political and theoretical airing [particularly in the succession of official reports from the Hadow Report of 1926 through to the Plowden Report of 1967]. Certainly this whole debate and corpus of intellectual work may well have given a form to, and set limits for, educational reform, but I would argue that they have in no real sense determined downwards a new pedagogic practice. In the actual school the two main approaches anyway have an 'elective affinity' with patterns I previously characterised as from 'below'. Though they are interlinked, relevance is concerned *mainly* with what the teacher offers, and progressivism with how the child is supposed to respond. Teachers select from the repertoire of teaching styles and developments which are currently available to deal with the problems as they know them. These still centre on the maintenance of the basic teaching paradigm — which seems the only possible one and which is anyway minutely supported by material infrastructures which have been only marginally changed. The 'new' techniques may or may not have had a radical genesis (there is certainly a case here to be argued for progressivism) but they have been taken up on very different and more ancient grounds. If the new techniques seemed revolutionary they were profoundly post-revolutionary solutions to pre-revolutionary problems. They have been taken up often, in real situations, for control purposes or for the justification and rationalisation of existing tendencies....

During *differentiation* the basic paradigm (no matter how modified) is to some extent delegitimised. The teacher's superiority is denied because the axis in which it is held has been partially dislodged. Because what the teacher offers is seen to be less than an equivalent the establishment of the framework which guarantees the teaching exchange is regarded with suspicion and is seen more and more obviously in its repressive mode. For 'the lads' other ways of valuing the self and other kinds of possible exchange present themselves. The teacher's authority becomes increasingly the random one of the prison guard, not the necessary one of the pedagogue. Where 'the private' was penetrated and controlled before it now becomes shared, powerful and oppositional. In a system where exchange of knowledge and the educational paradigm is used as a form of social control, denial of knowledge and refusal of its educational 'equivalent', respect, can be used as a barrier to control. 'The lads' become 'ignorant', 'awkward' and 'disobedient'....

This challenge to the formal paradigm, and re-evaluation of the self and the group, comes from those 'private' areas now *shared* and made visible which were held in check before. These private areas are nothing more nor less, of course, than the class experiences of the working class boy and derive basically from outside the school. Where the basic paradigm excludes class from the educational realm, its *differentiation* invites it in.

It is interesting to trace in the accounts of how individuals joined 'the lads', just how the development, both of the culture, and of the individuals in or moving towards it, starts from the school and steadily moves out to the street and neighbourhood, drawing with it a larger and larger content of working class values, attitudes and practices. It is clearly this expanding area which supplies informal and unofficial materials for the *differentiation* of the educational paradigm in the school. Where the cultural location of the school is not working class, then there is of course a different set-up: there is much less for the educational paradigm to be *differentiated* with respect to, and therefore a much greater possibility of the paradigm holding in the long run.

In the working class area, though, there is a huge reservoir of class feeling to be drawn upon once trust has been decisively withdrawn from the school. Neighbourhood, street and the larger symbolic articulations of working class youth cultures supply themes for, and are themselves strengthened dialectically by counterschool culture. Of course parents and family are very important and influential bearers of working class culture too. Stories are told in the home about shopfloor culture, the things which happen and the attitudes which prevail there — especially attitudes towards authority. The language in the home reproduces (minus the swearwords) that of work culture. There is also a characteristic division of labour and a form of male supremacy in the home. The man earns the living and does practical work around the house, and the wife works for the 'extras' and services the needs of the family. There is also an interface here with the more extreme aspects of working class culture so that the father may 'tip the wink' occasionally about what to do in a fight ('Get one in, then ask questions') or how to approach theft ('Small fish are sweet, son').

Nevertheless parents should only be considered as one set — though important — of many possible 'bearers' of working class culture. Not all parents act in the same way or share the same values. Parents have their own complex and creative relations to class themes and in no sense press their children into a simple standard working class mould. There is a degree of relative independence between parents and kids. Some very conformist, 'respectable' parents who visit the school and try to back it up in everything have kids who inexplicably, to them, 'go wrong' and join 'the lads'. Other parents who are indifferent or even hostile to the school have 'ear'ole' kids — sometimes to their discomfort and dislike....

Still, there is an undoubted sense in which working class values and feelings — importantly though not always borne by parents — work against the school and provide concrete materials for *differentiation*. Spanksy's father, for instance, voices a profound working class suspicion of formal institutions and their modes of working. Ultimately he is not willing to legitimise the teacher's authority either. It is seen as basically artificial even though fearsome as it exploits, for instance, his own felt weakness in expression. Here he is talking about the last school open night he had attended:

> The headmaster irritated me, I can't put me finger on it now ... 'cos I could see ... could see, I was 'im, I was 'im, I was standing there, and I was 'im. I thought, 'Aye, aye, he's talking to hisself', you know, wa'nt talking to me (...) he put my back up (...) and then there was this person, you know, family, father or something, instead of coming out, asking the teacher a question he knew what he'd gotta ask, he knew what answer he wanted to get, you see, I don't know how to explain it, like. I thought like, 'Mate you'm only asking that question, just to let people know you'm in the room', know what I mean, 'cos he wasn't listening to the bloke's answer, he'd already accepted whatever the bloke was going to say was right, you know what I mean, how can I explain that. I don't know how to put it ... See now, I can't get up in a room and talk against teachers, like, I couldn't talk against you, because I'd be flabbergasted, I'd be 'umming' and 'ahhing', and I'd be worried stiff you know (...) I dunno how to say it, how to put it, 'cos I'd look around me and I'd think, 'These people don't want to know anyway' (...) If I could have been in a room with 'im [the head] you know on his own, without anybody hearing us, I could have said...
>
> *PW* Could have said what?
>
> *Father* You're full of bull....

The letter of invitation for the open night has a tear-off strip saying that unless it is filled in and returned the head will assume parents are not going. It also says that questions must be submitted in writing beforehand and that only selected questions will be called.... Add to this the curiously pompous and elliptical style which can be used to parents about their children's misbehaviour (Spanksy's father received a letter beginning, 'I would like to discuss with you your son's *possible* future in the school' — my italics) and it can be seen that this working class mistrust is responding to something real. This is not necessarily a criticism of the school. It is doing its own job well in its own terms. But the axis of moral authority underlying its certainties and its style is quite different from the profane confusions, compromises and underlying spirit of resistance in working class culture. Once the working class boy begins to differentiate himself from school authority there is a powerful cultural charge behind him to complete the process:

[In an individual interview]
Spanksy He [father] doesn't want me to cheek the teachers, but he wouldn't want me to be a wanker, sitting there working, you know ... My old man called me an ear'ole once, in the second years, playing football and comin' to the school. It upset me it did, I was surprised (...) I'd like to be like him, you know, he can't stand no bull, if anybody tries it on him, he hates it. It's the same with me, I think I'm gonna be little and fat like him, I'd love to be. I'd love to be like him, he's a great bloke.

It is not quite that the parents become any more influential during the period of *differentiation*, of return to, and regeneration of, working class themes. In a crucial sense they become less influential as their world becomes more so. The development of the young boy and his growing cultural confidence often put him in a role of competition with his father and a kind of attempted half-domination of his mother. He becomes not so much like his father as of the same world: the working class male world of independence, physicality and symbolic intimidation — and standing up to these things. The boy becomes a force to be reckoned with in this world. Despite filial affection there can be a definite tension in the domestic atmosphere where 'measuring up to dad' can mean being able 'to put one on 'im'. Often parents say, 'He goes his own way, like they do', or 'You can't tell 'im a thing', or there is a fatalistic recognition that certain profound cultural processes are already in train strengthened especially by the need for cash.

Spanksy's father This is probably one factor you don't... people don't probably think it's important, is money today. There's a group of chaps here, they go out every day (...) then there's little [his son], 'cos he goes to school, he has to rely on me to give him a pound. I can't afford to give him any more but how does he feel amongst them others. Education's gone by the board now, they'm out there ain't they. Somewhere to go, a discotheque or something, they go and buy sandwiches, ice cream, cake ... can't, he ain't got it, he's the same age as them or he might be a few months younger you know (...) Education is right at the back of their minds you see. Their pockets you see, that's in their minds.

From the boy's side this fatalism can come across as indifference. This underlines the harsh importance of finding your own way through.

[In an individual interview]
Joey I asked the old lady ... 'Ain't you fucking bothered what I become, don't you worry about it like?' Her never said, 'What do you want to be?' Nor the old man never said anything. But she answered it in a nutshell. She said, 'What difference would it make if I fucking said anything?' Her said, 'You'll still be what you want to be'. So I thought, 'Oh well'.

The middle class pattern is different. Though disillusion with the school and affiliation with some group form can be seen, these things do not occur with reference to a distinctive outside culture. Authority is not properly differentiated with respect to class dynamics. The emergent culture does not benefit from the force of working class themes. Consequently optimal conditions exist for the dominant educational axis to recoup its former position. The second term necessary for institutional differentiation is basically lacking.

When the middle class child is thrown back on to his indigenous culture, instead of finding strengthening and confirming oppositional themes there, he finds the same ones. Centripetal forces act to throw him back to the institution.

His relationship at home is not one of competition but of dependence. The axis at home is similar to that at school. Knowledge and guidance are exchanged for hoped-for respect in a relationship of superior/inferior. This relationship is secured particularly by the parents' likely financial ability to support the child. Thus no matter what the crisis, there is likely to be a parental notion of responsibility to a dependent instead of the working class notion of indifference to an independent. This reproduces to some extent the relationship which obtains at school. In particular, there is likely to be a reinforcement of a certain view of the social importance and value of knowledge, though on somewhat different grounds from the school's more idealistic paradigm. Middle class parents, in fact, are more likely than the teacher to insist on the importance of the school as a source not of theory for application to concrete practice, but of qualifications as a means of mobility in the chain of exchanges which characterise our society....

Post-differentiated relationships

We should not underestimate the hostilities which can develop in the *post-differentiated* school situation. Just because we have looked at the 'richness' of the cultural response of 'the lads' we should not forget what that response is to. Where knowledge becomes devalued or worthless, authority, stripped of its educational justifications, can appear very harsh and naked. That is why it is opposed. The teaching paradigm is seen more and more in its coercive mode. The total experience of school is something 'the lads' most definitely want to escape from.

One of the most oppressive forces is the belittling and sarcastic attitude of some teachers. This attitude arises from the particular conjunction of class and institution as it is exposed after *differentiation.* We may call it the 'class insult': it occurs in class but its referent is social class. Understandably enough, many teachers are outraged when the received educational paradigm breaks down. They register this breakdown as an affront: a breach in those manners which they expect as a matter of course. As we have seen, one of the essential equivalents in the educational exchange is respect. For good reasons of their own, therefore, after *differentiation* 'the lads' stop being polite to staff — at least as the main mode of their relationship, and this change is expressed at the very heart of the general style of their culture. All some staff see, of course, is wholesale impertinence and rudeness — not the logic of a changed relationship. Their frustration and anger takes the form of withdrawing their own equivalent, 'knowledge' — or, more precisely, revaluing its nature to make it utterly beyond the reach of 'the lads' anyway no matter whether they offer anything in exchange or not. Now whilst this has a certain logic of its own, and may even be successful in reasserting the old relationship where *differentiation* has not gone too far, its essentially *institutional* dynamic is perceived as a *class* dynamic by 'the lads'. There is a double articulation of meanings which is absolutely characteristic of institutions in a class society. We are faced with a mystifying and exacerbating process of the conversion and reconversion of institutional into class, and class into institutional, meanings. The teacher's frustration and attempts to re-orientate himself to the changed relationship and the changed notion of 'knowledge' at stake between him and his pupils, though taking place within the institution, are taken by 'the lads' as insults, not to their institutional identity, but to that whole class identity which they have turned to and reworked. These class insults are given an extra bite by the facility with which they are delivered. The teacher still has the mastery of formal words and expression. It is an area increasingly abandoned by 'the lads'. Examples of this kind of ridicule are extremely common:

> *Various teachers* to class '*The Midwich Cuckoos* is about children with frightening mental powers — that won't concern us here'....
> 'It's a good job you didn't have to learn to breathe, Y, you wouldn't be here now'.

'The lads' are very sensitive to this kind of approach. Where it fails, of course, or is incompetently executed (as in 'Shut your mouth when you're talking to me'), they make hay of it. Often, though, it really strikes home. It is the most hurtful barb of what they increasingly take to be the essentially arbitrary nature of authority in school.

> *Spanksy* What gets me about teachers [is] when they try and embarrass you in class, like [they did with] Fuzz, for instance.
> *Bill* In front of all your mates.
> *Spanksy* They says to him, you know, 'I'll get a sand pit for you next week', don't they? [Laughter] They started reading my essay out and it was really crap it was.
> *Derek* Made it sound worse than it was.

In an increasingly vicious circle 'the lads' respond to the overall pressure on their culture with attempts to hit back in any way that is open to them:

> *Joey* You do anything you can here to, you know, go against them. Well, I mean, you vandalise books.
> *Spike* Yeah, you smash chairs up, take the screws out of...
> *Joey* Really afterwards, you think, 'Well, stuff me, our old lady paid for that lot out of tax', but at the time you're doing it, you don't think and you don't really care.
> *PW* But do you think of it in the same way as smashing bottles or thieving?
> *Joey* It's opportunity, getting your own back on the teachers when you're caned or something. If you think, if you can get your own back on *him* you'll do anything you can (...) revenge, sort of thing, getting revenge.

As the pressure increases, so does misbehaviour, opposition to authority, vandalism, and the exploitation of any weakness or mistake on the part of the staff. They threaten to overwhelm the staff particularly towards the end of term. But the mark of commitment and of the 'good' school is the refusal to give way:

A senior teacher You're faced with a tide, you can't stop it, we try, we try to stem it ... at some places they let the tide go over them.

At the highest levels of the staff hierarchy something very like the old paradigm can be maintained, though with a somewhat altered balance of coercion and consensus and perhaps a shift towards the 'right attitudes' variant of the exchange relationship. The progressive distance of the head of the upper school, deputy head, and finally headmaster from day to day class life means they are held in a degree of awe. The weight of the material structure and organisation of the school and the knowledge that what formal and coercive power there is resides here, makes 'the lads' generally subdued, if not exactly tamed, in front of them. Over really fundamental issues senior staff have to hold the line. The basic paradigm is enforced if only as a lesson to others and as a general defence of the legitimacy of the institution....

Where senior staff take individual classes containing members of 'the lads' something of their larger authority remains, and disruption is rare. The culture of 'the lads' is suppressed on such occasions, and a reified form of the traditional paradigm enforced.

The most horrific classroom breakdowns seem to occur where more junior teachers try to assert the old educational paradigm when it is simply not tenable: the moral basis for the educational exchange having disappeared. Nothing brings out the viciousness of certain working class cultural traits like the plain vulnerability of the mighty fallen. Nothing annoys senior staff more than being brought in to try to sort out the wreckage.

In such classes advertising jingles are sung in unison to break the period up like a television programme. Regular 'news flashes' contain wicked mixtures of all that is known to give the teacher apoplexy. In one case the teacher has told 'the lads' never again to mention the school moped which they had been pestering him to let them ride, and never again to mention Picasso whom he had once unwisely been drawn into describing at length. A raucous advertising jingle — 'Beer at home means Davenports' — is interrupted for an 'important announcement': 'Picasso has just been seen riding through the school gate on a stolen school moped'. It takes the teacher twenty minutes to get the five offenders to the head's office because they keep circling back to their seats after he has lined them up by the door.

On another occasion 'the lads' are reading a play, and in a fine symbolic homologue of their submersion of the educational paradigm, slowly begin to take over the play and substitute their own. It begins with individual words, 'bastard' for 'blasted' and 'jam rag' for 'towel', to the insertion of whole lines, 'my mother bought a sink from a supermarket', and whole jokes, 'daddy bear says "Who's been eating my porridge", baby bear says, "who's been eating my porridge", and mummy bear says, "shut your 'ole, I ain't made it yet",' to a final chaotic climax of simulated battle scenes with bangs and clashes, loud rapping desk knuckles, and stomping feet.

In this permanent guerrilla war 'the lads' give no quarter to a weak opponent. Their own culture provides a commonsense map by which to judge what they take to be a failure in nerve and authority:

> [In a group discussion]
> *Eddie* Anybody these days who puts up with what he does, they'll be played up for the rest of his life. If you don't show your authority straight away when somebody starts to pick on you, like, they'll keep on all the time, like, all the kids if they know somebody you can pick on like, or summat, they'll play on him for the rest of their life as long as they know him, they'll keep playing up. You gotta show him that you ain't gonna stand for it in the first place.
> *Spike* It happens with us, like Spratt in the first and second year, I used to be a right cunt I did. I was shit scared of everybody I was, I was a right little wanker, especially him, Spanksy, he used to push me around left, right and centre Spanksy did (...) Then one day, I'd had enough and 'cos Spratt was one of the hard boys then, you know, he was a little tufty, and we was in Science, and he got me fucking mad, he kicked me in the fucking back, and everything, so I chased him round and I fucked him, really, I really done him, y'know all his face was smashed up and ever since then, y'know, if you show a bit of authority, show you ain't fucking scared of 'em.

In a mutation of the basic paradigm many teachers operate with a schizophrenic notion of the pupil. In a half-recognition of the basic shift of 'the lads' from an institutional to a class identity they are seen as simultaneously carrying sets of referents to both. This acts as a double-bind on 'the lads'. Typical comments are: 'I'll start helping you when you start helping yourself'; 'You're your own worst enemy'; 'Would you give me just some common decency, you haven't even got manners to listen to me, so why should you be treated like men?'. It is as if pupils were composed of two people one of whom is supposed to save the other. They are continually exhorted to behave in precisely those ways of which they are supposedly incapable of behaving. This nagging vestigal but insulting attempt to reassert the old authority further disqualifies the authority of the school in the eyes of 'the lads'.

The most 'successful' teachers, those who survive with 'the lads' and do not burden senior staff with their problems (the main criterion of success in the view of hard-pressed senior staff), are those who have adapted, somewhat, the basic paradigm whether or not it is their usual style just enough to contain the counterculture without provoking incidents on the one hand or collapse on the other. This tactical withdrawal for strategic containment is often dignified with the rubric of progressivism and 'relevance'. The justification concerns 'individual learning', 'discovery', 'self-direction' and 'relevance' but their logic in use concerns control. Though such classes may appear noisy, aimless and undisciplined, they rarely degenerate into chaos or psychic, symbolic or real violence towards the teacher.

For 'the lads' such classes are a matter of 'riding' the formal to extend, use and celebrate their own values of independence, the 'laff' and opposition, without pushing the teacher to the point of a final confrontation in which they might suffer. If things have gone too far there is a momentary return to the old paradigm. Priming questions or sudden interests die, though, as soon as the threat of an explosion has been averted. The following of instructions becomes mindless and literal so that the teacher is forced to qualify or even contradict himself. 'The lads' know the nature of the informal dimension much better than the staff, and especially the techniques for playing it off against the formal and its weaknesses. 'The lads' are experimenting and playing with themes of authority and of the containment of authority. The following example is from a general science class discussion about a possible syllabus for the coming term:

Fuzz Please sir, Joey's talking to Bill.
Teacher Why are you telling me?
Fuzz Oh, I just felt like doing a bit of tell-taling sir.
Eddie Let's measure the football pitch, and then the girls' netball pitch ... then the girls' hall.
Teacher Yes, right, that's a fairly small job ... what are you going to do then, what are you going to do with the results?
Spanksy [Sarcastically] Well it's like this sir, we'll get a big piece of paper — green paper if you like — then we'll draw out the pitch and the semicircles and everything, [Laughter] and then we'll put little footballers on and play Subbuteo. [More laughter]
Fuzz No sir, we can find the area of the semicircles, and all that, and the different areas of the pitch.
Teacher What's your long term aim then ... what are you trying to do?
Spanksy We can go all round the school measuring and that.
Teacher Now (to Spanksy) I don't want you to approach it with silliness, or a couldn't care less attitude, it's got to be useful.
Fuzz It would sir, we'd have to find out all the areas of everything and go into the girl's school and take measurements [Laughter]
Joey I'd prefer to stay in sir. The way I see it we might as well waste time

here in the warm as outside in the cold....

Here 'the lads' are talking about such classes:

PW (...)Just how far can you push the teacher around without them coming right down on you?

Joey Really, it's an instinctive thing, really. Actually you always know (...) Mr Archer, you don't play him up 'cos you can have a laugh with him, but you don't have to play up. Mr Bird, he's got a sort of effect about him, like, he'll shout when you're playing up and uh ... we carry on talking when we go in his lesson, just sit there talking to Bill and as long as you aren't disrupting the rest of the class, he doesn't mind (...).

PW Can you tell when you've gone too far?

Joey You can tell by just looking at 'em, really by what he sez to you, what you can say back.

Spanksy Or when they start getting mad, y'know like this in the face [straining].

Joey Mr Samuels, his neck goes all red, it's his neck.

Fuzz His neck, not his face, just about that far [indicating a point on his neck]....

Techniques which attempt to get too close to 'the lads' are simply rejected because they come from 'teachers' and are imbued with what 'teaching' already stands for in the institution.

Spanksy Some teachers try to get down to your level like, and try to be like, you know ... like Chapman, he gets us all in the gym.

Spike He calls him Eddie.

Eddie Yeah, I can't stand that, a teacher to call me Eddie.

Spanksy He was talking to us, he was goin' 'Bloody' you know, he was saying, 'The boss', you know Simmondsy.

PW What did you think of that?

Spanksy We thought it was good at the time, you know, now we realise he was only trying to bring us round to his ways, you know what I mean? Split us all up.

Fred Reagan used to come over and sit by me and he used to talk to us. I got really fed up with it one time. I just told him to fuck off. He says, 'Go to the headmaster', I had four [canings] war'n it?

For all their much lauded differences, in the real situation both traditional and modern techniques are basically about winning a form of consent from students within as tightly controlled an axis as possible. It is quite wrong, as we have seen, to assume that the traditional paradigm is about any simple domination of the students. Indeed an overcompliance with the teacher's wishes is registered as 'girlishness' and 'lack of backbone' even in the traditional model. The crucial relationship even here is predicated on the *consent* of the pupils to reciprocate — willingly and from their own resources — in acts of educational exchange. Progressivism as it is usually practised can be seen as a continuation of traditionalism in the sense that it attempts to preserve a version of the consent which has always been at the heart of the older method. In the concrete situation progressivism is a broadening of its terms in the face of reality, not an overthrow of traditionalism.

4 Settling Accounts with Subcultures: A Feminist Critique

Angela McRobbie

Although 'youth culture' and the 'sociology of youth' — and particularly critical and Marxist perspectives on them — have been central strands in the development of Cultural Studies over the past fifteen years, the emphasis from the earliest work of the National Deviancy Conference onwards has remained consistently on *male* youth cultural forms.[1] There have been studies of the relation of male youth to class and class culture, to the machinery of the State, and to the school, community and workplace. Football has been analysed as a male sport, drinking as a male form of leisure, the law and the police as patriarchal structures concerned with young male (potential) offenders. I don't know of a study that considers, never mind prioritises, youth and the family; women and the whole question of sexual division have been marginalised. This failure by subcultural theorists to dislodge the male connotations of 'youth' inevitably poses problems for feminists teaching about these questions. As they cannot use the existing texts straight, what other options do they have?

One is to dismiss the existing literature as irrevocably male-biased and to shift attention towards the alternative terrain of girls' culture, to the construction of ideologies about girlhood as articulated in and through various institutions and cultural forms — in schools, in the family, in law and in the popular media.[2] The danger of this course is that the opportunity may be missed of grappling with questions which, examined from a feminist perspective, can increase our understanding of masculinity, male culture and sexuality, and their place within class culture. This then is the other option: to combine a clear commitment to the analysis of girls' culture with a direct engagement with youth culture as it is constructed in sociological and cultural studies. Rather than simply being dismissed, the subcultural 'classics' should be re-read critically so that questions hitherto ignored or waved aside in

Source: *Screen Education*, no. 34, 1980, pp. 37-49.

embarrassment become central. An examination of their weaknesses and shortcomings can raise questions of immediate political relevance for feminists. What, for example, is the nature of women's and girls' leisure? What role do hedonism, fantasy escapes and imaginary solutions play in their lives? What access to these spheres and symbols do women have anyway?

In this article I am going to explore some questions about youth culture and subcultures by attempting this sort of feminist re-reading of two recent books, Paul Willis's *Learning to Labour* and Dick Hebdige's *Subculture*. The point, therefore, is not to condemn them — they represent the most sophisticated accounts to date of youth culture and style — but to read 'across' them to see what they say (or fail to say) about working class male sexuality, bravado and the sexual ambiguity of style. Willis investigates the relation for a group of 'lads' between working-class youth cultural 'gestures' and the places to which they are allocated in production. The expressions of resistance and opposition which characterise this relation are fraught with contradiction. Willis suggests that the vocabulary articulating their distance from structures of authority in school and workplace simultaneously binds the 'lads' to the basically rigid positions they occupy in these spheres; their rowdy shouts of disaffiliation quickly become cries of frustration and incorporation. A particular mode of class culture is thus seen in a complex way to serve two masters ... Capital *and* labour. The emphasis of Hebdige's *Subculture* is quite different. He focuses elliptically on subcultural style as *signifier* rather than as a series of distinct cultural expressions. Style, he claims, takes place several steps away from the material conditions of its followers' existence and continually resists precise historical analysis. One of its objectives, then, is to be forever out of joint with mainstream dominant culture: it evaporates just as it crystallises.

Willis and Hebdige both show how male adolescents take already coded materials from their everyday landscapes (and, though this is not spelt out, from their fantasies) and mould them into desirable shapes, into social practices and stylish postures. Both accounts draw on the notion that control and creativity are exercised from within subordinate class positions and that, as a result of this subordination, cultural gestures often appear in partial, contradictory and even amputated forms. These insights can be taken further by focussing on the language of adolescent male sexuality embedded in these tests. Questions around sexism and working-class youth and around sexual violence make it possible to see how class and patriarchal relations work together, sometimes with an astonishing brutality and at other times in the teeth-gritting harmony of romance, love and marriage. One of Willis's 'lads' says of his girlfriend:

She loves doing fucking housework. Trousers I brought up yesterday, I took 'em up last night and her turned 'em up for me. She's as good as gold and I wanna get married as soon as I can. [Willis, 1977, p.45]

Until we come to grips with such expressions as they appear across the subcultural field, our portrayal of girls' culture will remain one-sided and youth culture will continue to 'mean' in uncritically masculine terms. Questions about girls, sexual relations and femininity in youth will continue to be defused or marginalised in the ghetto of Women's Studies.

Silences

One of the central tenets of the women's movement has been that the personal is political. Similarly, feminists recognise the close links between personal experience and the areas we choose for study — our autobiographies invade and inform what we write. Even if the personal voice of the author is not apparent throughout the text, she will at least announce her interest in, and commitment to, her subject in an introduction or foreword. Although few radical (male) sociologists would deny the importance of the personal in precipitating social and political awareness, to admit how their own experience has influenced their choice of subject-matter (the politics of selection) seems more or less taboo. This silence is particularly grating in the literature on the hippie and drug countercultures, where it seems to have been stage-managed only through a suspiciously exaggerated amount of 'methodological' justification [See, for example, Willis, 1978].

...This absence of self and the invalidating of personal experience in the name of the more objective social sciences goes hand in hand with the silencing of other areas, which are for feminists of the greatest importance.... If we look for the structured absences in this youth literature, it is the sphere of family and domestic life that is missing. No commentary on the hippies dealt with the countercultural sexual division of labour, let alone the hypocrisies of 'free love'; few writers seemed interested in what happened when a mod went home after a weekend on speed. Only what happened out there on the streets mattered.

Perhaps these absences should be understood historically.. . Many of the radical young sociologists in the vanguard of the attack on functionalist sociology were recruited from the New Left, from the student movement of the late Sixties and even from the hippie counterculture. At this time, before the emergence of the women's movement in the early Seventies, the notions of escaping from the family, the bourgeois commitments of children and the whole sphere of family consumption formed a distinct strand in left politics. Sheila Rowbotham has described how women were seen in some left circles as a temptation provided by Capital to divert workers and militants alike from the real business of revolution, and she has also shown how hypocritical these anti-family, anti-women platitudes were [Rowbotham, 1973, p 19]. Clearly things have changed since then but, although the work of feminists has enabled studies of the family to transcend functionalism, the literature on subcultures and youth culture has scarcely begun to deal with the contradictions that patterns of cultural resistance pose in relation to women. The writers, having defined themselves as against the family and the trap of romance as well as against the boredom of meaningless labour, seem to be drawn to look at other, largely working-class, groups who appear to be doing the same thing.

In documenting the temporary flights of the Teds, Mods or Rockers, however, they fail to show that it is monstrously more difficult for women to escape (even temporarily) and that these symbolic flights have often been at the expense of women (especially mothers) and girls. The lads may get by with — and get off on — each other alone on the streets but they did not eat, sleep or make love there. Their peer-group consciousness and pleasure frequently seem to hinge on a collective disregard for women and the sexual exploitation of girls. And in the literary sensibility of urban romanticism that resonates across most youth cultural discourses, girls are allowed little more than the back seat on a draughty motor bike.

> Just wrap your legs around these velvet rims
> And strap your hands across my engines
> We'll run till we drop baby we'll never go back
> I'm just a scared and lonely rider
> But I gotta know how it feels.
> [Born to Run, © Bruce Springsteen, 1975]

Writing about subcultures isn't the same thing as being in one. Nonetheless, it's easy to see how it would be possible in sharing some of the same symbols — the liberating release of rock music, the thrill of speed, of alcohol or even of football — to be blinded to some of their more oppressive features.

I have oversimplified in this account, of course — there is a whole range of complicating factors. In the first place, feminists also oppose the same oppressive structures as the radical sociologists and have visions of alternative modes of organising domestic life — although ones which are *primarily* less oppressive of women, because historically women have always suffered the greatest exploitation, the greatest isolation in the home. Secondly, to make sense of the literature on subculture *purely* in terms of male left identification with male working-class youth groups would mean devaluing the real political commitment behind the work and ignoring its many theoretical achievements. The attempts to explain the ways in which class fears on the part of the dominant class have been inflected during the post-war period onto sectors of working-class youth — and dealt with at this level — remains of vital significance; also important has been the ascription of a sense of dignity and purpose, an integrity and a rationale, to that section of youth commonly labelled 'animals' in the popular media. Thirdly, there have been political and theoretical developments. The NDC of the late Sixties grew out of a libertarianism which rejected both reformist and old left politics in favour of 'grass-roots' politics (especially cultural and 'alternative' politics) and which emphasised the importance of community work and action research [see Taylor, Walton and Young, 1975]. Many of these ideas have since been refined in an engagement with the work of Althusser and of Gramsci.

Yet the question of sexual division still remains more or less unexplored. In *Learning to Labour,* Paul Willis convincingly argues that the culture which the lads bring to the school and workplace and its consequent relation to the position they occupy in the labour hierarchy provides the key to many of the more contradictory aspects of male working-class culture. But what do these expressions mean for girls and female working-class culture? One striking feature of Willis's study is how unambiguously degrading to women is the language of aggressive masculinity through which the lads kick against the oppressive structures they inhabit — the text is littered with references of the utmost brutality. One teacher's authority is undermined by her being labelled a 'cunt'. Boredom in the classroom is alleviated by the mimed masturbating of a giant penis and by replacing the teacher's official language with a litany of sexual 'obscenities'. The lads demonstrate their disgust for and fear of menstruation by substituting 'jam rag' for towel at every opportunity. What Willis fails to confront, I think, is the violence underpinning such imagery and evident in one lad's description of sexual intercourse as having 'a good maul on her'. He does not comment on the extreme cruelty of the lads' sexual double standard or tease out in sufficient detail how images of sexual power and domination are used as a kind of last defensive resort. It is in these terms that the book's closing lines can best be understood. When Paul Willis gently probes Joey about his future, he replies 'I don't know, the only thing I'm interested in is fucking as many women as I can if you really want to know'.

Although Willis shows how male manual work has come to depend on the elaboration of certain values — the cultural reproduction of machismo from father to son, the male pride in physical labour and contempt for 'penpushing' — he does not integrate these observations on masculinity and patriarchal culture into the context of the working-class family. The family is the obverse face of hard, working-class culture, the softer sphere in which fathers, sons and boyfriends expect to be, and are, emotionally serviced. It is this link between the lads' hard outer image and their private experiences — relations with parents, siblings and girlfriends — that still needs to be explored. Willis's emphasis on the cohesion of the tight-knit groups tends to blind us to the ways that the lads' immersion in and expression of working-class culture also takes place outside the public sphere. It happens as much around the breakfast table and in the bedroom as in the school and the workplace.

Shopfloor culture may have developed a toughness and resilience to deal with the brutality of capitalist productive relations, but these same 'values' can be used internally. They are evident, for example, in the cruel rituals to which the older manual workers subject school-leavers newly entering production [Willis, 1977, p.96]. They can also be used, and often are, against women and girls in the form of both wife and girlfriend battering. A full *sexed* notion of working-class culture would have to consider such features more centrally.

Discourses of Disrespect

Because it consistently avoids reduction to one essential meaning and because its theses are almost entirely decentred, it's not easy to contain Dick Hebdige's *Subculture* within the normal confines of a critical review. Ostensibly his argument is that it is on the concrete and symbolic meeting-ground of black and white (implicitly male) youth that we have to understand the emergence and form of subcultural style, its syncopations and cadences. From an account of the 'Black Experience', he works outwards to the ways in which this culture has been taken up and paid homage to by white male intellectuals and by sections of working class youth. At the heart of this process he places rock music — black soul and reggae, white rock (especially the music and style of David Bowie) and, of course, the 'mess' of punk....

Whereas in the earlier *Resistance through Rituals* [Hall et al, 1976] it is class that provides the key to unlocking subcultural meanings (though not, the authors stress, in a reductionist way), in *Subculture* style and race are selected as the organising principles for prising them open. Although neither book takes us very far in understanding youth and gender, Hebdige's account at least makes it possible to explore the theme *without* continual recourse to class and so may disrupt (in a positive sense) some of our own commonsense wisdoms about class and class culture. But although his method draws on the work of feminists like Kristeva and is one widely used by feminists working in Media Studies, Hebdige by and large reproduces yet another 'silence'. The pity is that he thereby misses the opportunity to come to grips with subculture's best kept secret, its claiming of style as a male but never unambiguously masculine prerogative. This is not to say that women are denied style, rather that the style of a subculture is primarily that of its men. Linked to this are the collective celebrations of itself through its rituals of stylish public self-display and of its (at least temporary) sexual self-sufficiency. As a well-known ex-Mod put it:

> You didn't need to get too heavily into sex or pulling chicks, or sorts as they were called ... Women were just the people who were dancing over in the corner by the speakers. [Interview with Pete Meader, *New Musical Express,* 17 November 1979].

If only he had pushed his analysis of style further, Hebdige might well have unravelled the question of sexuality, masculinity and the apparent redundancy of women in most subcultures.

What is clear, though, is that Hebdige revels in style. For him it is a desirable mode of narcissistic differentiation — 'You're still doing things I gave up years ago,' as Lou Reed put it. There's nothing inherently wrong with that; the problem is that as a signifier of desire, as the starting point for innumerable fantasies or simply as a way of sorting friends from enemies, Hebdige's usage of 'style' structurally excludes women. This is ironic, for in 'straight' terms it is accepted as primarily a female or feminine interest. What's more, women are so obviously inscribed (marginalised, abused) within subcultures as static objects (girlfriends, whores or 'faghags') that access to its thrills, to hard fast rock music, to drugs, alcohol and 'style', would hardly be compensation even for the most adventurous teenage girl. The signs and codes subverted and reassembled in the 'semiotic guerrilla warfare' conducted through style don't really speak to women at all. The attractions of a subculture — its fluidity, the shifts in the minutiae of its styles, the details of its combative bricolage — are offset by an unchanging and exploitative view of women.

Homages to Masculinity

Rather than just cataloguing the 'absences' in *Subculture,* I want to deal with three questions raised by a feminist reading: the extent to which subcultural bricoleurs draw on patriarchal meanings, the implications of ambiguous sexuality for youth cultures, and the question of gender and the moral panic.

Dick Hebdige claims that style breaks rules and that its 'refusals' are complex amalgams taken from a range of existing signs and meanings. Their 'menace' lies in the extent to which they threaten these meanings by demonstrating their frailty and the ease with which they can be thrown into disorder. But just as the agents who carry on this sartorial terrorism are inscribed as subjects within patriarchal as well as class structures, so too are the meanings to which they have recourse. These historical, cultural configurations cannot be free of features oppressive to women. Machismo suffuses the rebel archetypes in Jamaican culture which, Hebdige claims, young British blacks plunder for suitable images. The Teds turned to the style of Edwardian 'gents'. The Mods, locating themselves within the 'modernism' of the new white-collar working class, looted its wardrobe as well as that of smart young blacks around town. The Skins, similarly, turned simultaneously to both black style and that of their 'fathers' and 'grandfathers'. More tangentially, Punks appropriated the 'illicit iconography of pornography', the male-defined discourse *par excellence.* Of course, it would be ludicrous to expect anything different. The point I'm stressing is how highly differentiated according to gender style (mainstream or subcultural) is — it's punk girls who wear the suspenders, after all.

If, following Eco's dictum, [see Hebdige, 1979, p.100] we speak through our clothes, then we still do so in the accents of our sex. Although Hebdige does fleetingly mention sexual ambiguity in relation to style (and especially to the various personae of David Bowie), he doesn't consider it as a central feature right across the subcultural spectrum — for him subcultural style *is* Sta-prest trousers, Ben Sherman shirts or pork pie hats. I'm not suggesting that all subcultures value transvestism — far from it — but that subcultural formations and the inflections of their various 'movements' raise questions about sexual identity which Hebdige continuously avoids. Does subcultural elevation of style threaten the official masculinity of straight society which regards such fussiness as cissy? Does the Skinheads' pathological hatred of 'queers' betray an uneasiness about their own fiercely defended male culture and style? Are subcultures, as Ned Polsky suggests, ways of providing relatively safe frameworks within which boys and young men can escape the pressures of heterosexuality? [Polsky, 1971, pp 161-2].

For feminists the main political problem is to assess the significance of this for women. If subculture offers a (temporary?) escape from the demands of traditional sex roles, then the absence of predominantly girl subcultures — their denial of access to such 'solutions' — is evidence of their deeper oppression and of the monolithic heterosexual norms which surround them and find expression in the ideology of romantic love. Whereas men who 'play around' with femininity are nowadays credited with some degree of power to choose, gender experimentation, sexual ambiguity and homosexuality among girls are viewed differently. Nobody explains David Bowie's excursions into female personae (see the video accompanying his 'gay' single *Boys Keep Swinging)* in terms of his inability to attract women. But any indication of such ambiguity in girls is still a sure sign that they couldn't make it in a man's world. Failure replaces choice; escape from heterosexual norms is still synonymous with rejection. .... My point, then, is not to label subcultures as potentially gay, but to show that the possibility of escaping oppressive aspects of adolescent heterosexuality within a youth culture or a gang with a clearly signalled identity remains more or less unavailable to girls. For working-class girls especially, the road to 'straight' sexuality still permits few deviations.

Finally I want to comment on the way in which Hebdige deals with the processes of reaction and incorporation accompanying the subcultural leap into the limelight of the popular press and media.... For again, because his model is not gendered, he fails to recognise that these are gender-specific processes. Ultimately the shock of subcultures can be partially defused because they can be seen as, among other things, boys having fun. That is, reference can be made *back* to the idea that boys should 'sow their wild oats' — a privilege rarely accorded to young women. This does not mean that the 'menace' altogether disappears, but at least there are no surprises as far as gender is concerned. Even male sexual ambiguity can be dealt with to some extent in this way. (Boys with ear-rings, dyed hair and mascara? No problem: they do it every week in *It Ain't Half Hot, Mum.*) But if the Sex Pistols had been an all-female band spitting and swearing their way into the limelight, the response would have been more heated, the condemnation less tempered by indulgence. Such an event would have been greeted in the popular press as evidence of a major moral breakdown and not just as a fairly common, if 'shocking', occurrence.

Walking on the Wild Side — It's Different for Girls

... I now want to look briefly at some of the meanings ensconced within some of the objects and practices constituting the subcultural artillery.

Rock music has been so much a part of post-war youth cultures that its presence has often just been noted by writers; the meanings signified by its various forms have not received the attention they deserve. Dick Hebdige does something to redress this, but again without developing a perspective sensitive to gender and sexual division. My points here are tentative and simple. Such a perspective would have to realise that rock does not signify alone, as pure sound. The music has to be placed within the discourses through which it is mediated to its audience and within which its meanings are articulated. Just as Elizabeth Cowie has shown how reviews construct the sense of a particular film in different ways, [Cowie, 1979] so an album or concert review lays down the terms and the myths by which we come to recognise the music. One myth energetically sustained by the press is the overwhelming male-ness of the rock scene. Writers and editors seem unable to imagine that girls could make up a sizable section of their readership: although at a grass-roots level virulent sexism has been undermined by punk, Rock Against Racism and Rock Against Sexism, journalistic treatment remains much the same. As 'the exception', women musicians are now treated with a modicum of respect in the *New Musical Express* or *Melody Maker,* but women are dealt with more comfortably in the gossip column on the back page, as the wives or girlfriends of the more flamboyant rock figures.

The range of drug scenes characterising subcultures reveals a similar pattern. The inventory is familiar — alcohol for Teds, Rockers and Skins, speed and other pills for Mods, Punks and Rudies, hallucinogenics for Hippies, cocaine and to a lesser extent heroin for other groups closer to the rock scene. So intransigently male are the mythologies and rituals attached to regular drug taking that few women feel the slightest interest in their literary, cinematic or cultural expressions — from William Burroughs's catalogues of destructive self- abuse and Jack Kerouac's stream-of-consciousness drinking sprees to Paul Willis's lads and their alcoholic bravado. It would be foolish to imagine that women don't take drugs — isolated young housewives are amongst the heaviest drug users and girls in their late teens are one of the largest groups among attempted suicides by drug overdose. Instead I'm suggesting that for a complex of reasons the imaginary solutions which drugs may offer boys do not have the same attraction for girls. One reason is probably the commonsense wisdom deeply inscribed in most women's consciousnesses — that boys don't like girls who drink, take speed and so on; that losing control spells sexual danger; and that drinking and taking drugs harm physical appearance. A more extreme example would be the way that the wasted male junkie can in popular mythology, in novels and films, retain a helpless sexual attraction which places women in the role of potential nurse or social worker. Raddled, prematurely aged women on junk rarely prompt a reciprocal willingness.

The meanings that have sedimented around other objects, like motorbikes or electronic musical equipment, have made them equally unavailable to women and girls. And although girls are more visible (both in numbers and popular representation) in punk than earlier subcultures, I have yet to come across the sight of a girl 'gobbing'. Underpinning this continual marginalisation is the central question of street visibility. It has always been on the street that most subcultural activity takes place (save perhaps for the more middle-class oriented hippies): it both proclaims the publicisation of the group and at the same time ensures its male dominance. For the street remains in some ways taboo for women (think of the unambiguous connotations of the term streetwalker): 'morally dubious' women are the natural partners of street heroes in movies like Walter Hill's *The Warriors* and in rock songs from the Rolling Stones to Thin Lizzy or Bruce Springsteen. Few working-class girls can afford flats and so for them going out means either a date — an escort and a place to go — or else a disco, dance hall or pub. Younger girls tend to stay indoors or to congregate in youth clubs; those with literally nowhere to go but the street frequently become pregnant within a year and disappear back into the home to be absorbed by childcare and domestic labour.

There are of course problems in such large-scale generalisations. Conceptually it is important to separate popular public images and stereotypes from lived experience, the range of ideological representations we come across daily from empirical observation and sociological data. But in practice the two sides feed off each other. Everyday life becomes at least partly comprehensible within the very terms and images offered by the media, popular culture, education and the 'arts', just as material life creates the preconditions for ideological and cultural representation. This complexity need not paralyse our critical faculties altogether, however. It is clear from my recent research[3], for example, that girls are reluctant to drink precisely because of the sexual dangers of drunkenness. This doesn't mean that girls don't occasionally 'get pissed'; my data suggest that they will drink with more confidence and less tension only when they have a reliable steady boyfriend willing to protect them from more predatory, less scrupulous males. It's difficult to deal so schematically with drug usage, and particularly involvement in hard drug subcultures. Particularly interesting, however, are the warnings to girls against hard drugs in the West German media (the addiction rate there is much higher than in Britain). These are couched entirely in terms of the damage heroin can do to your looks, your body and your sexuality. They reinforce and spell out just how 'its different for girls': a girl's self-evaluation is assumed to depend on the degree to which her body and sexuality are publicly assessed as valuable.

The Politics of Style — Two Steps Beyond

... In order to understand questions about youth culture and politics more fully, it will be necessary to supplement the established conceptual triad of class, sex and race with three more concepts — *populism, leisure* and *pleasure*. It's not possible to develop a full-blown theoretical justification for that project here, however. And as I opened this article by condemning the self-effacement of male writers, it would perhaps be appropriate to end on a personal note about the ambivalence of my own responses to subcultures (I too lace my texts with rock lyrics) and the possible links between youth subcultures and feminist culture.

For as long as I can remember, collective expressions of disaffiliation from Authority and the hegemony of the dominant classes (by either sex) have sent shivers of excitement down my spine. Despite their often exaggerated romanticism and their bankrupt (frequently sexist) politics, the 'spectacle' of these symbolic gestures has got a hold on my consciousness which I cannot completely exorcise. Sitting on a train in West Germany, surrounded by carefully coiffeured businessmen and well-manicured businesswomen, the sight of two Felliniesque punks (male) in the next compartment cannot fail to make me smile, just as it cannot fail to make some convoluted political statement.

In a similar way, punk is central to an understanding of the resurgence of 'youth politics' in Britain over recent years. It's not a *deus ex machina* which will banish the unpopularity of left politics but, as a set of loosely linked gestures and forms, it has proved a mobilising and energising force which has helped to consolidate developments like Rock Against Racism. There have also been overlaps between the nuances of punk style and feminist style which are more than just coincidental. Although the stiletto heels, mini-skirts and suspenders will, despite their debunking connotations, remain unpalatable to most feminists (with the exception of Nina Hagen), both punk girls and feminists want to overturn accepted ideas about what constitutes femininity. And they often end up using similar stylish devices to upset notions of 'public propriety'.

What this indicates is a mysterious symbiosis between aspects of subcultural life and style in post-war Britain and aspects of a 'new' left and even feminist culture. However precious or trivial the question of style may seem in contrast to concrete forms of oppression and exploitation (unemployment, for example, or the strengthening of the State apparatus), it cannot be hived off into the realm of personal hedonism. The sort of style Dick Hebdige describes is central to the contradictory nature of working-class male culture, and it plays a visible role in the resistances by youth in Britain today. The style of West Indian boys *and* girls is as much an assault on authority as outright confrontation. In our daily lives, feminists wage a similar semiotic warfare. Knitting in pubs, breast-feeding in Harrods, the refusal to respond to expressions of street sexism, the way we wear our clothes — all the signs and meanings embodied in the way we handle our public visibility play a part in the culture which, like the various youth cultures, bears the imprint of our collective, historical creativity. They are living evidence that although inscribed within structures, we are not wholly prescribed by them. For many of us too, escaping from the family and its pressures to act like a real girl remains the first political experience. For us the objective is to make this flight possible for all girls, and on a long term basis.

I'm not arguing that if girls were doing the same as some boys (and subcultures are always minorities) all would be well. The 'freedom' to consume alcohol and chemicals, to sniff glue and hang about the street staking out only symbolic territories is scarcely less oppressive than the pressures keeping girls in the home. Yet the classic subculture does provide its members with a sense of oppositional sociality, an unambiguous pleasure in style, a disruptive public identity and a set of collective fantisies. As a pre-figurative form and set of social relations, I can't help but think it could have a positive meaning for girls who are pushed from early adolescence into achieving their feminine status through acquiring a 'steady'. The working-class girl is encouraged to dress with stylish conventionality (see the fashion pages of *Jackie);* she is taught to consider boyfriends more important than girlfriends and to abandon the youth club or disco for the honour of spending her evenings watching television in her boyfriend's house, so saving money for an engagement ring. Most significantly, she is forced to relinquish youth for the premature middle age induced by childbirth and housework. It's not so much that girls do too much too young: rather they have the opportunity of doing too little too late. To the extent that all-girl subcultures, where the commitment to the gang comes first, might forestall these processes and provide their members with a collective confidence which could transcend the need for 'boys', they could well signal an important progression in the politics of youth culture.

Notes

1 Among the more important books have been Jock Young *The Drugtakers: The Social Meaning of Drug Use* Paladin 1971; Stan Cohen *Folk Devils and Moral Panics: The Creation of the Mods and Rockers* MacGibbon and Kee 1972; Stuart Hall and Tony Jefferson (eds) *Resistance through Rituals* Hutchinson 1976; David Robbins and Philip Cohen *Knuckle Sandwich* Penguin 1978; Paul Corrigan *Schooling the Smash Street Kids* Macmillan 1979; Paul Willis *Learning to Labour* Saxon House 1977; Dick Hebdige *Subculture: The Meaning of Style* Methuen 1979.

2 See, for example, Sue Sharpe *Just Like a Girl* Penguin 1977; Anne Marie Wolpe *Some Processes in Sexist Education* WRRC Pamphlet 1977; Angela McRobbie 'Working Class Girls and the Culture of Femininity' in CCCS Women's Studies Group (eds) *Women Take Issue* Hutchinson 1978; Deirdre Wilson 'Sexual Codes and Conduct' in Carol Smart and Barry Smart (eds) *Women, Sexuality and Social Control* RKP 1978; Maggie Casburn *Girls Will Be Girls: Sexism and Juvenile Justice in a London Borough* WRRC Pamphlet 1979.

3 Angela McRobbie *Young Women and Leisure: How Working-Class Girls Get Working-Class Husbands* (forthcoming).

References

COWIE, E., 'The Popular Film as Progressive Text: a discussion of *Coma*', Part 1 in *m/f*, no. 3, 1979.

HALL, S., and JEFFERSON, T., (eds.), *Resistance Through Rituals*, Hutchinson, 1976.

HEBDIGE, D., *Subculture: The meaning of style*, Methuen, 1979.

POLSKY, N., *Beats, Hustlers and Others*, Penguin, 1971.

ROWBOTHAM, S., *Woman's Consciousness, Man's World*, Penguin, 1973.

TAYLOR, I., WALTON, P., and YOUNG, J., (eds) *Critical Criminology*, Routledge and Kegan Paul, 1975.

WILLIS, P., *Profane Culture*, Routledge and Kegan Paul, 1978.

WILLIS, P., *Learning to Labour: How working class kids get working class jobs*, Saxon House, 1977.

SECTION 3

Structuralist Approaches

Structuralist approaches, both to the social practices and to the 'texts' in various forms (verbal, visual, musical) involved in the study of culture and ideology, have in common an emphasis on the system of signification in whose terms practices and texts are enabled to have 'meaning', as distinct from the specific 'meanings' which the human participants (individual or group) find in them. Raymond Williams's early work proposed the notion of 'a structure of feeling' shared by different writers in a specific period, which attempted to combine both the 'culturalist' emphasis on individual texts and a governing set of constraints whose analysis could be shown to yield general meanings which over-rode the specific group of texts, revealing a set of objective relationships between the authors and their historical period. The impact of structuralism, as a general intellectual event, has been to encourage that search beyond groups of texts for the underlying rules and conventions of which each can be seen to be a variant utterance. The theoretical model lay in Saussurean linguistics with its conception of a language as a closed system of interacting elements, while the application of this model to anthropological research by Lévi-Strauss offered a dramatic example of its potential in the field of cultural phenomena.

In the first essay in this Section, Jonathan Culler notes the general dependence of structuralist analysis on Saussure's original proposal in the *Course in General Linguistics* for a general 'science of signs', i.e. for the development of semiology, in which the study of language would necessarily be prominent. Culler distinguishes amongst the different kinds of 'sign', underlining the special nature of the system on which literary texts depend. The codes, or sign-systems, of literature differ from unambiguous codes like Morse or Braille because of their elusive and mobile character.

> As soon as an aesthetic code comes to be generally perceived as a code... then works of art tend to move beyond this code. They question, parody, and generally undermine the code while exploring its possible mutations and extensions.

For this reason the semiological investigation of such codes is peculiarly challenging and (it has to be admitted) not yet far advanced.

The two essays that follow outline a principal criticism of the Saussurean concept of underlying system. For Volosinov, the 'sign is a phenomenon of the external world'. Human consciousness only exists in sign-systems, which are therefore the material basis of ideology. '*Without signs, there is no ideology*'. The disengagement of the sign-system from its concrete historical existence as a medium of ideological creativity thus involves an abstractionism as damaging as the economic reductionism which a different version of Marxism applied to cultural phenomena. Volosinov also reminds us that the understanding of the non-verbal arts is indissolubly linked to language, not in the sense that words can substitute for or translate music or pictures or dance, but in the deeper sense that verbal language remains the predominant signifying system, which mediates our grasp of the others.

R. Coward and J. Ellis point out that Saussure's sharp distinction between 'synchronic structure and diachronic change' necessarily entails as the user of language 'a transcendent subject', beyond and outside the historical process, ultimately the abstraction to which Lévi-Strauss attributed the final source of the *langue* of myth, the 'human mind'. This tendency can be countered, however, by insisting on the role of the 'signifying chain' both in the production of new signifiers and the construction of specific historical human subjects. 'Man is constructed in the symbol, and is not pre-given or transcendent.' The symbol, the signifying system is not a fixed Platonic structure, a 'ghostly paradigm', but itself a source of ceaseless productivity.

Even the briefest selection of material illustrating the structuralist approach would be incomplete without an extract from the work of Barthes. In his essay on narrative, Barthes offers a theoretical approach to the fine linguistic tissue of narrative, a subject on which traditional literary criticism has had almost nothing to say. Narrative as a second-order language system can be conceived on the basic linguistics model, as having the structure of a 'sentence', made up of linguistic units which can be described and whose sequential interconnections are responsible for the fugue-like interweaving that characterizes narrative:

> Sequences move in counterpoint; functionally the structure of narrative is fugued: thus it is that narrative at once 'holds' and 'pulls on'.

One kind of unit constructs the sequence, or syntagm, while another is 'integrationist', this interaction of elements accounting both for the forward momentum of narrative, and for its existence as a single a-temporal structure from which we abstract 'characters' and 'plots'. It is only when the source of narrative in specific arrangements of language has been accounted for, that we can move on to narrative as discourse, as the manipulation and production of the codes by whose means narrative persuades us of its hold on 'reality'.

1 Semiology: The Saussurian legacy

Jonathan Culler

Very few paragraphs of the *Course in General Linguistics* are devoted to semiology, and this is no doubt one of the reasons why linguists generally neglected to follow Saussure's lead in developing a general science of signs which would situate and orient linguistics. But for Saussure the semiological perspective was central to any serious study of language. 'So is it not obvious', he wrote, 'that language is above all a system of signs and that therefore we must have recourse to the science of signs if we are to define it properly?' (Engler, 47).

> Language is a system of signs that express ideas and is thus comparable to the system of writing, to the alphabet of deaf-mutes, to symbolic rituals, to forms of etiquette, to military signals, etc. It is but the most important of these systems.
>
> We can therefore imagine *a science which would study the life of signs within society* ... We call it *semiology*, from the Greek *semeion* ('sign'). It would teach us what signs consist of, what laws govern them. Since it does not yet exist we cannot say what it will be; but it has a right to existence; its place is assured in advance. Linguistics is only a part of this general science; and the laws which semiology discovers will be applicable to linguistics, which will thus find itself attached to a well-defined domain of human phenomena (*Course*, 16; *Cours*, 33).

Since human beings make noises, use gestures, employ combinations of objects or actions in order to convey meaning, there is a place for a discipline which would analyse this kind of activity and make explicit the systems of convention on which it rests. And, Saussure argues, if linguistics is conceived as a part of semiology there will be important consequences:

Source: Jonathan Culler, *Saussure*, Fontana, 1976, Chapter 4.

> ... aspects of language which may at first seem extremely important (such as the use of vocal mechanisms) will become secondary considerations if they serve only to distinguish language from other semiological systems. This procedure will not only clarify the problems of linguistics; rituals, customs, etc., will, we believe, appear in a new light if they are studied as signs, and one will come to see that they should be included in the domain of semiology and explained by its laws (*Course*, 17; *Cours*, 35).

Semiology is thus based on the assumption that insofar as human actions or productions convey meaning, insofar as they function as signs, there must be an underlying system of conventions and distinctions which makes this meaning possible. Where there are signs there is system. This is what various signifying activities have in common, and if one is to determine their essential nature one must treat them not in isolation but as examples of semiological systems. In this way, aspects which are often hidden or neglected will become apparent, especially when nonlinguistic signifying practices are considered as 'languages'.

But why should linguistics, the study of one particular though very important signifying system, be thought to provide the model for studying other systems? Why should linguistics be as Saussure called it, 'le patron général' of semiology? The answer takes us back to a familiar starting point, the arbitrary nature of the sign.

Linguistics may serve as a model for semiology, Saussure argued, because in the case of language the arbitrary and conventional nature of the sign is especially clear. Non-linguistic signs may often seem natural to those who use them, and it may require some effort to see that the politeness or impoliteness of an action is not a necessary and intrinsic property of that action but a conventional meaning. But if linguistics is taken as a model it will compel the analyst to attend to the conventional basis of the non-linguistic signs he is studying.

This is not to say that all signs are wholly arbitrary. There are some intrinsic constraints on the meanings action can bear and, reciprocally, on the class of actions appropriate to express a particular meaning. It is difficult to imagine a culture where a punch on the mouth might be a friendly greeting. But within such constraints there is a whole range of actions which would serve perfectly well as friendly greetings. Within this realm of available possibilities one can speak of signs as conventional and arbitrary. In fact, Saussure writes,

> every means of expression used in a society is based, in principle, on a collective norm – in other words, on convention. Signs of politeness, for instance, often have a certain natural expressivity (one thinks of the way a

> Chinese prostrates himself nine times before the Emperor by way of salutation), but they are nonetheless determined by a rule; and it is this rule which leads one to use them, not their intrinsic value. We can therefore say that wholly arbitrary signs are those which come closest to the semiological ideal. This is why language, the most complex and widespread of systems of expression, is also the most characteristic. And for this reason linguistics can serve as a model for semiology as a whole, though language is only one of its systems (*Course*, 68; *Cours*, 100-101).

By taking linguistics as a model one may avoid the familiar mistake of assuming that signs which appear natural to those who use them have an intrinsic meaning and involve no conventions.

Why is this important? Why should one wish to stress the conventional nature of non-linguistic signs? The answer is quite simple. If signs were natural, then there would really be nothing to analyse. One would say that opening a door for a woman simply *is* polite, and that's all there is to it. But if one starts with the assumption that signs are likely to be conventional, then one will seriously seek out the conventions on which they are based and will discover the underlying system which makes these signs what they are. Just as, in linguistics, the arbitrary nature of the sign leads one to think about the system of functional differences which create signs, so in other cases one will focus on significant differences: differences and oppositions which bear meaning. What differentiates a polite from an impolite greeting, a fashionable from an unfashionable garment? One comes to study not isolated signs but a system of distinctions.

The Domain of Semiology

Saussure's proposals concerning semiology were not immediately taken up, and it was only towards the middle of this century, many years after the publication of the *Course*, that others began to realize the importance of his suggestions. It is as if the individual disciplines had to develop in their own ways and rediscover Saussure's insights for themselves before they could become properly semiological. Indeed, what is now called 'structuralism' arose when anthropologists, literary critics, and others saw that the example of linguistics could help to justify what they sought to do in their own disciplines; and as they began to take linguistics as a model they realized that they were in fact developing the semiology which Saussure had so long ago proposed.

Thus, it was not until 1961, in his inaugural lecture at the Collège de France, that the anthropologist Claude Lévi-Strauss defined anthropology as a branch of semiology and paid homage to Saussure as the man who, in his discussion of semiology, had laid the foundations for the proper conception of anthropology. But fifteen years earlier, in an epoch-making article on 'Structural Analysis in Linguistics and Anthropology', [Lévi-Strauss, 1968] Lévi-Strauss had already drawn upon the concepts and methods of linguistics to establish his brand of structuralism.

In this article Lévi-Strauss speaks of the advances in linguistics, especially in phonology, which have made it a scientific discipline and remarks that 'phonology cannot help but play the same renovating role for the social sciences that nuclear physics, for example, played for the exact sciences.' He proposes that the anthropologist follow the example of the linguist and reproduce in his own field something comparable to the 'phonological revolution'. Phonology studies not isolated terms but relations between terms, systems of relation; and phonology passes from the study of phenomena which are consciously grasped or known by speakers of a language to their 'unconscious infrastructure'. It seems to identify, that is to say, systems of relations which are known only subconsciously. What lesson can the anthropologist draw from this? He can take it, Lévi-Strauss says, as an example in method: in order to analyse signifying phenomena, in order to investigate actions or objects which bear meaning, he should postulate the existence of an underlying system of relations and try to see whether the meaning of individual elements or objects is not a result of their contrasts with other elements and objects in a system of relations of which members of a culture are not already aware.

Indeed, Nikolai Trubetzkoy, in his seminal *Principles of Phonology* (1939), had already outlined the methodological implications of phonological theory for the social sciences and thus had advanced the semiology proposed by Saussure. Whereas the phonetician is concerned with the properties of actual speech sounds, the phonologist is interested in the differential features which are functional in a particular language; he asks what phonic differences are linked with differences of meaning, how the differential elements are related to one another and how they combine to form words or phrases. It is clear, Trubetzkoy continues, that these tasks cannot be accomplished by the methods of the natural sciences, which are concerned with the intrinsic properties of natural phenomena themselves and not with the differential features which are the bearers of social significance. In other words, in the natural sciences there is nothing corresponding to the distinction between *langue* and *parole:* there is no institution or conventional system to be studied. The social and human sciences, on the other hand, are concerned with the social use of material objects and must therefore distinguish between the objects themselves and the system of distinctive or differential features which give them meaning and value.

Attempts to describe such systems, Trubetzkoy argues, are closely analogous to work in phonology. The example he cites is the study of clothing, as it might be carried out by an anthropologist or a sociologist. Many features of physical garments themselves which would be of great importance to the wearer are of no interest to the anthropologist, who is concerned only with those features that carry a social significance. Thus, the length of skirts might carry a lot of significance in the social system of a culture, while the material from which they were made did not. Or again, if I were to wear a yellow suit rather than a grey suit, that might have considerable social meaning, but the fact that I have a strong preference for grey suits rather than brown suits, or a dislike for woollen materials, might be purely personal choices which carried no social significance. Just as the phonologist tries to determine which differences in sound bear meaning and which do not, so the anthropologist or sociologist studying clothing would be trying to isolate those features of garments which carried social significance. He attempts to reconstruct the system of relations and distinctions which members of a society have assimilated and which they display in taking certain garments as indicating a particular life-style, social role, or social attitude. He is, in short, interested in those features by which garments are made into signs.

Like the linguist, the anthropologist or sociologist is attempting to make explicit the implicit knowledge which enables people within a given society to communicate and understand one another's behaviour. The facts he is trying to explain are facts about people's implicit knowledge: that a particular action is regarded as polite while another is impolite; that a particular garment is appropriate in one situation but inappropriate in another. Where there is knowledge or mastery of any kind, there is a system to be explained. This is the fundamental principle which guides one's extrapolation from linguistics into other disciplines. If the meanings assigned to objects or actions by members of a culture are not purely random phenomena, then there must be a semiological system of distinctions, categories, and rules of combination which one might hope to describe.

One could thus assign to semiology a vast field of enquiry: if everything which has meaning within a culture is a sign and therefore an object of semiological investigation, semiology would come to include most disciplines of the humanities and the social sciences. Any domain of human activity, be it music, architecture, cooking, etiquette, advertising, fashion, literature, could be approached in semiological terms.

The immediate objection to an imperialistic semiology, which sought in this way to encompass so many other disciplines, might be that the signifying phenomena which one encounters in these various domains are not all alike. Even if most human objects and activities are signs, they are not signs of the same type. This is an important objection, and one of the major tasks of semiology is to distinguish between different types of signs, which may need to be studied in different ways.

Various typologies of signs have been proposed, but three fundamental classes of signs seem to stand out as requiring different approaches: the icon, the index, and the sign proper (sometimes misleadingly called 'symbol'). All signs consist of a signifier and a signified, a form and an associated meaning or meanings; but the relations between signifier and signified are different for each of these three types of sign. An *icon* involves actual resemblance between signifier and signified: a portrait signifies the person of whom it is a portrait less by an arbitrary convention than by resemblance. In an *index* the relation between signifier and signified is causal: smoke means fire because fire is generally the cause of smoke; clouds mean rain if they are the sort of clouds which produce rain; tracks are signs of the type of animal likely to have produced them. In the *sign proper,* however, the relation between signifier and signified is arbitrary and conventional: shaking hands conventionally signifies greeting; cheese is by convention an appropriate food with which to end a meal.

What are the implications of this three-way division for semiology? The main consequence is to make the sign proper the central object of semiology and to make the study of other signs a specialized and secondary activity. Study of the way in which a drawing or a photograph of a horse represents a horse might form part of semiology; but it seems more properly the concern of a philosophical theory of representation than of a linguistically based semiology. Semiology must identify and characterize iconic signs, but the study of icons is not likely to be one of its central activities.

Indices are, from the semiologist's point of view, more worrying. If he places them within his domain then he risks taking all human knowledge for his province, for any science which attempts to establish causal relations among phenomena could be seen as a study of indices and thus placed within semiology. Medicine, for example, tries to relate diseases to symptoms: to have discovered the symptoms of a disease is to have identified the signs which betray the presence of that disease and, reciprocally, to have learned what these symptoms are signs of. Meteorology attempts to construct a system in order to relate atmospheric conditions to their causes and consequences and thus to read them as signs: as signs of weather conditions. Economic prediction depends on a proper reading of economic signs; economics is the discipline which identifies these signs and enables one to read them. In short, a whole range of disciplines tries to decipher the natural or social world; the methods of these disciplines are different, and there is no reason to think that they would gain substantially by being brought under the banner of an imperialistic semiology.

Signs proper, where the relation between signifier and signified is arbitrary or conventional, are then the central domain of semiology. Indeed, they require semiological investigation if their mechanisms are to be understood. In the absence of a causal link between signifier and signified which would enable one to treat each sign individually, one must try to reconstruct the semiotic system, the system of conventions, from which a whole group of signs derive. Precisely because the individual signs are unmotivated, one must attempt to reconstruct the system, which alone can explain them.

However, one cannot exclude indices altogether from the domain of semiology, for they form an interesting and important borderline case. The fact is that any index may be used as a conventional sign. Once the causal or indexical relationship between a signifier and a signified is recognized by a culture, the particular signifier becomes associated with its signified and can be used to evoke that meaning even in cases where the causal relation is absent. For example, once it is generally recognized that smoke means fire I can use smoke to signify fire. The smoke produced by a smoke machine may be used in a play to signify fire, even though the smoke is not in this case being caused by fire. The index is here being used as a conventional sign.

Many indices, of course, can be used as conventional signs in this theatrical way: if an actor is made up to look as if he has measles we read his spots as signifying measles in a conventional way and do not believe that the spots are in his case causally connected with measles. But there is a large set of conventionalized indices which are especially interesting to the semiologist because they come to constitute what one might call the conventional social mythology of a culture. What we call 'status-symbols' are perhaps the best example. As the name itself suggests, these are not just indices of status but symbols of status; though they have some causal or intrinsic relation to the status they signify, they have been promoted by the conventions of a society to the rank of symbol and carry more meaning than their causal or indexical nature would entail. Thus, a Rolls-Royce is certainly an index of wealth in that one must be wealthy to own one, but social convention has made it a symbol of wealth, a mythical object which signifies wealth more imperiously than other objects which might be equally expensive. Among the many objects which are indices of wealth in that they are all expensive, it has been singled out by social usage as a symbol of wealth. The semiologist who is studying social life as a system of signs will certainly want to include conventionalized indices of this kind within his domain. [See Barthes, 1972].

Moreover, there is another way in which indices enter the domain of the semiologist. Within particular sciences the meanings of indices change with the configurations of knowledge. Medical symptoms, for example, are read and interpreted differently from one era to another as knowledge advances.

There are changes both in what are identified as symptoms and in the way symptoms are interpreted. It thus becomes possible for the semiologist to study the changes in medicine as an interpretive system, as a way of reading and identifying signs. He would be trying to discover the conventions which determine or make possible the medical discourse of a period and permit indices to be read. In this investigation the semiologist would be interested not in the symptoms or indices themselves, nor in the 'real' causal relation between index and meaning, but in the reading of indices within a system of conventions.

What then is the domain of semiology? How far does its empire extend? It will obviously have variable boundaries; there are many things which can be treated semiologically but which need not necessarily be studied in this way. In fact, to characterize the domain of semiology one must simply identify the different sorts of cases it can encounter.

I. At the heart of the semiological enterprise are systems of conventional signs used for direct communication. These include, first, the various codes used to convey messages which are composed in an existing natural language such as English. Morse code, semaphore codes, braille, and all the codes devised for secrecy can be used to convey an English message. Secondly, there is a whole series of specialized codes used to convey a particular type of information to groups who may not share the same natural language: chemical symbols, traffic signals and road signs, silver assay marks, mathematical symbols, the signs used in airports, trains, etc., and finally the recondite symbolisms of heraldic or alchemical codes [See Mounin, 1970]. All these cases involve conventional signs based on explicit codes: since they are designed for easy and unambiguous communication there is an explicit procedure for encoding and decoding, such as looking up the item in question in a code book. Such codes are pure examples of semiological systems, but precisely because they are so straightforward it is usually an easy matter to describe the principles on which they are constructed and so they often prove much less interesting to the semiologist than less explicit and more complicated systems which fall into our next category.

II. More complicated than explicit codes are systems where communication undoubtedly takes place but where the codes on which the communication depends are difficult to establish and highly ambiguous or open-ended. Such is the case, for example, with literature. To read and understand literature one requires more than a knowledge of the language in which it is written, but it is very difficult to establish precisely what supplementary knowledge is required for satisfactory interpretation of literary works. Certainly one is not dealing with the sort of codes for which keys or code books could be supplied. However, precisely because one is dealing with an extremely rich and complicated communicative system, the semiological study of literature and of other aesthetic codes (such as the codes of painting and music) can be extraordinarily interesting.

The reason for the evasive complexity of these codes is quite simple. Codes of the first type are designed to communicate directly and unambiguously messages and notions which are already known; the code simply provides an economical notation for notions which are already defined. But aesthetic expression aims to communicate notions, subtleties, complexities which have not yet been formulated, and therefore, as soon as an aesthetic code comes to be generally perceived as a code (as a way of expressing notions which have already been articulated) then works of art tend to move beyond this code. They question, parody, and generally undermine the code while exploring its possible mutations and extensions. One might even say that much of the interest of works of art lies in the ways in which they explore and modify the codes which they seem to be using; and this makes semiological investigation of these systems both highly relevant and extemely difficult.

III. The third sort of case which semiology must confront covers social practices which may not at first seem to involve communication but which are highly codified and certainly employ a whole series of distinctions in order to create meaning. Ritual and etiquette of various kinds and the systems of convention governing food and clothing are obviously semiological systems: to wear one set of clothes rather than another is certainly to communicate something, albeit indirectly. But one can go further and say that the buildings we inhabit, the objects we purchase, and the actions we perform are of interest to the semiologist because all the categories and operations through which they are invested with meaning are fundamentally semiological. This is not to say that purchasing a house, for example, is primarily or essentially a communicative action, but only that the differences between houses are invested with meaning by a semiological system and that in choosing one house rather than another one is dealing with the image projected by the particular house (a country cottage, a modern maisonette, a crumbling Victorian semi). One may, for purely practical reasons, choose to purchase a house whose image seems uncongenial, but one is nonetheless involved in a semiological system. The task of the semiologist in dealing with clothing, commercial objects, pastimes, and all these other social entities, is to make explicit the implicit meanings they seem to bear and to reconstruct the system of connotations on which these meanings are based.

IV. Finally we come to the cases which I initially set aside as involving indices rather than signs proper: the disciplines of the social and natural sciences which try to establish relations of cause and effect between phenomena and for which the meaning of an object or an action is likely to be its causal antecedent or consequence, its significance in a causal scheme. As I have already mentioned, though these disciplines are not in themselves semiological, that does not mean that they need escape the attention of the semiologist. The objects which these disciplines study are not signs proper, but they themselves, as disciplines, as 'languages' or systems of articulation, may be studied as semiotic systems.

This is obvious in the case of sciences which are now discredited, such as astrology. Since we do not believe in the causal relations which astrologists established between the movements of the planets and the events of people's lives, it is easy to consider astrology as a system of conventions. The semiologist studying astrology would ask what were the rules or conventions which astrologers employed in attributing meaning to the configurations of the heavens. What were the conventions which one had to accept to be an astrologer?

We would not hesitate to admit that we are here dealing with a system of signs which might be elucidated. But in fact, if we think about the matter we can see that our semiological analysis would not be fundamentally affected if future discoveries were to prove that everything the astrologers had said were true. The same set of rules would still underlie astrological discourse, whether the predictions they yield are true or false. And so we can extend the bounds of semiology somewhat further: semiology can study the conventions which govern the discourse and interpretations of any discipline. But notice what this involves. To the semiologist the truth or falsity of the propositions of a discipline will be irrelevant. If everything which botany now asserts were to be disproved, that would not affect a semiological analysis of the conventions of botany as a system of signs. Botany is not the sum of true statements about plants but a system of discourse. At any given period there are a great many things which could be truly said about plants which do not fall within the realm of botany (e.g. that roses are systematically cultivated and dandelions systematically uprooted), and the semiologist is interested in the conventions which exclude some statements from the realm of botany and permit others. Though some disciplines, such as medicine, meteorology, psychoanalysis, and astrology, might lend themselves more easily to a semiological analysis, in that they are more obviously concerned with the reading and interpretation of signs, in fact at this level any system of discourse can be studied semiologically since it is itself a system of signs.

Semiological Analysis

Linguistics has served as the model for semiology and, as Saussure suggested, has drawn attention to the conventional nature of signs and the differential nature of meaning. But it will perhaps be evident from the diversity of the sign systems I have mentioned that the concepts and techniques of linguistic analysis may be much better suited for the investigation of some systems than of others. In all cases the analyst distinguishes *langue* from *parole,* tries to go behind the actions or objects themselves to the system of rules and relations which enables them to have meaning. And in most cases he will be able to identify syntagmatic and paradigmatic relations: the relations between elements which can be combined to form higher-level units and relations between elements which can replace one another and which therefore contrast with one another to produce meaning. But in some systems the syntax is so weak as to make syntagmatic relations almost non-existent. Traffic signs, for example, generally do not involve the combination of more than one unit, or if they do (as in signs where the shape indicates the presence of a hazard and the device specifies the sort of hazard) the syntagmatic relation is very simple and uninteresting. Alternatively, in some systems the set of elementary paradigmatic oppositions is extremely limited. In Morse code, for example, there are only two oppositions: noise versus pause and short versus long. Other systems are semantically very weak. The abominations of Leviticus list the animals one is permitted and forbidden to eat. One can, with some ingenuity, reconstruct the system of rules which assign significance to particular animals, but this system only produces two meanings: clean and unclean (i.e. permitted and forbidden).

But for most systems there do seem to be syntagmatic relations, paradigmatic contrasts, and a variety of meanings which can be produced by various contrasts and relations. In the food system, for example, one defines on the syntagmatic axis the combinations of courses which can make up meals of various sorts; and each course or slot can be filled by one of a number of dishes which are in paradigmatic contrast with one another (one wouldn't combine roast beef and lamb chops in a single meal: they would be alternatives on any menu). These dishes which are alternatives to one another often bear different meanings in that they connote varying degrees of luxury, elegance, etc.

Many semiological systems are complicated, however, by the fact that they rest on other systems, particularly that of language, and thus become 'second order' systems. Literature is one such system: it has language as its basis and its supplementary conventions are conventions about special uses of language. Thus, to take a simple example, the rhetorical figures such as metaphor, metonymy, hyperbole, synecdoche can be seen as operations of a second-order literary code. When Shakespeare writes 'But thy eternal summer shall not fade', his words are signs which have a literal meaning in the linguistic code of English, but the rhetorical figure of metaphor is part of a second-order literary code which allows one to use the linguistic signs, *eternal summer,* to mean something like 'a full, languorous beauty which will always remain at its peak'. And, furthermore, there is a convention of love poetry making hyperbolic compliment of this kind, which draws upon metaphors of nature and natural processes, an appropriate form of praise.

Now it is obvious that the system of literature – the knowledge one must acquire, over and above knowledge of the language, in order to read and interpret literary works – does not involve explicit codes like those of traffic signs or of etiquette. One can learn about various ways of interpreting figurative language, about the conventions governing different literary genres, about types of literary structure or organization. But literature continually undermines, parodies, and escapes anything which threatens to become a rigid code or explicit rules for interpretation. Traffic signs do not violate the code of traffic signs, but literary works are continually violating codes. And this is because literature is fundamentally an exploration of the possibilities of experience, a questioning and deepening of the categories in and through which we ordinarily view ourselves and the world. Literary codes have an important role in that they make possible this questioning and deepening process, just as rules of etiquette make it possible to be impolite. But literary works never lie wholly within the codes that define them, and, as I have argued elsewhere, this is what makes the semiological investigation of literature such a tantalizing enterprise [See Culler, 1975].

In a series of unpublished reflections on medieval German legends, Saussure shows his interest in the semiology of literature and his awareness of some of the problems it poses. A legend, he writes, 'is composed of a series of symbols in a sense which remains to be defined.' These symbols, though more difficult to define than the units of a language, are doubtless governed by the same principles as other signs, and 'they all form part of semiology' [quoted in Starobinski, 1971, p.15]. In the case of literature, as in that of language and other semiotic systems, the fundamental problem is one of identity. One is not dealing with fixed signs such that a given form will always have the same meaning wherever it appears. On the contrary, the literary work is always drawing upon signs which exist prior to it, 'combining them and continually drawing from them new meaning'. Indeed, considering the problem of characters in his German legends, Saussure reaches the conclusion that one is confronted with a whole series of elements (proper names, attributes, relations with other characters, actions) and that what one speaks of as the character himself is nothing other than the creation of the reader, the result of drawing together and combining all the disparate elements which one encounters as one reads through the text [See Avalle, 1973, p.33].

Saussure has here hit upon an important system of convention in literature. The production of characters is governed by a set of cultural models which enable us, for example, to infer motives from action or the qualities of a person from his appearance. And so if we say that in the course of a given novel or story a character changes, what we are saying is that, in terms of our literary models of character, two actions or attributes which are attached to a single character are in opposition, are incompatible: that according to our notions of character if someone first does X and later does Y we can only make sense of this by saying that the character himself changed. ...

Conclusions

'In the whole history of science,' wrote the philosopher Ernst Cassirer, 'there is perhaps no more fascinating chapter than the rise of the new science of linguistics. In its importance it may very well be compared to the new science of Galileo which in the seventeenth century changed our whole concept of the physical world.'... Ferdinand de Saussure's role in the rise of modern linguistics is no doubt a fascinating episode in recent intellectual history. But Cassirer's bold comparison of modern linguistics with the new science of Galileo is more difficult to evaluate. What does it mean and how could it be substantiated?

For Cassirer the crucial and revolutionary aspect of modern linguistics is Saussure's insistence on the primacy of relations and systems of relations. Here, in its fundamental concepts and methodological premises, Saussure's theory of language is an exceptionally clear expression of the formal strategies by which a whole series of disciplines, from physics to painting, transformed themselves in the late nineteenth and early twentieth centuries and became modern.

The strategy can be stated most simply as a shift in focus, from objects to relations. It is relationships that create and define objects, not the other way around. The philosopher of science, Alfred North Whitehead, offers a general statement of the problem:

> The misconception which has haunted philosophic literature throughout the centuries is the notion of 'independent existence'. There is no such mode of existence; every entity is to be understood in terms of the way it is interwoven with the rest of the universe.

And in his book *Science and the Modern World* he shows that new discoveries in science produced so many complexities that a fundamental shift in perspective was necessary if the various disciplines were to come to terms with themselves and their objects. Physics discovered that it was exceedingly difficult to explain electricity and electromagnetic phenomena in terms of discrete units of matter and their movement. The solution seemed to be to reverse the problem: instead of taking matter as prime and trying to define the laws governing its behaviour, why not take energy itself, electrical energy, as prime and define matter in terms of electromagnetic forces. This change in perspective leads to the discovery of new scientific objects: an electron is not a positive entity in the old sense; it is a product of a field of force, a node in a system of relations, which, like a phoneme, does not exist independently of these relations.

What Whitehead calls the 'materialism' of the nineteenth century, the empiricism which grants ontological primacy to objects, gives way, he says, to a 'theory of relativity' in the broadest sense: a theory based on the primacy of relations. 'On the materialist theory,' Whitehead writes, 'there is material which endures. On the organic theory the only endurances are structures of activity.' Emphasis falls on the structures. 'The event is what it is by reason of the unification within itself of a multiplicity of relationships.' Outside these systems of relations, it is nothing.

Saussure, of course, states these themes clearly, not as aspects of some diffuse world view but as methodological postulates which are necessary if language is to be properly analysed. And alongside Saussure's affirmations we may place the unequivocal statement of the painter Georges Braque: 'I do not believe in things; I believe in relationships.' This is, perhaps, the true Modernist credo. What is Cubism if not an assertion of the primacy of relationships? In Cubist paintings objects lose their hitherto unquestioned primacy; they emerge with difficulty from the interaction of lines and planes; the three-dimensional space which supports ordinary objects is broken down in an attempt to represent a variety of perspectives and relations simultaneously. Or again, in Modernist literature one can observe the shift by which both poetry and the novel become less directly mimetic, less concerned with the representation of recognizable objects and scenes, and more interested in effects of juxtaposition, where relational values – relations between words or among various types of discourse – become the primary constituents of the work of art.

In various fields or disciplines shifts in technique have led to a concentration on systems of relation. This is the basis of Cassirer's bold claim: that for the thought of our century the world is no longer essentially a collection of independent entities, of autonomous objects, but a series of relational systems.

This move from object to structure is indeed a major shift in our conception of the world, but it is not clear how far the role of Galileo should fall to Saussure and Saussurian linguistics. From a historical point of view, his theory of language seems an exceptionally clear expression of a shift which was taking place simultaneously, if less explicitly, in a variety of fields: an expression or example more than a primary cause. Indeed, it seems likely that if Saussure is ever to be cast in the role of twentieth-century Galileo, his right to that position will depend on the discipline and mode of thought which he was actually instrumental in founding: semiology. To bring us to see social life and culture in general as a series of sign systems which a linguistic model can help us to analyse – this is the contribution which might eventually make him comparable to Galileo.

But of course it is too early to judge the real significance of Saussure in the intellectual history of our century, for work in the field of semiology has only recently begun, and it is not yet clear whether it will indeed become a dominant intellectual movement of our time. If it does become a major presence, a central discipline, this will be due to the efforts of many people besides Saussure; but his vision of a semiology which would encompass linguistics while taking it as a model has led others to give concrete expression to the semiological perspective: man is a creature who lives among signs and must try not only to grasp their meaning but especially to understand the conventions responsible for their meaning. It is Saussure who stands behind the claim, which many people would today espouse, that to study man is essentially to study the various systems by which he and his cultures organize and give meaning to the world.

References

A Saussure's writings

Course – Ferdinand de Saussure, *Course in General Linguistics*, trans. W Baskin (London: Peter Owen, 1960; Fontana, 1974).
Cours – Ferdinand de Saussure, *Cours de Linguistique générale* edited by Tullio de Mauro (Paris: Payot, 1973).
Engler – Ferdinand de Saussure, *Cours de linguistique générale* Critical Edition by Rudolf Engler (Wiesbaden: Otto Harrassowitz, 1967-74)

B Other Sources

AVALLE, D'ARCO SILVIO, 'La sémiologie de la narrativité chez Saussure' in Bouazis, C. (ed) *Essais de la théorie du texte,* Galilee, 1973.
BARTHES, R., *Mythologies* Jonathan Cape, 1972.
CULLER, J., *Structuralist Poetics: Structuralism, linguistics and the study of literature,* Routledge and Kegan Paul, 1975.
LÉVI-STRAUSS,C., 'Structural Analysis in Linguistics and in Anthropology' in *Structural Anthropology,* Allen Lane, 1968.
MOUNIN, G., *Introduction à la semiologie,* Minuit, 1970.
STAROBINSKI, J., *Les Mots sur les mots: les anagrammes de F de Saussure,* Gallimard, 1971.
TRUBETZKOY, N., *Principles of Phonology,* University of California Press, 1969.

2 The study of ideologies and philosophy of language

V. N. Volosinov

The problem of the ideological sign. The ideological sign and consciousness. The word as an ideological sign par excellence. The ideological neutrality of the word. The capacity of the word to be an inner sign. Summary.

Problems of the philosophy of language have in recent times acquired exceptional pertinence and importance for Marxism. Over a wide range of the most vital sectors in its scientific advance, the Marxist method bears directly upon these problems and cannot continue to move ahead productively without special provision for their investigation and solution.

First and foremost, the very foundations of a Marxist theory of ideologies – the bases for the studies of scientific knowledge, literature, religion, ethics, and so forth – are closely bound up with problems of the philosophy of language.

Any ideological product is not only itself a part of a reality (natural or social), just as is any physical body, any instrument of production, or any product for consumption, it also, in contradistinction to these other phenomena, reflects and refracts another reality outside itself. Everything ideological possesses *meaning:* it represents, depicts, or stands for something lying outside itself. In other words, it is a *sign. Without signs, there is no ideology.* A physical body equals itself, so to speak; it does not signify anything but wholly coincides with its particular, given nature. In this case there is no question of ideology.

However, any physical body may be perceived as an image; for instance, the image of natural inertia and necessity embodied in that particular thing. Any such artistic-symbolic image to which a particular physical object gives rise is already an ideological product. The physical object is converted into a sign. Without ceasing to be a part of material reality, such an object, to some degree, reflects and refracts another reality.

Source: V. N. Volosinov, *Marxism and the Philosophy of Language*, Seminar Press, 1973, Chapter 1.

The same is true of any instrument of production. A tool by itself is devoid of any special meaning; it commands only some designated function – to serve this or that purpose in production. The tool serves that purpose as the particular, given thing that it is, without reflecting or standing for anything else. However, a tool also may be converted into an ideological sign. Such, for instance, is the hammer and sickle insignia of the Soviet Union. In this case, hammer and sickle possess a purely ideological meaning. Additionally, any instrument of production may be ideologically decorated. Tools used by prehistoric man are covered with pictures or designs – that is, with signs. So treated, a tool still does not, of course, itself become a sign.

It is further possible to enhance a tool artistically, and in such a way that its artistic shapeliness harmonizes with the purpose it is meant to serve in production. In this case, something like maximal approximation, almost a coalescence, of sign and tool comes about. But even here we still detect a distinct conceptual dividing line: the tool, as such, does not become a sign; the sign, as such, does not become an instrument of production.

Any consumer good can likewise be made an ideological sign. For instance, bread and wine become religious symbols in the Christian sacrament of communion. But the consumer good, as such, is not at all a sign. Consumer goods, just as tools, may be combined with ideological signs, but the distinct conceptual dividing line between them in not erased by the combination. Bread is made in some particular shape; this shape is not warranted solely by the bread's function as a consumer good; it also has a certain, if primitive, value as an ideological sign (e.g., bread in the shape of a figure eight *(krendel)* or a rosette).

Thus, side by side with the natural phenomena, with the equipment of technology, and with articles for consumption, there exists a special world – the *world of signs.*

Signs also are particular, material things; and, as we have seen, any item of nature, technology, or consumption can become a sign, acquiring in the process a meaning that goes beyond its given particularity. A sign does not simply exist as a part of a reality – it reflects and refracts another reality. Therefore, it may distort that reality or be true to it, or may perceive it from a special point of view, and so forth. Every sign is subject to the criteria of ideological evaluation (i.e., whether it is true, false, correct, fair, good, etc.). The domain of ideology coincides with the domain of signs. They equate with one another. Wherever a sign is present, ideology is present, too. *Everything ideological possesses semiotic value.*

Within the domain of signs – i.e., within the ideological sphere – profound differences exist: it is, after all, the domain of the artistic image, the religious symbol, the scientific formula, and the judicial ruling, etc. Each field of ideological creativity has its own kind of orientation towards reality and each refracts reality in its own way. Each field commands its own special function within the unity of social life. *But it is their semiotic character that places all ideological phenomena under the same general definition.*

Every ideological sign is not only a reflection, a shadow, of reality, but is also itself a material segment of that very reality. Every phenomenon functioning as an ideological sign has some kind of material embodiment, whether in sound, physical mass, color, movements of the body, or the like. In this sense, the reality of the sign is fully objective and lends itself to a unitary, monistic, objective method of study. A sign is a phenomenon of the external world. Both the sign itself and all the effects it produces (all those actions, reactions, and new signs it elicits in the surrounding social milieu) occur in outer experience.

This is a point of extreme importance. Yet, elementary and self-evident as it may seem, the study of ideologies has still not drawn all the conclusions that follow from it.

The idealistic philosophy of culture and psychologistic cultural studies locate ideology in the consciousness. Ideology, they assert, is a fact of consciousness; the external body of the sign is merely a coating, merely a technical means for the realization of the inner effect, which is understanding.

Idealism and psychologism alike overlook the fact that understanding itself can come about only within some kind of semiotic material (e.g., inner speech), that sign bears upon sign, that *consciousness itself can arise and become a viable fact only in the material embodiment of signs.* The understanding of a sign is, after all, an act of reference between the sign apprehended and other, already known signs; in other words, understanding is a response to a sign with signs. And this chain of ideological creativity and understanding, moving from sign to sign and then to a new sign, is perfectly consistent and continuous: from one link of a semiotic nature (hence, also of a material nature) we proceed uninterruptedly to another link of exactly the same nature. And nowhere is there a break in the chain, nowhere does the chain plunge into inner being, nonmaterial in nature and unembodied in signs.

This ideological chain stretches from individual consciousness to individual consciousness, connecting them together. Signs emerge, after all, only in the process of interaction between one individual consciousness and another. And the individual consciousness itself is filled with signs. Consciousness becomes consciousness only once it has been filled with ideological (semiotic) content, consequently, only in the process of social interaction.

Despite the deep methodological differences between them, the idealistic philosophy of culture and psychologistic cultural studies both commit the same fundamental error. By localizing ideology in the consciousness, they transform the study of ideologies into a study of consciousness and its laws; it makes no difference whether this is done in transcendental or in empirical-psychological terms. This error is responsible not only for methodological confusion regarding the interrelation of disparate fields of knowledge, but for a radical distortion of the very reality under study as well. Ideological creativity – a material and social fact – is forced into the framework of the individual consciousness. The individual consciousness, for its part, is deprived of any support in reality. It becomes either all or nothing.

For idealism it has become all: its locus is somewhere above existence and it determines the latter. In actual fact, however, this sovereign of the universe is merely the hypostatization in idealism of an abstract bond among the most general forms and categories of ideological creativity.

For psychological positivism, on the contrary, consciousness amounts to nothing: it is just a conglomeration of fortuitous, psychophysiological reactions which, by some miracle, results in meaningful and unified ideological creativity.

The objective social regulatedness of ideological creativity, once misconstrued as a conformity with laws of the individual consciousness, must inevitably forfeit its real place in existence and depart either up into the superexistential empyrean of transcendentalism or down into the presocial recesses of the psychophysical, biological organism.

However, the ideological, as such, cannot possibly be explained in terms of either of these superhuman or subhuman, animalian, roots. Its real place in existence is in the special, social material of signs created by man. Its specificity consists precisely in its being located between organized individuals, in its being the medium of their communication.

Signs can arise only on *interindividual territory*. It is territory that cannot be called 'natural' in the direct sense of the word*. Signs do not arise between any two members of the species *Homo sapiens*. It is essential that the two individuals be *organized socially*, that they compose a group (a social unit); only then can the medium of signs take shape between them. The individual consciousness not only cannot be used to explain anything, but, on the contrary, is itself in need of explanation from the vantage point of the social, ideological medium.

The individual consciousness is a social-ideological fact. Not until this point is recognized with due provision for all the consequences that follow from it will it be possible to construct either an objective psychology or an objective study of ideologies.

It is precisely the problem of consciousness that has created the major

*Society, of course, is also a *part of nature,* but a part that is qualitatively separate and distinct and possesses its own *specific* systems of laws.

difficulties and generated the formidable confusion encountered in all issues associated with psychology and the study of ideologies alike. By and large, consciousness has become the *asylum ignorantiae* for all philosophical constructs. It has been made the place where all unresolved problems, all objectively irreducible residues are stored away. Instead of trying to find an objective definition of consciousness, thinkers have begun using it as a means for rendering all hard and fast objective definitions subjective and fluid.

The only possible objective definition of consciousness is a sociological one. Consciousness cannot be derived directly from nature, as has been and still is being attempted by naive mechanistic materialism and contemporary objective psychology (of the biological, behaviouristic, and reflexological varieties). Ideology cannot be derived from consciousness, as is the practice of idealism and psychologistic positivism. Consciousness takes shape and being in the material of signs created by an organized group in the process of its social intercourse. The individual consciousness is nurtured on signs; it derives its growth from them; it reflects their logic and laws. The logic of consciousness is the logic of ideological communication, of the semiotic interaction of a social group. If we deprive consciousness of its semiotic, ideological content, it would have absolutely nothing left. Consciousness can harbor only in the image, the word, the meaningful gesture, and so forth. Outside such material, there remains the sheer physiological act unilluminated by consciousness, i.e., without having light shed on it, without having meaning given to it, by signs.

All that has been said above leads to the following methodological conclusion: *the study of ideologies does not depend on psychology to any extent and need not be grounded in it.* As we shall see in greater detail in a later chapter, it is rather the reverse: *objective psychology must be grounded in the study of ideologies.* The reality of ideological phenomena is the objective reality of social signs. The laws of this reality are the laws of semiotic communication and are directly determined by the total aggregate of social and economic laws. Ideological reality is the immediate superstructure over the economic basis. Individual consciousness is not the architect of the ideological superstructure, but only a tenant lodging in the social edifice of ideological signs.

With our preliminary argument, disengaging ideological phenomena and their regulatedness from individual consciousness, we tie them in all the more firmly with conditions and forms of social communication. The reality of the sign is wholly a matter determined by that communication. After all, the existence of the sign is nothing but the materialization of that communication. Such is the nature of all ideological signs.

But nowhere does this semiotic quality and the continuous, comprehensive role of social communication as conditioning factor appear so clearly and fully expressed as in language. *The word is the ideological phenomenon par excellence.*

The entire reality of the word is wholly absorbed in its function of being a sign. A word contains nothing that is indifferent to this function, nothing that would not have been engendered by it. A word is the purest and most sensitive medium of social intercourse.

This indicatory, representative power of the word as an ideological phenomenon and the exceptional distinctiveness of its semiotic structure would already furnish reason enough for advancing the word to a prime position in the study of ideologies. It is precisely in the material of the word that the basic, general-ideological forms of semiotic communication could best be revealed.

But that is by no means all. The word is not only the purest, most indicatory sign but is, in addition, *a neutral sign.* Every other kind of semiotic material is specialized for some particular field of ideological creativity. Each field possesses its own ideological material and formulates signs and symbols specific to itself and not applicable in other fields. In these instances, a sign is created by some specific ideological function and remains inseparable from it. A word, in contrast, is neutral with respect to any specific ideological function. It can carry out ideological functions of *any* kind – scientific, aesthetic, ethical, religious.

Moreover, there is that immense area of ideological communication that cannot be pinned down to any one ideological sphere: the area of *communication in human life, human behavior.* This kind of communication is extraordinarily rich and important. On one side, it links up directly with the processes of production; on the other, it is tangent to the spheres of the various specialized and fully fledged ideologies. In the following chapter, we shall speak in greater detail of this special area of behavioral, or life ideology. For the time being, we shall take note of the fact that the material of behavioral communication is preeminently the *word.* The locale of so-called conversational language and its forms is precisely here, in the area of behavioral ideology.

One other property belongs to the word that is of the highest order of importance and is what makes the word the primary medium of the individual consciousness. Although the reality of the word, as is true of any sign, resides between individuals, a word, at the same time, is produced by the individual organism's own means without recourse to any equipment or any other kind of extracorporeal material. This has determined the role of word as *the semiotic material of inner life — of consciousness* (inner speech). Indeed, the consciousness could have developed only by having at its disposal material that was pliable and expressible by bodily means. And the word was exactly that kind of material. The word is available as the sign for, so to speak, inner employment: it can function as a sign in a state short of outward expression. For this reason, the problem of individual consciousness as the *inner word* (as an *inner sign* in general) becomes one of the most vital problems in philosophy of language.

It is clear, from the very start, that this problem cannot be properly approached by resorting to the usual concept of word and language as worked out in nonsociological linguistics and philosophy of language. What is needed is profound and acute analysis of the word as social sign before its function as the medium of consciousness can be understood.

It is owing to this exclusive role of the word as the medium of consciousness that *the word functions as an essential ingredient accompanying all ideological creativity whatsoever.* The word accompanies and comments on each and every ideological act. The processes of understanding any ideological phenomenon at all (be it a picture, a piece of music, a ritual, or an act of human conduct) cannot operate without the participation of inner speech. All manifestations of ideological creativity — all other nonverbal signs — are bathed by, suspended in, and cannot be entirely segregated or divorced from the element of speech.

This does not mean, of course, that the word may supplant any other ideological sign. None of the fundamental, specific ideological signs is replacable wholly by words. It is ultimately impossible to convey a musical composition or pictorial image adequately in words. Words cannot wholly substitute for a religious ritual; nor is there any really adequate verbal substitute for even the simplest gesture in human behavior. To deny this would lead to the most banal rationalism and simplisticism. Nonetheless, at the very same time, every single one of these ideological signs, though not supplantable by words, has support in and is accompanied by words, just as is the case with singing and its musical accompaniment.

No cultural sign, once taken in and given meaning, remains in isolation: it becomes part of the *unity of the verbally constituted consciousness.* It is in the capacity of the consciousness to find verbal access to it. Thus, as it were, spreading ripples of verbal responses and resonances form around each and every ideological sign. Every *ideological refraction of existence in process of generation,* no matter what the nature of its significant material, *is accompanied by ideological refraction in word* as an obligatory concomitant phenomenon. Word is present in each and every act of understanding and in each and every act of interpretation.

All of the properties of word we have examined - *its semiotic purity, its ideological neutrality, its involvement in behavioral communication, its ability to become an inner word and, finally, its obligatory presence, as an accompanying phenomenon, in any conscious act* - all these properties make the word the fundamental object of the study of ideologies. The laws of the ideological refraction of existence in signs and in consciousness, its forms and mechanics, must be studied in the material of the word, first of all. The only possible way of bringing the Marxist sociological method to bear on all the profundities and subtleties of 'immanent' ideological structures is to operate from the basis of the philosophy of language as the *philosophy of the ideological sign*. And that basis must be devised and elaborated by Marxism itself.

3 Structuralism and the subject: a critique

R. Coward and J. Ellis

Language, as Lévi-Strauss claims, in some sense lays the foundations for culture as it is made of the same material: structural relations, systems of difference, signs, relations of exchange. Structuralist thought bases its analysis of the social process upon this analogy between society and language as it is conceived in structural linguistics. For Lévi-Strauss, linguistics presents itself as a systematic science, whose methods are exemplary for the 'human sciences'. The discipline of anthropology, along with the other human sciences, can exploit the fundamental discoveries of modern linguistics. These reveal that signification, which appears to be a natural relation, is in reality an arbitrary system of differences in which elements gain their meanings only from their relation with all other elements. This conception of language, with its concomitant modes of study, was originated by Ferdinand de Saussure in his lectures from 1907 to 1911, published after his death as the *Course in General Linguistics*.

Saussure's initial gesture was to introduce an order into the inchoate mass of speech acts that compose a language. He produced the distinction between *langue*, the system of language, and *parole*, the individual acts of realisation of that system. The speech act is only comprehensible on the basis of the whole system from which it gains its validity; and the system itself only exists in the multitude of individual speech acts. The structure of language is the systematicity which informs every individual act of speech: it is a system which can be constructed by an analyst but has no concrete existence as such. The system only exists in the fact that the potential infinity of individual utterances is comprehensible. In Saussure's initial distinction, language is revealed to be a system whose only reality is its realisations. This is the preliminary definition of a structure.

Source: R. Coward and J. Ellis, *Language and Materialism*, Routledge and Kegan Paul, 1977, Chapter 2.

The elements of the structure of language are signs, and it is the notion of the sign which provided the founding moment for structuralism... Saussure demonstrated that signs are composed of two faces, two sides, neither of which pre-exists the other nor has any meaning outside their relation. These are the sound-image or *signifier,* and the concept, or *signified.* Thus the sign /cat/ consists of a signifier the sounds 'k-a-t' and a signified, the conception of a cat. These two, the signifier and signified together, comprise the sign, and neither has any meaning outside their relation in the sign. In French, there are different signifiers, 'chat' or 'chatte', and a difference introduced into the signified, as French is capable of making a sexual differentiation where English has no gender system. From this example, two aspects of the sign can be deduced. First, the link between the signifier and the signified is an arbitrary convention. Nothing 'in nature' decrees that a certain signifier should articulate a certain signified. There is no so-called natural link between a particular sound and its concept, for even onomatopoeic sounds, which are meant to resemble their signifieds physically, still differ from language to language. The sign is constituted in the social fixing of the appearance of a relation of equivalence between signifier and signified: in language the signifier and the signified appear as symmetrical. Second, the concept and sound-image are produced in the same movement: the signifier cuts out, articulates, a certain space which becomes through this articulation, a signified, that is, meaning. The linguistic signifier in isolation has no intrinsic link with the signified: it only refers to meaning inasmuch as it forms part of a system of signification characterised by differential oppositions.

It is therefore artificial to speak of 'a' sign, as signs are only comprehensible within systems of signification and not in any ideal way 'on their own'. The structure is that which endows signifiers and signifieds with the possibility of signification: they are constituted in a process of differentiation from each other.

> In language there are only differences *without positive terms.* Whether we take the signified or the signifier, language has neither ideas nor sounds that existed before the linguistic system, but only conceptual and phonic differences that have issued from the system (Saussure, 1974, p.120).

Thus the structure not only sets in place but also creates both signifiers and signifieds, and the structure is a system of difference. Each signifier differs from others that sound similar but are not identical; and it differs from those that precede and follow it in the signifying chain. Language is a structure whose elements constitute each other in difference. Hjelmslev defines this structure as 'an autonomous entity composed of internal dependencies', and adds that

> the analysis of this entity allows one constantly to disengage the elements which condition each other reciprocally, each of which depends on certain others and could neither be conceived nor defined without these other elements. This analysis returns its object to a network of dependencies by considering linguistic facts as proportional to each other... (Hjelmslev, 1944)

Structural linguistics abandoned the question of bourgeois linguistics, the question of the origin and history of language, to make its object the relational composition in the interior of language itself. In this, it implied two dominant modes of analysis. One mode analyses the structural form at any one moment, the substitutions that are possible within it, the analysis of a particular state of *langue*. This is analysis of the paradigm, synchronic analysis of that which exists at a certain moment or during a definite epoch. The second form of analysis is that of the actual combinations that are generated, the signifying chains that are produced, the analysis of *parole*. This is analysis of the syntagm, the diachronic analysis of that which unfolds through the passing of time. It can be seen that whereas syntagmatic analysis deals with the combination of elements that are actualised in the sentence, paradigmatic analysis reveals the sets and codes to which these elements belong, any member of which could be legitimately substituted for them. If this is conceived spatially, syntagmatic analysis deals with a horizontal axis of present elements: paradigmatic analysis deals with the vertical axis of the system which renders each element intelligible. This separation of modes was initially necessary for linguistics in order to combat the atomistic historicism which dominated the late nineteenth century, and it has proved valuable in other disciplines to overcome similar tendencies, as Lévi-Strauss's work demonstrates. However, the distinction is in some ways too rigid as it fails to deal with the productivity of structures: it tends to separate the product from its production, the subject from the structure...

The strengths and weaknesses of the structuralism which developed from Saussure's linguistics are well demonstrated by the work of one of the originators of modern structuralism, Lévi-Strauss. He transposed the structuralist conceptions to the study of anthropological data, relying on the sign as a central term. It was not simply an analysis of the transmission of signs which functions within sociality, but also a matter of envisaging structures as symbolic systems, that is, the structural arrangement as productive of meaning: 'any culture may be looked upon as an ensemble of symbolic systems, in the front rank of which are to be found language, marriage laws, economic relations, art, science and religion' (Lévi-Strauss, 1950).

Lévi-Strauss's work is paradoxical: it uses rigid structural models which emphasise a synchronic moment in a process rather than the diachronic process of production and change, yet his writing seethes with evocation of the specificity of each moment, which, he claims, analysis cannot reconstruct. This tension has to be remembered throughout this schematic account of his structuralism: it is a tension that cannot be resolved except by a radical transformation of the structuralist mode of thought.

As an anthropologist, Lévi-Strauss examines the multitude of different forms of social organisation that, despite the remorseless spread of Western bourgeois modes, still exist in the world. He sees his task as taking these societies on their own terms; then to translate their terms into ours, to explain the logic by which the people of these societies conceive of and organise their relations to each other and to the world. This necessarily entails going behind the subjective accounts given of these relations, to find the basic relations which generate them. So, with his analysis of kinship structures, he takes the mass of disparate evidence from various cultures and deduces the basic 'unit of kinship' that gives rise to this multitude of different forms. Similarly, when analysing myths he finds oppositions which, whilst they reduplicate themselves to infinity in a body of myths, nevertheless express a basic contradiction or relation which underpins the attitudes and behaviour of a particular society. Summarising this method of analysing basic structures in a society, he wrote that

> the method we adopt . . . consists of the following operations:
> (i) define the phenomenon under study as a relation between two or more terms, real or supposed;
> (ii) construct a table of possible permutations between these terms:
> (iii) take this table as the general object of analysis which, at this level only, can yield the necessary connections, the empirical phenomenon considered at the beginning as being only one possible combination among others, the complete system of which must be constructed beforehand (Lévi-Strauss, *Totemism*, p.16).

His analysis of kinship systems demonstrates this method and its contrast with previous approaches.

'The error of traditional anthropology, like that of traditional linguistics, was to consider the terms, and not the relations between the terms' (Lévi-Strauss, [1968] p.46). Traditional anthropology ran up against a problem with kinship structures: it had to explain the recurrence of instances such as special relationships which exist between sons and their mother's brothers, the maternal uncle. Anthropologists like Radcliffe-Brown encountered this problem because they thought of kinship from the point of view of a Western bourgeois family: a unit consisting of a man, wife and children; this results in three special relationships, those between parents, between children, and between parents and children. The special relationship of children to the maternal uncle in certain societies is thus inexplicable. Lévi-Strauss begins not from the established 'family unit', but by positing the 'universal' incest taboo and resulting exchange of women. The incest taboo is the prerequisite of any form of social organisation whatsoever: Lévi-Strauss claims that women are exchanged between one family and another, creating bonds of mutual obligation and relation, instead of being kept by the brother for himself. He can find no society where this does not take place: there is always exchange of women by men, and for this reason it has been asserted (e.g. Kristeva, 1977) that despite varied forms of descent (matrilinear, patrilinear, matrifocal, etc.), all known social organisations have been partriarchal. It is an exchange (one woman for another) which takes place over generations, amongst a whole social group, and for small tribes it is the principal form in which the society is held together. The mechanisms take place in a variety of forms in differing societies, and they are expressed in the often complex taboos on marriage with cousins: it is possible to marry a cousin on the father's side, but not on the mother's and vice versa. It is clear from this way of viewing kinship structures that the place of the maternal uncle is no anomaly: he is the brother who gives his sister in the exchange, expecting, as his 'natural right', a wife in a similar exchange with another member of the society. In this analysis of the social formation, the maternal uncle is a structural function from the start.

The result is that Lévi-Strauss distinguishes a basic unit consisting of four relations: brother/sister, husband/wife, father/son, mother's brother/sister's son. Furthermore, this structural functioning makes it possible to predict and analyse the forms of those relations, for they always occur in two contrasting pairs. There are modifications to this model, concerning the different forms of relationships that are possible (mutuality, reciprocity, rights, obligations), but it reveals the basic pattern of kinship systems, based not on the 'biological family' of traditional anthropology but on the incest taboo and the resultant exchange of women. The traditional view only describes what appears to be the 'biological reproduction' of the species and does not account for the reproduction of social structures and their role in determining the form of reproduction of the species. Lévi-Strauss's method accomplishes both by revealing the way in which the demands of sociality form the kinship structure. This description of what structures interhuman reality, introduced by Lévi-Strauss, is referred to as the symbolic order. The assertion is that the human subject is inserted into a pre-existent linguistic order, which forms its relation to 'meaning' (in this case, the forms of familial relations). Lacan takes up and elaborates this term, as we will see later, to describe the construction of the subject in relation to meaning: but, in opposition to Lévi-Strauss, Lacan stresses that a signifier can never be permanently bound to any signified.

Kinship structures are one element in the organisation of a society. Men need at once to form relations with nature (of which they are a part), and to mark themselves off from nature. This complex relationship between Nature and Culture, together with the taboos and preferred forms of behaviour that it entails, are expressed in the form of myths and totemism. Similarly, the form of kinship and its taboos are explained in these practices. Myths themselves are oblique, repetitive tales of men intermingling with animals, fabulous events in the cosmos, strange distinctions made between apparently homogeneous materials, etc. Lévi-Strauss shows how myths cannot be understood singly, but only – like language – as a corpus of differences and oppositions. Each myth is incomplete, full of irrelevant details and events; when understood as a part of a corpus, it is seen to carry basic oppositions, messages about the organisation of nature, culture, and their interpenetration and difference. These relationships are expressed in the form of relations between: men, animals and supernatural beings; forms of food; useful animals and plants; categories of landscape, climate, heavenly bodies, etc.; sounds and silences; smells and tastes. The material of myth is not necessarily words; the signs also include such totemic substances as food, as the example of honey and tobacco demonstrates.

Food is particularly important since it is a direct manifestation of the interpenetration of man and nature: it is a natural process for man to consume food (as animals do), but the ways in which it is consumed are entirely cultural. So Lévi-Strauss elaborates a system of difference between kinds of cooking that expresses an opposition between Nature and Culture. The system has two poles, constituted by the two ways in which raw food can be transformed: the cultural use of fire to cook, and the natural method of rotting. He then shows that, in the mythology of the South American Indians of whom he writes, there exist two crucial kinds of food which transgress this system of differentiation. One is honey, which is naturally pre-cooked, and requires no cultural intervention to make it edible; the other is tobacco, which has to be entirely consumed by the cultural means of fire before it can be enjoyed as smoke. Honey is over-natural; tobacco is over-cultural. Each of these then becomes a totemic substance for this reason: as transgressors of the differentiation between Culture and Nature, their transgressing power has to be neutralised in rituals which confirm this basic division of the world into two categories, with man as irreducibly different from animals.

The structural analysis of myth emphatically does not 'pin down' the meaning of a myth system, even if that meaning were only ascertainable from a whole corpus of individual cases. Myths are endlessly transformable into each other: any structure is a structure of transformations, not of eternally fixed oppositions between terms. As Lévi-Strauss puts it: 'all our analyses show – and this is the very justification for their monotony and proliferation – that the divergent differences worked by myths do not inhere so much in things as in a body of common properties which can be expressed in geometric terms and transformed one into another through operations which are already an algebra' [Lévi-Strauss, 1966, p.407]. Thus myths are not a static system of prohibitions, but a dynamic logic for explaining the world and the society of the subject tribe. The complexity of this transformational logic is shown in the four volumes of *Mythologiques* (published 1964-8). Its subject is the myth-system of South American Indians. The first volume begins with the birth of culture, which according to the myths comes about with the cooking of meat. This demands an alliance between man and the master of fire, the jaguar. The relation is established and elaborated above all in the codes of cooking and kinship, because they deal with the interpenetration of Culture and Nature. In the second volume, it is the excessive modes of cooking which confront each other: honey and tobacco draw the balance between man and nature in their very excessiveness. These excesses are found again in the myths of the Honey-Mad-Woman, who consumes honey, disregarding all the rules for its correct usage. In these myths, the 'mad' consumption of honey corresponds to a breaking of the rules of marriage, for she is 'consumed' sexually in defiance of the kinship system. Thus the third volume deals with the rules that men impose upon women: table manners, on the level of the transformation of myth, are seen as one of the possible ways of introducing order into a menacing disorder that has woman as its centre. Woman transgresses the division between Nature and Culture by her very reproductive capacity: she is at once natural, because of reproductive capacities, and equally entirely cultural, speaking, thinking and acting as a human. Thus there is a disorder within the classification of Culture and Nature; and myth, with its endless transformations, exists to express such contradictions and to provide (ritual or religious) ways of settling them. The endless transformations of myth work towards producing this ordering of the world in which men and women can act.

Thus we see how it is that the central categories of Nature and Culture themselves are transitory, or as Lévi-Strauss puts it, the very distinction itself is a '*product of culture*': the activity of signification. The structural system appears to have no fixed points, but rather a play of differences in which the establishment of fixed points is one moment in the endless transformations of the system.

There exists no real end for the analysis of myth, no secret unity that can be

> seized at the end of a work of deconstruction. The themes divide to infinity. When it seems that they have been untangled and are held separately, this is the very moment when it is realised that they knit together again in response to unforeseen affinities. As a result, the unity of myth is only tendential and projective, it never reflects a state or moment of the myth. As an imaginary phenomenon implicated in the effort to interpret, its role is to give a synthesising form to myth, and to prevent it from dissolving into a confusion of contraries (Lévi-Strauss, 1964, p.139).

This process of difference and of transformation means that human beings cannot be regarded as the transcendent subjects of this system, operating it from outside. They are defined by the systems of kinship, myth and ritual: they do not rest undefined by these systems, full and complete subjects born to operate them. A structure is what 'sets in place an experience for a subject which it includes...' (J. A. Miller, 1968, p.95). The structure defines the human subject within its play of transformations. The subject is, then, not a full and self-sufficient 'I' in the sense of classic bourgeois philosophy:

> What Rousseau asserts – a truth which is surprising even though psychology and ethnology have made it more familiar to us – is that there exists an 'it' which thinks in me, and makes me doubt whether it is I that think. To the 'what do I know' of Montaigne (from which everything sprang), Descartes thought himself able to reply that I know what I know because I think: to which Rousseau's response is a 'what am I?'; to which there is no certain solution, inasmuch as inner experience provides us only with that 'it' which Rousseau discovered... (Lévi-Strauss, 1962, p.241).

Thus Lévi-Strauss's structuralism shows us that the human subject is not homogeneous and in control of himself, he is constructed by a structure whose very existence escapes his gaze. The self-presence of the human subject is no longer tenable; instead the subject is seen as subject to the structure and its transformations.

To see the subject as subjected, constructed by the symbol, is the most radical moment of this structuralism. However, this very structuralist method prevents Lévi-Strauss from going any further: the implication of seeing the structure as a process of production should be that the subject is also constructed by and in an imaginary relation to the real relations, which produce that subject which they include. This implies a diversity of structuring practices, including imaginary relations, real relations, and relations between these two. These relations are necessary if the subject is to produce itself at all in the structure, when the action of the structure presupposes that the subject (as what seems to 'produce' the structure) is absent from the activity of the structure. Only the articulation of psychoanalysis and Marxism can hope to give an account of such practices. Such a philosophy has no ultimate full stop, or centre, to its process of structuring: it has no 'God', no 'human essence', no 'presence' as the transcendent term which makes the system possible. There is only the play of difference, and the multiplicity of mutually conditioning contradictions. Instead of moving to this conception of structuration, Lévi-Strauss finally posits a transcendent centre to his structures: he locates them in the 'human mind', a term which by definition remains beyond analysis.

> And if we are asked to what final signified do these significations return, significations which signify each other, but which must finally relate together to something else, the only answer suggested by this book is that myths signify the mind which elaborates them by means of the world of which it is itself a part. Thus simultaneously the myths themselves are generated by the mind that causes them, and through the myths is generated an image of the world that is already inscribed in the architecture of the mind (Lévi-Strauss, 1964, p.346).

The generalised human mind becomes the repository of these structures, and this human mind constitutes the unconscious of each individual. In this way, Lévi-Strauss's structuralism does not have to conceive of the structure as a continuous process of production. In spite of the radical potentiality of structuralist thought, therefore, there remains the danger of thinking of an immanent structure made up of fully finished subjects and objects. Lévi-Strauss can therefore conceive of structure in terms of a spatial diagram. On the surface, there is empirical richness, whose multiple specificity always escapes analysis; this is assigned to the uniquely individual. This is the realm of diachronic analysis, the place where time passes and events occur. The notion of process is left at this level. Beneath (or behind) this is the structure which generates this surface empirical richness: this structure is itself only comprehensible as a totality of relations, it is constituted by oppositions between terms, and undergoes transformations and substitutions. This structure is englobed by the human mind, which constitutes the play of the structure yet remains outside it. Hence the form of his analysis of kinship structures: there are many societies with a huge number of different kinship relations between individuals, but these are generated by a basic arrangement of relations. Although it is explicit that this kinship structure functions to reproduce society and individuals within it, the model constructed exists on the level of one generation of parents and children. In other words, the diachronic development of the structure and the actual engendering of children, is left out of the model which thus deals with the synchronic only. There are mere gestures to the diachronic. As J. A. Miller put it, in a seminal essay, this form of structure,

> demands an 'empirical' content from a 'natural' object to which it adds 'intelligibility'. If one is content to display an object using the dimensions of a framework so as to describe the interaction of elements, then the product is isolated from its production, a relation of exteriority is established between them (op.cit., p.94).

Lévi-Strauss's structuralism can be expressed in terms of a spatial model, just as it uses geometric forms to explain its structures. But the notion of process cannot be expressed in this way, as will become clear.

We have seen that, in the most radical moment, the categories of Nature and Culture are no more than products of a system of difference which provides their interrelation and intelligibility. For instance, the kinship system, the foundation of society, straddles the division between Nature and Culture, being at once natural (universal) and cultural (a system of taboos and customs). The difference, Nature/Culture, has to be produced across this discrepancy; it is in no way inherent. However, such moments are finally treated as transgressions of the system, a notion around which the explication of the role of honey and tobacco finally rests. These moments are treated as transgressions of an already-constituted system, rather than as evidence of its very process of constitution, which then would have to be analysed as a continuous process of contradiction. Rather than objects and subjects which are constituted of contradictions (as in both Marxist and psychoanalytic thought), this structuralism thinks in terms of systematic oppositions between objects that are already fully constituted, held in a system of oppositions that gains its internal balance and limits from a transcendent subject. The structuralist system relies on the sign having a real referent: the arbitrary relation between signifier and signified is established in this schema by a natural bond between the human mind and a real referent. What is arbitrary in this schema, is the signifier produced for that reference. This is a tendency implicit in Saussure, who, despite realising that the designated object was not important – replacing it with the notion of a 'referent' – nevertheless, still seemed committed to the idea of a real referent. This was clear from his assertion that several signifiers have the same signified. By establishing the separability of signifier and signified, Saussure left the way open for linguistics and structuralism to found themselves on the basis that meaning, the signified, pre-existed the realisation of it in the individual speech act. By this, structuralism bypasses the question posed by materialism which asks, what relation exists between the linguistic symbol, in its totality, and the real outside that it symbolises? This question can only be posed if the radical potentiality of Saussure's separation of the signifier and signified is realised. The separation would make it possible to ask what is arbitrary in the relation of the sign (signifier/signified) to the reality which it names.

The limitation, imposed by a 'real referent' appears in much of Saussure's work; and his less radical followers exploit this side of his work exclusively. His rigid division of language into synchronic structure and diachronic change, obscures his fundamental discovery that the establishment of signification by a process of difference is not static, but is a constant process of articulation of new signifieds by the signifying chain. This idea of difference has two implications. In emphasising the indissolubility of the signifier and the signified in the sign, it is also necessary to stress their separation. In other words, it is the signifying chain which produces the chain of signifieds. Language, then, becomes a ceaseless productivity. As we shall see in the following chapter, this radical rethinking of Saussure's (synchrony – diachrony, signifier – signified) came about when his schema was applied to the analysis of those uses of language which exceed communication: poetry, the *avant-garde* text and the discourse of the unconscious. These practices also reveal the second aspect of language as a continuous productivity: the social use of language necessitates the fixing of certain positions for the speaking subject in order that predication can take place, in order that an 'I' is constituted who can utter a remark. It is psycho-analysis which shows how this subject is constituted in the positions that enable predication, precisely through the limitation of the productivity of the signifying chain. In Saussure's own work, however, the question of the constitution of the subject who speaks, is never asked. Throughout, he assumes a pre-given user for the linguistic system which is the object of his analysis. He assumes, in fact, a transcendent human subject who uses language in order to 'sort himself out': 'psychologically our thought – apart from its expression in words – is only a shapeless and indistinct mass... The characteristic role of language with respect to thought is not to create a material phonic means for expressing ideas but to serve as a link between thought and sound, under conditions that of necessity bring about the reciprocal delimitations of units' (Saussure, op.cit.,p.112). These are consequences of Saussure's initial positing of a transcendent subject, the user of language. Thought is then deemed to pre-exist language in some way.

It can be seen that structuralism can only operate its divisions of synchrony and diachrony, *langue* and *parole*, structure and product, etc. by presupposing a transcendent subject of some kind: the human mind, the language-user, etc.

If, on the other hand, the radical nature of Saussure's concept of difference is realised, the continuous productivity of the system of signification becomes clear, showing the ineffectuality of such rigid divisions. The concept of productivity implies that it is the play of difference of the signifying chain that produces signifieds; the fixing of this relation is provided by the positionality of the speaking subject, a subject who is produced in this movement of productivity. Man is constructed in the symbol, and is not pre-given or transcendent.

It is the task of the following chapters to extend this critique of structuralism. First, the development of semiology in France in the late 1950s and early 1960s shows the strengths and limitations of what Saussure had foreseen as 'a science that studies the life of signs within society' (op.cit.,p.16). The problems of this mode of analysis become clear with the examination of literature: it reveals the process of language, both in the fixity of social positions in realism, and in their crisis in texts which exploit language as more than a medium of communication. Then the persistent metaphor of exchange (exchange of meanings between pre-existent subjects) that underlies both Saussure's linguistics and Lévi-Strauss's anthropology is shown to be inadequate through an examination of both Marxism and psychoanalysis. With Marxism, the notion that economic relations are relations of exchange appears as a representation that is produced in a particular social practice, a representation which functions to provide a positionality for subjects within a system of contradictions. With psychoanalysis, the constitution of the human subject is a constant process of splitting as the unformed infant encounters the contradictory outside analysed by Marxism. Finally, this conception of the human subject is shown to undercut any notion of language as a system of exchange between complete individuals. Its notion of the subjective moment and of the productive dissolution of structures is a theory of revolutionary practice.

References

HJELMSLEV, L., 'Linguistique structurale', *Acta Linguistica,* iv, 1944.
KRISTEVA, J., *On Chinese Women,* Marion Boyars, 1977.
LÉVI-STRAUSS, C., *Structural Anthropology, Allen Lane, 1968.*
LÉVI-STRAUSS, C., *Mythologies I: Le Cru et le cuit,* Paris, Plon, 1964.
LÉVI-STRAUSS, C., *Mythologies II: Du miel aux cendres,* Paris, Plon, 1966.
LÉVI-STRAUSS, C., 'J.J. Rousseau, fondateur des sciences des hommes' in *Jean Jacques Rousseau,* Neuchâtel, Editions de la Baconnière, 1962.
MILLER, J.A., 'Action de la structure', *Cahiers de l'analyse,* vol. 9, 1968.
SAUSSURE, F., *Course in General Linguistics,* Fontana, 1974.

4 Introduction to the structural analysis of narratives

Roland Barthes

The narratives of the world are numberless. Narrative is first and foremost a prodigious variety of genres, themselves distributed amongst different substances – as though any material were fit to receive man's stories. Able to be carried by articulated language, spoken or written, fixed or moving images, gestures, and the ordered mixture of all these substances; narrative is present in myth, legend, fable, tale, novella, epic, history, tragedy, drama, comedy, mime, painting (think of Carpaccio's *Saint Ursula*), stained glass windows, cinema, comics, news items, conversation. Moreover, under this almost infinite diversity of forms, narrative is present in every age, in every place, in every society; it begins with the very history of mankind and there nowhere is nor has been a people without narrative. All classes, all human groups, have their narratives, enjoyment of which is very often shared by men with different, even opposing, cultural backgrounds. Caring nothing for the division between good and bad literature, narrative is international, transhistorical, transcultural: it is simply there, like life itself.

Must we conclude from this universality that narrative is insignificant? Is it so general that we can have nothing to say about it except for the modest description of a few highly individualized varieties, something literary history occasionally undertakes? But then how are we to master even these varieties, how are we to justify our right to differentiate and identify them? How is novel to be set against novella, tale against myth, drama against tragedy (as has been done a thousand times) without reference to a common model? Such a model is implied by every proposition relating to the most individual, the most historical, of narrative forms. It is thus legitimate that, far from the abandoning of any idea of dealing with narrative on the grounds of its universality, there should have been (from Aristotle on) a periodic interest in

Source: Roland Barthes, trans. Stephen Heath, *Image, Music, Text,* Fontana, 1977, pp. 79-117.

narrative form and it is normal that the newly developing structuralism should make this form one of its first concerns – is not structuralism's constant aim to master the infinity of utterances [*paroles*] by describing the 'language' ['*langue*'] of which they are the products and from which they can be generated. Faced with the infinity of narratives, the multiplicity of standpoints – historical, psychological, sociological, ethnological, aesthetic, etc. – from which they can be studied, the analyst finds himself in more or less the same situation as Saussure confronted by the heterogeneity of language [*langage*] and seeking to extract a principle of classification and a central focus for description from the apparent confusion of the individual messages. Keeping simply to modern times, the Russian Formalists*, Propp and Lévi-Strauss have taught us to recognize the following dilemma: either a narrative is merely a rambling collection of events, in which case nothing can be said about it other than by referring back to the storyteller's (the author's) art, talent or genius – all mythical forms of chance – or else it shares with other narratives a common structure which is open to analysis, no matter how much patience its formulation requires....

Where then are we to look for the structures of narrative? Doubtless, in narratives themselves. *Each and every* narrative? Many commentators who accept the idea of a narrative structure are nevertheless unable to resign themselves to dissociating literary analysis from the example of the experimental sciences; nothing daunted, they ask that a purely inductive method be applied to narrative and that one start by studying all the narratives within a genre, a period, a society. This commonsense view is utopian. Linguistics itself, with only some three thousand languages to embrace, cannot manage such a programme and has wisely turned deductive, a step which in fact marked its veritable constitution as a science and the beginning of its spectacular progress, it even succeeding in anticipating facts prior to their discovery. So what of narrative analysis, faced as it is with millions of narratives? Of necessity, it is condemned to a deductive procedure, obliged first to devise a hypothetical model of description (what American linguists call a 'theory') and then gradually to work down from this model towards the different narrative species which at once conform to and depart from the model. It is only at the level of these conformities and departures that analysis will be able to come back to, but now equipped with a single descriptive tool, the plurality of narratives, to their historical, geographical and cultural diversity.

Thus, in order to describe and classify the infinite number of narratives, a 'theory' (in this pragmatic sense) is needed and the immediate task is that of

*A group of literary theorists, active in immediately post-revolutionary Russia, often regarded as the progenitors of structuralism.

finding it, of starting to define it. Its development can be greatly facilitated if one begins from a model able to provide it with its initial terms and principles. In the current state of research, it seems reasonable that the structural analysis of narrative be given linguistics itself as founding model.

I. The Language of Narrative

1. Beyond the sentence

As we know, linguistics stops at the sentence, the last unit which it considers to fall within its scope. If the sentence, being an order and not a series, cannot be reduced to the sum of the words which compose it and constitutes thereby a specific unit, a piece of discourse, on the contrary, is no more than the succession of the sentences composing it. From the point of view of linguistics, there is nothing in discourse that is not to be found in the sentence: ... Hence there can be no question of linguistics setting itself an object superior to the sentence, since beyond the sentence are only more sentences - having described the flower, the botanist is not to get involved in describing the bouquet.

And yet it is evident that discourse itself (as a set of sentences) is organized and that, through this organization, it can be seen as the message of another language, one operating at a higher level than the language of the linguists. Discourse has its units, its rules, its 'grammar': beyond the sentence, and though consisting solely of sentences, it must naturally form the object of a second linguistics. For a long time indeed, such a linguistics of discourse bore a glorious name, that of Rhetoric. As a result of a complex historical movement, however, in which Rhetoric went over to belles-lettres and the latter was divorced from the study of language, it has recently become necessary to take up the problem afresh. The new linguistics of discourse has still to be developed, but at least it is being postulated, and by the linguists themselves. This last fact is not without significance, for, although constituting an autonomous object, discourse must be studied from the basis of linguistics. If a working hypothesis is needed for an analysis whose task is immense and whose materials infinite, then the most reasonable thing is to posit a homological relation between sentence and discourse insofar as it is likely that a similar formal organization orders all semiotic systems, whatever their substances and dimensions. A discourse is a long 'sentence' (the units of which are not necessarily sentences), just as a sentence, allowing for certain specifications, is a short 'discourse'. This hypothesis accords well with a number of propositions put forward in contemporary anthropology. Jakobson and Lévi-Strauss have pointed out that mankind can be defined by the ability to create secondary - 'self-multiplying' - systems (tools for the manufacture of other tools, double articulation of language, incest taboo permitting the fanning out of families) while the Soviet linguist Ivanov supposes that artificial languages can only have been acquired after natural language: what is important for men is to have the use of several systems of meaning and natural language helps in the elaboration of artificial languages. It is therefore legitimate to posit a 'secondary' relation between sentence and discourse – a relation which will be referred to as homological, in order to respect the purely formal nature of the correspondences....

2. Levels of meaning

From the outset, linguistics furnishes the structural analysis of narrative with a concept which is decisive in that, making explicit immediately what is essential in every system of meaning, namely its organization, it allows us both to show how a narrative is not a simple sum of propositions and to classify the enormous mass of elements which go to make up a narrative. This concept is that of *level of description*.

A sentence can be described, linguistically, on several levels (phonetic, phonological, grammatical, contextual) and these levels are in a hierarchical relationship with one another, for, while all have their own units and correlations (whence the necessity for a separate description of each of them), no level on its own can produce meaning. A unit belonging to a particular level only takes on meaning if it can be integrated in a higher level; a phoneme, though perfectly describable, means nothing in itself: it participates in meaning only when integrated in a word, and the word itself must in turn be integrated in a sentence. The theory of levels (as set out by Benveniste) gives two types of relations: distributional (if the relations are situated on the same level) and integrational (if they are grasped from one level to the next); consequently, distributional relations alone are not sufficient to account for meaning. In order to conduct a structural analysis, it is thus first of all necessary to distinguish several levels or instances of description and to place these instances within a hierarchical (integrationary) perspective.

The levels are operations. It is therefore normal that, as it progresses, linguistics should tend to multiply them. Discourse analysis, however, is as yet only able to work on rudimentary levels.... Today, in his analysis of the structure of myth, Lèvi-Strauss has already indicated that the constituent units of mythical discourse (mythemes) acquire meaning only because they are grouped in bundles and because these bundles themselves combine together. [Lévi-Strauss 1968 p.211]. As too, Tzvetan Todorov, reviving the distinction made by the Russian Formalists, proposes working on two major levels, themselves subdivided: *story* (the argument), comprising a logic of actions and a 'syntax' of characters, and *discourse,* comprising the tenses, aspects and modes of the narrative [Todorov 1966]. But however many levels are proposed and whatever definition they are given, there can be no doubt that narrative is a hierarchy of instances. To understand a narrative is not merely to follow the unfolding of the story, it is also to recognize its construction in 'storeys', to project the horizontal concatenations of the narrative 'thread' on to an implicitly vertical axis; to read (to listen to) a narrative is not merely to move from one word to the next, it is also to move from one level to the next. Perhaps I may be allowed to offer a kind of apologue in this connection. In *The Purloined Letter,* Poe gives an acute analysis of the failure of the chief commissioner of the Paris police, powerless to find the letter. His investigations, says Poe, were perfect *'within the sphere of his speciality'*; he searched everywhere, saturated entirely the level of the 'police search', but in order to find the letter, protected by its conspicuousness, it was necessary to shift to another level, to substitute the concealer's principle of relevance for that of the policeman. Similarly, the 'search' carried out over a horizontal set of narrative relations may well be as thorough as possible but must still, to be effective, also operate 'vertically': meaning is not 'at the end' of the narrative, it runs across it; just as conspicuous as the purloined letter, meaning eludes all unilateral investigation.

A great deal of tentative effort is still required before it will be possible to ascertain precisely the levels of narrative. Those that are suggested in what follows constitute a provisional profile whose merit remains almost exclusively didactic; they enable us to locate and group together the different problems, and this without, I think, being at variance with the few analyses so far. It is proposed to distinguish three levels of description in the narrative work: the level of '*functions*' (in the sense this word has in Propp and Bremond), the level of '*actions*' (in the sense this word has in Greimas when he talks of characters as actants) and the level of '*narration*' (which is roughly the level of 'discourse' in Todorov). These three levels are bound together according to a mode of progressive integration: a function only has meaning insofar as it occupies a place in the general action of an actant, and this action in turn receives its final meaning from the fact that it is narrated, entrusted to a discourse which possesses its own code.

II. Functions

1. The determination of the units

Any system being the combination of units of known classes, the first task is to divide up narrative and determine the segments of narrative discourse that can be distributed into a limited number of classes. In a word, we have to define the smallest narrative units.

Given the integrational perspective described above, the analysis cannot rest satisfied with a purely distributional definition of the units. From the start, meaning must be the criterion of the unit: it is the functional nature of certain segments of the story that makes them units – hence the name 'functions' immediately attributed to these first units. Since the Russian Formalists a unit has been taken as any segment of the story which can be seen as the term of a correlation. The essence of a function is, so to speak, the seed that it sows in the narrative, planting an element that will come to fruition later – either on the same level or elsewhere, on another level. If in *Un Coeur simple* Flaubert at one point tells the reader, seemingly without emphasis, that the daughters of the Sous-Préfet of Pont-l'Evêque owned a parrot, it is because this parrot is subsequently to have a great importance in Félicité's life; the statement of this detail (whatever its linguistic form) thus constitutes a function, or narrative unit.

Is everything in a narrative functional? Does everything, down to the slightest detail, have a meaning? Can narrative be divided up entirely into functional units? We shall see in a moment that there are several kinds of functions, there being several kinds of correlations, but this does not alter the fact that a narrative is never made up of anything other than functions: in differing degrees, everything in it signifies. This is not a matter of art (on the part of the narrator), but of structure; in the realm of discourse, what is noted is by definition notable. Even were a detail to appear irretrievably insignificant, resistant to all functionality, it would nonetheless end up with precisely the meaning of absurdity or uselessness: everything has a meaning, or nothing has....

From the linguistic point of view, the function is clearly a unit of content: it is 'what it says' that makes of a statement a functional unit, not the manner in which it is said. This constitutive signified may have a number of different signifiers, often very intricate. If I am told (in *Goldfinger*) that *Bond saw a man of about fifty*, the piece of information holds simultaneously two functions of unequal pressure: on the one hand, the character's age fits into a certain description of the man (the 'usefulness' of which for the rest of the story is not nil, but diffuse, delayed); while on the other, the immediate signified of the statement is that Bond is unacquainted with his future interlocutor, the unit thus implying a very strong correlation (initiation of a threat and the need to establish the man's identity). In order to determine the initial narrative units, it is therefore vital never to lose sight of the functional nature of the segments under consideration and to recognize in advance that they will not necessarily coincide with the forms into which we traditionally cast the various parts of narrative discourse (actions, scenes, paragraphs, dialogues, interior monologues, etc.) still less with 'psychological' divisions (modes of behaviour, feelings, intentions, motivations, rationalizations of characters).

In the same way, since the 'language' ['*langue*'] of narrative is not the language [*langue*] of articulated language [*langage articulé*] though very often vehicled by it – narrative units will be substantially independent of linguistic units; they may indeed coincide with the latter, but occasionally, not systematically. Functions will be represented sometimes by units higher than the sentence (groups of sentences of varying lengths, up to the work in its entirety) and sometimes by lower ones (syntagm, word and even, within the word, certain literary elements only). When we are told that – the telephone ringing during night duty at Secret Service headquarters – *Bond picked up one of the four receivers,* the moneme *four* in itself constitutes a functional unit, referring as it does to a concept necessary to the story (that of a highly developed bureaucratic technology). In fact, the narrative unit in this case is not the linguistic unit (the word) but only its connoted value (linguistically, the word/four/never means 'four'); which explains how certain functional units can be shorter than the sentence without ceasing to belong to the order of discourse: such units then extend not beyond the sentence, than which they remain materially shorter, but beyond the level of denotation, which, like the sentence, is the province of linguistics properly speaking.

2. Classes of units

The functional units must be distributed into a small number of classes. If these classes are to be determined without recourse to the substance of content (psychological substance for example), it is again necessary to consider the different levels of meaning: some units have as correlates units on the same level, while the saturation of others requires a change of levels; hence, straightaway, two major classes of functions, distributional and integrational. The former correspond to what Propp and subsequently Bremond (in particular) take as functions but they will be treated here in a much more detailed way than is the case in their work. The term *'functions'* will be reserved for these units (though the other units are also functional), the model of description for which has become classic since Tomachevski's analysis: the purchase of a revolver has for correlate the moment when it will be used (and if not used, the notation is reversed into a sign of indecision, etc.): picking up the telephone has for correlate the moment when it will be put down; the intrusion of the parrot into Félicité's home has for correlate the episode of the stuffing, the worshipping of the parrot, etc. As for the latter, the integrational units, these comprise all the *'indices'* (in the very broad sense of the word), the unit now referring not to a complementary and consequential act but to a more or less diffuse concept which is nevertheless necessary to the meaning of the story: psychological indices concerning the characters, data regarding their identity, notations of 'atmosphere', and so on. The relation between the unit and its correlate is now no longer distributional (often several indices refer to the same signified and the order of their occurrence in the discourse is not necessarily pertinent) but integrational. In order to understand what an indicial notation 'is for', one must move to a higher level (characters' actions or narration), for only there is the indice clarified: the power of the administrative machine behind Bond, indexed by the number of telephones, has no bearing on the sequence of actions in which Bond is involved by answering the call; it finds its meaning only on the level of a general typology of the actants (Bond is on the side of order). Indices, because of the, in some sort, vertical nature of their relations, are truly semantic units: unlike 'functions' (in the strict sense), they refer to a signified, not to an 'operation'. The ratification of indices is 'higher up', sometimes even remaining virtual, outside any explicit syntagm (the 'character' of a narrative agent may very well never be explicitly named while yet being constantly indexed), is a paradigmatic ratification. That of functions, by contrast, is always 'further on', is a syntagmatic ratification. *Functions* and *indices* thus overlay another classic distinction:... the former correspond to a functionality of doing, the latter to a functionality of being.

These two main classes of units, functions and indices, should already allow a certain classification of narratives. Some narratives are heavily functional (such as folktales), while others on the contrary are heavily indicial (such as 'psychological' novels); between these two poles lies a whole series of intermediary forms, dependent on history, society, genre. But we can go further. Within each of the two main classes it is immediately possible to determine two sub-classes of narrative units. Returning to the class of functions, its units are not all of the same 'importance': some constitute real hinge-points of the narrative (or of a fragment of the narrative); others merely 'fill in' the narrative space separating the hinge functions. Let us call the former *cardinal functions* (or *nuclei*) and the latter, having regard to their complementary nature, *catalysers*. For a function to be cardinal, it is enough that the action to which it refers open (or continue, or close) an alternative that is of direct consequence for the subsequent development of the story, in short that it inaugurate or conclude an uncertainty. If, in a fragment of narrative, *the telephone rings,* it is equally possible to answer or not answer, two acts which will unfailingly carry the narrative along different paths. Between two cardinal functions however, it is always possible to set out subsidiary notations which cluster around one or other nucleus without modifying its alternative nature: the space separating *the telephone rang* from *Bond answered* can be saturated with a host of trivial incidents or descriptions – *Bond moved towards the desk, picked up one of the receivers, put down his cigarette*, etc. These catalysers are still functional, insofar as they enter into correlation with a nucleus but their functionality is attenuated, unilateral, parasitic; it is a question of a purely chronological functionality (what is described is what separates two moments of the story), whereas the tie between two cardinal functions is invested with a double functionality, at once chronological and logical. Catalysers are only consecutive units, cardinal functions are both consecutive and consequential. Everything suggests, indeed, that the mainspring of narrative is precisely the confusion of consecution and consequence, what comes *after* being read in narrative as what is *caused by*; in which case narrative would be a systematic application of the logical fallacy denounced by Scholasticism in the formula *post hoc, ergo propter hoc* – a good motto for Destiny, of which narrative all things considered is no more than the 'language'.

It is the structural framework of cardinal functions which accomplishes this 'telescoping' of logic and temporality. At first sight, such functions may appear extremely insignificant; what defines them is not their spectacularity (importance, volume, unusualness or force of the narrated action), but, so to speak, the risk they entail: cardinal functions are the risky moments of a narrative. Between these points of alternative, these 'dispatchers', the catalysers lay out areas of safety, rests, luxuries. Luxuries which are not, however, useless: it must be stressed again that from the point of view of the story a catalyser's functionality may be weak but not nil. Were a catalyser purely redundant (in relation to its nucleus), it would nonetheless participate in the economy of the message; in fact, an apparently merely expletive notation always has a discursive function: it accelerates, delays, gives fresh impetus to the discourse, it summarizes, anticipates and sometimes even leads astray. Since what is noted always appears as being notable, the catalyser ceaselessly revives the semantic tension of the discourse, says ceaselessly that there has been, that there is going to be, meaning. Thus, in the final analysis, the catalyser has a constant function which is, to use Jakobson's term, a phatic one: it maintains the contact between narrator and addressee. A nucleus cannot be deleted without altering the story, but neither can a catalyst without altering the discourse....

A distinction can be made, however, between *indices* proper, referring to the character of a narrative agent, a feeling, an atmosphere (for example suspicion) or a philosophy, and *informants*, serving to identify, to locate in time and space. To say that through the window of the office where Bond is on duty the moon can be seen half-hidden by thick billowing clouds, is to index a stormy summer night, this deduction in turn forming an index of atmosphere with reference to the heavy, anguish-laden climate of an action as yet unknown to the reader. Indices always have implicit signifieds. Informants, however, do not, at least on the level of the story: they are pure data with immediate signification. Indices involve an activity of deciphering, the reader is to learn to know a character or an atmosphere; informants bring ready-made knowledge, their functionality, like that of catalysers, is thus weak without being nil. Whatever its 'flatness' in relation to the rest of the story, the informant (for example, the exact age of a character) always serves to authenticate the reality of the referent, to embed fiction in the real world. Informants are realist operators and as such possess an undeniable functionality not on the level of the story but on that of the discourse.

Nuclei and catalysers, indices and informants (again, the names are of little importance), these, it seems, are the initial classes into which the functional level units can be divided..... [It should be noted however that] a unit can at the same time belong to two different classes: to drink a whisky (in an airport lounge) is an action which can act as a catalyser to the (cardinal) notation of *waiting*, but it is also, and simultaneously, the indice of a certain atmosphere (modernity, relaxation, reminiscence, etc.). In other words, certain units can be mixed, giving a play of possibilities in the narrative economy. In the novel *Goldfinger*, Bond, having to search his adversary's bedroom, is given a master-key by his associate: the notation is a pure (cardinal) function. In the film, this detail is altered and Bond laughingly takes a set of keys from a willing chamber-maid: the notation is no longer simply functional but also indicial, referring to Bond's character (his easy charm and success with women)....

3. *Functional syntax*

How, according to what 'grammar', are the different units strung together along the narrative syntagm? What are the rules of the functional combinatory system? Informants and indices can combine freely together: as for example in the portrait which readily juxtaposes data concerning civil status and traits of character. Catalysers and nuclei are linked by a simple relation of implication: a catalyser necessarily implies the existence of a cardinal function to which it can connect, but not vice-versa. As for cardinal functions, they are bound together by a relation of solidarity: a function of this type calls for another function of the same type and reciprocally. It is this last relation which needs to be considered further for a moment – first, because it defines the very framework of the narrative (expansions can be deleted, nuclei cannot); second, because it is the main concern of those trying to work towards a structure of narrative.

It has already been pointed out that structurally narrative institutes a confusion between consecution and consequence, temporality and logic. This ambiguity forms the central problem of narrative syntax. Is there an atemporal logic lying behind the temporality of narrative? Researchers were still quite recently divided on this point. Propp, whose analytic study of the folktale paved the way for the work going on today, is totally committed to the idea of the irreducibility of the chronological order: he sees time as reality and for this reason is convinced of the necessity for rooting the tale in temporality. Yet Aristotle himself, in his contrast between tragedy (defined by the unity of action) and historical narrative (defined by the plurality of actions and the unity of time), was already giving primacy to the logical over the chronological. As do all contemporary researchers (Lévi-Strauss, Greimas, Bremond, Todorov), all of whom (while differing on other points) could subscribe to Lévi-Strauss's proposition that 'the order of chronological succession is absorbed in an atemporal matrix structure' [Lévi-Strauss 1960, p.29]. Analysis today tends to 'dechronologize' the narrative continuum and to 'relogicize' it, to make it dependent on what Mallarmé called with regard to the French language '*the primitive thunderbolts of logic*'; [Mallarmé 1961 p.386] or rather, more exactly (such at least is our wish), the task is to succeed in giving a structural description of the chronological illusion – it is for narrative logic to account for narrative time. To put it another way, one could say that temporality is only a structural category of narrative (of discourse), just as in language *(langue)* temporality only exists in the form of a system; from the point of view of narrative, what we call time does not exist, or at least only exists functionally, as an element of a semiotic system. Time belongs not to discourse strictly speaking but to the referent; both narrative and language know only a semiotic time, 'true' time being a 'realist', referential illusion, as Propp's commentary shows. It is as such that structural analysis must deal with it.

What then is the logic which regulates the principal narrative functions? It is this that current work is actively trying to establish and that has so far been the major focus of debate. Three main directions of research can be seen. The first (Bremond) is more properly logical in approach: it aims to reconstitute the syntax of human behaviour utilized in narrative, to retrace the course of the 'choices' which inevitably face the individual character at every point in the story and so to bring out what could be called an energetic logic, since it grasps the characters at the moment when they choose to act. The second (Lévi-Strauss, Jakobson) is linguistic: its essential concern is to demonstrate paradigmatic oppositions in the functions, oppositions which ... are 'extended' along the line of the narrative.... The third (Todorov) is somewhat different in that it sets the analysis at the level of the 'actions' (that is to say, of the characters), attempting to determine the rules by which narrative combines, varies and transforms a certain number of basic predicates.

There is no question of choosing between these working hypotheses; they are not competitive but concurrent, and at present moreover are in the throes of elaboration. The only complement we will attempt to give them here concerns the dimensions of the analysis. Even leaving aside the indices, informants and catalysers, there still remains in a narrative (especially if it is a novel and no longer a tale) a very large number of cardinal functions and many of these cannot be mastered by the analyses just mentioned, which until now have worked on the major articulations of narrative. Provision needs to be made, however, for a description sufficiently close as to account for *all* the narrative units, for the smallest narrative segments. We must remember that cardinal functions cannot be determined by their 'importance', only by the (doubly implicative) nature of their relations. A 'telephone call', no matter how futile it may seem, on the one hand itself comprises some few cardinal functions (telephone ringing, picking up the receiver, speaking, putting down the receiver), while on the other, taken as a whole, it must be linkable – at the very least proceeding step by step – to the major articulations of the anecdote. The functional covering of the narrative necessitates an organization of relays the basic unit of which can only be a small group of functions, hereafter referred to (following Bremond) as a *sequence*.

A sequence is a logical succession of nuclei bound together by a relation of solidarity: the sequence opens when one of its terms has no solidary antecedent and closes when another of its terms has no consequent. To take a deliberately trivial example, the different functions order a drink, obtain it, drink it, pay for it, constitute an obviously closed sequence, it being impossible to put anything before the order or after the payment without moving out of the homogeneous group '*Having a drink*'. The sequence indeed is always nameable. Determining the major functions of the folktale, Propp and subsequently Bremond have been led to name them (*Fraud, Betrayal, Struggle, Contract, Seduction,* etc.); the naming operation is equally inevitable in the case of trivial sequences, the 'micro-sequences' which often form the finest grain of the narrative tissue. Are these namings solely the province of the analyst? In other words, are they purely metalinguistic? No doubt they are, dealing as they do with the code of narrative. Yet at the same time they can be imagined as forming part of an inner metalanguage for the reader (or listener) who can grasp every logical succession of actions as a nominal whole: to read is to name; to listen is not only to perceive a language, it is also to construct it..... The narrative language [*la langue du récit*] within us comprises from the start these essential headings; the closing logic which structures a sequence is inextricably linked to its name; any function which initiates a *seduction* prescribes from the moment it appears, in the name to which it gives rise, the entire process of seduction such as we have learned it from all the narratives which have fashioned in us the language of narrative.

However minimal its importance, a sequence, since it is made up of a small number of nuclei (that is to say, in fact, of 'dispatchers'), always involves moments of risk and it is this which justifies analysing it. It might seem futile to constitute into a sequence the logical succession of trifling acts which go to make up the offer of a cigarette (*offering, accepting, lighting, smoking*), but precisely, at every one of these points, an alternative – and hence a freedom of meaning – is possible. Du Pont, Bond's future partner, offers him a light from his lighter but Bond refuses; the meaning of this bifurcation is that Bond instinctively fears a booby-trapped gadget. A sequence is thus, one can say, a *threatened logical unit,* this being its justification *a minimo*. It is also founded *a maximo:* enclosed on its function, subsumed under a name, the sequence itself constitutes a new unit, ready to function as a simple term in another, more extensive sequence. Here, for example, is a micro-sequence: *hand held out, hand shaken, hand released.* This *Greeting* then becomes a simple function: on the one hand, it assumes the role of an indice (flabbiness of Du Pont, Bond's distaste); on the other, it forms globally a term in a larger sequence, with the name *Meeting*, whose other terms(*approach, halt, interpellation, sitting down*) can themselves be micro-sequences. A whole network of subrogations structures the narrative in this way, from the smallest matrices to the largest functions. What is in question here, of course, is a hierarchy that remains within the functional level: it is only when it has been possible to widen the narrative out step by step, from Du Pont's cigarette to Bond's battle against Goldfinger, that functional analysis is over – the pyramid of functions then touches the next level (that of the Actions).... What needs to be noted, however, is that the terms from several sequences can easily be imbricated in one another: a sequence is not yet completed when already, cutting in, the first term of a new sequence may appear. Sequences move in counterpoint; functionally, the structure of narrative is fugued: thus it is this that narrative at once 'holds' and 'pulls on'. Within the single work, the imbrication of sequences can indeed only be allowed to come to a halt with a radical break if the sealed-off blocks which then compose it are in some sort recuperated at the higher level of the Actions (of the characters). *Goldfinger* is composed of three functionally independent episodes, their functional stemmas twice ceasing to intercommunicate: there is no sequential relation between the swimming-pool episode and the Fort Knox episode; but there remains an actantial relation, for the characters (and consequently the structure of their relations) are the same....

III. Actions

1. Towards a structural status of characters

In Aristotelian poetics, the notion of character is secondary, entirely subsidiary to the notion of action: there may be actions without 'characters', says Aristotle, but not characters without an action; a view taken over by classical theoreticians (Vossius). Later the character, who until then had been only a name, the agent of an action, acquired a psychological consistency, became an individual, a 'person', in short a fully constituted 'being', even should he do nothing and of course even before acting. Characters stopped being subordinate to the action, embodied immediately psychological essences; which essences could be drawn up into lists, as can be seen in its purest form in the list of 'character parts' in bourgeois theatre (the coquette, the noble father, etc.). From its very outset, structural analysis has shown the utmost reluctance to treat the character as an essence, even merely for purposes of classification; Tomachevski went so far as to deny the character any narrative importance, a point of view he subsequently modified. Without leaving characters out of the analysis altogether, Propp reduced them to a simple typology based not on psychology but on the unity of the actions assigned them by the narrative (*Donor of a magical agent, Helper, Villain,* etc.).

Since Propp, the character has constantly set the structural analysis of narrative the same problem. On the one hand, the characters (whatever one calls them – *dramatis personae* or *actants*) form a necessary plane of description, outside of which the slightest reported 'actions' cease to be intelligible; so that it can be said that there is not a single narrative in the world without 'characters', or at least without agents. Yet on the other hand, these – extremely numerous – 'agents' can be neither described nor classified in terms of 'persons' – whether the 'person' be considered as a purely historical form, limited to certain genres (those most familiar to us it is true), in which case it is necessary to leave out of account the very large number of narratives (popular tales, modern texts) comprising agents but not persons, or whether the 'person' is declared to be no more than a critical rationalization foisted by our age on pure narrative agents. Structural analysis, much concerned not to define characters in terms of psychological essences, has so far striven, using various hypotheses, to define a character not as a 'being' but as a 'participant'. For Bremond, every character (even secondary) can be the agent of sequences of actions which belong to him (*Fraud, Seduction*); when a single sequence involves two characters (as is usual), it comprises two perspectives, two names (what is *Fraud* for the one is *Gullibility* for the other); in short, every character (even secondary) is the hero of his own sequence. Todorov, analysing a 'psychological' novel (*Les liaisons dangereuses*), starts not from the character-persons but from the three major relationships in which they can engage and which he calls base predicates (love, communication, help). The analysis brings these relationships under two sorts of rules: rules of *derivation,* when it is a question of accounting for other relationships, and rules of *action,* when it is a question of describing the transformation of the major relationships in the course of the story. There are many characters in *Les liaisons dangereuses* but 'what is said of them' (their predicates) can be classified. Finally, Greimas has proposed to describe and classify the characters of narrative not according to what they are but according to what they do (whence the name *actants*), inasmuch as they participate in three main semantic axes (also to be found in the sentence: subject, object, indirect object, adjunct) which are communication, desire (or quest) and ordeal [Greimas, 1966 p.129f]. Since this participation is ordered in couples, the infinite world of characters is, it too, bound by a paradigmatic structure (*Subject/Object, Donor/Receiver, Helper/Opponent*) which is projected along the narrative; and since an actant defines a class, it can be filled by different actors, mobilized according to rules of multiplication, substitution or replacement.

These three conceptions have many points in common. The most important, it must be stressed again, is the definition of the character according to participation in a sphere of actions, these spheres being few in number, typical and classifiable; which is why this second level of description, despite its being that of the characters, has here been called the level of Actions: the word *actions* is not to be understood in the sense of the trifling acts which form the tissue of the first level but in that of the major articulations of *praxis* (desire, communication, struggle.)

2. The problem of the subject

...The real difficulty posed by the classification of characters is the place (and hence the existence) of the *subject* in any actantial matrix, whatever its formulation. *Who* is the subject (the hero) of a narrative? Is there – or not – a privileged class of actors? The novel has accustomed us to emphasize in one way or another – sometimes in a devious (negative) way – one character in particular. But such privileging is far from extending over the whole of narrative literature. Many narratives, for example, set two adversaries in conflict over some stake; the subject is then truly double, not reducible further by substitution. Indeed, this is even perhaps a common archaic form, as though narrative, after the fashion of certain languages, had also known a *dual* of persons. This dual is all the more interesting in that it relates narrative to the structures of certain (very modern) games in which two equal opponents try to gain possession of an object put into circulation by a referee; a schema which recalls the actantial matrix proposed by Greimas, and there is nothing surprising in this if one is willing to allow that a game, being a language, depends on the same symbolic structure as is to be found in language and narrative: a game too is a sentence. If therefore a privileged class of actors is retained (the subject of the quest, of the desire, of the action), it needs at least to be made more flexible by bringing that actant under the very categories of the grammatical (and not psychological) person. Once again, it will be necessary to look towards linguistics for the possibility of describing and classifying the personal (*je/tu*, first person/second person) or apersonal (*il*, third person), singular, dual or plural, instance of the action. It will – perhaps – be the grammatical categories of the person (accessible in our pronouns) which will provide the key to the actional level; but since these categories can only be defined in relation to the instance of discourse, not to that of reality, characters, as units of the actional level, find their meaning (their intelligibility) only if integrated in the third level of description, here called the level of Narration (as opposed to Functions and Actions).

IV. Narration

1. *Narrative communication*

Just as there is within narrative a major function of exchange (set out between a donor and a beneficiary), so, homologically, narrative as object is the point of a communication: there is a donor of the narrative and a receiver of the narrative. In linguistic communication, *je* and *tu* (*I* and *you*) are absolutely presupposed by one another; similarly, there can be no narrative without a narrator and a listener (or reader). Banal perhaps, but still little developed. Certainly the role of the sender has been abundantly enlarged upon (much study of the 'author' of a novel, though without any consideration of whether he really is the 'narrator'); when it comes to the reader, however, literary theory is much more modest. In fact, the problem is not to introspect the motives of the narrator or the effects the narration produces on the reader, it is to describe the code by which narrator and reader are signified throughout the narrative itself. At first sight, the signs of the narrator appear more evident and more numerous that those of the reader (a narrative more frequently says *I* than *you*); in actual fact, the latter are simply more oblique than the former. Thus, each time the narrator stops 'representing' and reports details which he knows perfectly well but which are unknown to the reader, there occurs, by signifying failure, a sign of reading, for there would be no sense in the narrator giving himself a piece of information. *Leo was the owner of the joint*[1], we are told in a first-person novel: a sign of the reader, close to what Jakobson calls the conative function of communication. Lacking an inventory however, we shall leave aside for the moment these signs of reception (though they are of equal importance) and say a few words concerning the signs of narration.

[1]*Double Bang à Bangkok* [secret agent thriller by Jean Bruce, Paris 1959]. The sentence functions as a 'wink' to the reader, as if he was being turned towards. By contrast, the statement '*So Leo had just left*' is a sign of the narrator, part of a process of reasoning conducted by a 'person'.

Who is the donor of the narrative? So far, three conceptions seem to have been formulated. The first holds that a narrative emanates from a person (in the fully psychological sense of the term). This person has a name, the author, in whom there is an endless exchange between the 'personality' and the 'art' of a perfectly identified individual who periodically takes up his pen to write a story: the narrative (notably the novel) then being simply the expression of an *I* external to it. The second conception regards the narrator as a sort of omniscient, apparently impersonal, consciousness that tells the story from a superior point of view, that of God: the narrator is at once inside his characters (since he knows everything that goes on in them) and outside them (since he never identifies with any one more than another). The third and most recent conception (Henry James, Sartre) decrees that the narrator must limit his narrative to what the characters can observe or know, everything proceeding as if each of the characters in turn were the sender of the narrative. All three conceptions are equally difficult in that they seem to consider narrator and characters as real – 'living' – people (the unfailing power of this literary myth is well known), as though a narrative were originally determined as its referential level (it is a matter of equally 'realist' conceptions). Narrator and characters, however, at least from our perspective, are essentially 'paper beings'; the (material) author of a narrative is in no way to be confused with the narrator of that narrative. The signs of the narrator are immanent to the narrative and hence readily accessible to a semiological analysis; but in order to conclude that the author himself (whether declared, hidden or withdrawn) has 'signs' at his disposal which he sprinkles through his work, it is necessary to assume the existence between this 'person' and his language of a straight descriptive relation which makes the author a full subject and the narrative the instrumental expression of that fullness. Structural analysis is unwilling to accept such an assumption: *who speaks* (in the narrative) is not *who writes* (in real life) and *who writes* is not *who is*[2].

In fact, narration strictly speaking (the code of the narrator), like language, knows only two systems of signs: personal and apersonal. These two narrational systems do not necessarily present the linguistic marks attached to person (*I*) and non-person (*he*): there are narratives or at least narrative episodes, for example, which though written in the third person nevertheless have as their true instance the first person. How can we tell? It suffices to rewrite the narrative (or the passage) from *he* to *I*: so long as the rewriting entails no alteration of the discourse other than this change of the grammatical pronouns, we can be sure that we are dealing with a personal system. The whole of the beginning of *Goldfinger*, though written in the third person, is in fact 'spoken' by James Bond. For the instance to change, rewriting must

[2]J. Lacan: 'Is the subject I speak of when I speak the same as the subject who speaks?'

become impossible; thus the sentence 'he saw a man in his fifties, still young-looking...' is perfectly personal despite the *he* ('I, James Bond, saw...'), but the narrative statement 'the tinkling of the ice against the glass appeared to give Bond a sudden inspiration' cannot be personal on account of the verb 'appeared', it (and not the *he*) becoming a sign of the apersonal. There is no doubt that the apersonal is the traditional mode of narrative, language having developed a whole tense system peculiar to narrative (based on the aorist), designed to wipe out the present of the speaker. As Benveniste puts it: 'In narrative, no one speaks'. The personal instance (under more or less disguised forms) has, however, gradually invaded narrative, the narration being referred to the *hic et nunc* of the locutionary act (which is the definition of the personal system). Thus it is that today many narratives are to be found (and of the most common kinds) which mix together in extremely rapid succession, often within the limits of a single sentence, the personal and the apersonal; as for instance this sentence from *Goldfinger*:

His eyes,	*personal*
grey-blue,	*apersonal*
looked into those of Mr Du Pont who did not know what face to put on	*personal*
for this look held a mixture of candour, irony and self-deprecation.	*apersonal*

The mixing of the systems is clearly felt as a facility and this facility can go as far as trick effects. A detective novel by Agatha Christie (*The Sittaford Mystery*) only keeps the enigma going by cheating on the person of the narration: a character is described from within when he is already the murderer – as if in a single person there were the consciousness of a witness, immanent to the discourse, and the consciousness of a murderer, immanent to the referent, with the dishonest tourniquet of the two systems alone producing the enigma....

2. *Narrative situation*

...The narrational code is the final level attainable by our analysis, other than by going outside of the narrative-object, other, that is, than by transgressing the rule of immanence on which the analysis is based. Narration can only receive its meaning from the world which makes use of it: beyond the narrational level begins the world, other systems (social, economic, ideological) whose terms are no longer simply narratives but elements of a different substance (historical facts, determinations, behaviours, etc.). Just as linguistics stops at the sentence, so narrative analysis stops at discourse –

from there it is necessary to shift to another semiotics. Linguistics is acquainted with such boundaries which it has already postulated – if not explored – under the name of *situations*. Halliday defines the 'situation' (in relation to a sentence) as 'the associated non-linguistic factors' [Halliday, 1966 p.4] Prieto as 'the set of facts known by the receiver at the moment of the semic act and independently of this act' [Prieto, 1964 p.36]. In the same way, one can say that every narrative is dependent on a 'narrative situation', the set of protocols according to which the narrative is 'consumed'. In so-called 'archaic' societies, the narrative situation is heavily coded nowadays, avant-garde literature alone still dreams of reading protocols – spectacular in the case of Mallarmé who wanted the book to be recited in public according to a precise combinatory scheme, typographical in that of Butor who tries to provide the book with its own specific signs. Generally, however, our society takes the greatest pains to conjure away the coding of the narrative situation: there is no counting the number of narrational devices which seek to naturalize the subsequent narrative by feigning to make it the outcome of some natural circumstance and thus, as it were, 'disinaugurating' it: epistolary novels, supposedly rediscovered manuscripts, author who met the narrator, films which begin the story before the credits. The reluctance to declare its codes characterizes bourgeois society and the mass culture issuing from it: both demand signs which do not look like signs. Yet this is only, so to speak, a structural epiphenomenon: however familiar, however casual may today be the act of opening a novel or a newspaper or of turning on the television, nothing can prevent that humble act from installing in us, all at once and in its entirety, the narrative code we are going to need. Hence the narrational level has an ambiguous role: contiguous to the narrative situation (and sometimes even including it), it gives on to the world in which the narrative is undone (consumed), while at the same time, capping the preceding levels, it closes the narrative, constitutes it definitively as utterance of a language [*langue*] which provides for and bears along its own metalanguage.

References

GREIMAS, A. J., *Semantique structurale,* Paris, Larousse, 1966.

HALLIDAY, M. A. K., 'General linguistics and its application to language teaching' in Halliday and McIntosh, *Patterns of Language,* Longman, 1966.

LÉVI-STRAUSS, C., *Structural Anthropology,* Allen Lane, 1968.

LÉVI-STRAUSS, C., 'La structure et la forme', *Cahiers de l'Institute de Science Economique Appliquée,* No. 99, March 1960.

MALLARMÉ, *Oeuvres complètes,* Paris, Bibliothèque de la Pléiade, 1961.

PRIETO, L. J., *Principes de noologie,* Paris and the Hague, 1964.
TODOROV, T., 'Les catégories du récit littéraire', *Communications,* No. 8, 1966.

SECTION 4

Class, Culture and Hegemony

In previous sections there have been various references to the work of the Italian Marxist, Antonio Gramsci. Here, we include passages from his own writings, a theoretical overview of his importance for the analysis of culture and ideology and two analyses which deploy a broadly 'gramscian' framework for historical and cultural analysis.

Within the Marxist tradition, Gramsci's work represents a decisive innovation with respect to the analysis of the complex areas of culture and ideology. This is not all of what Gramsci is about, but it is perhaps the most important and original aspect of his work and, of course, it is the most important for the analysis of popular culture.

Where does Gramsci's originality lie? The central dynamic, particularly of those writings carried out in prison, consists in a critique of, on the one hand, the traditional tendency to separate out the areas of culture and politics, and, on the other hand, the orthodox Marxist tendency to reduce the complexity of culture to the status of a 'transmission belt' for the dominant class in any given society. This dual critique is mobilised around a central concept: hegemony.

Quite literally, and according to the *Oxford English Dictionary*, hegemony means 'leadership' or 'preponderance'. More frequently it is used by political commentators to designate, quite simply, domination. But for Gramsci, as we will see from his own writings and the articles which use his work, the concept of hegemony signifies something much more complex. Inflected in a variety of directions, Gramsci uses the concept to examine the precise political, cultural and ideological forms through which, in any given society, a fundamental class is able to establish its *leadership* as distinct from the more coercive forms of domination. Hegemony, though in the first instance dependent on the 'decisive nucleus of economic activity' introduces the dimension of 'intellectual and moral leadership' absent from more orthodox forms of Marxist analysis, and indicates the diverse ways in which that 'leadership' has been established historically.

There are various ways in which Gramsci does this. If Gramsci remains within the overall framework of Marxism, then he does so by introducing areas and forms of analysis which had previously been absent from it or only crudely and schematically formulated. He examines, for example, the range of functions and effects of those strata which he terms the 'functionaries' of hegemony — the intellectuals — and also the various sites of hegemony — education, the various forms of 'high' and 'popular' culture, and their 'cement' in ideology, popular beliefs, and 'common sense'. If orthodox Marxism had emphasized the repressive role of the state in class societies, then Gramsci introduces the dimension of 'civil society' to locate the complex ways in which *consent* to certain forms of domination is produced.

It is this 'extra dimension' of hegemony which enables Gramsci to reformulate the whole question of the relationship between class and culture; to suggest the ways in which the terrain of culture is a strategic field for the establishment of forms of consent and to mark out the ways in which cultural and ideological forms are historically *negotiated* between dominant and subordinate groups.

In her article, Chantal Mouffe takes up the themes of ideology and hegemony in Gramsci's work and shows how, in the originality of their formulation, they represent a decisive innovation within Marxism. Whereas, for earlier Marxists, the analysis of the relationship between class and ideology was guided by the principle of *reduction* (i.e., that this or that ideology could be reduced to or 'belonged to' this or that class), the guiding principle in Gramsci's work, she suggests, is that of *articulation*. What is meant by this is that no ideology can be seen as unified or homogeneous, but that it is made up of diverse and sometimes conflicting elements. Hegemony here means the ways in which these elements are made to 'hang together' in a relative, though never complete, unity. Ideological forms are not fixed and immobile, they do not express or 'reflect' a class, but over a long historical period, are articulated to it through assimilation, absorption and active intervention by the dominant class. In this sense there can be no 'pure' working class ideology and no 'pure' bourgeois ideology. As Mouffe shows, Gramsci rejects any notion of a unified class consciousness and insists instead upon the diverse forms of ideology and on the 'material institutional nature of ideological practice'. Ideology does not 'descend from above', nor does it emanate 'from below': it is rather the result of complex forms of negotiation between various groups and on specific sites.

To examine this last assertion we shift from the broader theoretical overview offered by Mouffe to examine the ways in which some of these concepts can be tried out in historical and cultural analysis in Britain. Robert Gray's analysis of hegemony in Victorian Britain uses a gramscian framework to examine the complex forms of interaction and of political, cultural and ideological negotiation between the dominant groups (aristocracy and bourgeoisie) and the various sub-groups or class-fractions. He assesses the nature of political parties and allegiances, of intellectual formations and of various cultural and social practices in order to discern the composite elements of bourgeois hegemony in late nineteenth-century Britain. Combining the findings of both liberal and Marxist historians, he assesses the ways in which these can be more fruitfully deployed through using the concept of hegemony to explain the complexity of the relationship between capital and labour during this formative historical period.

Tony Davies considers the question in similar terms, though from a different point of view, in his analysis of education, ideology and literature. In the emergent education system — one of the primary sites for the production and reproduction of hegemony — Davies analyses the genesis of certain dominant, and still pervasive, meanings around the apparently innocent term 'literature'. In this context, the theme of 'intellectual and moral leadership' is very clearly foregrounded and we can begin to locate, even at the level of values and meanings, the ways in which hegemony operates discretely and in areas which are not apparently or immediately political.

1 Antonio Gramsci

Introduction

Requesting Antonio Gramsci's condemnation and imprisonment in 1926, the Italian Fascist Prosecutor repeated Mussolini's demand that 'We must stop this brain from functioning for twenty years'. Fortunately this demand was not met: over the next ten years until his death in prison, Gramsci undertook, in severely restrained and difficult circumstances, a project which, in intensity and intellectual breadth, is quite astonishing. The result of this period of isolated intellectual activity is known today as the *Prison Notebooks.* In their entirety these comprise almost two and a half thousand pages of notes, essays and analyses on politics, history, philosophy, literature, culture and many other areas. They represent what is probably the most sustained attempt over the past fifty years to advance what, to avoid the censor's pen, he called the 'philosophy of praxis', that is, Marxism.

Gramsci was not just an essayist. He was, during a crucial period in Italian history, a prominent political figure prior to his imprisonment. An active socialist since the age of about fourteen, he was to play a leading role in the Italian Socialist Party in its early years and then, in 1920, to play a major role in the formation of the Italian Communist Party, eventually becoming its General Secretary. He became a Deputy (MP) for one of the Rome constituencies in 1924. It was this role, combined with his active and organised resistance to Fascism, which led to his arrest in 1926, his imprisonment and ultimately his death.

Gramsci was not a politician in the narrow sense of the term. His theory and practice of politics were expansive. From his early years in the Socialist Party he considered the theoretical and practical questions of culture to be of the utmost importance for politics. The first passage in the following section indicates why. He recognised that the diverse forms of national and international culture were never neutral, never separable from politics: they were, for him, inextricably bound up with questions of 'leadership' or, in his own terms, with *hegemony*. This is the central concept in Gramsci's *Prison Notebooks* and the fulcrum around which all other concepts revolve, whether he is writing of politics, history, the intellectuals, education, his fellow Marxists, or culture in general. It is in fact the basis for the complex and sophisticated ways in which he approaches all of these questions. This will become clearer as you read through the passages, discerning the connections, the general direction of the argument and its originality.

This originality has to be placed in its own historical context. In working through the concept of hegemony in a variety of contexts, Gramsci is making three distinct challenges. The first challenge is to the liberal idealist tradition which conceives of culture and cultural questions as essentially a-political or as a question of the 'spirit' untainted by politics. The second challenge is to his fellow Marxists who had reversed the procedure and reduced culture to a mere 'reflection' of the economic base of society. Gramsci called this tendency, dominant in the Marxism of his time, 'economism' or, sometimes, 'vulgar materialism'. The third challenge, related to the first two, was to his contemporaries to transform the existing, fragile, hegemony of the Italian State into a new 'intellectual and moral leadership' which would be expansive and democratic. The call went unheeded of course as Mussolini and his forces imposed quite a different form of domination on Italian society. Gramsci's years in prison were to be a broad-ranging reflection on the causes of this failure.

So for Gramsci there is a crucial link between culture and politics but the link is far from being a simple or mechanical one. Culture has to be broken down into its diverse forms, whether they be 'high' or 'low' culture, elite culture or popular culture, philosophy or 'common sense', and analysed in terms of their effectivity in 'cementing' complex forms of leadership. Gramsci rejects the cruder and more orthodox Marxist conceptions of 'class-domination' in favour of a more nuanced and sophisticated coupling of 'force and consent' (or 'coercion plus hegemony' as he puts it). He is primarily concerned with the ways in which a whole complex series of cultural, political and ideological practices work to 'cement' a society into a relative — though never complete — unity. Gramsci makes connections where we may not have noticed them before; he throws into question areas such as common sense which we may have thought of as innocent or spontaneous; he interrogates a wide range of cultural forms from the apparently 'highest' to the apparently 'lowest' and marks out the historical and political sites of their interaction and formation. His work enables us to ask questions about why, historically, a given cultural form was considered to be 'low' or 'high', what effects this sort of division had and how it is reproduced today. These forms of questioning would seem to be central to the domain of popular culture.

The following passages cannot do justice to the immense range of Gramsci's work. They have been selected in the hope that some of the key concepts and forms of analysis may emerge in embryonic form at least. It is divided into five sections: Culture, Hegemony, Ideology and Popular Beliefs, The Intellectuals and The State. These are necessarily schematic and imposed by the process of editing rather than laid out by Gramsci himself. It is hoped that this division will not obscure the nature of the connection between the various areas of his work.

Key to references
All but two of the passages come from Antonio Gramsci, *Selections from the Prison Notebooks,* trans. and ed. Quintin Hoare and Geoffrey Nowell-Smith, Lawrence and Wishart, London, 1971 (designated *SPN*). The exceptions are from *Selections from the Political Writings* and *Letters from Prison* (cited fully as they occur).

i Culture
The *raison d'etre* and driving force behind the importance which Gramsci conferred on the analysis of culture was set out by him at the age of 24. It is a zealous and polemical article, but only the more idealist elements were to be abandoned as his work developed over the next twenty years:

> We need to free ourselves from the habit of seeing culture as encyclopaedic knowledge, and men as mere receptacles to be stuffed full of empirical data and a mass of unconnected raw facts, which have to be filed in the brain as in the columns of a dictionary, enabling their owner to respond to the various stimuli from the outside world. This form of culture is really dangerous, particularly for the proletariat. It serves only to create maladjusted people, people who believe they are superior to the rest of humanity because they have memorized a certain number of facts and dates and who rattle them off at every opportunity, so turning them almost into a barrier between themselves and others. It serves to create the kind of weak and colourless intellectualism... which has given birth to a mass of pretentious babblers who have a more damaging effect on social life than tuberculosis or syphilis germs have on the beauty and physical health of the body. The young student who knows a little Latin and history, the young lawyer who has been successful in wringing a scrap of paper called a degree out of the laziness and lackadaisical attitude of his professors — they end up seeing themselves as different from and superior to even the best skilled workman, who fulfils a precise and indispensable task in life and is a hundred times more valuable in his activity than they are in theirs. But this is not culture,

but pedantry, not intelligence, but intellect, and it is absolutely right to react against it.

Culture is something quite different. It is organization, discipline of one's inner self, a coming to terms with one's own personality; it is the attainment of a higher awareness, with the aid of which one succeeds in understanding one's own historical value, one's own function in life, one's own rights and obligations. But none of this can come about through spontaneous evolution, through a series of actions and reactions which are independent of one's own will — as is the case in the animal and vegetable kingdoms where every unit is selected and specifies its own organs unconsciously, through a fatalistic natural law. Above all, man is mind, i.e. he is a product of history, not nature. Otherwise how could one explain the fact, given that there have always been exploiters and exploited, creators of wealth and its selfish consumers, that socialism has not yet come into being? The fact is that only by degrees, one stage at a time, has humanity acquired consciousness of its own value and won for itself the right to throw off the patterns of organization imposed on it by minorities at a previous period in history. And this consciousness was formed not under the brutal goad of physiological necessity, but as a result of intelligent reflection, at first by just a few people and later by a whole class, on why certain conditions exist and how best to convert the facts of vassalage into the signals of rebellion and social reconstruction. This means that every revolution has been preceded by an intense labour of criticism, by the diffusion of culture and the spread of ideas amongst masses of men who are at first resistant, and think only of solving their own immediate economic and political problems for themselves, who have no ties of solidarity with others in the same condition. The latest example, the closest to us and hence least foreign to our own time, is that of the French Revolution. The preceding cultural period, called the Enlightenment, which has been so misrepresented by the facile critics of theoretical reason, was not in any way or at least was not entirely a flutter of superficial encyclopaedic intellectuals discursing on anything and everything with equal imperturbability.... in short it was not solely a phenomenon of pedantic and arid intellectualism.... The Enlightenment was a magnificent revolution in itself... it gave all Europe a bourgeois spiritual International in the form of a unified consciousness, one which was sensitive to all the woes and misfortunes of the common people and which was the best possible preparation for the bloody revolt that followed in France.

In Italy, France and Germany, the same topics, the same institutions and same principles were being discussed. Each new comedy by Voltaire, each new pamphlet moved like a spark along the lines that were already stretched between state and state, between region and region, and found the same supporters and the same opponents everywhere and every time. The bayonets of Napoleon's armies found their road already smoothed by an invisible army of books and pamphlets that had swarmed out of Paris from the first half of the eighteenth century and had prepared both men and institutions for the necessary renewal. Later, after the French events had welded a unified consciousness, a demonstration in Paris was enough to provoke similar disturbances in Milan, Vienna and the smaller centres. All this seems natural and spontaneous to superficial observers, yet it would be incomprehensible if we were not aware of the cultural factors that helped to create a state of mental preparedness for those explosions in the name of what was seen as a common cause.

The same phenomenon is being repeated today in the case of socialism. It was through a critique of capitalist civilization that the unified consciousness of the proletariat was or is still being formed, and a critique implies culture, not simply a spontaneous and naturalistic evolution. A critique implies... self consciousness.... Consciousness of a self which is opposed to others, which is differentiated and, once having set itself a goal, can judge facts and events other than in themselves or for themselves but also in so far as they tend to drive history forward or backward. To know oneself means to be oneself, to be master of oneself, to distinguish oneself, to free oneself from a state of chaos, to exist as an element of order — but of one's own order and one's own discipline in striving for an ideal. And we cannot be successful in this unless we also know others, their history, the successive efforts they have made to be what they are, to create the civilization they have created and which we seek to replace with our own. In other words, we must form some idea of nature and its laws in order to come to know the laws governing the mind. And we must learn all this without losing sight of the ultimate aim: to know oneself better through others and to know others better through oneself.

If it is true that universal history is a chain made up of the efforts man has exerted to free himself from privilege, prejudice and idolatry, then it is hard to understand why the proletariat, which seeks to add another link to that chain, should not know how and why and by whom it was preceded, or what advantage it might derive from this knowledge.
(*Selections from the Political Writings 1910-20*, ed. Q. Hoare, Lawrence and Wishart, London, 1977, pp. 11-13).

Twenty years later, writing from prison now, he was to be more specific and analytical;

It would be interesting to study concretely the forms of cultural organisation which keep the ideological world in movement within a given country, and to examine how they function in practice. A study of the numerical relationship between the section of the population professionally engaged in active cultural work in the country in question and the population as a whole, would also be useful, together with an approximate calculation of the unattached forces. The school, at all levels, and the Church, are the biggest cultural organisations in every country, in terms of the number of people they employ.* Then there are newspapers, magazines and the book trade and private educational institutions, either those which are complementary to the state system, or cultural institutions like the Popular Universities.† Other professions include among their specialised activities a fair proportion of cultural activity. For example, doctors, army officers, the legal profession. But it should be noted that in all countries, though in differing degrees, there is a great gap between the popular masses and the intellectual groups, even the largest ones, and those nearest to the peripheries of national life, like priests and school teachers. The reason for this is that, however much the ruling class may affirm to the contrary, the State, as such, does not have a unitary, coherent and homogenous conception, with the result that intellectual groups are scattered between one stratum and the next, or even within a single stratum. The Universities, except in a few countries, do not exercise any unifying influence: often an independent thinker has more influence than the whole of university institutions, etc. (*SPN* pp.341-2)

Why would it be interesting? Because, he argues:

From this one can deduce the importance of the 'cultural aspect', even in practical (collective) activity. An historical act can only be performed by 'collective man', and this presupposes the attainment of a 'cultural-social' unity through which a multiplicity of dispersed wills, with heterogeneous aims, are welded together with a single aim, on the basis of an equal and common conception of the world, both general and particular, operating in transitory bursts (in emotional ways) or permanently (where the intellectual base is so well rooted, assimilated and experienced that it becomes passion. Since this is the way things happen, great importance is assumed by the general question of language, that is, the question of collectively attaining a single cultural 'climate'. (*SPN* p.349).

*Gramsci is writing at a time and in a context where the Church's role was considerably more significant than it is today.

†Literally, 'universities for the people' organised by the Italian Socialist Party. Gramsci was extremely critical of them for handing out 'trashy baubles' to the natives.

These criteria, derived from the analysis of culture: 'collective man', 'cultural-social' unity, and the welding of 'heterogeneous aims' and 'dispersed wills' are key terms for the more general concept of hegemony. We will see how they develop through the various analyses and concepts which Gramsci deploys.

ii Hegemony

Gramsci sets out his own analytic protocols in the following terms:

> The methodological criterion on which our own study must be based is the following: that the supremacy of a social group manifests itself in two ways, as 'domination' and as 'intellectual and moral leadership'. A social group dominates antagonistic groups, which it tends to 'liquidate', or to subjugate perhaps even by armed force; it leads kindred and allied groups. A social group can, and indeed must, already exercise 'leadership' before winning governmental power (this indeed is one of the principal conditions for the winning of such power); it subsequently becomes dominant when it exercises power, but even if it holds it firmly in its grasp, it must continue to 'lead' as well. (*SPN* pp. 57-8)

and elsewhere, with an eye to *future* political strategy, Gramsci adds:

> ... a class is dominant in two ways, i.e. 'leading' and 'dominant'. It leads the classes which are its allies, and dominates those which are its enemies. Therefore, even before attaining power a class can (and must) 'lead'; when it is in power it becomes dominant, but continues to 'lead' as well ... there can and must be a 'political hegemony' even before the attainment of governmental power, and one should not count solely on the power and material force which such a position gives in order to exercise political leadership or hegemony. (*SPN* p.57n).

Later, Gramsci goes on to define the complex *nature* of hegemony, as both economic and as 'ethical-political':

> Undoubtedly the fact of hegemony presupposes that account be taken of the interests and the tendencies of the groups over which hegemony is to be exercised, and that a certain compromise equilibrium should be formed — in other words, that the leading group should make sacrifices of an economic-corporate kind. But there is also no doubt that such sacrifices and such a compromise cannot touch the essential; for though hegemony is ethical-political, it must also be economic, must necessarily be based on the

decisive function exercised by the leading group in the decisive nucleus of economic activity. (*SPN* p.161)

This 'nucleus of economic activity' is the first principle to be taken into account, but it is far from being the only determinant.

Also important is the relation of political forces; in other words, an evaluation of the degree of homogeneity, self-awareness, and organisation attained by the various social classes. This moment can in its turn be analysed and differentiated into various levels, corresponding to the various moments of collective political consciousness, as they have manifested themselves in history up till now. The first and most elementary of these is the economic-corporate level: a tradesman feels *obliged* to stand by another tradesman, a manufacturer by another manufacturer, etc., but the tradesman does not yet feel solidarity with the manufacturer; in other words, the members of the professional group are conscious of its unity and homogeneity, and of the need to organise it, but in the case of the wider social group this is not yet so. A second moment is that in which consciousness is reached of the solidarity of interests among all the members of a social class — but still in the purely economic field. Already at this juncture the problem of the State is posed — but only in terms of winning politico-juridical equality with the ruling groups: the right is claimed to participate in legislation and administration, even to reform these — but within the existing fundamental structures. A third moment is that in which one becomes aware that one's own corporate interests, in their present and future development, transcend the corporate limits of the purely economic class, and can and must become the interests of other subordinate groups too. This is the most purely political phase, and marks the decisive passage from the structure to the sphere of the complex superstructures; it is the phase in which previously germinated ideologies become 'party', come into confrontation and conflict, until only one of them, or at least a single combination of them, tends to prevail, to gain the upper hand, to propagate itself throughout society — bringing about not only a unison of economic and political aims, but also intellectual and moral unity, posing all the questions around which the struggle rages not on a corporate but on a 'universal' plane, and thus creating the hegemony of a fundamental social group over a series of subordinate groups. It is true that the State is seen as the organ of one particular group, destined to create favourable conditions for the latter's maximum expansion. But the development and expansion of the particular group are conceived of, and presented, as being the motor force of a universal expansion, of a

> development of all the 'national' energies. In other words, the dominant group is coordinated concretely with the general interests of the subordinate groups, and the life of the State is conceived of as a continuous process of formation and superseding of unstable equilibria (on the juridical plane) between the interests of the fundamental group and those of the subordinate groups — equilibria in which the interests of the dominant group prevail, but only up to a certain point, i.e. stopping short of narrowly corporate economic interest. (*SPN* pp.181-2)

For Gramsci, history is a process of conflicts and compromises where one fundamental class will emerge as both dominant and directive not only in economic but also in moral and intellectual terms. Here, and we shall see more of this later, the state emerges as the unifier and arbitrator of diverse interests and conflicts. In an effective and extensive form of hegemony there will be a relative equilibrium and harmony. But, Gramsci stresses the importance of recognising that this is only *relative*: that there are periods when hegemony, for various reasons, can begin to come apart, and when the dominant class will resort to coercive measures. Gramsci defines this as a 'crisis of authority';

> If the ruling class has lost its consensus, i.e. is no longer 'leading' but only 'dominant', exercising coercive force alone; this means precisely that the great masses have become detached from their traditional ideologies, and no longer believe what they used to believe previously, etc. The crisis consists precisely in the fact that the old is dying and the new cannot be born; in this interregnum a great variety of morbid symptoms appear. (*SPN* p.275)

Here, hegemony defines the complex nature of the connection between the mass of the people and the leading groups of society: a connection which is not only 'political' in the narrow sense, but also a question of ideas or of *consciousness*. It is this emphasis which marks the originality of the concept of hegemony. Where orthodox Marxism had overemphasised the importance of the economic base of society and liberal philosophy had put too much stress on the role of ideas, Gramsci insists upon bringing both these aspects together. One of the ways in which 'leaders' and 'led' are kept together is through 'popular beliefs'.

iii Ideology, popular beliefs and common sense

Criticising the negligence of the dimension of consciousness by some of his fellow Marxists, Gramsci states;

> Furthermore, another proposition of the philosophy of praxis [Marxism] is... that 'popular beliefs' and similar ideas are themselves material forces. The search for 'dirty-Jewish'* interests has sometimes led to monstrous and comical errors of interpretation, which have consequently reacted negatively on the prestige of the original body of ideas. (*SPN* p.165)

Ideas are 'material forces' for Gramsci. Here, he is following and elaborating Marx's assertion that 'social being determines social consciousness'. Consciousness is therefore not just spontaneously 'born' but is structured in certain ways corresponding to the general structure of society. He argues against the notion that

> ...numbers decide everything, and that the opinions of any idiot who knows how to write (or in some countries even of an illiterate) have exactly the same weight in determining the political course of the State as the opinions of somebody who devotes his best energies to the State and the nation, etc. But the fact is that it is not true, in any sense, that numbers decide everything, nor that the opinions of all electors are of 'exactly' equal weight. Numbers, in this case too, are simply an instrumental value, giving a measure and a relation and nothing more. And what then is measured? What is measured is precisely the effectiveness, and the expansive and persuasive capacity, of the opinions of a few individuals, the active minorities, the elites, the avant-gardes, etc. — i.e. their rationality, historicity or concrete functionality. Which means it is untrue that all individual opinions have 'exactly' equal weight. Ideas and opinions are not spontaneously 'born' in each individual brain: they have had a centre of formation, of irradiation, of dissemination, of persuasion -... (*SPN* p.192)

This may sound a bit too conspiratorial but the ways in which certain ideas or a certain 'philosophy' become dominant is a very complex process. To explain this process, Gramsci introduces three dimensions which 'link' elites with the people, language, common sense and 'folklore':

> It is essential to destroy the widespread prejudice that philosophy is a strange and difficult thing just because it is the specific intellectual activity of a particular category of specialists or of professional and systematic philosophers. It must first be shown that all men are 'philosophers', by

*Gramsci is referring here to Marx's first thesis on Feuerbach in which Marx argues that Feuerbach conceives practice 'only in its dirty — judaical manifestation' and hence failed to 'grasp the significance of "revolutionary", of practical — critical, activity.'

> defining the limits and characteristics of the 'spontaneous philosophy' which is proper to everybody. This philosophy is contained in: 1. language itself, which is a totality of determined notions and concepts and not just of words grammatically devoid of content; 2. 'common sense' and 'good sense'; 3. popular religion and, therefore, also in the entire system of beliefs, superstitions, opinions, ways of seeing things and of acting, which are collectively bundled together under the name of 'folklore'. (*SPN* p.323).

He goes on to explain the social basis of these ideas in the following terms:

> In acquiring one's conception of the world one always belongs to a particular grouping which is that of all the social elements which share the same mode of thinking and acting. We are all conformists of some conformism or other, always man-in-the-mass or collective man. The question is this: of what historical type is the conformism, the mass humanity to which one belongs? When one's conception of the world is not critical and coherent but disjointed and episodic, one belongs simultaneously to a multiplicity of mass human groups. The personality is strangely composite: it contains Stone Age elements and principles of a more advanced science, prejudices from all past phases of history at the local level and intuitions of a future philosophy which will be that of a human race united the world over. To criticise one's own conception of the world means therefore to make it a coherent unity and to raise it to the level reached by the most advanced thought in the world. It therefore also means criticism of all previous philosophy, in so far as this has left stratified deposits in popular philosophy. The starting-point of critical elaboration is the consciousness of what one really is, and is 'knowing thyself'* as a product of the historical process to date which has deposited in you an infinity of traces, without leaving an inventory.
>
> Philosophy cannot be separated from the history of philosophy, nor can culture from the history of culture. In the most immediate and relevant sense, one cannot be a philosopher; by which I mean have a critical and coherent conception of the world, without having a consciousness of its historicity, of the phase of development which it represents and of the fact that it contradicts other conceptions or elements of other conceptions. One's conception of the world is a response to certain specific problems posed by reality, which are quite specific and 'original' in their immediate relevance. How is it possible to consider the present, and quite specific present, with a mode of thought elaborated for a past which is often remote

*'Know thyself' was the inscription written above the gate of the Oracle at Delphi, and became a principle of Socratic philosophy.

> and superseded? When someone does this, it means that he is a walking anachronism, a fossil, and not living in the modern world, or at the least that he is strangely composite. And it is in fact the case that social groups which in some ways express the most developed modernity, lag behind in other respects, given their social position, and are therefore incapable of complete historical autonomy. (*SPN* pp.324-5)

These 'conceptions of the world' will be significantly affected by the nature of the national language:

> If it is true that every language contains the elements of a conception of the world and of a culture it could also be true that from anyone's language one can assess the greater or lesser complexity of his conception of the world. Someone who only speaks dialect, or understands the standard language incompletely, necessarily has an intuition of the world which is more or less limited and provincial, which is fossilised and anachronistic in relation to the major currents of thought which dominate world history. His interests will be limited, more or less corporate or economistic,* not universal. While it is not always possible to learn a number of foreign languages in order to put oneself in contact with other cultural lives, it is at the least necessary to learn the national language properly. A great culture can be translated into the language of another great culture, that is to say a great national language with historic richness and complexity, and it can translate any other great culture and can be a world-wide means of expression. But a dialect cannot do this. (*SPN* p.325)

The notion of 'common sense' is perhaps the most important to grasp here. For Gramsci common sense is pervasive but unsystematic; it has a basis in popular experience but does not represent a unified conception of the world as philosophy does:

> Philosophy is intellectual order, which neither religion nor common sense can be. It is to be observed that religion and common sense do not coincide either, but that religion is an element of fragmented common sense. Moreover common sense is a collective noun, like religion: there is not just one common sense, for that too is a product of history and a part of the historical process. Philosophy is criticism and the superseding of religion and 'common sense'. In this sense it coincides with 'good' as opposed to 'common' sense. But then, philosophy in general does not in fact exist. Various philosophies or conceptions of the world exist, and one always

*i.e. restricted to immediate and self interested concerns.

> makes a choice between them. How is this choice made? Is it merely an intellectual event, or is it something more complex? And is it not frequently the case that there is a contradiction between one's intellectual choice and one's mode of conduct? Which therefore would be the real conception of the world: that logically affirmed as an intellectual choice? or that which emerges from the real activity of each man, which is implicit in his mode of action? And since all action is political, can one not say that the real philosophy of each man is contained in its entirety in his political action? (*SPN* p.326)

Gramsci explains the relationship between philosophy and commonsense in these terms:

> Every social stratum has its own 'common sense' and its own 'good sense', which are basically the most widespread conception of life and of man. Every philosophical current leaves behind a sedimentation of 'common sense': this is the document of its historical effectiveness. Common sense is not something rigid and immobile, but is continually transforming itself, enriching itself with scientific ideas and with philosophical opinions which have entered ordinary life. 'Common sense' is the folklore of philosophy, and is always half-way between folklore properly speaking and the philosophy, science, and economics of the specialists. Common sense creates the folklore of the future, that is as a relatively rigid phase of popular knowledge at a given place and time. (*SPN* p.326)

and elsewhere;

> Perhaps it is useful to make a 'practical' distinction between philosophy and common sense in order to indicate more clearly the passage from one moment to the other. In philosophy the features of individual elaboration of thought are the most salient: in common sense on the other hand it is the diffuse, unco-ordinated features of a generic form of thought common to a particular period and a particular popular environment. But every philosophy has a tendency to become the common sense of a fairly limited environment (that of all the intellectuals). It is a matter therefore of starting with a philosophy which already enjoys, or could enjoy, a certain diffusion, because it is connected to and implicit in practical life, and elaborating it so that it becomes a renewed common sense possessing the coherence and the sinew of individual philosophies. But this can only happen if the demands of cultural contact with the 'simple' are continually felt. (*SPN* p.330)

Here we can see how Gramsci's conception of common-sense begins to dovetail into his more general notion of hegemony for 'intellectual and moral leadership' demands precisely this sort of connection between 'leaders and led': a culture or a philosophy are only hegemonic when they can establish these diverse forms of contact:

> The question posed here was the one we have already referred to, namely this: is a philosophical movement properly so called when it is devoted to creating a specialised culture among restricted intellectual groups, or rather when, and only when, in the process of elaborating a form of thought superior to 'common sense' and coherent on a scientific plane, it never forgets to remain in contact with the 'simple' and indeed finds in this contact the source of the problems it sets out to study and to resolve? Only by this contact does a philosophy become 'historical', purify itself of intellectualistic elements of an individual character and become 'life'. (*SPN* p.330)

More directly and polemically, he asserts

> the relation between common sense and the upper level of philosophy is assured by 'politics' (*SPN* p.331)

Gramsci, of course, did not just want to explain the existing order of things, but to confront it, criticize it and transform it; to establish a new hegemony for the hitherto subordinate groups. Thus,

> a philosophy of praxis [Marxism] cannot but present itself at the outset in a polemical and critical guise, as superseding the existing mode of thinking and existing concrete thought (the existing cultural world). First of all, therefore, it must be a criticism of 'common sense', basing itself initially, however, on common sense in order to demonstrate that 'everyone' is a philosopher and that it is not a question of introducing from scratch a scientific form of thought. (*SPN* pp.330)

The starting point for this critique is the 'active man-in-the-mass':

> The active man-in-the-mass has a practical activity, but has no clear theoretical consciousness of his practical activity, which nonetheless involves understanding the world in so far as it transforms it. His theoretical consciousness can indeed be historically in opposition to his activity. One might almost say that he has two theoretical consciousnesses

> (or one contradictory consciousness): one which is implicit in his activity and which in reality unites him with all his fellow-workers in the practical transformation of the real world; and one, superficially explicit or verbal, which he has inherited from the past and uncritically absorbed. But this verbal conception is not without consequences. It holds together a specific social group, it influences moral conduct and the direction of will, with varying efficacity but often powerfully enough to produce a situation in which the contradictory state of consciousness does not permit of any action, any decision or any choice, and produces a condition of moral and political passivity. Critical understanding of self takes place therefore through a struggle of political 'hegemonies' and of opposing directions, first in the ethical field and then in that of politics proper, in order to arrive at the working out at a higher level of one's own conception of reality. Consciousness of being part of a particular hegemonic force (that is to say, political consciousness) is the first stage towards a further progressive self-consciousness in which theory and practice will finally be one. Thus the unity of theory and practice is not just a matter of mechanical fact, but a part of the historical process, whose elementary and primitive phase is to be found in the sense of being 'different' and 'apart', in an instinctive feeling of independence, and which progresses to the level of real possession of a single and coherent conception of the world. This is why it must be stressed that the political development of the concept of hegemony represents a great philosophical advance as well as a politico-practical one. For it necessarily supposes an intellectual unity and an ethic in conformity with a conception of reality that has gone beyond common sense and has become, if only within narrow limits, a critical conception. (*SPN* pp. 333-4)

The fact that every person is in some sense a 'philosopher' provides the potential for change:

> Having first shown that everyone is a philosopher, though in his own way and unconsciously, since even in the slightest manifestation of any intellectual activity whatever, in 'language', there is contained a specific conception of the world, one then moves on to the second level, which is that of awareness and criticism. That is to say, one proceeds to the question — is it better to 'think', without having a critical awareness, in a disjointed and episodic way? In other words, is it better to take part in a conception of the world mechanically imposed by the external environment, i.e. by one of the many social groups in which everyone is automatically involved from the moment of his entry into the conscious world (and this can be one's village or province; it can have its origins in the parish and the 'intellectual

> activity' of the local priest or aging patriarch whose wisdom is law, or in the little old woman who has inherited the lore of the witches or the minor intellectual soured by his own stupidity and inability to act)? Or, on the other hand, is it better to work out consciously and critically one's own conception of the world and thus, in connection with the labours of one's own brain, choose one's sphere of activity, take an active part in the creation of the history of the world, be one's own guide, refusing to accept passively and supinely from outside the moulding of one's personality? (*SPN* pp.323-4)

And, importantly, this is not an individual act, but a social one;

> Creating a new culture does not only mean one's own individual 'original' discoveries. It also, and most particularly, means the diffusion in a critical form of truths already discovered, their 'socialisation' as it were, and even making them the basis of vital action, an element of co-ordination and intellectual and moral order. For a mass of people to be led to think coherently and in the same coherent fashion about the real present world, is a 'philosophical' event far more important and 'original' than the discovery by some philosophical 'genius' of a truth which remains the property of small groups of intellectuals. (*SPN* p.325)

Gramsci is clearly extending the definition of 'philosophy' beyond its traditional academic location to include more general cultural elements. At the same time this makes it a *political* question:

> ...at this point we reach the fundamental problem facing any conception of the world, any philosophy which has become a cultural movement, a 'religion', a 'faith', any that has produced a form of practical activity or will in which the philosophy is contained as an implicit theoretical 'premiss'. One might say 'ideology' here, but on condition that the word is used in its highest sense of a conception of the world that is implicitly manifest in art, in law, in economic activity and in all manifestations of individual and collective life. This problem is that of preserving the ideological unity of the entire social bloc which that ideology serves to cement and to unify. The strength of religions, and of the Catholic church in particular, has lain, and still lies, in the fact that they feel very strongly the need for the doctrinal unity of the whole mass of the faithful and strive to ensure that the higher intellectual stratum does not get separated from the lower. The Roman church has always been the most vigorous in the struggle to prevent the 'official' formation of two religions, one for the 'intellectuals' and the other for the 'simple souls'. (*SPN* p.328)

But this 'faith' is not completely harmonious or stable: at the same time as it dominates it is resisted by incursions from the collective action of subordinate groups:

> ... the social group in question may indeed have its own conception of the world, even if only embryonic; a conception which manifests itself in action, but occasionally and in flashes — when, that is, the group is acting as an organic totality. But this same group has, for reasons of submission and intellectual subordination, adopted a conception which is not its own but is borrowed from another group; and it affirms this conception verbally and believes itself to be following it, because this is the conception which it follows in 'normal times' – that is when its conduct is not independent and autonomous, but submissive and subordinate. Hence the reason why philosophy cannot be divorced from politics. And one can show furthermore that the choice and the criticism of a conception of the world is also a political matter. (*SPN* p.327)

Gramsci calls common-sense the 'sub-stratum of ideology'. Ideology is the more general term for the ways in which certain sets of ideas and assumptions become dominant material forces in society. Gramsci attempts to rescue the concept of 'ideology' from its traditional connotations:

> 'Ideology' was an aspect of 'sensationalism',* i.e. eighteenth-century French materialism. Its original meaning was that of 'science of ideas,' and since analysis was the only method recognised and applied by science it means 'analysis of ideas,' that is, 'investigation of the origin of ideas.' Ideas had to be broken down into their original 'elements,' and these could be nothing other than 'sensations.' Ideas derived from sensations. (*SPN* p.375)

He goes on to suggest that the ways in which

> ... the concept of Ideology passed from meaning 'science of ideas' and 'analysis of the origin of ideas' to meaning a specific 'system of ideas' needs to be examined historically. (*SPN* p.376)

and criticises his fellow Marxist Bukharin in these terms:

> One should examine the way in which... Bukharin... has remained trapped in Ideology; whereas the philosophy of praxis [Marxism]

*By 'sensationalism' Gramsci means that school of philosophy which took the immediate senses – sensations – as their empirical starting-point.

> represents a distinct advance and historically is precisely in opposition to Ideology. Indeed the meaning which the term 'ideology' has assumed in Marxist philosophy implicitly contains a negative value judgment and excludes the possibility that for its founders the origin of ideas should be sought for in sensations, and therefore, in the last analysis, in physiology. 'Ideology' itself must be analysed historically, in the terms of the philosophy of praxis, as a superstructure. (*SPN* p.376)

So ideology is not just a question of 'ideas' or of political beliefs in the explicit sense. It is both more *material* and more *specific*. Gramsci criticises the vagueness with which the term is applied;

> It seems to me that there is a potential element of error in assessing the value of ideologies, due to the fact (by no means casual) that the name ideology is given both to the necessary superstructure of a particular structure and to the arbitrary elucubrations of particular individuals. The bad sense of the word has become widespread, with the effect that the theoretical analysis of the concept of ideology has been modified and denatured. The process leading up to this error can be easily reconstructed. (*SPN* p.376)

What Gramsci means by this is that the term 'ideology' is applied in two distinctive ways which frequently become confused. On the one hand it is deployed, usually by Marxists, to explain the 'system of ideas' which corresponds to the economic base of a given society; and on the other hand it is deployed, usually by non-Marxists, to explain specific sets of ideas held by individuals. Or, frequently enough, both conceptions are shared by the different traditions of thought.

Gramsci is clearly criticising his fellow Marxists when

> 1 ideology is identified as distinct from the structure, and it is asserted that it is not ideology that changes the structures but vice versa;
> 2 it is asserted that a given political solution is 'ideological' – i.e. that it is not sufficient to change the structure, although it thinks that it can do so; it is asserted that it is useless, stupid, etc.;
> 3 one then passes to the assertion that every ideology is 'pure' appearance, useless, stupid, etc. (*SPN* p.376)

So, given that there are, simultaneously, general and social structures which may determine the ways in which we think, and room also for individual and group opinions to hold sway, how should we approach the question of ideology? Gramsci is clear about this:

> One must therefore distinguish between historically organic ideologies, those, that is, which are necessary to a given structure, and ideologies that are arbitrary, rationalistic, or 'willed'. To the extent that ideologies are historically necessary they have a validity which is 'psychological'; they 'organise' human masses, and create the terrain on which men move, acquire consciousness of their position, struggle, etc. To the extent that they are arbitrary they only create individual 'movements', polemics and so on (though even these are not completely useless, since they function like an error which by contrasting with truth, demonstrates it).
>
> It is worth recalling the frequent affirmation made by Marx on the 'solidity of popular beliefs' as a necessary element of a specific situation. What he says more or less is 'when this way of conceiving things has the force of popular beliefs', etc. Another proposition of Marx is that a popular conviction often has the same energy as a material force or something of the kind, which is extremely significant. (*SPN* p.377)

Gramsci is saying here that ideology is not just a question of explicit political beliefs, but that it is also a material force; it 'organises' human masses, and 'creates the terrain'; that it has an 'internal' psychological dimension and that it is the way in which consciousness itself is structured. Also, there is the very important distinction between 'organic' and 'arbitrary' ideologies. Briefly we could say that the former represent the ideological *core* of society while the latter are, in varying degrees, its 'fringe benefits'. The general social structure and the individual are brought together in this formulation in a complex relationship of dominance and subordination.

Gramsci goes on to stress that there is an interdependent, interactive relationship between the 'ideal' and the 'material':

> The analysis of these propositions tends, I think, to reinforce the conception of *historical bloc** in which precisely material forces are the content and ideologies are the form, though this distinction between form and content has purely didactic value, since the material forces would be inconceivable historically without form and the ideologies would be individual fancies without the material forces. (*SPN* p.377)

There is a constant and dialectical relationship between ideologies and

*'Historical bloc' is a term which Gramsci uses to describe what we generally call 'society'. As used by Gramsci it means a 'contradictory and discordant ensemble': not a unified whole but the result of conflicts, compromises and negotiations.

material forces. This is Gramsci's interpretation of Marx's assertion that 'social being' [material forces] determines 'social consciousness' [ideologies]. But as we can see, it has been considerably 'loosened up' to suggest a two-way process.

iv The intellectuals

How is ideology disseminated? We have seen that it does not just descend 'from above', nor does it emerge spontaneously 'from below': it is always structured somewhere between those extremes. Earlier, Gramsci insisted that 'Ideas and opinions are not spontaneously "born" in each individual brain: they have had a centre of formation, of irradiation, of dissemination, of persuasion' (see above p 200). Here he means the nature of received ideas, forms of schooling and teaching, the relative maturity or immaturity of the 'national language' and the nature of the dominant social groups in any given society. But, almost uniquely among Marxists, Gramsci insists upon the importance of the various 'functionaries' of these centres: the intellectuals.

Here again Gramsci extends the traditional meaning of this term:

> By 'intellectuals' must be understood not those strata commonly described by this term, but in general the entire social stratum which exercises an organisational function in the wide sense – whether in the field of production, or in that of culture, or in that of political administration. They correspond to the NCOs and junior officers in the army, and also partly to the higher officers who have risen from the ranks. (*SPN* p.97n)

He goes on to emphasise that these strata are to be located in relation to the fundamental structure of society:

> Every social group, coming into existence on the original terrain of an essential function in the world of economic production, creates together with itself, organically, one or more strata of intellectuals which give it homogeneity and an awareness of its own function not only in the economic but also in the social and political fields. The capitalist entrepreneur creates alongside himself the industrial technician, the specialist in political economy, the organisers of a new culture, of a new legal system, etc. (*SPN* p.5)

But it is not quite the case that each class has its own united *corps* of intellectuals because

> ...every 'essential' social group which emerges into history out of the

> preceding economic structure, and as an expression of a development of this structure, has found (at least in all of history up to the present) categories of intellectuals already in existence and which seemed indeed to represent an historical continuity uninterrupted even by the most complicated and radical changes in political and social forms. (*SPN* pp.6-7)

We should remember that society – the 'historical bloc' – is 'contradictory and discordant'. The first group of intellectuals described above are called 'organic intellectuals' by Gramsci and the latter group 'traditional intellectuals'. In the first group we should include, roughly, managers, technicians, policy-makers and so on while in the second group we would include the more 'academic' functions of philosophers, critics, writers, clergy and so on. But we should be wary of being too sociological here: in different cultures and at different times there may be considerable overlap of these varying functions. What is important is that the nature of the relationship between these groups will affect the very nature of hegemony: whether there is conflict or stability between them or whether there are effective political and cultural links between them and the mass of the people. Gramsci cites the example of England;

> In England the development is very different from France. The new social grouping that grew up on the basis of modern industrialism shows a remarkable economic-corporate development but advances only gropingly in the intellectual-political field. There is a very extensive category of organic intellectuals — those, that is, who come into existence on the same industrial terrain as the economic group — but in the higher sphere we find that the old land-owning class preserves its position of virtual monopoly. It loses its economic supremacy but maintains for a long time a politico-intellectual supremacy and is assimilated as 'traditional intellectuals' and as directive ... group by the new group in power. The old land-owning aristocracy is jointed to the industrialists by a kind of suture which is precisely that which in other countries unites the traditional intellectuals with the new dominant classes.
> (*SPN* p.18)

Here, Gramsci is attempting to locate the importance of the intellectuals (in the broad sense) to the nature of hegemony in England. Because there is this dislocation between the dominant (traditional) intellectuals and the newly-emergent dominant class, there are political and cultural implications for the nature of hegemony thereafter: in the case of England it meant that the more 'naked' forms of class-confrontation in the English Revolution were de-fused and diffused through other negotiated channels in comparison to, say, the violent and confrontational nature of the French Revolution a century and a half later.

Above we have an example of the historical importance of intellectuals for the nature of hegemony. But Gramsci's reflections here have a more general theoretical significance in so far as:

> All men are intellectuals, one could therefore say: but not all men have in society the function of intellectuals.
>
> When one distinguishes between intellectuals and non-intellectuals, one is referring in reality only to the immediate social function of the professional category of the intellectuals, that is, one has in mind the direction in which their specific professional activity is weighted, whether towards intellectual elaboration or towards muscular-nervous effort. This means that, although one can speak of intellectuals, one cannot speak of non-intellectuals, because non-intellectuals do not exist. But even the relationship between efforts of intellectual-cerebral elaboration and muscular-nervous effort is not always the same, so that there are varying degrees of specific intellectual activity. There is no human activity from which every form of intellectual participation can be excluded: *homo faber* cannot be separated from *homo sapiens*.* Each man, finally, outside his professional activity, carries on some form of intellectual activity, that is, he is a 'philosopher', an artist, a man of taste, he participates in a particular conception of the world, has a conscious line of moral conduct, and therefore contributes to sustain a conception of the world or to modify it, that is, to bring into being new modes of thought.
> (*SPN* p.9)

Intellectualism then is not, in its narrow sense, a 'gift' but a function in relation to the general social structure of society:

> Thus there are historically formed specialised categories for the exercise of the intellectual function. They are formed in connection with all social groups, but especially in connection with the more important, and they undergo more extensive and complex elaboration in connection with the dominant social group. One of the most important characteristics of any group that is developing towards dominance is its struggle to assimilate and to conquer 'ideologically' the traditional intellectuals, but this assimilation and conquest is made quicker and more efficacious the more the group in question succeeds in simultaneously elaborating its own organic

*Roughly, 'man who makes' and 'man who knows'.

intellectuals.

The enormous development of activity and organisation of education in the broad sense in the societies that emerged from the medieval world is an index of the importance assumed in the modern world by intellectual functions and categories. Parallel with the attempt to deepen and to broaden the 'intellectuality' of each individual, there has also been an attempt to multiply and narrow the various specialisations. This can be seen from educational institutions at all levels, up to and including the organisms that exist to promote so-called 'high culture' in all fields of science and technology. (*SPN* p.10)

Here we begin to touch upon the institutional location of intellectuals: specifically and most obviously in the educational apparatus but also in relation to the state in general. The intellectuals have a general function in relation to the state in the organisation of hegemony. To locate this range of functions and effects, Gramsci first of all adds complexity to the traditional notion of the state and then goes on to describe why intellectuals are important:

What we can do, for the moment, is to fix two major superstructural 'levels': the one that can be called 'civil society', that is the ensemble of organisms commonly called 'private', and that of 'political society' or 'the State'. These two levels correspond on the one hand to the function of 'hegemony' which the dominant group exercises throughout society and on the other hand to that of 'direct domination' or command exercised through the State and 'juridicial' government. The functions in question are precisely organisational and connective. The intellectuals are the dominant group's 'deputies' exercising the subaltern functions of social hegemony and political government. These comprise:

1 The 'spontaneous' consent given by the great masses of the population to the general direction imposed on social life by the dominant fundamental group; this consent is 'historically' caused by the prestige (and consequent confidence) which the dominant group enjoys because of its position and function in the world of production.

2 The apparatus of state coercive power which 'legally' enforces discipline on those groups who do not 'consent' either actively or passively. This apparatus is, however, constituted for the whole of society in anticipation of moments of crisis of command and direction when spontaneous consent has failed.

This way of posing the problem has as a result a considerable extension of the concept of intellectual, but it is the only way which enables one to reach a

concrete approximation of reality. It also clashes with preconceptions of caste. The function of organising social hegemony and state domination certainly gives rise to a particular division of labour and therefore to a whole hierarchy of qualifications in some of which there is no apparent attribution of directive or organisational functions.
(*SPN* pp.12-13)

v The State

This brings us directly to the question of the state. As we have seen above, Gramsci distinguishes two specific realms within the state: that of *civil society* – 'the ensemble of organisms commonly called "private"' – and that of *political society* – or the state apparatuses of administration, law, services etc., in the traditional sense of the term. The former realm – civil society – is crucial for Gramsci's concept of hegemony; it is the realm of consent, of 'free will', etc., whereas the realm of *political society* is that of coercion, force and intervention. This is an important distinction but, as Gramsci says, a 'methodological' and not an 'organic' (i.e. essential, permanent,) one. An historical comparison is provided by Gramsci to help define the specific nature of the modern state;

> A further criterion of research must be borne in mind, in order to emphasise the dangers inherent in the method of historical analogy as an interpretative criterion. In the ancient and medieval State alike, centralisation, whether political-territorial or social (and the one is merely a function of the other), was minimal. The State was, in a certain sense, a mechanical bloc of social groups, often of different race: within the circle of political-military compression, which was only exercised harshly at certain moments, the subaltern groups had a life of their own, institutions of their own, etc., and sometimes these institutions had State functions which made of the State a federation of social groups with disparate functions not subordinated in any way.... The modern State substitutes for the mechanical bloc of social groups their subordination to the active hegemony of the directive and dominant group, hence abolishes certain autonomies, which nevertheless are reborn in other forms, as parties, trade unions, cultural associations. The contemporary dictatorships legally abolish these new forms of autonomy as well, and strive to incorporate them within State activity: the legal centralisation of the entire national life in the hands of the dominant group becomes 'totalitarian'. (*SPN* p.54n)

What are the implications of this more complex and active modern structure of the state?

> ...in the case of the most advanced States... 'civil society' has become a very complex structure and one which is resistant to the catastrophic 'incursions' of the immediate economic element (crises, depressions, etc.). The superstructures of civil society are like the trench-systems of modern warfare. In war it would sometimes happen that a fierce artillery attack seemed to have destroyed the enemy's entire defensive system, whereas in fact it had only destroyed the outer perimeter; and at the moment of their advance and attack the assailants would find themselves confronted by a line of defence which was still effective. The same thing happens in politics, during the great economic crises. A crisis cannot give the attacking forces the ability to organise with lightning speed in time and in space; still less can it endow them with fighting spirit. Similarly, the defenders are not demoralised, nor do they abandon their positions, even among the ruins, nor do they lose faith in their own strength or their own future. (*SPN* p.235)

In the letters which Gramsci wrote from prison to his sister-in-law Tatiana, he set out his project as follows:

> This research will also concern the concept of the State, which is usually thought of as political society – i.e., a dictatorship or some other coercive apparatus used to control the masses in conformity with a given type of production and economy – and not as a balance between political society and civil society, by which I mean the hegemony of one social group over the entire nation, exercised through so-called private organizations like the Church, trade unions, or schools. (*Letters from Prison*, trans. and ed. Lynne Lawner, Cape, London, 1975, p.204)

Gramsci is attempting to maintain a balance between these distinct realms of the state: to avoid an overemphasis on either its coercive or its consensual elements. He insists that

> by 'State' should be understood not only the apparatus of government, but also the 'private' apparatus of 'hegemony' or civil society. (*SPN* p.261)

and goes on to criticize those forms of political analysis (Marxist, liberal or otherwise) which identify the state simply with the realm of government;

> We are still on the terrain of the identification of State and government — an identification which is precisely a representation of the economic-corporate form, in other words of the confusion between civil society and political society. For it should be remarked that the general notion of State includes elements which need to be referred back to the notion of civil

society (in the sense that one might say that State = political society + civil society, in other words hegemony protected by the armour of coercion). (*SPN* pp.262-3)

and further;

In politics the error occurs as a result of an inaccurate understanding of what the State (in its integral meaning: dictatorship + hegemony) really is. (*SPN* p.239)

Finally, he arrives at the following definition:

the State is the entire complex of practical and theoretical activities with which the ruling class not only justifies and maintains its dominance, but manages to win the active consent of those over whom it rules. (*SPN* p.244)

Clearly this is a much more expansive definition of the state than we may be accustomed to. This is primarily because of the importance of 'culture' in relation to hegemony. In the currency of contemporary debate, this question was posed as the 'ethical State', about which Gramsci had this to say:

In my opinion, the most reasonable and concrete thing that can be said about the ethical State, the cultural State, is this: every State is ethical in as much as one of its most important functions is to raise the great mass of the population to a particular cultural and moral level, a level (or type) which corresponds to the needs of the productive forces for development, and hence to the interests of the ruling classes. The school as a positive educative function, and the courts as a repressive and negative educative function, are the most important State activities in this sense: but, in reality, a multitude of other so-called private initiatives and activities tend to the same end — initiatives and activities which form the apparatus of the political and cultural hegemony of the ruling classes. (*SPN* p.258)

Elaborating these ideas, Gramsci suggests that

In reality, the State must be conceived of as an 'educator', in as much as it tends precisely to create a new type or level of civilisation. Because one is acting essentially on economic forces, reorganising and developing the apparatus of economic production, creating a new structure, the conclusion must not be drawn that superstructural factors should be left to themselves, to develop spontaneously, to a haphazard and sporadic

> germination. The State, in this field, too, is an instrument of 'rationalisation', of acceleration... It operates according to a plan, urges, incites, solicits, and 'punishes'; for, once the conditions are created in which a certain way of life is 'possible', then 'criminal action or omission' must have a punitive sanction, with moral implications, and not merely be judged generically as 'dangerous'. The Law is the repressive and negative aspect of the entire positive, civilising activity undertaken by the State. The 'prize-giving' activities of individuals and groups, etc., must also be incorporated in the conception of the Law; praiseworthy and meritorious activity is rewarded, just as criminal actions are punished (and punished in original ways, bringing in 'public opinion' as a form of sanction). (*SPN* p.247)

What is at stake in these complex and diverse functions of the modern state?

> Government with the consent of the governed - but with this consent organised, and not generic and vague as it is expressed in the instant of elections. The State does have and request consent, but it also 'educates' this consent, by means of the political and syndical associations; these, however, are private organisms, left to the private initiative of the ruling class. (*SPN* p.259)

Gramsci insists that this is not a neutral process. If the state organises and coheres the various elements of hegemony, it does so in a directed and directive way and towards a *particular* form of hegemony:

> The revolution which the bourgeois class has brought into the conception of law, and hence into the function of the State, consists especially in the will to conform (hence ethicity of the law and of the State). The previous ruling classes were essentially conservative in the sense that they did not tend to construct an organic passage from the other classes into their own, i.e. to enlarge their class sphere 'technically' and ideologically: their conception was that of a closed caste. The bourgeois class poses itself as an organism in continuous movement, capable of absorbing the entire society, assimilating it to its own cultural and economic level. The entire function of the State has been transformed; the State has become an 'educator', etc. (*SPN* p.260)

We have seen that from the general concept of culture Gramsci moves through the various theoretical tools and empirical resources for the analysis of culture: through hegemony, common-sense, ideology, consent and the state. Using these concepts he is able to deconstruct apparent unities and locate forces at work where we may not have noticed them: not just at the 'centre' of the political stage but also at the unnoticed cultural and ideological 'edges'. If he was asked why this was important, Gramsci would reply:

> On the ideological front...the defeat of the auxiliaries and the minor hangers-on is of all but negligible importance. Here it is necessary to engage battle with the most eminent of one's adversaries. (*SPN* p.433)

2 Hegemony and ideology in Gramsci

Chantal Mouffe

1 Economism and ideology

The theory of ideology was for a long time one of the most neglected areas of the marxist analysis of society. Yet this is a key area involving some extremely important issues which are not only theoretical but also political. It is vital, therefore, to attempt to understand the nature of those obstacles which have hindered the formulation of a theory which offers an adequate explanation of the significance and role of ideology, since it is no exaggeration to say that these have constituted the main impediment to the development of marxism, both as a theory and as a political movement.

At first sight the answer seems fairly simple. The various obstacles all seem in effect to proceed from the unique phenomenon which a vast body of contemporary literature has termed *economism*. However, the apparent obvious simplicity of the term hides a whole series of problems which begin to emerge as soon as one attempts a rigorous definition of its specificity and extent. Although it is clear that all forms of economism imply a misrecognition of the distinct autonomy of politics and ideology, this generic definition is inadequate, as it gives rise to two possible spheres of ambiguity. The first stems from the fact that the notion of the economic is indeed ambiguous and far from being clear itself (it is not clear for example, what is the relative importance attributed to the forces of production and the relations of production in this area). The second is the result of the vagueness and imprecision characterising the mechanism of the subordination of politics and ideology to economics, since this is always defined resorting to purely allusive metaphors, ('subordination', 'reduction', 'reflexion'). In this way one is left with the possibility of the existence of complex forms of economism which are not easy to detect since they do not appear as such at first sight....

Source: C. Mouffe (ed), *Gramsci and Marxist Theory*, Routledge and Kegan Paul, 1979, chapter 5.

> ... Antonio Gramsci must surely be the first to have undertaken a complete and radical critique of economism, and it is here that his main contribution to the marxist theory of ideology lies. It is the object of this article, therefore, to analyse Gramsci's contribution within this perspective.... I will attempt to show how the gramscian conception of *hegemony* involved, *in the practical state,* the operation of an anti-reductionist problematic of ideology. I shall go even further and maintain that it is this whole anti-reductionist conception of ideology which is the actual condition of *intelligibility* of Gramsci's conception of hegemony, and that the difficulties encountered in the interpretation of this conception stem from the fact that this anti-reductionist problematic has not so far been stressed....

2 Gramsci and hegemony

The concept of hegemony first appeared in Gramsci's work in 1926 in *Notes on the Southern Question*. It was introduced in the following way:

> The Turin communists posed concretely the question of the 'hegemony of the proletariat': i.e. of the social basis of the proletarian dictatorship and the workers' State. The proletariat can become the leading *(dirigente)* and the dominant class to the extent that it succeeds in creating a system of alliances which allows it to mobilise the majority of the working population against capitalism and the bourgeois State. In Italy, in the real class relations which exist there, this means to the extent that it succeeds in gaining the consent of the broad peasant masses. [*Selections from Political Writings 1921-26 (SPW)* p.443]

This work marked a step forward in Gramsci's thought. Naturally he had understood the importance of an alliance with the peasantry before 1926, since already in 1919, in an article entitled 'Workers and Peasants', he had insisted on the role which the peasants had to play in the proletarian revolution. It was in his *Notes on the Southern Question,* however, that he was to put the question of this alliance in terms of hegemony for the first time and to stress the political, moral and intellectual conditions which were necessary to bring this about. Hence he insisted, for example, on the fact that the working class had to free itself entirely of corporatism in order to be capable of winning over the Southern intellectuals to its cause, since it was through them that it would be able to influence the mass of the peasantry. The existence of an intellectual and moral dimension in the question of hegemony was already something typical of Gramsci and was later to take on its own importance. However, we are still at the stage of the leninist conception of hegemony seen as the leadership of the proletariat over the peasantry, that is to say that it was political leadership which constituted the essential element of this conception in view of the fact that hegemony was thought of in terms of a *class alliance*. It is only later in the *Prison Notebooks* that hegemony in its typically gramscian sense is to be found, and here it becomes the indissoluble union of political leadership and intellectual and moral leadership, which clearly goes beyond the idea of a simple class alliance.

The problematic of hegemony is to be found right from the first of the *Prison Notebooks*, but with an important innovation: Gramsci no longer applied it only to the *strategy* of the proletariat, but uses it to think of the practices of the ruling classes in gener ..

> The following historical and political criterion is the one on which research must be based: a class is dominant in two ways, that is to say it is dominant and ruling. It rules the allied classes and dominates the opposing classes. [*Prison Notebooks (PN)*p.57]

There is no doubt that in mentioning the direction of the allied classes Gramsci is referring here to hegemony, and there are innumerable statements to this effect throughout the *Prison Notebooks*. For example, a few pages further on in the same *Notebook* 1, in his examination of the role of the Jacobins in the French Revolution, he declares:

> not only did they organise a bourgeois government, i.e. make the bourgeoisie the dominant class – they did more. They created the bourgeois State, made the bourgeoisie into the leading, hegemonic class of the nation, in other words gave the new State a permanent basis and created the compact modern French nation. [*PN*, p.79]

He indicates that it was by forcing the bourgeoisie to overcome its corporatist nature that the Jacobins managed to make it a hegemonic class. They in fact forced it to widen its class interests and to discover those interests which it had in common with the popular sectors, and it was on this basis that they were able to put themselves in command and to lead those sectors into the struggle. Here, therefore, we find once more the opposition between corporatist and hegemonic classes encountered in *Notes on the Southern Question*, but this time it is applied to the bourgeoisie. Gramsci had in fact begun to understand that the bourgeoisie had also needed to ensure itself popular support and that the political struggle was far more complex than had ever been thought by reductionist tendencies, since it did not consist in a simple confrontation between antagonistic classes but always involved complex relations of forces.

Gramsci analyses the relations of forces in all societies and studies the transition from a corporate to a hegemonic stage in a fundamental passage in *Notebook* 4 [*PN* pp.180-3]. He begins by distinguishing three principal levels at which the relations of forces exist:

1 the relation of social forces linked to the structure and dependent on the degree of development of the material forces of production;
2 the relation of political forces, that is to say the degree of consciousness and organisation within the different social groups;
3 the relation of military forces which is always, according to Gramsci, the decisive moment.

In his analysis of the different moments of political consciousness he distinguished three more degrees:

a the *primitive economic* moment in which the consciousness of a group's own professional interests are expressed but not as yet their interests as a social class;
b the *political economic* moment which is the one in which the consciousness of class interests is expressed, but only at an economic level;
c the third moment is that of *hegemony*, 'in which one becomes aware that one's own corporate interests, in their present and future development, transcend the corporate limits of the purely economic class, and can and must become the interests of other subordinate groups too.' [ibid] For Gramsci this is where the specifically political moment is situated, and it is characterised by ideological struggle which attempts to forge unity between economic, political and intellectual objectives, 'placing all the questions around which the struggle rages on a "universal," not a corporate level, thereby creating the hegemony of a fundamental social group over a series of subordinate ones' [ibid].

This text (which was to be reworked by Gramsci into its definitive form two years later in *Notebook* 13) is, I believe, one of the key texts for an understanding of the gramscian conception of hegemony and it is surprising that until now little importance has been attached to it. It is here in fact that Gramsci sets out a very different conception of hegemony from the one found in *Notes on the Southern Question*, since here it is no longer a question of a simple political alliance but of a complete fusion of economic, political, intellectual and moral objectives which will be brought about by one fundamental group and groups allied to it *through the intermediary of ideology* when an ideology manages to 'spread throughout the whole of society determining not only united economic and political objectives but also intellectual and moral unity.' [*PN*, pp.180-5] From *Notebook* 4 the leninist conception of hegemony is doubly enriched: firstly its extension to the bourgeoisie and then the addition of a new and fundamental dimension (since it is through this that unity at the political level will be realised), that of intellectual and moral direction. It was only later that Gramsci was to develop all the implications of this enrichment, but from *Notebook* 4 onwards hegemony does assume its specifically gramscian dimension. It is therefore already possible on the basis of what has so far been discussed, to advance a tentative initial definition of a *hegemonic class*: it is a class which has been able to articulate the interests of other social groups to its own by means of ideological struggle. This, according to Gramsci, is only possible if this class renounces a strictly corporatist conception, since in order to exercise leadership it must genuinely concern itself with the interests of those social groups over which it wishes to exercise hegemony – 'obviously the fact of hegemony presupposes that one takes into account the interests and the tendencies of the groups over which hegemony will be exercised, and it also presupposes a certain equilibrium, that is to say that the hegemonic groups will make some sacrifices of a corporate nature [*Quaderni,* vol 1 p.461]..

Concerning the methods by which a class can become hegemonic, Gramsci distinguishes two principal routes: the first is that of transformism and the second is that of expansive hegemony. Let us first take *transformism.* This is the method by which the Moderate Party during the Risorgimento managed to secure its hegemony over the forces fighting for unification. Here what was involved was 'the gradual but continuous absorption, achieved by methods which varied in their effectiveness, of the active elements produced by allied groups – and even those which came from the antagonistic groups...'[*PN,* p. 59]. This naturally was only a bastard form of hegemony and the consensus obtained with these methods was merely a 'passive consensus.' In fact the process whereby power was taken was termed a 'passive revolution' by Gramsci, since the masses were integrated through a system of absorption and neutralisation of their interests in such a way as to prevent them from opposing those of the hegemonic class. Gramsci contrasted this type of hegemony through absorption by what he called successful hegemony, that is to say, *expansive hegemony.* This had to consist in the creation of an active, direct consensus resulting from the genuine adoption of the interests of the popular classes by the hegemonic class, which would give rise to the creation of a genuine 'national-popular will.' Unlike the passive revolution, in fact, where vast sectors of the popular classes are excluded from the hegemonic system, in an expansive hegemony the whole society must advance. This distinction of two methods of hegemony makes it possible to specify further the tentative definition of hegemony already put forward. In fact, if hegemony is defined as the ability of one class to articulate the interest of other social groups to its own, it is now possible to see that this can be done in two very different ways: the interests of these groups can either be articulated so as to neutralise them and hence to prevent the development of their own specific demands, or else they can be articulated in such a way as to promote their full development leading to the final resolution of the contradictions which they express.

These texts prompt a series of further observations. First, only a fundamental class (that is to say one which occupies one of the two poles in the relations of production of a determinate mode of production) can become hegemonic, as Gramsci unequivocally states: 'though hegemony is ethico-political, it must also be economic, must necessarily be based on the decisive function exercised by the leading group in the decisive nucleus of economic activity.' [*PN*, p.161] This condition not only restricts the possible number of hegemonic classes, it also indicates the possible limitations of any forms of hegemony. If in fact the exercise of hegemony involves economic and corporate sacrifices on the part of the aspiring leading class, the latter cannot, however, go so far as to jeopardise its basic interests. Sooner or later, therefore, the bourgeoisie comes up against the limitations of its hegemony, as it is an exploiting class, since its class interests must, at a certain level, necessarily clash with those of the popular classes. This, says Gramsci, is a sign that it has exhausted its function and that from then on 'the ideological bloc tends to crumble away; then "spontaneity" may be replaced by "constraint" in ever less disguised and indirect forms, culminating in outright police measures and *coups d'etat.*' *[PN* pp.60-1] Thus only the working class, whose interests coincide with the limitation of all exploitation, can be capable of successfully bringing about an expansive hegemony.

The most important aspect of Gramsci's hegemony still remains to be studied. This is the aspect of *intellectual and moral leadership* and the way in which this is achieved. In fact, all the points which have been raised could be entirely compatible with a conception of hegemony seen as alliance of classes. However, if Gramsci's hegemony were limited to political leadership it would only differ from Lenin's concept in that Gramsci does not restrict its use to the strategy of the proletariat, but also applies it to the bourgeoisie. Now it has been pointed out that the conception of hegemony is doubly enriched with respect to Lenin, as it also involves the addition of a new dimension which is inextricably linked to political direction, and that is intellectual and moral leadership. As a result, the establishing of hegemony became a phenomenon which went far beyond a simple class alliance. In fact, for Gramsci – and it is this which constitutes his originality – hegemony is not to be found in a purely instrumental alliance between classes through which the *class demands* of the allied classes are articulated to those of the fundamental class, with each group maintaining its own individuality within the alliance as well as its own ideology. According to him hegemony involves the creation of a *higher synthesis,* so that all its elements fuse in a 'collective will' which becomes the new protagonist of political action which will function as the protagonist of political action during that hegemony's entire duration. It is through ideology that this collective will is formed since its very existence depends on the creation of ideological unity which will serve as 'cement'. [*Quaderni* vol 2, p.1380]. This is the key to the indissoluble unity of the two aspects of gramscian hegemony, since the formation of the collective will and the exercise of political leadership depends on the very existence of intellectual and moral leadership....

If, therefore, we wish finally to manage to establish a comprehensive definition of Gramsci's conception of hegemony which accounts for its specificity and does not ignore any of its potentialities, it is important to be able to think theoretically the kind of relation established between its two components, that is, the secret of their unity, and to see what are the main characteristics resulting from this. To do this the following question needs to be answered: how can one forge genuine ideological unity between different social groups in such a way as to make them unite into a single political subject? To answer this problem it is of course necessary to discuss the conception of ideology which is present — both explicitly and implicitly — in Gramsci's work. It will then be shown how it is impossible to give a coherent account of the specificity of Gramsci's conception from the perspective of an economistic problematic of ideology.

3 Hegemony and ideology

The best point of departure for an analysis of the conception of ideology operating in the gramscian problematic of hegemony is to study the way in which he envisaged the process of the formation of a new hegemony. The notes referring to how a new collective will must be formed through moral and intellectual reform which will be the work of the 'Modern Prince' are, therefore, the most revealing on this subject. [*PN*, pp123-202] But first the few texts in which Gramsci explicitly sets out his conception of ideology must be discussed.

The problematic of ideology

Gramsci immediately places himself on entirely different ground from those viewing ideology as false consciousness or as a system of ideas, and he rebels against all epiphenomenalist conceptions which reduce it to mere appearances with no efficacy:

> The claim, presented as an essential postulate of historical materialism, that every fluctuation of politics and ideology can be presented and expounded as an immediate expression of the structure, must be contested in theory as primitive infantilism, and combated in practice with the authentic testimony of Marx, the author of concrete political and historical works. [*PN*, p.407]

According to Gramsci, the starting point of all research on ideology must be Marx's assertion that 'men gain consciousness of their tasks on the ideological terrain of the superstructures'. [*PN,* p.365] So that the latter, he declares, must be considered 'operating realities which possess efficacy' [*PN*, p.377], and if Marx sometimes terms them illusions it is only in a polemical sense in order to clearly specify their historical and transitory nature. Gramsci was to formulate his own definition of ideology as the terrain 'on which men move, acquire consciousness of their position, struggle'. [*PN*, p.377] Ideology, he declares, must be seen as a battle field, as a continuous struggle, since men's acquisition of consciousness through ideology will not come individually but always through the intermediary of the ideological terrain where two 'hegemonic principles' confront each other. [*Quaderni,* vol. 2, p.1236] ... One finds here, in fact, the idea that the subjects are not originally given but are always produced by ideology through a socially determined ideological field, so that subjectivity is always the product of social practice. This implies that ideology has a material existence and that far from consisting in an ensemble of spiritual realities, it is always materialised in practices.... In fact what Gramsci was trying to do was to think the role of subjectivity, but so as not to present it as the irruption of the individual consciousness into history. To achieve this he posits consciousness not as originally given but as the effect of the system of ideological relations into which the individual is inserted. Thus it is ideology which creates subjects and makes them act.

Ideology as a practice producing subjects is what appears to be the real idea implicit in Gramsci's thoughts on the operative and active nature of ideology and its identification with politics....

Another very new aspect of the gramscian problematic of ideology is the importance which he attributes to the *material and institutional nature of ideological practice.* In effect Gramsci insists on the fact that this practice possesses its own agents, that is to say, the *intellectuals.* They are the ones in charge of elaborating and spreading organic ideologies, and they are the ones who will have to realise moral and intellectual reform. Gramsci classes the intellectuals into two main categories depending on whether they are linked to one of the two fundamental classes (organic intellectuals), or to classes expressing previous modes of production (traditional intellectuals). Apart from stressing the role of the intellectuals, Gramsci insists on the importance of the material and institutional structure for the elaboration and spreading of ideology. This is made up of different *hegemonic apparatuses:* schools, churches, the entire media and even architecture and the names of the streets. This ensemble of apparatuses is termed the *ideological structure* of a dominant class by Gramsci, and the level of the superstructure where ideology is produced and diffused is called *civil society.* This constitutes the ensemble of 'private' bodies through which the political and social hegemony of a social group is exercised.

It is now obvious that we are far from the economistic problematic of ideology and that Gramsci is clearly situated on a different terrain. What is quite new in him is the awareness of the material nature of ideology and of the fact that it constitutes a practice inscribed in apparatuses which plays an indispensable practical-social role in all societies. He intuited the fact that this practice consists in the production of subjects, but he did not quite manage to formulate this theoretically. Besides, one should never forget that all these new ideas are expressed by Gramsci in an ambiguous form which is now outdated.... In any case, Gramsci never set out to elaborate a theory of ideology and his thought is not presented in a systematic way. Having said all this, however, it does nevertheless seem possible to assert that Gramsci's problematic anticipated Althusser in several respects: the material nature of ideology, its existence as the necessary level of all social formations and its function as the producer of subjects are all implicit in Gramsci, although it was Althusser who was to be the first to formulate this conception in a rigorous fashion.

A non-reductionist conception

Gramsci's contribution to the marxist theory of ideologies, however, is not limited to his having shown that they were objective and operative realities, as real as the economy itself, and that they played a crucial role in all social formations. Such a conception, however, only definitively supersedes the first facet of economism and still leaves room for the possible existence of complicated forms of reductionism. Now Gramsci was not simply content to criticise the epiphenomenal conception as he went much further and queried the reductionist conception which made ideology a function of the class position of the subjects. There can be no doubt that it is here that the most important and original aspect of his contribution is to be found....

It must be admitted here that this is a much more difficult area, since Gramsci never presented the anti-reductionist problematic in an explicit fashion, although it does exist *in the practical state* in the way in which he conceived hegemony. This problematic must, therefore, be clearly brought out, and it must be shown that it provides the *actual condition of intelligibility* of Gramsci's hegemony. However, before embarking on a study of texts which will serve as points of reference, it is worth briefly recapitulating the three principles underlying the reductionist problematic of ideology, since this will make it easier to bring out the difference between Gramsci's conception and this one. The three principles are as follows:

1 all subjects are class subjects;
2 social classes have their own paradigmatic ideologies;
3 all ideological elements have a necessary class belonging.

Gramsci's opposition to the first principle emerges clearly at once. According to him the subjects of political action cannot be identified with social classes. As has already been seen, they are 'collective wills' which obey specifically formed laws in view of the fact that they constitute the political expression of hegemonic systems created through ideology. Therefore, the subjects (the social classes) which exist at the economic level, are not duplicated at the political level; instead, different 'inter class' subjects are created. This constitutes Gramsci's break with the first principle of reductionism and provides him with the necessary theoretical basis to enable him to think hegemony beyond a simple class alliance as the creation of a superior unity where there will be a fusion of the participant elements of the hegemonic bloc. We know that this fusion will be realised through ideology, but the question remains, how and on what basis? We have now, in effect, reached the point of having to answer our previously formulated question: how can genuine ideological unity between different social groups be created?

There are two possible solutions to the problem. The first is the only one which can be formulated within a reductionist problematic of ideology (as exemplified by principles 2 and 3). It consists in viewing this ideological unity as the imposition of the class ideology of the main group upon the allied groups. This leads one to define a hegemonic class as one which has been capable of creating ideological consensus with other groups on the basis of the role played by its own ideology as the dominant one, and to reduce the problematic of ideology to a mere phenomenon of ideological inculcation....

The second solution – the one to be found in Gramsci – does not consist in the imposition of the class ideology of one of the groups over the others. An analysis of the way in which Gramsci visualises the process leading to the constitution of a new hegemony through *intellectual and moral reform* will throw light on the subject.

As already previously mentioned, the importance of intellectual and moral reform lies in the fact that the hegemony of a fundamental class consists in the creation of a 'collective will' (on the basis of a common world-view which will serve as a unifying principle) in which this class and its allies will fuse to form a 'collective man':

> From this one can deduce the importance of the 'cultural aspect', even in practical (collective) activity. An historical act can only be performed by 'collective man', and this presupposes the attainment of a 'cultural-social' unity through which a multiplicity of dispersed wills, with heterogeneous aims, are welded together with a single aim, on the basis of an equal and common conception of the world. [*PN*, p.348].

The creation of a new hegemony, therefore, implies the transformation of the previous ideological terrain and the creation of a new world-view which will serve as a unifying principle for a new collective will. This is the process of ideological transformation which Gramsci designates with the term 'intellectual and moral reform'. What is important now is to see how this process is envisaged by Gramsci. The two following passages are extremely significant in this context:

> What matters is the criticism to which such an ideological complex is subjected by the first representatives of the new historical phase. This criticism makes possible a process of differentiation and change in the relative weight that the elements of the old ideologies used to possess. What was previously secondary and subordinate, or even incidental, is now taken to be primary – becomes the nucleus of a new ideological and theoretical complex. The old collective will dissolves into its contradictory elements since the subordinate ones develop socially... [*PN*, p.195]

> How, on the other hand should this historical consciousness, proposed as autonomous consciousness, be formed? How should everyone choose and combine the elements for the constitution of such an autonomous consciousness? Will each element imposed have to be repudiated *a priori*? It will have to be repudiated inasmuch as it is imposed, but not in itself, that is to say that it will be necessary to give it a new form which is specific to the given group. [*Quaderni*, vol. 2, p.1875]

Here Gramsci indicates extremely clearly that intellectual and moral reform does not consist in making a clean sweep of the existing world-view and in replacing it with a completely new and already formulated one. Rather, it consists in a process of transformation (aimed at producing a new form) and of rearticulation of existing ideological elements. According to him, an ideological system consists in a particular type of articulation of ideological elements to which a certain 'relative weight' is attributed. The objective of ideological struggle is not to reject the system and all its elements but to rearticulate it, to break it down to its basic elements and then to sift through past conceptions to see which ones, with some changes of content, can serve to express the new situation. Once this is done the chosen elements are finally rearticulated into another system.

It is obvious that viewed in this way moral and intellectual reform is incomprehensible within a reductionist problematic which postulates the existence of paradigmatic ideologies for each social class, and the necessary class-belonging of all ideological elements. If, in effect, one does accept the reductionist hypothesis, moral and intellectual reform can only amount to replacing one class ideology by another. In the case of the hegemony of the working class, therefore, the latter would have to extricate the social groups which it required as allies from the influence of bourgeois ideology and impose its own ideology upon them. In order to do this it would have to combat bourgeois ideology by totally rejecting all its elements since these would be intrinsically and irremediably bourgeois, and since the presence of one of these elements within socialist discourse would prove that working class ideology had been contaminated by bourgeois ideology; in this event ideological struggle would always be reduced to the confrontation of two closed and previously determined systems. This, of course, is not Gramsci's conception, and the information so far available already makes it possible to assert that his conception of ideology *cannot be reductionist* since in that case the way in which he visualises moral and intellectual reform would be totally incomprehensible.

What, then, is the conception of ideology developed in Gramsci's theory of hegemony? In order to clarify this it is first necessary to determine what kind of answers Gramsci gives to the following questions:

1 What constitutes the unifying principle of an ideological system?
2 How can one determine the class character of an ideology or of an ideological element?

... We know that according to Gramsci hegemony (which is only possible for a fundamental class) consists in the latter exercising a political, intellectual and moral role of leadership within a hegemonic system which is cemented by a common world-view (organic ideology). We also know that intellectual and moral leadership exercised by the hegemonic class does not consist in the imposition of the class ideology upon the allied groups. Time and time again Gramsci stresses the fact that every single hegemonic relation is necessarily 'pedagogic and occurs amongst the different forces of which it is composed.' [*PN* p.350] He also insists that in a hegemonic system there must exist democracy between the ruling group and the ruled groups. This is also valid at the ideological level, of course, and it implies that this common world-view unifying the hegemonic bloc is really the organic expression of the whole bloc (and here we have the explanation of the chief meaning of the term 'organic ideology'). This world-view will therefore include ideological elements from varying sources, but its unity will stem from its articulating principle which will always be provided by the hegemonic class. Gramsci calls this articulating principle a *hegemonic principle*. He never defines this term very precisely, but it seems that it involves a system of values the realisation of which depends on the central role played by the fundamental class at the level of the relations of production. Thus the intellectual and moral direction exercised by a fundamental class in a hegemonic system consists in providing the articulating principle of the common world-view, the value system to which the ideological elements coming from the other groups will be articulated in order to form a unified ideological system, that is to say an organic ideology. This will always be a complex ensemble whose contents can never be determined in advance since it depends on a whole series of historical and national factors and also on the relations of forces existing at a particular moment in the struggle for hegemony. It is, therefore, by their articulation to a hegemonic principle that the ideological elements acquire their class character which is not intrinsic to them. This explains the fact that they can be 'transformed' by their articulation to another hegemonic principle. Ideological struggle in fact consists of a process of *disarticulation – rearticulation* of given ideological elements in a struggle between two hegemonic principles to appropriate these elements; it does not consist of the confrontation of two already elaborated, closed world-views. Ideological ensembles existing at a given moment are, therefore, the result of the relations of forces between the rival hegemonic principles and they undergo a perpetual process of transformation.

It is now possible to answer our two questions:

1 The unifying principle of an ideological system is constituted by the hegemonic principle which serves to articulate all the other ideological elements. It is always the expression of a fundamental class.
2 The class character of an ideology or of an ideological element stems from the hegemonic principle which serves as its articulating centre.

However, we are still a long way from having solved all the problems. There remains for example the problem of the nature of those ideological elements which do not have a necessary class character. It is not clear what they express, and Gramsci does not give us an answer. But, in spite of this, it is possible to find a few very significant definite pointers to a solution. In a passage where he reflects on what will determine the victory of one hegemonic principle over another, Gramsci declares that a hegemonic principle does not prevail by virtue of its intrinsic logical character but rather when it manages to become a 'popular religion' [*Quaderni* vol. 2 p.1084] What are we supposed to understand by this? Elsewhere Gramsci insists that a class wishing to become hegemonic has to 'nationalise itself,' [*PN*, p.241] and further on he declares:

> the particular form in which the hegemonic ethico-political element presents itself in the life of the state and the country is 'patriotism' and 'nationalism', which is 'popular religion', that is to say it is the link by means of which the unity of leaders and led is effected. [*Quaderni* p. 1084]

In order to understand what Gramsci means it is necessary to relate all these statements to his conception of the 'national-popular'. Although this conception is not fully formulated, it plays an important role in his thought. For Gramsci everything which is the expression of the 'people-nation' is 'national-popular.' [*PN,* pp.421ff] A successful hegemony is one which manages to create a 'collective national-popular will', and for this to happen the dominant class must have been capable of articulating to its hegemonic principle all the national-popular ideological elements, since it is only if this happens that it (the class) appears as the representative of the general interest. This is why the ideological elements expressing the 'national-popular' are often at stake in the fierce struggle between classes fighting for hegemony. As regards all this Gramsci points out some changes of meaning undergone by terms like 'nationalism' and 'patriotism' as they are appropriated by different fundamental classes and articulated to different hegemonic principles. [*Quaderni,* vol. 2 p.1237]. He also stresses the role which those terms play as a link leading to the creation of the union between leaders and led and in providing a base for a popular religion.

It is now possible to understand Gramsci's statement in which he declares that a hegemonic principle asserts itself when it manages to become a popular religion. What he means is that what has to be chiefly at stake in a class's struggle for hegemony is the attempt to articulate to its discourse all national-popular ideological elements. This is how it can 'nationalise itself' [see, further, Laclau, 1977].

The conception of ideology found in the practical state in Gramsci's problematic of hegemony consists therefore of a practice which transforms the class character of ideological elements by the latter's articulation to a hegemonic principle differing from the one to which they are at present articulated. This assumes that these elements do not in themselves express class interests, but that their class character is conferred upon them by the discourse to which they are articulated and by the type of subject thus created....

Conclusion

In this article I have argued that in Gramsci's conception of hegemony one finds in the practical state a radically *anti-economistic* problematic of ideology and that it constitutes the condition of intelligibility of the specificity of his conception of hegemony. However, I am not claiming that all the problems of the marxist theory of ideology are solved by Gramsci – even in the practical state. In any case the conceptual tools which he had to use have been completely superseded, and nowadays we are equipped to deal with the problem of ideology in a far more rigorous fashion thanks to the development of disciplines such as linguistics and psycho-analysis. Nevertheless, Gramsci's contribution to the marxist theory of ideology must be considered of crucial importance for several reasons:

1 Gramsci was the first to stress the material nature of ideology, its existence as a necessary level of all social formations, its inscription in practices and its materialisation into apparatuses.
2 He broke away radically from the conception of ideology as false consciousness, i.e. a distorted representation of reality because it is determined by the place occupied by the subject in the relations of production, and he anticipated the conception of ideology as a practice producing subjects.
3 Finally, he also queried the general principle of reductionism which attributes a necessary class-belonging to all ideological elements.

As regards the first two points, Gramsci's thought has been taken up and thoroughly developed by Louis Althusser – although the latter reached the same point of view in quite a different way — and so his ideas have spread through the althusserian school. As regards his criticism of reductionism, however, it is unfortunate that his contribution has not been fully recognised as it is in this area that the theoretical potentialities of his thought urgently need developing. This is particularly so since the marxist theory of ideology has not yet managed to free itself entirely of the reductionist problematic and hence remains trapped by insidious forms of economism.

The topicality and importance which Gramsci's work has for marxist researchers working in the field of ideology lies in the fact that Gramsci's conception points the way to a possible solution to the most serious problem of marxist theory of ideology. The problem consists in superseding economism while at the same time adhering to the problematic of historical materialism. In fact once the elementary phase of ideology seen as an epiphenomenon has been superseded, marxist theory still has to face the following difficulty: how to show to what extent ideological practice actually has real autonomy and efficacity while still upholding the principle of the determination in the last instance by the economic. This is a problem which Althusser himself has not yet been capable of solving satisfactorily, and it is why he has recently been accused of economism [see Hirst 1976]. However, if his critics propose a solution which effectively resolves the problem of economism, this is done at the expense of abandoning historical materialism. In effect, by identifying economism with the thesis of the determination in the last instance by the economy, and by proposing the total autonomy of ideological practices as a solution, they call into question the basic tenets of historical materialism.

In Gramsci's work the outline of another kind of solution to the problem can be found and it is worth analysing it before deciding whether the solution to the problem of economism is really impossible within the theoretical framework of marxism. As presented here the problematic of hegemony contains in the practical state the broad outlines of a possible articulation between the relative autonomy of ideology and the determination in the last instance by the economy. In fact the conception of ideology brought out by Gramsci's conception of hegemony attributes real autonomy to it, since the ideological elements which ideological practice aims at transforming do not possess a necessary class-belonging and hence do not constitute the ideological representation of interests existing at the economic level. On the other hand, however, this autonomy is not incompatible with the determination in the last instance by economy, since the hegemonic principles serving to articulate these elements are always provided by the fundamental classes. Here, of course, I am only designating the area where a solution might be found, and if work is to be done in this direction there are a large number of problems still to be solved before it will be possible to formulate a theoretical solution. It does nevertheless seem to be an area which ought to prove fruitful....

References

GRAMSCI, A., *Selections from Political Writings, 1921-26,* ed. and trans. Q. Hoare, Lawrence and Wishart, 1978.

GRAMSCI, A., *Selections from the Prison Notebooks,* ed. and trans. Q. Hoare and G. Nowell-Smith, Lawrence and Wishart, 1971.

GRAMSCI, A., *Quaderni dal Carcere,* ed. V. Gerratana, Turin, Einaudi, 1975.

HIRST, P. Q., 'Althusser and the Theory of Ideology', *Economy and Society,* vol. 5, no. 4, 1976.

LACLAU, E., *Politics and Ideology in Marxist Theory,* New Left Books, 1977.

3 Bourgeois hegemony in Victorian Britain

Robert Gray

This paper analyses the relationships between the economically dominant bourgeoisie, ideology and the state during the nineteenth century, in terms of the concepts of hegemony and the power bloc, formulated by Gramsci (1971) and developed by Poulantzas. (1975).... I follow Thompson (1965) and Poulantzas (1967) in locating hegemony in the bourgeoisie, and amplify this thesis in a discussion of the nature of the Victorian ruling class, relations among its fractions, and the 'hegemonizing' practices through which consent was organized, both among the allied fractions constituting the dominant power bloc and in their relations to the classes they ruled.

One major theoretical difficulty should be noted at the outset. It is extremely difficult to avoid formulations that suggest a conspiratorial and mechanistic view of the class struggle. This reflects limitations to the concepts and language available to a British Marxist historian in the 1970s. Thus it is now widely recognized as a general principle that Marxism is not a 'conspiracy thesis'; that politics and ideology cannot be reduced to mere instruments of the subjective will of the dominant class, and that classes are not heavenly hosts to be 'marshalled, sent on manoeuvres, and marched up and down whole centuries'. (Thompson, 1965, p.357) But it is not easy to move from these general caveats to specific analyses without adopting formulations that personify classes; the implicit model of class struggle is a boxing match or a game of chess between two rival class-subjects. I certainly would not claim to resolve this problem; we probably lack the concepts and language to do so. But I do want to suggest that Gramsci provides an indispensable point of approach. The necessary theoretical advances will come from deploying the resources he provides in concrete historical research, with a conscious effort to purge conspiratorial and mechanistic formulations from the vocabulary of Marxist analysis.

Source: Jon Bloomfield (ed) *Class, Hegemony and Party,* Lawrence and Wishart, 1977, pp.73-90

Characteristics of the Victorian bourgeoisie

Nineteenth-century capitalism was competitive capitalism, and this has important implications for the nature of its ruling class. Industrial, commercial and banking capital were separately owned, in contrast to their merger into finance capital during the twentieth-century monopoly era; and each fraction was itself composed of many competing rival capitals, as yet little affected by concentration and centralization. Big landowners still constituted either a separate class or a very distinctive fraction.

The competitive industrial capitalism of the period was, moreover, one of family businesses and private partnerships, with a localized basis (decreasingly so from the 1880s, but still significantly so – especially as compared to the more newly industrialized countries of Germany and the USA – down to 1914). Even quite big industrialists had strong local roots in the factory towns of the North and Midlands. Banking capital, on the other hand, was probably growing in importance, as overseas investment grew, and gathered around itself a 'rentier' bourgeoisie. Concentrated especially in London and the southern counties (and in Scotland in Edinburgh), this fraction diverged in attitudes and probably at times in interests from industrial capital. It had close links with the central State apparatus (located of course in the capital city), perhaps because direct day-to-day influence on government was vital to its interests (e.g. imperialist intervention in support of bondholders).

This schematic characterization of the Victorian ruling class breaks with the conventional wisdom of contemporaries, and many historians, who saw society as divided into an 'aristocracy', 'middle classes' and 'working classes'. The 'middle classes' embraced both sections of the dominant bourgeoisie and sections of the 'middle strata' (shopkeepers, tradesmen, many professional practitioners, white-collar employees, etc.). The prevalence of this notion is a measure of the success with which such strata were subordinated to bourgeois hegemony – to the point where the real differences in class position were obscured – but also a measure of the economic realities which made this possible: the predominance of local-based businesses, whose owners were not too remote from a broader base of medium and small 'petty bourgeois' businessmen. This means that to identify members of the ruling class is often a complicated matter, demanding close analysis of a range of sources for the local formation under study. There was also doubtless a good deal of individual movement between the top layers of the middle strata and the fringes of the ruling class. The distinction between the class positions of these groups is nonetheless a real one, whatever the limitations of our information about particular cases (an empirical difficulty which cannot be allowed to dictate the conceptual framework we adopt).

The relationship of the bourgeoisie to the landowners (I say, 'landowners' as a deliberately neutral descriptive term) also poses problems. To what extent can the landowners (whose position rested on the success of capitalist agriculture conducted by their tenant farmers, but increasingly also on other forms of investment) be seen as a separate class, as opposed to a fraction of the bourgeoisie? How real was their apparent antagonism to the urban-industrial bourgeoisie in the first half of the nineteenth century? Does their dominance over key sectors of the state and their indisputable wealth, social prestige and influence mean that they, rather than the owners of industrial capital, were the hegemonic fraction of the ruling class? The class determination of the landowners can perhaps be treated as an open question for the purposes of the present discussion;... what is important is to recognize their existence as a highly distinctive group, whose interests were strongly articulated and whose culture and values were in important respects different from those of the urban ruling class.

Finally, we must note the particular position and role of the ruling class intellectuals, those groups to be found exercising leadership at the head of the State apparatus and in the elaboration and reproduction of the dominant ideology. The term 'urban gentry' has been aptly applied to these groups. (Stedman Jones, 1971, part III) Particularly concerned with the administrative and ideological organization of society, they were to be found as members of statistical societies and Royal Commissions, writers and readers of the quarterly press, organizers of charity and social discipline. Drawn from the professions (though by no means every professional man could be placed in the category), from intellectually gifted protégés of the wealthy, or from established wealth whose owners could devote time (like Charles Booth) to 'social problems,' they played a crucial role in the organization of hegemony. Their social affinities and attitudes varied in ways which show a complex correspondence to the different bourgeois fractions; but they also, as is characteristic of intellectuals, had particular 'caste-like' modes of cohesion, and links with socially broader based intellectual strata; the definition of 'genteel' professional status and qualifications, and the associated transformation and growth of high prestige educational institutions, were important developments of the period, forming hierarchies of intellectuals, but at the same time fostering their cohesion on a 'professional' basis.

The power bloc

Most historians would agree that the late 1840s and early 50s saw an important shift in the economic, political and ideological relations in British society. The various accounts of this process have in common an emphasis on the establishment of stable relations of political and ideological domination in an industrial-urban society. This historically unprecedented transition was rendered more problematic by the fact that Britain was the first industrial nation; but this same peculiarity gave certain historic advantages to British capital. The early bourgeois revolution, and subsequent development of the State and relations of hegemony, limited the challenges to capitalism. The emerging working-class political tradition had a dynamic sense of class identity and interest, and a developing concern to theorize the experience of class exploitation; yet the early forms of socialism never displaced the dominance of a radical-democratic tradition.

The stabilization and diversification of the economy in the years after 1850 was an important precondition for political stabilization. But the crisis was clearly not 'purely economic' (no historical phenomenon ever is) and stabilization had political and ideological dimensions that were not just mechanical reflections of the economic shift. Stable class rule depended on the construction of a power bloc of allied dominant classes and fractions. In periods of 'organic crisis' the power bloc becomes unworkable (e.g. because it fails to represent newly important fractions of the bourgeoisie, such as industrial capital in the early nineteenth century, to mobilize the consent of new classes and strata, etc.) and tends to disintegrate;* the social instability of the second quarter of the century represents just such a crisis. In the power bloc constructed in the period of stabilization, landowners continued (despite the sharp antagonisms of the preceding decades, in whose diminution the solidarity of the 'propertied classes' against the Chartist threat had played a large part) to dominate important sectors of the State, 'as the *aristocratic representatives* of the bourgeoisie, of the industrial and commercial middle class'. [Marx, 1973, p.259]

State power thus presents the appearance of a kind of equilibrium. In the 1830s the new urban areas had gained parliamentary representation and the right to constitute ratepayer-controlled municipal corporations, to establish police forces controlled by watch committees, etc. Politics in such areas contained some popular elements, generally channelled by groups and parties representing the local bourgeoisie. (Local government was often the preserve of shopkeepers and tradesmen, who manifested a certain antagonism to the local ruling class, but were unable to use their electoral power to strike at its position.) Rural areas were still administered by gentry sitting on the magistrates' bench, and parliamentary representation was normally in the gift of the biggest of these landowners; politics there was not unlike what it had been in the eighteenth century. The landowners were strongly represented in party leadership and cabinets, whose formal political complexion was a range of loose and shifting Whig-Liberal and Liberal-Whig coalitions, until the

*For the concept of 'organic crisis' see Gramsci, 1971 pp.201-11

extension of the urban vote in 1867 led to a more clear-cut party system adapted to mass urban politics. 'Territorial influence', 'virtual representation' and 'a stake in the community' were pervasive political concepts. Put together, they amounted to the notion that the leading property-holders (whether gentry or merchants and industrialists) were the natural representatives of their communities, and that the political participation of other groups should be dependent on a properly rational social demeanour, as defined by their superiors (a notion modified, but not entirely overthrown, by the extension of the vote in 1867 to many urban workers, who were held to have a kind of corporate stake by virtue of saving in friendly societies, co-ops, etc.)

Hegemony in the power bloc

The effect of this political configuration was to reproduce capitalist relations, and to foster especially the expansion of industrial capital. The industrial bourgeoisie constituted the *hegemonic fraction* within the power bloc – that whose interests preponderate in the exercise of state power, and whose particular social relations figure in dominant ideological representations. This hegemonic position is not synonomous with the *governing fraction* (in this period partly landowners) which staffs the top levels of the State apparatus, or the groups which elaborate and reproduce dominant ideology (the leading intellectuals: in this case the 'urban gentry'). (Cf. Poulantzas, 1975, p.183) Hegemony should not be located in those groups which visibly exercise political and ideological leadership in society, but rather in the *effects* of dominant forms of political and ideological practice, the particular social relations they reproduce. The location of hegemony is historically problematic and may show complex shifts and displacements within the dominant class and its forms of political representation.

It is therefore necessary to look in more detail at the ways in which the industrial bourgeoisie exerted hegemony over the power bloc and the State apparatus. Two important aspects of this should be mentioned. First, the pervasive power of bourgeois ideas about economic life and the absence of theoretically articulated alternatives. Various overlapping intellectual and literary networks produced administrative cadres strongly committed to utilitarianism and free trade, who staffed key new branches of the State apparatus. Moreover 'divinity and economics ran together' (Best, 1971 p.257) and the laws of political economy were closely entangled with moral, and often religiously sanctioned, norms of 'rational conduct'. The secularized prescriptions of utility and economic progress and the strong religious components of hegemonic ideology in practice reinforced each other; the utilitarians offered the only available techniques for dealing with the 'merely *business* side of the social arrangements'. A new notion of 'public opinion' – the influence of the élite press, the legitimizing functions of professional expertise, the political technique of the Royal Commission, whose proceedings could be stagemanaged and anyhow reflected unspoken shared assumptions – developed with the activities of utilitarian and Evangelical pressure-groups.

The terrain of the State and of public discussion and policy-making was thus re-shaped by the intellectuals of the industrial bourgeoisie;* the landowners, as the Whigs realized in 1832 and as Peel realized in the 1840s, had to adapt to this terrain. Their adaptation occurred at many levels, from the supremacy of vulgarized political economy and of the national goal of industrial progress, to the 'reform of manners' noted by many contemporaries and historians. While it is doubtful if 'Victorian middle-class' norms of conduct ever really captured the hearts of the landowners (or even of the urban bourgeoisie themselves) as a whole, there was a significant measure of external conformity to norms of domestic life and sexual morality, religious observance, and serious application to public service as the obligation of social privilege.

Secondly, the local character of much State power – including such key coercive organs as the police and the poor law – and the correspondingly local 'provincial' basis of industry make the composition of the central State apparatus a misleading guide; with the limited role of the State, 'hegemony over its historical development belongs to private forces, to civil society – which is "State" too', (Gramsci, 1971, p.261) and among these 'private forces' industrial capital dominated in the expanding urban areas. The power bloc of the third quarter of the nineteenth century rested on the local predominance of industrialists, merchants and bourgeois intellectuals in the towns, together with a measure of direct urban bourgeois representation in parliament and key branches of civil service, and ideological hegemony cemented by the institutions of 'informed public opinion'. The role of landowners in government and the state has to be set firmly in this context; 'let them govern, but let them be fit to govern', (cited in Best, 1971, p.242) as one industrialist put it, summing up in ten words the relation between hegemonic and governing fractions.

The power bloc should not be seen as monolithic. In every social formation the State apparatus has important internal contradictions, but also specific modes of cohesion as an apparatus. 'This unity ... is not established in a simple fashion, either by some kind of united act of will ..., or because the ... [hegemonic fraction] have got a physical stranglehold on the state-instrument as a whole.... It is rather established in a complex fashion, depending on the class contradiction, by means of a whole chain involving the subordination of certain apparatuses to others which particularly condense the power of the

*According to Gramsci every class has its own intellectuals, and the same may apply to fractions of classes: see Gramsci, 1971, pp.5-9.

hegemonic fraction; involving under-determinations, short-circuits and doublings-up between real power and formal power; shifts of apparatuses from the ideological field to the field of the repressive apparatus and vice versa; finally, significant changes within each apparatus itself'. (Poulantzas, 1975, p.164)

To establish the location of hegemony thus demands a close study of differences within the state apparatus and of relations between its branches. Such a study does not sustain Perry Anderson's thesis of a 'symbiotic fusion' of bourgeoisie and aristocracy, in which the bourgeoisie abandoned any claim to ideological hegemony; the features he notices – utilitarian empiricism, indifference to any global theory of society, the mystique of 'tradition' and the dominance of a narrowly commonsensical practicality – may rather be interpreted as measures of the depth and strength of the hegemony of industrial capital (Anderson, 1964).

Political parties (understood in a broad sense of the term) played a crucial part in hegemony over the State apparatus. The construction of viable power blocs does not emanate from a far-sighted plan elaborated by some secret committee of the dominant class; it is the effect of struggles between parties, which always represent *combinations* of classes and fractions (including some measure of representation of dominated classes and strata). *Its existence can never be taken for granted, as a datum of political life, but is reproduced through political struggle in every historical conjuncture. It is for this reason that it is in my view mystifying to write in ways that impute to classes and fractions a kind of individual subjectivity, as though they took decisions, adopted stategies, formed alliances, and so on in a unitary and un-problematic fashion; in effect, this treats parties – and hence the whole political and ideological level – as epiphenomenal, whereas in reality classes are constituted by class struggle, which always involves their representation in parties.† And party cleavages – whether within the power bloc or in the social formation as a whole – do not reflect class differences in a simple reductive fashion; parties are efficacious in so far as they have *some* support in *all* classes and fractions, and cohere partly through specifically ideological (in the nineteenth century often religious) differences and traditions.

*This is so even where the subordinate class is largely excluded from formal participation in the policy, as the British working class was before 1867. It was nevertheless still necessary to take account of its existence as a socio-political force — not least to prevent the recurrence of militant mass protests against its political exclusion. It is of course true that the extension of formal political rights brought about a qualitative change in the nature of the problem.

†This may occur, as implied in the previous note, by their representation in parties dominated by other classes; in this case the class struggle is still a political (i.e. party) struggle, with one class at a large – but never infinite – strategic advantage.

The term 'party' is here used in the broad sense of Gramsci, not in the more restricted sense of the formal party system. It is perhaps particularly those institutions and practices held to be 'outside politics', to stand above the struggle of formal parties (which are confined to the representative parts of the state) that condense the power of the hegemonic fraction. The State itself, Gramsci suggests, cements the power bloc under the hegemony of a particular class or fraction, and in this sense acts as a 'party' organizing the dominant class. (Gramsci, 1971, pp.206-7 and Poulantzas, 1978, p.98). The ideology of the bourgeois intellectuals was characterized by a disdain for the rough and tumble of party politics, and a belief that sound administration and public service (based of course on a sound knowledge of the indisputable 'laws' of political economy) stood 'above politics'; they thus constituted 'an élite of men of culture, who have the function of providing leadership of a cultural and general ideological nature for a great movement of interrelated parties (which in reality are fractions of one and the same organic party)'. [Gramsci, 1971, pp.149-50]

To see formal party differences as 'in reality fractions of one and the same organic party' is in no sense to reduce their importance. Hegemonic ideology had differentiated versions and interpretations, and was constantly argued out and re-formulated within the ruling class. The debate about factory legislation, for example, was at this level a debate around the bourgeois value of the integrity of the family, which was held to be threatened by the employment of women and children, and thus came into contradiction with the ideology of freedom of contract, including freedom to buy and sell female and child labour. A whole series of debates about the proper limits of public regulation – sanitation, housing, education, etc. – can be viewed in similar terms....

The power bloc should therefore not be seen as static, but as constantly re-constituted, modified, strengthened or undermined in party struggles.... The power bloc was therefore the result of party struggles, in which real antagonisms were at stake. The areas of 'aristocratic' domination were often challenged by political leaders claiming to speak for the dynamic urban society of free competition and industrial progress against hereditary privilege, patronage and corruption. Marx, perhaps with the idea that the historic mission of the bourgeoisie was to make a revolution on the French model lurking at the back of his mind, expected such antagonisms to be fought through to a conclusion, and thus greatly under-estimated the solidity and permanency of the power bloc whose lineaments he correctly discerned. For there can be no doubt that the continuing 'aristocratic' presence had objective advantages for the urban bourgeoisie. Bagehot's analysis of mass deference and the 'dignified part of the constitution' is often correctly cited in this context. But its significance did not lie merely in the 'deferential' support it attracted, but equally in the opposition it provoked from the radical workers and petty bourgeoisie, whose demagogic leadership by bourgeois politicians (the Anti-Corn Law League in the 1840s, the agitation for parliamentary reform in the 60s, Joseph Chamberlain in the 80s) helped cement Liberal hegemony over mass popular radicalism....

Hegemony and the subordinate classes

The period after c.1850 is generally seen as one during which the working class became less combative and less united, beginning to pursue limited interests within a society whose general framework was rarely questioned. This consent to capitalist relations was organized through a complex set of processes, which certainly cannot be reduced, as vulgarizations of the concept of hegemony would have it, to some notion of 'social control', or the unilateral imposition 'from above' of ideological uniformity. To talk of the 'organization of consent' implies a political practice ('hegemonization') through which diverse, and often potentially 'subversive,' ideological practices are subordinated and contained. Conversely, the adoption 'for reasons of submission and intellectual subordination' (Gramsci, 1971, p.327) of a language drawn from the ideological practice of the dominant class always implies a shift in the meanings of that language. Ideology is the 'lived relation between men and their world', (Althusser, 1969, p.251) and in a differentiated social formation can never be uniform. Hence there are contradictions within the practices which maintain the hegemony of the dominant class, and this hegemony should be seen as a dynamic and historically shifting set of relations, not as a static system of manipulative control.

Nor should we oversimplify the distinction between 'coercion' and 'consent'. As Gramsci himself emphasized, any form of hegemony presupposes particular relations of coercion, and vice versa; effective domination depends on a workable combination of 'voluntary' and 'coercive' relations. (Gramsci, 1971 pp. 80n, 263) One feature of the containment of working-class opposition in the 1830s and 40s was the extremely discriminating use of legal repression, often with considerable care to ensure the prior political isolation of its victims. Coercion itself may, moreover, have symbolic aspects, as the rituals of legal repression testify. No set of relations is ever 'purely' coercive, since all systems of coercion require at the very least effective hegemony over the personnel of the coercive organs themselves; the organization of consent is a precondition of stable rule even in fascist dictatorships. My emphasis on hegemony should not therefore be taken to imply the absence of force; indeed the growth of the state apparatus, including new repressive organs such as the police, was a feature of the period, which its liberal rhetoric should not be permitted to obscure.

Hegemony, then, should not be seen as reproduced solely through institutions of a self-evidently 'political' or 'ideological' character; the political and ideological are present in *all* social relations. (Poulantzas, 1975 p.21) Thus the most important aspect of hegemony over the working class (both in the nineteenth and twentieth centuries) is their forced habituation to the relations of industrial wage-labour, and the ideological practices involved in this process; the cycle of capitalist production reproduces the capitalist as capitalist and the wage-labourer as wage-labourer at the ideological, as well as economic, level. One aspect of the explosive class struggles before 1850 was the newness of factory employment, and the struggle to resist the real subordination of wage-labour to capital in the process of production itself, as opposed to the merely 'formal' subordination characteristic of domestic industry. In the 1850s the new mode of production was more firmly established; the possibility of transforming it seemed remote, and economic diversification and stabilization meant that visible advances, albeit of a highly sectional character, could be won by bargaining within the system. Capitalist production was a relatively fixed environment, to which all sections of the working class had, in varying ways, to adapt. And this adaptation, the necessary condition of individual survival, extended to areas of life-style, personal conduct, even in some cases religious belief and observance. The enormous relative strength of Victorian employers (even in trades with 'strong' craft unions by the standards of the time, still more so in unorganized sectors) accentuated the inherent despotism of industrial capital.

But it was not only at work that the bourgeoisie sought to produce an ideological environment to which workers had to adapt. One response to the social crisis of the 1830s and 40s was an 'evangelistic' (in both a specifically religious and general metaphorical sense of the term) drive to assert control over the urban masses. This is especially clear in the concern with education, whose ideological assumptions were stated with an explicitness that seems remarkable to anyone accustomed to the more veiled terms of such discussions nowadays (this 'frankness' is presumably related to the self-confidence of the bourgeoisie at a period when capitalism could be seen as synonymous with economic progress). Social unrest was seen as the result of indiscipline, the lack of moral control by social superiors, and 'ignorance'. Remedies were believed to include poor law reform, the beginnings of elementary education, religious evangelism, propaganda against dangerous 'economic heresies', the fostering of more acceptable expressions of working-class self help (friendly societies, co-ops, etc.) and of safe forms of 'rational recreation'.

In all these activities the urban gentry were very much to the fore. Common to all of them was the attempt to propagate an ideology common to the ruling class as a whole, but also with certain traits specific to the urban gentry. Economic, moral and religious concerns were fused into a single image of urban social danger; iron laws, whether of calvinist theology or classical economics, dictated discipline and restraint, the slightest backsliding would lead to disaster, and individual weakness could spread contagiously to demoralize society and reverse the precarious conquest of scarcity achieved through industriousness and foresight. To convince the working class of the truth of this, through varying forms of persuasion and coercion, was the common theme of a range of bourgeois endeavours in the urban community. The urban gentry were distinguished by the rigour with which they elaborated this outlook (e.g. they agitated against dilutions of the 1834 poor law, while other bourgeois groups adopted a more pragmatic attitude). The second distinctive feature is a paternalistic colouring, the attempt to reproduce in urban society the harmonious social hierarchy supposed, in a highly ideological view of social conflict, to characterize a lost rural world. Both features reflect their social location as bourgeois intellectuals, distanced from the realities of industrial production. Hence, perhaps, the centrality of the family, where ideologies of subordination and control (over women, children and servants) could be acted out, as they could not in the world of industrial production. Conversely, the moral decay of the working class was seen above all in terms of its deficient patterns of family life, the apparent absence of values of domesticity, family responsibility, thrift and accumulation. The concern with the urban environment reflected a preoccupation, not with bad conditions as such, but with their disintegrating effect on family relations (as, for example, in the 1884 Royal Commission on Housing where incest in overcrowded dwellings is a recurring preoccupation).

The urban gentry sought, then, to resolve the problems of capitalist society by a network of direct or indirect controls designed to reform the individual behaviour of the working class. During the crisis of the 1830s and 40s this was pursued with an almost hysterical evangelism. Its success was limited until the crisis period ended, but from the 1850s changes in the working class (the emergence of the labour aristocracy) could be read as comforting signs of 'progress', and evangelical zeal was tempered by social complacency.

Does this evangelical re-structuring of the urban community represent the successful imposition of bourgeois values? It is often so treated. But to see it like that is to read contemporary statements at face value, and to reduce hegemony to the subjective intentions of members of the ruling class, or to a functionalist problematic of 'social control'. The most effective ideological influences came, not from the evangelical social reform that sought to eradicate working-class identity altogether, but from more complex and indirect agencies, through which fragments of dominant ideology were 'spontaneously' reproduced by members of the working class. Those programmes through which a group seeks to influence ways of thinking and acting are not necessarily the most adequate or effective forms of hegemony (though they may be extremely important to the cohesion and morale of the ruling class itself, as they were in this case): nor should behaviour that apparently corresponds to dominant ideology be read at face value as a direct product of ruling class influence.

Viable forms of hegemony had to take account of the situation and aspirations of the working class, especially of its organized and articulate sections: the labour aristocracy. Thus behaviour corresponding to such central values as 'thrift' and 'respectability' was certainly articulated and rationalized in the terms of dominant ideology, but it has still to be seen in relation to the distinctive social experience of different groups. Thrift was linked to survival under the conditions of life confronting skilled labour; and self-help could take collective forms. Those labour aristocratic groups most likely to adopt such behaviour patterns were also most resistant to any form of patronage and direct control (indeed this independence was part of the meaning they attached to the values of 'respectability'). As the signs of a striving for 'respectability' among higher-paid workers were read as indicating social harmony and progress, so it became apparent that the distinctive identity of the working class could not simply be eradicated, but that the reproduction of dominant values rested on a more subtle process of negotiated re-definition, in which the conditional independence of working-class institutions came to be recognized. The ideological function of the law is apparent in discussions about such institutions as friendly societies and trade unions; the legal framework defined the boundaries of those forms of 'respectable' working-class behaviour considered legitimate.

Because bourgeois hegemony involved negotiated re-definitions of values and the emergence of distinctive versions of the dominant ideology, and because that ideology could give no convincing account of aspects of real social experience, there were important tensions and contradictions in ideological relations between the classes. The independence of the labour aristocracy was only grudgingly and suspiciously accepted. Many institutions were rejected by their intended upper working-class clientele because of their heavy management by patrons, as, for instance, were the mechanics' institutes; others, like the working men's clubs, had sharp internal struggles to throw off patronage. Even those institutions that were strongly approved and assiduously fostered had a side the bourgeoisie found impenetrable, bewildering and disturbing (saving for funerals, ritual and conviviality in friendly societies). The extent to which working people could be trusted to run such institutions, and the terms on which they should be licensed to do so, is a main theme in official enquiries of the period.

Class tensions keep breaking through the rhetoric of 'respectability'. Class consciousness could be contained and eroded, but never eradicated. The high wages that underpinned the pursuit of 'respectability' depended on the organization and struggle of the craft unions. Trade unionism always drew a sharp line between the outlook of the labour aristocracy and that of their social superiors. Attempts by both sides to define 'acceptable' forms of trade unionism always proved exceedingly fragile.

Hegemony over the working class should therefore not be seen in terms of a re-moulding of the 'respectable' skilled strata in the bourgeois image. It arose from a complex set of social relations, in which bourgeois reform aimed at imposing social discipline was one, but only one, element. It would be equally true to say that relations of hegemony involved the imposition *on the bourgeoisie* of some form of representation, at all levels of social practice, of working-class interests (especially, but not exclusively, those of the labour aristocracy). When bourgeois intellectuals like Alfred Marshall praised the enlightened moderation of the 'largest and best managed unions' this was something the bourgeoisie had been *forced* to accept, and to legitimize through shifts in its ideology, not a cunning scheme to 'integrate' the labour aristocracy. Any 'integration' was a two-edged affair, as the whole history of working-class struggle indicates.

The network of overlapping activities in the urban community which I have labelled 'bourgeois evangelism' was, however, significant for hegemony in two related ways. First, it fostered the cohesion and morale of the ruling class itself, provided a sense of mission, and a set of inter-related ideological accounts of the palpable social realities of Victorian capitalism. The norms of domestic life, religious observance, etc., helped draw ideological boundaries between those members of society able and willing to behave 'rationally', and the unregenerate urban masses. (This does not mean, as it often implied, that any recognition of 'environmental' aspects of working-class behaviour was necessarily excluded by the dominant ideology; the point is that whether one started with the 'environment' or the 'individual' the analysis remained within the same given ideological assumptions.) Secondly, evangelistic reform played an important part in bourgeois hegemony over the middle strata, and especially in the production of 'subaltern intellectuals'.* The whole problem of hegemony over these groups has been veiled by the very strength of that hegemony. Yet the small businessmen, white-collar employees, etc., had different relations of production from those of the bourgeoisie and inhabited

*A term used by Gramsci, 1971, p.13, by which he means those strata of 'divulgators of pre-existing, traditional, accumulated intellectual wealth' who are closely tied to the popular masses ... and function to reproduce ruling-class hegemony at this social level.

a distinct social world, even though its upper fringes might overlap the world of the bourgeoisie.

Two features of dominant ideology seem important for hegemony over these strata: family and religion. Domestic life-style, often though not necessarily including the employment of domestic service, had an important symbolic function in defining membership of the 'middle class'; even for groups whose social relations were not those of capital, the pervasive metaphors of restraint, accumulation, and advance through the exercise of rational self-control could be applied to the visible status of the family. (These metaphors also, of course, could plausibly apply to the realities of incremental salaries, promotion, or the modest prosperity which the professional practitioner or small businessman saw as the reward of hard work.) Many churches, especially the English nonconformists and the Free Church of Scotland, drew their congregations from these strata. The greatest response to the urban missionary efforts seems to have come from the middle strata, rather than from the working class whose irreligion loomed so large in the social anxieties of some bourgeois intellectuals.

It was particularly from these sections of society that the 'subaltern intellectuals' of Victorian Britain were drawn – and also, in the case of intellectuals in the narrow professional sense (teachers, etc.), belonged by virtue of their occupational function. Elementary schoolteachers were recruited from the middle strata and upper layers of the working class; criteria of family respectability entered into their selection, and their relations with the school inspectors – at this period often urban gentry, who themselves had neither attended nor taught in elementary schools – symbolized their subordinate social role. Other occupations have been less studied but are probably of equal significance in this respect; all the professions, for example, were heterogeneous in composition, divided between leading (bourgeois) and subaltern (middle strata) intellectuals. (The recruitment and function of the clergy might be especially interesting.) Other groups performed the social function of subaltern intellectuals without having the occupational status of an intellectual.* One effect of the party struggle was to form 'intellectuals' (in the broadest sense of the term) among the subordinate classes. The local political role of shopkeepers has already been mentioned; this role appears to have extended beyond the political sphere narrowly defined, to a range of institutions, with churches often forming vital links in the local institutional network. The leaders of organized labour were another important

*The function of intellectuals is to foster the cohesion and organize the domination of a given social class, to give it 'homogeneity and an awareness of its own function not only in the economic but also in the social and political fields' (Gramsci, 1971, p.5); groups may perform this function without being 'intellectual' in a specific occupational sense.

grouping of intellectuals in the broad Gramscian sense; their significance certainly increased during the third quarter of the century, especially with the advent in the 1870s of working class representation in local and parliamentary government.

The period saw an expansion of such groups, which occupied a key position in the reproduction of relations of domination. But this should certainly not be interpreted in a mechanistic fashion; the subaltern intellectuals were more than mere 'transmission belts'. Their mode of life and, therefore, ideology were quite different from those of the bourgeoisie, and hegemony over them, and over the subordinate classes generally, depended on the representation within the hegemonic ideology of 'a number of "elements" which transcribe the way classes other than the hegemonic class live their conditions of existence'. (Poulantzas 1967 p.67) This is apparent in the relations between the bourgeoisie and the labour aristocracy, and the adaptations of bourgeois ideology to take account of the autonomous existence of working-class organizations. The same thing may hold for the middle strata, whose relations with the dominant class have been less well discussed by historians. Any electoral base in the towns depended on the mobilization of shop-keepers and tradesmen, and concessions (even if purely opportunistic concessions) to their outlook. And the proliferation of subaltern intellectuals led to modifications of the functions their social superiors had designed for them. 'Official' definitions of the scope and purposes of elementary education were, for example, modified in practice in the classroom – a process reinforced by the development of teachers' associations and after 1870 of elected School Boards. Religious institutions may also have undergone significant transformations, as evangelism found a response in the middle strata. Literary and scientific production by intellectuals from the subordinate classes might produce important innovations, to which the hegemonic ideology had to adapt.

The role of the subaltern intellectuals was therefore two-sided. On one hand, they did transmit elements of ideology adopted 'from above'; but this was itself an active process, necessarily involving re-interpretation of ideological forms, their adaptation so as to render them 'plausible' under diverse social conditions. On the other hand, they also transmitted 'upwards' innovative ideological practices, which might be imposed on the hegemonic class itself. (Indeed the capacity to adapt to such innovations, and thus retain ideological leadership of a social bloc, is one measure of the strength of hegemony.) Hegemony was a set of political relations between classes, fractions and strata, and was fractured by contradictions. Historical shifts in the class struggle can only be understood in terms of this inherently contradictory character of relations of hegemony. The last two decades of the nineteenth century, for example, were characterized by social transformations which eroded the forms of domination examined in this paper, with consequent shifts and dislocations in the patterns of hegemony.

References

ALTHUSSER, L. *For Marx,* trans, B. Brewster, Penguin Books, 1969, p.251.

ANDERSON, P. 'Origins of the Present Crisis', *New Left Review* 23, 1964.

BEST, G. *Mid-Victorian Britain,* Weidenfeld & Nicholson, (original edn.) 1971.

GRAMSCI, A. *Selections from the Prison Notebooks,* ed. and trans. Q. Hoare and G. Nowell-Smith, Lawrence and Wishart, 1971. See also the selections in this Reader.

MARX, K. *Surveys from Exile,* ed. D. Fernbach, Pelican Marx Library, 1973.

POULANTZAS, N. 'Marxist Political Theory in Great Britain', *New Left Review* 43, 1967.

POULANTZAS, N. *Classes in Contemporary Capitalism,* trans. D. Fernbach, New Left Books, 1975.

STEDMAN JONES, G. *Outcast London,* Clarendon Press, 1971.

THOMPSON, E. P. 'The Peculiarities of the English', *Socialist Register 1965* ed. R. Miliband and J. Saville, Merlin Press, 1965.

4 Education, Ideology and Literature

Tony Davies

...A glance at the *Oxford Dictionary* entry... confirms... that the word 'literature', far from designating a steady and self-evident object, has been the site of a series of conjunctural crises of meaning, of which the most decisive can be located with some precision in the 1860s and 70s. The entry reads in part as follows:

> Literary productions as a whole: the body of writings produced in a particular country or period, or in the world in general. Now also in a more restricted sense, applied to writing which has claim to consideration on the ground of beauty of form or emotional effect.

The appearance of that 'restricted sense', now of course the dominant and virtually exclusive one, is closely contemporary with the first major economic and ideological crisis in mature industrial capitalism, and with the resulting debate on the role of education in the reproduction of the national culture that prompted, among many others, Thomas Huxley's *Science and Education*, Dean Farrar's *Essays on a Liberal Education*, and Matthew Arnold's *Culture and Anarchy*. Nor was it merely or accidentally contemporary, as a reading of those texts makes clear. Here is Henry Sidgwick, champion of English as a university subject, in a contribution to Farrar's book:

> Let us demand that all boys, whatever be their special bent and destination, be really taught literature: so that as far as possible, they may learn to enjoy intelligently poetry and eloquence: that their interest in history may be awakened, stimulated, guided; that their views and sympathies may be enlarged and expanded by apprehending noble, subtle, and profound thoughts, refined and lofty feelings: that some apprehension

Source: *Red Letters*, no. 7, 1978, pp.4-13

of the varied development of human nature may ever abide with them, the source and essence of a truly humanising culture. (Sidgwick, 1867, pp.129-30)

And here is Arnold, rather later, in the 1880 report of the School Inspectorate:

> Good poetry does undoubtedly tend to form the soul and character; it tends to beget a love of beauty and of truth in alliance together; it suggests ... high and noble principles of action, and it inspires the emotion so helpful in making principles operative. Hence its extreme importance to all of us. (Mathieson, 1975 p.17)

'Noble, subtle and profound thoughts'; 'refined and lofty feelings'; 'humanising culture'; 'high and noble principles of action': reading through the educational propaganda of those years, phrases of this kind fall into a recognisable configuration of meanings, a moral-aesthetic ideology of literary consumption. This ideological formation is characterised by its *idealism* and its *universality:* Sidgwick demands that 'all boys ... be taught literature' (girls, of course, are educationally nonexistent); Arnold asserts the importance of poetry 'to all of us'.

This universal cultural-educational ideal, founded, as the phrase about 'beauty and truth' indicates, in the aesthetic of early romantic poetry, is constructed on the back of an often penetrating but pervasively moralising critique of industrial capitalism. Its principal targets are the divisive, reactionary classicism of Oxford and Cambridge, the utilitarian materialism of manufacturing industry, and, most fundamental of all, the growing danger of an organised and militant industrial working class. Arnold returns to this theme constantly, and with notable unease. In *Culture and Anarchy,* [his tone is solemn:]

> [Culture] does not try to teach down to the level of the inferior classes; it does not try to win them for this or that sect of its own, with ready-made judgments and watchwords. It seeks to do away with classes; to make the best that has been thought and known in the world current everywhere; to make all men live in an atmosphere of sweetness and light. (Arnold, 1967, p.439)

In *Friendship's Garland,* [it is ironic:]

> I observe a Jacobinical spirit growing up in some quarters which gives

> me more alarm than even household suffrage.... These things are very serious, and I say, if the masses are to have power, let them be instructed, and don't swamp with ignorance and unreason the education and intelligence which now bear rule amongst us. (Ibid p.530).

In the essay on *Democracy* there is an increasing urgency and directness:

> It is of itself a serious calamity for a nation that its tone of feeling and grandeur of spirit should be lowered or dulled. But the calamity appears far more serious still, when we consider that the middle classes, remaining as they are now, with their narrow, harsh, unintelligent and unattractive spirit and culture, will almost certainly fail to mould or assimilate the masses below them... at the same time I say that the middle classes have the right, in admitting the action of government, to make the condition that this government shall be one of their own adoption, one that they can trust. To ensure this is now in their own power (Ibid p.566)

In this last passage the verbs describing the cultural mediation of class have hardened significantly. Culture no longer 'suggests' principles or 'inspires' emotions. Indeed, the word 'culture', with its central refusal of the necessity of class conflict, has been overtaken by the naked rhetoric of political and ideological dominance. The bourgeoisie must seize state power in order to 'mould' and 'assimilate' the masses. We are near the limits of the ideology. The 'Ode on a Grecian Urn' seems a long way away.

This is familiar ground, and I don't return to it simply to repeat what others have said about the ideological character and intention of compulsory mass education. What I want to emphasise... is the central and determining position of *literature* in that formation. More than that, following the semantic shift in the word itself, I want to argue that, faced with a crisis of ideological dominance and unable to resort either to the classics or to a science increasingly feared as the voice of a soulless materialism, education *discovered* and therefore *created* literature as the principal material and object of its institutions and practices.

That may seem a preposterous claim. There were heroes before Agamemnon, and there were literary texts before Arnold. Indeed; but it was the effect of literary ideology, which came into being at the same moment as literature as its inseparable twin, to create that 'history' of literary productions without which it would have had nothing to speak of. Certainly there were texts, stretching back to the distant horizons of human culture: but not *literary* texts. The word has the precise function of designating the distinct, privileged status of 'literature' in the whole field of written and printed texts without which it would be unable to perform its specific role in the ideological practices of education. For Ben Jonson or Milton 'literature' meant no less than *everything in print:* poetry and fiction, certainly, but also law, politics, history, theology, even science — everything that it now excludes and even opposes. Perhaps we can begin to see more clearly the scope and effect of that restriction of meaning to 'writing which has claim to consideration on the ground of beauty of form or emotional effect.'

I have suggested that literature, literary ideology and literary history 'came into being' at the same moment, and I want to [illustrate] what I mean. Arnold published the first version of the *Democracy* essay in 1861. In the same year Francis Palgrave produced his *Golden Treasury of the Best Songs and Lyrical Poems in the English Language.* When I first began working in an English department, six or seven years ago, *The Golden Treasury* was still widely used in first year poetry courses. For all I know it still is in some places. In any case, for over a century that book has served, in schools and colleges, to form the first impression of the scope, character and history of English lyric poetry.* Of course there had been collections and miscellanies before, but *The Golden Treasury* differs from these previous anthologies in two ways. The poems in it are explicitly selected on *literary* grounds alone, and it aims overtly to *establish a canon* — a tradition. The selection on literary grounds I designate a region of literary ideology. 'The magic of this Art,' says Palgrave,

> can confer on each period of life its appropriate blessings: on early years experience, on maturity Calm, on age, Youthfulness. Poetry gives treasures 'more golden than gold,' leading us in higher and healthier ways than those of the world, and interpreting to us the lessons of Nature. (Palgrave, 1968, p.xii)

In considering 'what degree of merit should give rank among the best,' he insists

> that a Poem shall be worthy of the writer's genius — that it shall reach a perfection commensurate with its aim...that passion, colour, and originality cannot atone for serious imperfections in clearness, unity or truth — that a few good lines do not make a good poem ...above all, that Excellence should be looked for rather in the Whole than in the Parts.

A number of things are notable here: the pervasively moral and often explicitly religious language; the important role assigned to the concepts

*The *National Union Catalog* records 250 editions of *The Golden Treasury* in less than a century: and that list is certainly not exhaustive.

Genius and Nature; the assumption that poetry gives access to a world 'higher and healthier' than the everyday one. But above all I want to stress the central...notion of *unity*. This unity has nothing whatever to do with the formal and linguistic unities of classical and neo-classical criticism — that much is clear from its close relation in the critical discourse to mystified generalities like nature, genius and perfection. It belongs rather to a region of... 'organicism' (Eagleton, 1976, pp.103ff; Williams, 1961, p.256): that ideological formation (in which literature comes to play an indispensable role) whose function is to 'resolve' the ideological crisis and the intensifying class struggle of the latter decades of the nineteenth century into an image of organic *gemeinschaft* or unity. Just as a successful poem is an organic unity, so — mirroring the 'unity' of the nation itself — is the history, the 'evolution', of the national literature. 'The volume,' Palgrave claims, 'accurately reflects the natural growth and evolution of our poetry.' If mere chronological sequence fails adequately to bring out the unity of that 'natural growth,' literary ideology is entitled to adjust it:

> A chronological sequence...rather fits a collection aiming at instruction rather than at pleasure, and — within each book, therefore, the pieces have been arranged in gradations of feeling or subject... It is hoped that the contents of this Anthology will thus be found to present a certain unity, 'as episodes,' in the noble language of Shelley, 'to that great poem which all poets, like the cooperating thoughts of one great mind, have built up since the beginning of the world.'

If literary ideology is entitled to rewrite literary history in the interest of unity, it is naturally at liberty to do the same to individual poems whose 'unity' is suspect or defective. Palgrave, unlike some later literary ideologues, is at least explicit about this:

> The omissions (of the odd stanza) have been risked only when the piece could thus be brought to a closer lyrical unity.

His admiration for the 'noble language of Shelley' does not prevent him mutilating that poet's 'Stanzas written in dejection near Naples.'...Even Shakespeare is not exempt: the song from *Cymbeline* is cropped of its last verse by the imperious demands of 'unity.' Later, of course, the ideology imposed still sterner sacrifices. Those of you who recall the bemusing spectacle of F.R. Leavis throwing out almost the entire oeuvre of Dickens or dismembering the text of George Eliot's *Daniel Deronda* in precisely the same terms may not think Palgrave extreme in this respect.*

*cf Leavis, 1962 pp.93ff-249ff. One comment on Dickens is worth quoting here; 'I can think of only one of his books in which his distinctive creative genius is controlled throughout to a *unifying* and *organising* significance' (my emphases.)

I've looked at Palgrave's preface in some detail because there we can see literary ideology in a decisive moment of formation; and not only literary ideology, but also *the literature of which it speaks. The Golden Treasury* is not, in its own terms, just one of a number of possible versions of the 'growth and evolution' of English lyric poetry. It *produces* that poetry, as a coherent formal and historical unity, *at the same time as* and as inseparable from the terms in which it is to be read. Of course it must not seem to be doing anything so disconcertingly new. Ideology operates, Althusser remarks, through the effect of *recognition* — even though *mis*recognition — and Palgrave's readers must encounter their own 'literature' as something already entirely recognisable:

> Many familiar verses will here be met with; many also which should be familiar: — the Editor will regard as his fittest readers those who love Poetry so well that he can offer them nothing not already known and valued.

Literary ideology comes into being already equipped with a raw material (literature), a history (the 'growth and evolution' of that literature), and a subject (the reader). The circle of 'interpellation' is complete. The introductions made, ideology, like the perfect host, can tactfully... withdraw:

> [Poetry] speaks best for herself. Her true accents... may be heard throughout the following pages: — wherever the Poets of England are honoured, wherever the dominant language of the world is spoken, and it is hoped that they will find fit audience.

The original idea for *The Golden Treasury*, as well as a good deal of help with the selection of poems, came from Palgrave's friend Alfred Tennyson, the poet laureate, to whom the book is dedicated: a nice figure for that conjunction of writing and criticism in which... literary ideology, and consequently literature, is produced. For it's not simply a question, as I too mechanically proposed, of literary ideology 'inventing' literature like a criminal inventing an alibi. The relation between the two terms is mutually productive and reproductive: each depends on the other, makes the other visible, as a necessary condition of its own existence and effect. Obviously literary criticism — the name by which literary ideology most commonly goes — cannot exist without literature. But the reverse is equally true: *literature cannot exist without literary criticism.** I'm not speaking here only of the external

*The 'national literature' soon ceased to be a history, and became a tradition. It was not even, theoretically, all that had been written or all kinds of writing. It was a selection which culminated in, and in a circular way defined, the 'literary values' which 'criticism' was asserting... Selectivity and self-definition, which were the evident processes of 'criticism' of this kind were... projected as literature itself.

conditions of their constitution within an ideological apparatus. Each is produced and reproduced *internally* within the other. And that reciprocal internalisation, the constitutive condition of their existence and articulation one upon the other, is itself a determinate effect of their moral and educational function — specifically their function within the ideological institutions and practices ... of compulsory state education.

Literature cannot exist without literary criticism, without literary ideology operating in and for the educational apparatus. I'll give an example of what I mean in a moment. But in order to do that we must first look briefly at the raw material that is 'worked' by both: the English language. It's clear that the dominant assumptions behind Palgrave's principle of selection are linguistic. The 'unity' of the lyric poem, like the supposed unity of English poetry itself, is fundamentally a linguistic unity ... Before we can have a national literature, we must have a national language, a language characterised formally and historically by unity: 'standard English.' This is a complex topic, and I can only sketch the outlines here. An adequate account of the emergence from immense linguistic variety of the unitary national language would have to start in the sixteenth century, probably a good deal earlier. But 'standard English' does not become fully hegemonic until the latter half of the nineteenth century, when it becomes fully effective by being incorporated into the most fundamental routines of compulsory universal education. And what is this 'standard English,' the absolute basis of the school curriculum, the minimum requirement of educational competence? In its formal specifications, its prescriptive standards of spelling, grammar and pronunciation, it is the language of *literature* (as constructed by the ideological operations I have already described). In this respect the central text is neither Arnold nor Palgrave but a text already implicit in both, though it had to wait another fifty years to be completed: the *Oxford English Dictionary*, with which we started. That remarkable text, the very text of texts, provides not only a basic standard of spelling, usage and pronunciation over the whole range of the national language, but also an evolutionary history of that standard. It stands as the monument ... to the ideological dominance of the language of the dominant classes in the form of the language of literature.

... Like any dominance, this linguistic hegemony is achieved partly by repressive legal sanctions — the coercive and compulsory routines of elementary schooling — but more importantly by *winning consent*. In elementary schooling, and especially in its ... teaching of 'literacy,' the coercive element is uppermost. Many working-class children never experience 'their own' language as anything other than an oppressive orthodoxy imposed from outside. Indeed by strategies of 'failure' and refusal, a large number manage largely to avoid even that. For the rest of us, the 'successful' ones who negotiate the transition from coercion to consent and learn to 'recognise' and internalise the natural superiority and universality of the dominant linguistic practice, literature plays a crucial role. It is crucial, evidently, for those who go on to study it; but no less so for those who proceed to other subjects whose position in the curriculum is defined by the fact that *they are not literature*. This is not simply a matter, as my reading of Palgrave might have suggested, of the appropriation of certain texts to particular ideological uses within education, though that is an important function of literary ideology, as the great and continuing influence of F. R. Leavis indicates. Nor is it only that literature 'silently' testifies to the hegemony of the dominant language, even when it seems to be resisting or refusing it, though that is the case also. At the moment in which a certain corpus of texts, identified as 'literary', takes up its position in the contradictory unity of the dominant national language and in the institutions and practices of compulsory state education, literature ceases to be the passive raw material of certain processes of ideological production and reproduction and *actively* engages the terms of its own constitution. To make the point fully, across the whole range of literary types, would require a long and detailed analysis. I've only time here to indicate one example.

In the 1860s a new kind of fiction begins to appear: a version of the *bildungsroman* (the novel of childhood and adolescence) which actually narrates and thematises the terms of the formation I have been trying to describe - class, language and education. The best known examples of this genre are rather later (Hardy's *Jude the Obscure*, for instance, and [Williams 1977 pp.51-2] Lawrence's *Sons and Lovers*) but I want to say something about one of the earliest and I think most interesting of them: George Eliot's *The Mill on the Floss*, published in the spring of 1860 just a year before *The Golden Treasury*. There are aspects of this narrative that testify to the sentimental and complacent expectations of the novel-reading public, and perhaps also to certain contradictions in George Eliot's own history and predicament. There is a persistent, mawkish nostalgia for what she calls the 'golden gates of childhood', and a patronising facetiousness in the rendering of the petit-bourgeois Dobson sisters and their households. But these are far outweighed, in the first half of the text at least, by the clarity with which the ideological purposes and limitations of education are realised; a clarity available to this text by virtue of its *feminism*, of a position, that is, partly *outside* the formation I have been describing. The first book of the novel, called 'Boy and Girl', is centrally occupied with a detailed and compelling account of the imposition by a loving and affectionate family of gender identities onto the two protagonists, Tom and Maggie Tulliver — an imposition that takes the form, preeminently, of sending Tom away to school while his sister, cleverer and more bookish, stays at home. The advantages of education present themselves to the parents as primarily linguistic, as the acquisition of verbal accomplishments which will open the way to the bourgeois professions. The theme is announced in the first narrative chapter of the novel:

> 'What I want, you know,' said Mr Tulliver — 'what I want is to give Tom a good eddication; an eddication as'll be bread to him... The two years at th'academy 'ud ha' done well enough, if I'd meant to make a miller and farmer of him... But I should like Tom to be a bit of a scholard, so as he might be up to the tricks o' these fellows as talk fine and write with a flourish.' [Eliot, 1969. p.5]

And a moment later, deciding to seek the advice of the auctioneer Riley:

> 'Riley's as likely a man as any to know o' some school; he's had schooling himself, an' goes about to all sorts o' places — arbitatin' and vallyin' and that... I want Tom to be such a sort o' man as Riley, you know — as can talk pretty nigh as well as if it was all wrote out for him, and knows a lot o' words as don't mean much, so as you can't lay hold of 'em i' law; and a good solid knowledge o' business too.'

'Can talk pretty nigh as well as it if was all wrote out for him': the function of literature in the educational apparatus could hardly be put more succinctly, or more critically. 'Educated' speech is precisely that: the reproduction in speech of certain authorised modes of written discourse grounded... in literature. Tom Tulliver, 'being... abundant in no form of speech,' experiences the resulting education as an oppression, which the text, thanks to the presence in its formation of a critical feminism, is able to formulate in an unexpected and striking way:

> Under this vigorous treatment Tom became more like a girl than he had ever been in his life before. He had a large share of pride, which had hitherto found itself very comfortable in the world, despising Old Goggles (his previous schoolmaster), and reposing in the sense of unquestioned rights; but now this same pride met with nothing but bruisings and crushings. Tom was too clearsighted not to be aware that Mr Stelling's standard of things was quite different, was certainly something higher in the eyes of the world, than that of the people he had been living amongst, and that, brought into contact with it, he, Tom Tulliver, appeared uncouth and stupid; he was by no means indifferent to this, and his pride got into an uneasy condition which quite nullified his boyish self-satisfaction, and gave him something of a girl's susceptibility. [Ibid, pp. 130-1].

This is remarkable for the clarity with which it makes visible the very articulations of a complex ideological instance — class/gender/education — itself overdetermined by an ideology of linguistic 'competence.' Yet what is this text that can 'see' ideology so clearly, if not itself an outstanding exemplar of the very formation that it 'criticises'? A novel about the educational and sexual exploitation of lower-middle-class children written — how could it not be? — in the 'literary' language of the educated classes; written, furthermore, by a woman *disguised as a man.* Faced with contradictions of this order, the... 'failure' of the novel's ending, which has so preoccupied bourgeois criticism, seems a small thing indeed.

I offer this brief account in support of my thesis that literature, in all the variety of its texts, is grounded in the ideological unity of 'standard English,' which itself reflects the imaginary unity of the social formation as the 'nation.' Literature both reflects and reproduces that unity not in spite of but because of its capacity to 'see' the contradictions. A text with radical elements like *The Mill on the Floss* shows this particularly clearly. By rendering the position of the dominated classes (women, petit-bourgeois tradespeople dispossessed by finance capital and bourgeois law) in the language of — and therefore from the position of — the dominant classes, it exhibits contradictions, as Pierre Macherey puts it, 'in the form of their imaginary resolution.' It does this whatever its explicit or intended effect. Such is the ideological destiny of literature; it cannot break with that destiny, that determinate ideological effect, without ceasing to be literature.'*

*Describing 'the recognition of "literature"' as a specialised social and historical category and 'as the crucial theoretical break' Williams adds that 'it should be clear that this does not diminish its importance.' (Williams, 1977, p.53)

References

ARNOLD, M. *Poetry and Prose,* ed. J. Bryson, 1967.

EAGLETON, T. *Criticism and Ideology,* New Left Books, 1976.

ELIOT, G. *The Mill on the Floss,* Dent (Everyman edition), 1969.

LEAVIS, F. R. *The Great Tradition,* Penguin Books, 1962.

MATHIESON, M. *Preachers of Culture,* Allen and Unwin, 1975.

PALGRAVE, F.T. *The Golden Treasury of the Best Songs and Lyrical Poems in the English Language,* ed. J. Press, Oxford University Press, 1964.

SIDGWICK, H. 'The Theory of Classical Education,' *Essays on a Liberal Education,* ed. F. W. Farrar, 1867.

WILLIAMS, R. *Culture and Society,* Penguin Books, 1961.

WILLIAMS, R. *Marxism and Literature,* Oxford University Press, 1977.

SECTION 5

Debates with Marxism

The analysis of cultural production is a relative latecomer to the field of Marxist debate and in its current form, as the extracts in Section 4 indicate, owes much to Gramsci's attempt to construct a more complex and subtle model of class domination in the cultural field. It is this issue of class-domination, of a model that sets class-conflict at the centre of cultural theory, that Kenneth Roberts challenges in his account of research into the patterns of leisure in contemporary society. While social class is admitted to be a weighty factor, age, sex and marital status can be shown to be of equal importance in 'the social determinants of leisure conduct.' Detailed attention to the great variety of leisure pursuits, Roberts argues, indicates that a pluralistic model offers a less convoluted, more economical account than the kind entailed by the choice of a single over-arching theory. More generally:

> The model of society that best enables us to understand contemporary society is a pluralist model — the unofficial ideology of Western society. Sociology has always been a debunking subject, but in this case the conventional wisdom is less out of tune with reality than its more vociferous critics.

The freedom of choice exercised by consumers in the cultural market is therefore 'real,' Roberts concludes, and not the index of a hidden form of social control.

John Tagg's essay on the crucial contribution of photography to the development of forms of surveillance and control in the nineteenth century (police, asylums, orphanages) cuts across current Marxist cultural debate from a different angle. Drawing primarily on the work of Michel Foucault, Tagg identifies photography as a specific 'technology of power' necessary to the structure of industrial and post-industrial societies, asserting that

> we must cease once and for all to describe the effects of power in negative terms — as exclusion, repression, censorship, concealment, eradication. In fact, power produces. It produces reality. It produces domains of objects, institutions of language, rituals of truth.

Knowledge, truth, the products of scientific discovery are not antithetical to power, but its 'other face,' as inseparable from power as (in Saussure's definition) the signifier is inseparable from the signified. The 'knowledge' of persons embodied in the would-be neutrality of the photograph taken for purposes of identification constitutes an assertion of power, and belongs within an institutional structure for defining the boundaries between legal and criminal, sanity and madness, health and disease. Tagg extends to the notion of the photograph as transparent reflector of 'reality' Barthes's critique of narrative realism in the 19th century. Like the classic realist novelists, the police or scientific photographer suppresses all evidence of the production of the photograph as a guarantee of the product's untainted and objective 'truth'.

1 Culture, Leisure, Society – The Pluralist Scenario

Kenneth Roberts

I Theories of leisure, theories of society

It is hardly realistic to treat the class domination theory as a set of hypotheses to be rigorously tested through a strategically-designed research project, since this level of theory rarely proves wholly right or entirely wrong. Many writers have already proved that modern societies are sufficiently complex to offer numerous illustrations both in support and opposition. As the previous chapter has demonstrated, it is not difficult to illustrate the processes to which the class domination theory draws attention. There are scores of advertisers attempting to shape public taste, and many examples of governments promoting uses of leisure conducive to 'upright' citizenship. It was not just a desire to give young people a good time, but the concern engendered by an apparently anti-social youth culture that led to the appointment of the Albemarle Committee on the Youth Service whose report in 1960 led to a substantial injection of finance. [Albemarle Report 1960] Like the mass society analysis, the class domination theory spotlights genuine tendencies. Few would dispute that the theory also serves a purpose in sketching and alerting us to a scenario that *could* become a reality. But to exactly *what extent* does the theory explain leisure behaviour and provision in present-day society? While class domination theorists are mainly of left-wing persuasion, their theory is most readily reconciled with reality in the socialist world. In Western societies there are convincing grounds for insisting that the tendencies upon which the theory rivets attention remain, as yet, subservient to other processes. Furthermore, as we shall see, much of the evidence that the theory marshals is susceptible to alternative and, on balance, more convincing interpretation.

Source: K. Roberts, *Contemporary Society and the Growth of Leisure*, Longman, 1978, from Chapters 6 and 7.

The functions of leisure

Some correspondence between uses of leisure and the wider social order is inevitable. Leisure may help to consolidate the social system, offering gratifications which act as safety valves reconciling men to an otherwise unacceptable society. Leisure may also carry the imprint of values consistent with existing economic and political practices, thereby legitimising the social order. But does it necessarily follow that these functions of leisure are manifestations of an oppressive capitalist infrastructure together with its state apparatuses of social control? The truth is that leisure, or the alternative forms in which play can be institutionalised, performs comparable functions in all societies.

In his discussion of sport and games in Samoa, Dunlop describes how play integrates the community, provides an outlet for feelings of rivalry, celebrates socially significant occasions such as weddings, and teaches skills that are useful in other social roles from warfare to fishing. [Loy & Kenyon 1969]. It is difficult to see how uses of leisure could ever remain uninfluenced by the broader social contexts within which they are developed, and the fact that such influence can be discerned in our own society is hardly a ground for criticism.

The comparative research undertaken by J. M. Roberts and B. Sutton-Smith has identified some of the processes through which the surrounding context can shape leisure behaviour. [Loy & Kenyon 1969] These investigators collected information about the games played in a large number of relatively simple societies. They classified games according to whether physical skill, strategy or chance predominated, and found that each type of game tended to enjoy prominence within a particular type of culture. Games of physical skill proved most common in societies where mastery of the environment was a principal challenge. In contrast, games of strategy were prominent in more complex societies where child-training stressed obedience and following rules. Games of chance were most common in a different type of setting; where there existed a pervasive belief in an omnipotent, supernatural being. Roberts and Sutton-Smith interpret this evidence as suggesting that games perform an expressive function, relieving anxieties that broader patterns of social life generate. Hence the type of game that is popular depends upon the type of anxiety that a particular society engenders. When the emphasis is upon achievement and mastery of the environment, games of physical skill can offer a form of simulated achievement. In contemporary America, therefore, such games are most common among men in the higher socio-economic strata where childhood-training stresses individual achievement. In contrast, games of chance are prominent among women, reflecting the relative passivity of the female role.

In opposition to interpretations derived from conflict theory, functionalist sociologists have brought leisure within their own perspective. Whereas class analysts see leisure as reflecting and reinforcing broader patterns of conflict and domination, functionalists stress the contribution of leisure to the well-being of society as a whole. They draw attention to leisure as an arena in which individuals can develop and practice generally useful skills such as sociability, and how consorting with people who 'understand' enables life's tensions to be borne. [Smigel 1963] These are exactly the kinds of evidence to which the class domination theory draws attention, and the inescapable conclusion must be that this evidence is susceptible to alternative interpretation. Contemporary sport may display the imprint of the capitalist infrastructure. But so what? In a capitalist society enterprises are inevitably going to profit from leisure. Likewise the technology and styles of organisation in wider use are inevitably going to be incorporated into leisure industries. These extensions from the rest of life into leisure occur in all cultures. It is difficult to conceive of a society in which people will not use opportunities for play to release tensions, and to develop skills and personal attributes which are more generally rewarded. If such features of leisure can be discerned in our own society we should not be surprised, and neither should we rush to the conclusion that our leisure is particularly unfree. Gardner has illustrated the numerous ways in which American sport reflects the surrounding culture. [Gardner 1974] The commercialism and competitiveness that are valued in economic life spill over into sports, which are then prized for nurturing and rewarding these American values. To gain acceptance in America, it helps if sports can manifestly demonstrate their consistency with American values and character. Indeed, Gardner argues that the popularity of baseball can only be fully understood when account is taken of its advantage in being a peculiarly American game. These linkages between sport and the wider social order are not in dispute. But what do they prove? Do they reveal American sport as an apparatus of social control and domination? Or are we merely confronting interrelationships between leisure and other institutions that are inevitable in any society?

The role of the state

Without denying all credibility to the class domination theory we must recognise additional grounds for state involvement in recreation. It is possible to account for a great deal of state involvement in leisure without attributing any sinister motives. To begin with, it is difficult to imagine any society in which the state could adopt a completely *laissez-faire* approach to recreational tastes and behaviour. Rape and Paki-bashing might amuse sections of the contemporary British public, but the remainder surely have a right to protection. If we want to live in a society as opposed to anarchy, leisure activities must be contained within a framework of law. Until we have a totally consensual society, there will always be arguments about whether the public needs protecting from influences that some consider harmless. At the moment the availability of alcoholic drink, opportunities to gamble, and the right to witness sexual acts on screen and stage are cases in point. Government controls in these areas cannot be realistically interpreted as signs of a repressive state in action. That these issues are at all controversial simply reflects the fact that different sections of the public possess different tastes and values.

Second, if they attempt to plan the use of land, governments must inevitably become involved in planning for leisure activities that involve using large spaces in either urban or rural areas. If national parks and other places of 'natural beauty' are to be preserved as recreational resources and managed so as to cater for the visiting public with car parks, toilets and other facilities, is there any alternative to supervision by some public body? Similarly if land in urban areas and on the fringes of cities is to be kept available for sport and recreation, it is difficult to see how this can be guaranteed except by the state. Two-fifths of all the land in England and Wales is currently subject to some type of active conservation [Patmore 1972] and it is impossible to believe that the public's scope for recreational choice would be enhanced by removing this control. Likewise with other resources where the supply is finite, including broadcasting wavelengths, it is difficult to imagine the public being adequately served by anything other than a system of government regulation.

Third, a great deal of local and central government involvement in the leisure field is the inevitable by-product of quite different concerns. Rightly or wrongly, depending upon the political philosophy, since the nineteenth century governments in Britain and other industrial societies have been assuming a widening responsibility for public welfare by promoting, for example, health and education. These concerns unavoidably spread into leisure. Although today they are increasingly recognised as recreational services, the libraries, parks and swimming baths administered by local authorities in Britain were not originally developed merely to allow people to enjoy themselves, and they retain important non-recreational purposes. Similarly in America, before the First World War, what can now be recognised as recreation provision normally had other principal objectives, particularly conservation, health, and preservation of historic landmarks. [Van Doren and Hodges 1975].

Finally, if recreation opportunities are to be made available to economically disadvantaged groups, public provision is a logical if not the only method. If the state did not subsidise sport and other forms of recreation that involve the use of land, the majority of children would be unable to participate. The state does promote sport, particularly through education, but it is surely naive to see this as a subtle plot to implant acquiescent values into the minds of the young, or as a strategy to stimulate a profitable demand for sports equipment. Local government departments responsible for recreation are increasingly paying attention to the needs of other disadvantaged groups including the disabled and the ageing. Some of the services provided remain little known. For example, it is not widely broadcast that in 1974–75 local authorities helped to provide 104,800 people with holidays. [English Tourist Board and Trades Union Congress 1976] As with all other social services, whether or not this provision is desirable must be accepted as open to debate, but the points raised by the class domination theory hardly seem the central issues.

The charge of being laden with middle class values is easily hurled, but it is more difficult to make the indictment stick. Which recreational tastes are shared by the majority of middle class citizens but interest only a working class minority? The most popular forms of recreation including television and holidays transcend class boundaries, while other interests, such as the traditional arts, attract small taste publics rather than entire social classes. Public bodies like the Sports and Arts Councils certainly lie open to the charge that the working class is under-represented among their beneficiaries, but who doubts that if any critics could explain how to attract more working class participants the authorities would be happy to respond? In all formally organised activity, including politics and religion, the working class tends to be under-represented.

The entire spectrum of state-supported recreation cannot be whitewashed so casually. It is impossible to contend that all government enterprise in the leisure field is explicable in one or another of the ways outlined above. Why does the state in Britain support opera, squash, ballet and golf? Answers to these questions would hardly be complete without some reference to the social class compositions of the respective taste publics. Why do we subsidise British competitors in the Olympic Games? The preceding discussion has certainly not exhausted the reasons for state involvement in leisure. What has been illustrated is that there are numerous grounds for this involvement, and accounts that see social control writ large across all these endeavours are refusing to acknowledge the complexity of the picture.

The leisure market

Listing the diverse explanations for government involvement is not strictly an adequate answer to less vulgar versions of the class domination theory which disclaim conspiratorial overtones and rest content with identifying the covert social structural consequences of leisure provision. These arguments challenge not so much the motives of politicians and bureaucrats as the effects of their actions. A more satisfactory reply, therefore, is to explain that its impact upon the public's uses of leisure cannot be as impressive as the scale of government involvement since, in the leisure industries, the suppliers remain subservient to market forces. Consumer sovereignty remains a reality in the leisure market and one reason is that, to date, neither central government nor the local authorities in Britain have developed anything resembling coherent policies for recreation....

In leisure as in other spheres, there is a complex interactive relationship between demand and supply. Demand for a facility such as camping sites may provoke a supply, but it is easy to quote examples of supply-led demand. Until ten-pin bowling was commercially promoted in Britain no one was demanding to play it, and the visible availability of camp sites may increase demand for camping holidays. The relative weight of the influence flowing in each direction between supply and demand depends upon the state of the market. In leisure, as in other markets, a movement towards monopoly increases the power of the suppliers. While pluralism reigns in leisure supply, however, with the existence not only of voluntary and commercial sectors, but an uncoordinated public sector as well, it is the suppliers who are at the mercy of the market forces. It is public taste that has determined how television and radio broadcasting will be used in Britain. Whatever its early aspirations towards educating the public and raising levels of taste, the BBC has found that it can only win a mass audience, thereby justifying its revenue from the government, by catering for existing public interests. Likewise suppliers of sports complexes, arts centres and country parks have to wait and see what uses the public makes of their offerings and respond accordingly. Public provision accounts for only a small part even of organised recreation activity. [Mennell 1976] The providers have no captive audience. It is the public that can pick and choose.

Needless to say, the above comments about consumer sovereignty apply even more forcibly to the commercial sector. It is easy to talk about advertisers foisting their goods and services upon a susceptible public, but things never look so simple from the suppliers' side of the market. Advertisers may often try to shape public demand, but they are more rarely successful. Nine out of every ten new brands launched are failures. During the last 30 years the British public has largely deserted the cinema, the large dance palais, gents' hairdressers, and the bowling-alleys that were built during a short wave of popularity. Anyone who knows the advertising secret to tempt the missing customers back can make a fortune. The recreation business can be profitable, but leisure is a notoriously risky market. Public taste is fickle. Demand for basic necessities is easier to predict. And to complicate the problems of private enterprise, competition from a subsidised public sector is never far from the foreground. A secure position as a leisure supplier requires either a wealthy patron or a spread of risks across a large number of leisure industries so as to be waiting wherever demand might flow.

Socio-cultural pluralism

As far as uses of leisure are concerned, the public remains far from a single, undifferentiated mass. Our understanding of leisure is aided, but to no more than a limited extent by the mass society theory. Likewise the class domination theory offers insights, but cannot accommodate the greater part of the evidence about uses of and provision for leisure. The models of society offered in these theories are too simple to do full justice to a more complex reality.

Life-styles vary in a host of ways that cannot be explained by reference to the interests of a single dominant class. To explain these variations, it is usually more fruitful to refer to the interests and circumstances of the sections of the public directly concerned. Uses of leisure are related to social class. Working class households view more television, while the middle classes predominate at live theatre. There are few forms of recreation where participation is not somehow related to individuals' social class positions, usually assessed in terms of occupation. For the moment the point at issue is that while social class is certainly a useful predictor of leisure behaviour, the same applies to numerous other bases of social differentiation. We shall also see that age, sex, marital status and education are among the social determinants of leisure conduct. It is important to keep social class in perspective. Social class is important, but some sociologists of leisure display an unnecessary obsession with the subject.

Working class youth culture owes something to its working class foundations, but it also owes a great deal to the fact that its members are young and possess interests that differ from other age-groups. Class analysis never offers more than a partial explanation of leisure. Even with age and social class held constant, uses of leisure vary considerably between the sexes. The data in Table 1 derive from a study of 14-16 year-olds at one Dudley School, [E. Derrick et al.] and illustrate how sharply the life-styles of adolescent boys and girls differ. There are inevitable points of contact, but girls' lives are considerably more home and family centred. When they 'go out', dances and discos are among the most popular venues. Boys are more involved in hobbies, sport, and other forms of active outdoor recreation. Social class is but one among many influences upon uses of leisure, and the sum of the evidence simply will not justify making it the central explanatory concept.

From exposing the limitations of the mass society and class domination theories we can begin to identify a more valid approach to understanding leisure, and the senses in which its growth constitutes a problem. Both the

Table 1 Adolescent boys' and girls' involvement in selected leisure activities (percentages)

Leisure activities	Boys	Girls
Have a hobby	54	25
Dances/discos	49	84
Own a bicycle	64	17
Team sports	30	8
Watch sport	51	23
Visit relations	37	73
Help parents	49	84

mass society and class domination theories draw attention to tendencies that certainly operate but which are counterbalanced, in each case, largely by individuals and primary groups developing their own tastes and interests, and using the media and other facilities for their own purposes. The model of society that best enables us to understand contemporary leisure is a pluralist model — the unofficial ideology of Western society. Sociology has always been a debunking subject, but in this case the conventional wisdom is less out of tune with reality than its more vociferous critics. All grand theories necessarily simplify a more complex social reality, but the pluralist theory offers a better fit than its principal rivals, certainly as regards the analysis of leisure. In Britain and other Western societies there exists a variety of taste publics that possess contrasting interests generated by their different circumstances. The uses of leisure of these publics are certainly influenced by commercial and public provision, but the providers are at least as responsive to the public's tastes, and the public has a distinguished history of saying 'No'. In recreation and other spheres the public uses its leisure to nurture life-styles that supply experiences which the individuals concerned seek and value. 'Freedom from' is a condition for leisure. But there is also a positive side of the coin that involves individuals exploiting their 'freedom to' and leads logically to socio-cultural pluralism, meaning societies in which various taste publics are able to fashion life-styles reflecting their different interests and circumstances. This is the reality of modern leisure, and theories that fail to spotlight this aspect of reality prove only their own need of revision.

The pluralist theory incorporates a relatively complex model of society, but its explanations of leisure behaviour are characteristically economical. In contrast, the class domination theory with its more readily assimilated imagery of society consisting of dominant and oppressed strata, often has to resort to highly convoluted explanations when faced with the details of leisure conduct. For example, there are theories that purport to relate the appeal of competitive sport in general, and violence among both players and spectators in particular, to class structure and class struggle [Cohen 1971]. Some of these theories would benefit from a touch of Occam's razor. It is advisable to appraise more obvious explanations before embarking upon speculative class analysis. It is difficult not to sympathise with Petryszak's observation that, 'Unfortunately capitalism and its assumed agencies of manipulation including the media, all too often serve as the convenient scapegoats and explanatory catch-alls for sterile sociological thinking.' [Smith 1977] Petryszak's own preferred 'bio-social' explanation of violence in sport is theoretically economical and simultaneously persuasive. He commences with the observation that human beings possess a need for group membership, notes that competitive sport can meet this need for both participants and spectators, and proceeds to hypothesise that violence whether on the field or among spectators can heighten collective feeling. Students of leisure are well advised to try relating behaviour to the interests of those directly involved before speculating about the significance of the class struggle.

There are numerous patterns of attempted domination and exploitation in leisure, as is the case in most areas of social life. Middle class interests are more diverse than theories which persistently deplore the oppression of the working class suggest. The self-employed complain about expanding government bureaucracies triggering escalating rates and tax burdens, while the salary expectations and career prospects of new middle class armies of executives and professionals including civil servants, teachers, social workers and medical practitioners depend upon the further growth of public expenditure. [Roberts et al. 1977] Within the leisure industries exploitation is not the prerogative of commercial and political elites. Recreation professionals have their own diverse and vested interests. They include holiday camp workers who use campers as easy sources of money, and sometimes sex as well. Then there are the fairground gaff-lads who skilfully and systematically short-change customers. [Dallas 1971] In so far as exploitation is occurring it is not only the state and propertied classes that are the guilty parties....

There are romantics to whom formal organisation is anathema whether it is commercially or state sponsored and who insist that, to escape alienation, individuals and communities must organise their own leisure. However, there is already plenty of this communal organisation in our own society. This is the living proof of the pluralist case. There are participant-run dart and domino leagues, golf clubs and photography societies, while kids play street football and arrange their own informal games. We have this and more besides. And is anything lost when schools or recreation departments arrange regular football matches, erect goalposts and provide referees, and when supplies of kit can be purchased? The notion that technology and formal organisation along with their rational values are inherently alienating is surely a misconception. The study of leisure challenges such misconceptions, and the growth of leisure is rendering the broader theories of society from which these notions are derived increasingly suspect.

It is worth noting that despite their deep and often bitter differences, there is little disagreement on basic values between supporters of the class domination and pluralist theories. Both reveal a preference for societies in which members of the public can develop diverse life-styles, supported but not controlled by business and political apparatuses. The disagreement concerns whether this is possible within the present political economy. The pluralist case rests on the claim that while they are certainly at play, class domination tendencies are currently held in check, and that the form of political economy that has developed within Western societies offers a better protection against class domination than any of the known alternatives....

II Leisure and other social roles: The family and related influences.

Social networks

...Variations in uses of leisure are associated with the different roles that individuals play within the larger social system. With the pluralist theory in the background, it becomes possible to explain why some factors, such as the family exert a more powerful influence upon leisure than certain others, such as education. Furthermore, it becomes possible to explain *how* this influence is communicated — the processes whereby the family, education and other aspects of individuals' present circumstances and histories shape their leisure behaviour...

The Rapoports' study of *Leisure and the Family Life-Cycle* [Rapoport, 1975] is important for its insistence that specific uses of leisure are related to individuals' broader life-styles, and to the preoccupations and interests that characterise different social statuses. This is a sensible strategy in order to keep the 'experiencing' dimension in leisure analysis, and to capture the 'holistic' quality of people's systems of leisure behaviour. The meaning of any given leisure activity, whether listening to music, reading or watching sport can rarely be fully understood outside the broader life-style to which it contributes. The Rapoports move beyond palpable demand to explore preoccupations, interests and life-styles, and we can probe even further to relate individuals' life-styles to their personal social networks thereby recognising the importance of the people with whom leisure is spent.

This network concept refers to the total systems of social relationships by which individuals are surrounded; relationships that can have many bases including family, work, education and neighbourhood. Each individual's social network will possess unique characteristics, but as different types of work, family life and so on involve different patterns of social relationships, distinctive types of networks tend to arise among different sections of the public. Individuals' life-styles are built upon these networks, and it is within these frameworks that individuals express their interests and experience the various leisure activities in which they become involved.

To prove the value of this approach, the argument pursued in this and the following chapter draws extensively upon data from a survey investigation undertaken during 1972 involving interviews with 474 economically active males from a sample selected at random from the electoral registers covering a part of suburban Liverpool. This Liverpool enquiry was not concerned exclusively with uses of leisure, but one of its objectives was to operationalise and test the value of the ideas outlined above. Information was collected about each respondent's uses of five evening and weekend occasions during the week prior to each interview, and also about participation in specific leisure activities such as church-going, membership of clubs and entertaining friends at home. In analysing responses to the diary-type, open-ended questions in which respondents were simply asked to describe their behaviour on certain evening and weekend occasions, having first eliminated uses such as sleeping and working that could not be described as leisure, four main types of leisure behaviour were distinguished. First, watching *television* was classified separately to confirm what is already known about the large proportion of all leisure time that it accounts for. The second use of leisure distinguished covered other forms of *mass entertainment* including the cinema, the theatre and concerts. With the remaining uses of leisure a division was made between where respondents explained their use of an occasion in terms of pursuing a particular *activity* which could be anything from reading to sport, and when the occasion was described in terms of being with, visiting or meeting other people. How occasions were classified depended basically upon how respondents themselves described what they had been doing, and approximately one-third of all answers fell into this *social* category, confirming the importance of this use of leisure time. There are many other possible ways of classifying uses of leisure, and it is not being claimed that the method described above is the only valid approach. However, the analysis in Table 2 will show that it is one useful way of probing beyond the information that can be derived by simply enumerating activities.

Table 2 Types of leisure activity undertaken with different associates (percentages)

Uses of Leisure	Associates				
	Alone	Household	Relations	Friends	Total
Television	8	51	9	3	32
Other entertainment	2	3	5	9	4
Activities	65	14	17	27	24
Social	11	15	58	55	25
Other	15	17	11	7	14
n (of occasions) =	317	1,215	127	425	2, 084

In this table, and also in Table 3, respondents are reported as having been 'alone' on some occasions that are classified as having been spent 'socially'. This is not due to coding errors so much as to an almost inevitable degree of arbitrariness in allocating responses to a limited set of categories. For example, it is possible for a person to go out alone to meet friends in a public house.

The value of this classification is illustrated in Tables 2 and 3. Responses were analysed to seek relationships between leisure behaviour and variables such as age, income and marital status, and, as will become evident, many such relationships were established. However, in addition to asking respondents *what* they did on five occasions during the week preceding each interview, information was also sought concerning *who* each respondent was with at the time, and relationships between the types of participating groups and uses of leisure proved considerably stronger than connections between leisure behaviour and characteristics of individual respondents. Table 3 shows, for example, that television is primarily a household activity. Respondents rarely watched television when alone or in any other type of company. As many as 93 per cent of the occasions accounted for by television were family occasions, when respondents were at home and in the company only of other members of their households. Rather than simply expressing *individuals'* preferences, it is more useful to conceive recreation demand as arising from primary social networks. This is what the pluralist theory leads us to expect, and it is in these terms that we can explain how and why the family exerts a powerful influence upon leisure behaviour.

The strength of this influence has been previously documented, and the following evidence offers confirmation. Uses of leisure vary according to the

Table 3 Types of associates with whom different leisure activities are undertaken (in percentages)

Associates	**Uses of leisure**				
	Television	Entertain-ment	Activities	Social	Total
Alone	4	6	40	7	15
Household	93	42	34	34	56
Relations	2	7	4	14	6
Friends	2	45	22	45	22
n (of occasions) =	669	86	510	517	1,782

sex roles that individuals play within the family, the type of family concerned and its position in the life-cycle. All this is well known. The main interest in what follows, therefore, concerns the theoretical significance of the family's influence. How and why is the family so important in shaping uses of leisure? Answering these questions will illustrate and support the approach to leisure analysis proposed above, suggesting that particular uses of leisure are best understood by exploring their contributions to the broader life-styles of the persons concerned, and relating these life-styles to the types of social networks within which the individuals are located. As we shall see, the family's influence upon leisure derives from its pivotal position in structuring the public's social networks. The next chapter will endorse this theoretical position by showing that the influence of work upon leisure is less pronounced, for although the income, status and free time associated with different occupations must affect uses of leisure to some extent, work is normally a less potent influence in the construction of personal networks.

Gender

A point that cannot be overstressed in considering the influence of the family upon leisure is that we are not dealing with a source of minor variations. This area offers some sharp contrasts. To begin with there is the gender variable. In general leisure time is not evenly distributed between husbands and wives. Women are very much the second class citizens. Inequalities in the distribution of leisure time within families make the contrasts that can be drawn between social classes pale to insignificance.

Bell and Healey [Smith, 1973] have written about the decline of the traditional family and the emergence of new styles of marriage embodying joint conjugal roles with greater similarity of status between husbands and wives. As a result, they argue, leisure is gradually becoming available for women on the same terms as experienced by their husbands. An articulate body of opinion has certainly been urging the liberation of women, but if the trend that Bell and Healey discuss really is underway, recent findings do not suggest that is has progressed very far. The truly symmetrical family is still an only exceptionally realised ideal type. Trends towards jointness in the conjugal relationship have been uneven. During recent decades there has been a substantial movement of married women into the labour force, sharing out the breadwinner role. Housework, however, is rarely shared out equally. When housework is counted, the work-week of the contemporary wife frequently exceeds 60 hours. Despite the downward trend of hours worked in industry, it is doubtful whether the total work-week of married women has declined over the last generation.

In a sample of London couples each of whom was employed outside the home, Cullen found that the men spent only 36 per cent of the women's time on household chores. [Cullen 1974] Some women may regard cooking and shopping as leisure activities, but it is difficult to avoid concluding that women have substantially less leisure time than men, and this is one reason why men are the more active in virtually all types of out-of-home recreation.

Not only do women have less time free from household obligations, but their uses of the leisure time they do enjoy are relatively limited. This applies in all social classes but particularly for working class women.... When the women went outside their homes for recreation it was nearly always as a couple or as a family group; rarely alone or with friends. The trend towards sex equality has been less apparent in much of society-at-large than in the literature.

The source of these persistent inequalities in leisure opportunities lies in the woman's domestic role being of a more general, all-absorbing character than that of the man. Particularly when there are young children to care for, the family often becomes the only active base in a woman's social network. Studies in traditional working class districts have shown that a local extended kinship system can greatly enrich women's social lives. In the absence of kinfolk, however, a woman's home and family can bind her captive. The role of the husband/father makes less extensive demands. Men usually have jobs which act as a source of social relations, and as home and family continue to be treated primarily as the woman's responsibility, husbands are better able to maintain contact with friends during evenings and weekends. Males' social networks are spread over a larger number of bases supporting relatively diverse life-styles and leading to a wider range of leisure interests.

As children mature and parental responsibilities diminish, women become less tied to their homes but their life-styles continue to diverge from their husbands'.... Even when women enjoy similar amounts of leisure time, their social networks remain less extensive than their husbands' and their life-styles are accordingly narrow. It may not necessarily follow that women's life-styles are less satisfying than men's but they are certainly different.

The family life-cycle

Similarly impressive contrasts in uses of leisure are found between different stages in the family life-cycle. The changes in leisure behaviour that occur as individuals move from childhood, through adolescence, to marriage, parenthood, the post-parental stage and eventual retirement have been well documented. The Rapoports have illustrated how the unfolding of this life-cycle is associated with shifts in basic preoccupations and interests, while Sillitoe has coined the concept of 'domestic age' in portraying these developments. Data from the Liverpool investigation that was introduced earlier confirm the importance of the life-cycle, and, more importantly, enable the changes in uses of leisure that occur at particular junctures — with marriage, parenthood, and the later diminishing of parental responsibilities — to be examined in the depth necessary to clarify the underlying processes responsible for these changes.

The respondents interviewed were all economically active males and among this sample the group whose leisure was most emphatically 'different' comprised the unmarried under 30-year-olds. Compared with other informants, they were less occupied with television which accounted for only 20 per cent of the occasions examined. As Table 4 shows, in their uses of leisure time, the accent was upon social pastimes; meeting people in homes, pubs, cafés and other environments that support diffuse sociability. In addition to querying how occasions were spent, each respondent was asked whom he had been with at the time, and the unmarried under 30-year-olds also differed from the remainder of the sample in terms of their leisure companions. Their life-styles were not family centred: leisure was spent mainly with friends rather than members of their households, and these friends were exceptionally likely to be persons met 'socially' rather than relatives and other individuals met through the family, a very prominent source of leisure-time associates among other age groups.... Youth has long been recognised as a flowering period during which time and money are spent outside the home developing a style of life that is irrevocably lost upon marriage, and the results of our Liverpool enquiry confirm this impression...

Table 4 Uses of leisure and domestic age (Percentages)

	Unmarried Aged<30	Married Aged<30	Unmarried aged 30-44	Married aged 30-44		Married aged 45+
				No children	Children	
Use of occasions						
Non-leisure	9	19	5	11	17	10
Television	20	33	22	32	37	35
Entertainment	7	3	6	6	4	3
Activities	21	19	33	18	21	30
Social	43	26	33	32	21	22
n=	245	173	119	87	750	841
Companions						
Alone	11	15	24	6	15	17
Household	23	63	30	77	65	66
Relatives	2	5	8	3	5	7
Friends	64	17	38	13	14	11
Others	—	—	—	1	1	—
n =	249	160	142	88	737	880

Upon marriage the uses of leisure of the under 30-year-olds changed radically. With the advent of domestic responsibilities, hours of work increased as individuals set about building careers and maximising their earning potential, and a greater proportion of married respondents' occasions could not, therefore, be classified as leisure. Within the sample, the demands of work were allowed to recede to adolescent proportions only following the child-rearing phase. Furthermore, uses of the leisure occasions that remained were adjusted following marriage. Leisure became centred upon the home and television which subsequently accounted for 33 per cent of all occasions, while time spent with friends and upon social pastimes declined sharply. Following marriage the proportion of leisure occasions spent with friends declined from 64 to 17 per cent, and parenthood gave these trends a further push. With the arrival of children, time spent watching television rose further to account for 37 per cent of the occasions and the decline of social pastimes was accentuated. However, especially in terms of the companions with whom leisure is spent, the data indicate that it is marriage rather than parenthood that heralds the main break with adolescent life-styles....

Contrasts between the uses of leisure of older and younger unmarried individuals, and between both of these and married persons are best explained in terms of the social networks that typically surround these statuses. As suggested earlier, to understand leisure we need to push activities from the centre of the analysis. Relating lifestyles to social networks is a more effective approach towards clarifying variations in uses of leisure between different sections of the population, and its effectiveness is demonstrated in explaining the changes that occur during the family life-cycle.

Life-styles may be reshaped following the child-rearing phase. Diminishing domestic responsibilities can leave individuals less tied to their homes creating opportunities for more outgoing life-styles, and for some people middle age appears to be a leisure renaissance. It is known, for example, that activists in local political life and religious organisations are often drawn from this age-group and there was evidence of renewed interest in 'activities' among the Liverpool sample. Partly because family responsibilities were lighter, the 45-plus age group was able to relax the demands of work. With less need than in previous years to maximise earnings through overtime and shift-work, there were relatively few occasions about which the sample was questioned when this age-group was not at leisure. In view of the apparently greatly increased scope for choice, uses of leisure changed less than could possibly have been expected. For example, there was no trend whatsoever towards spending more time socially with friends, nor towards out-of-home entertainment, and television retained its appeal. The sole change compared with the previous stage in the life-cycle was the devotion of the greater quantity of time freed from work to activities. Children may depart but the conjugal relationship persists and usually continues to dominate leisure. At an earlier period in the life-cycle it is marriage rather than the arrival of children that decisively centres leisure upon home and television, and this is where leisure normally remains centred in middle-age. For married persons, irrespective of whether they are responsible for dependent children, their families are usually the central elements in their social networks and uses of leisure are shaped accordingly. It is possible to talk of opportunities being missed and of the life-styles of the middle-aged having fallen into ruts that resist recasting. Such judgements, however, overlook the fact that for married persons simply being with their families can be a major and valued aspect of leisure. Just spending time socially with people among whom one feels comfortable is not peripheral but a normal use of leisure time, and for many people the nexus of home, family and television is the most comfortable milieu available....

References

ALBEMARLE REPORT, *The Youth Service in England and Wales,* HMSO, 1960.

COHEN, S. (ed.), *Images of Deviance,* Penguin, 1971.

CULLEN, I., 'A Day in the Life of...' *New Society,* 11 April 1974.

DALLAS, D., *The Travelling People,* Macmillan, 1971.

DERRICK, E., *et al., Schoolchildren and Leisure: Interim Report,* Working Paper 19, Centre for Urban and Regional Studies, University of Birmingham, 1973.

ENGLISH TOURIST BOARD and TRADES UNION CONGRESS, *Holidays: The Social Need,* 1976.

GARDNER, P. A., *Nice Guys Finish Last,* Allen Lane, 1974.

LOY, J. W. and KENYON, G. S. (eds), *Sport, Culture and Society,* Macmillan, 1969.

MENNEL, S., *Cultural Policy in Towns,* Strasbourg, Council of Europe, 1976.

PATMORE, J. A., *Land and Leisure,* Penguin, 1972.

RAPOPORT, R. AND R. N., *Leisure and the Family Life-Cycle,* Routledge and Kegan Paul, 1975.

ROBERTS, K. *et al., The Fragmentary Class Structure,* Heinemann, 1977.

SMIGEL, E. O. (ed.) *Work and Leisure,* New Haven, College & University Press, 1963.

SMITH, M. A., (ed.), *Leisure and Urban Society,* Manchester, Leisure Studies Association, 1977.

VAN DOREN, C. S. and HODGES, L., *America's Park and Recreation Heritage,* Washington, U S Department of the Interior, 1975.

2 Power and photography – a means of surveillance: the photograph as evidence in law*

John Tagg

At the end of the nineteenth century, in the 1880s, photography underwent a double technical revolution enabling, on the one hand, the mass production of cheaply printed half-tone blocks and, on the other hand, the mass production of simple and convenient photographic equipment, such as the hand-held Kodak camera.... This double revolution stripped the image of what Walter Benjamin called its 'aura' by flooding the market with cheap and disposable photo-mechanical reproductions and by giving untrained masses the means to picture themselves. While aesthetes and pictorial photographers sought to salvage some prestige by preserving superseded techniques and arguing for the autonomy of photography as an art, an unabating technical development ensured the vast expansion of photography in the far from autonomous realms of advertising, of the family as a reconstructed unit of consumption, and of a whole range of scientific, technical, medical, legal and political apparatuses in which photography functioned as a means of record and a source of 'evidence'.

It is into the workings of these institutions that we must pursue photography if we are to understand the *power* that began to accrue to it in the latter half of the nineteenth century. It is in the emergence, too, of new institutions of knowledge that we must seek for the mechanism which could enable photography to function, in certain contexts, as a kind of *proof*, even while an ideological contradiction was negotiated so that photographic practice could be divided between the domain of art, whose privilege is a function of its lack of power, and the scientifico-technical domain, whose power is a function of its renunciation of privilege.

*This article is based on a lecture given, as part of a series on photography, at the Institute of Contemporary Arts, London, in February 1979. [The figures referred to in it follow p.308]

Source: *Screen Education*, no. 36, Autumn 1980, pp.17-55.

This analysis of power and photography will take us far beyond the boundaries of conventional art history into the institutional spaces of the modern state. Our starting point must be power itself and the attempts that have been made to theorise its functionings....

Power in the West, Foucault says, is what displays itself most and hides itself best. [Foucault, 1977, p.157] 'Political life', with its carefully staged debates, provides a little theatre of power — an image — but it is not there that power lies; nor is that how it functions. The relations of power are among the best hidden things in a social body, which may be why they are among the least studied.

On the left, the dominant tradition, following orthodox Marxism, has tended to neglect relations of elementary power in its concentration on the determining effectivity of the economy. It has also tended to see power only in the form of state power, wielded in the apparatus of the State, and has thus participated in the very *ideology of power* which conceals its pervasive workings...

In the classic texts of Marx and Lenin, too, the State is conceived as an explicitly repressive apparatus, a machine of repression which guarantees the domination and subjection of the working classes by the ruling class. It consists of specialised apparatuses such as the police, the law courts and the prisons, but also the army and, above this ensemble, the head of State, the government and the administration. All these apparatuses execute their functions and intervene according to 'the interests of the ruling class' in a class war conducted by the ruling class and its allies against the dominated working classes. Whatever the value of this description in casting light on all the direct and indirect forms of exploitation and domination through which is exercised what Marx, and later Lenin, rhetorically called 'the dictatorship of the bourgeoisie', it also prevents us seeing certain highly pertinent features — features it has become imperative to understand in highly developed modern states and in the historical aftermath of those twin aberrations of power: Fascism and Stalinism.

The theoretical development of the classic Marxist view of the State in keeping with these demands received new impetus in the analyses of the French Marxist philosopher Louis Althusser who took up the relatively unsystematised distinction made in the *Prison Notebooks* of the Italian Communist leader Antonio Gramsci, between the institutions of Civil Society — the Church, the schools, the trade unions, and so on — and those of the State apparatus proper. [see Gramsci, 1971, p.210ff] Gramsci saw that the State had undergone a crucial change of function in Western bourgeois democracies so that its real strength could no longer be understood only as the apparatus of government, the politico-juridicial organisation, but demanded attention to the 'private' apparatuses of 'hegemony' or Civil Society through which the bourgeois class sought to assimilate the entire society to its own cultural and economic level. In his more rigid theoretical framework, Althusser divided the State into two domains or kinds of apparatus: that which functioned primarily and predominantly by 'physical force', and that which functioned primarily and predominantly 'by ideology'. It is the State apparatuses which, principally by force, procure the political conditions for the action of the 'Ideological State Apparatuses' — the educational, religious, family, political, trade-union, communications and 'cultural' apparatuses — which, acting behind a 'shield', largely secure the reproduction of the relations of production. The Ideological State Apparatuses are 'on the side of the repressive State Apparatus', but they must not be confused with it. They are distinct, specialised and 'relatively autonomous' institutions which constitute a plurality, much of which lies outside the public domain as defined in bourgeois law, but which owe their unity to their functioning 'beneath the ruling ideology', that is, beneath the ideology of the ruling class. [See Althusser 1971]

There is still in Althusser's theoretical amplification something of an idea of power as a privilege to be captured and then exercised: a kind of 'fluid' which may be 'poured' into an apparatus as into a vessel.... Too often, Althusser sees the Ideological State Apparatuses as the *stake,* rather than the *site* of class struggle; though he has to acknowledge that the Ideological State Apparatuses are fraught with contradictions originating both in the residues of former ruling classes and in the resistances of the exploited classes. What he does not show is that it is in the representational practices of these apparatuses themselves that the ideological level is constituted, of necessity including that positionality which constitutes class identity.

This said, a decisive step has been taken towards seeing State power in more than its repressive functions; towards a total explanation which incorporates those apparently peripheral and independent institutions such as the family, the school and the communications media, in the reproduction of the social relations within which production takes place; and towards the most important realisation that, if these apparatuses function 'by ideology', by interpellating individual subjects in the positions created for them by the socio-technical division of labour, then 'an ideology always exists in an apparatus, and its practice, or practices. This existence is material'. [ibid. p. 156]

Part of the value of Althusser's account resides, therefore, in the way it opens on an extensive prospect of concrete historical work. It has been the French historian Michel Foucault who has done most to elaborate this materialist analysis in the concrete domain of real history; who has set out, in his own words, 'to investigate what might be most hidden in the relations of power; to anchor them in the economic infrastructures; to trace them not only in their governmental forms but also in the infra-governmental or para-governmental ones; to discover them in their material play'. [Foucault, 1977, p.158] Foucault has made what he calls 'the technology of power' the very principle, the central matrix, from which the particular processes of the present scientifico-juridical formation derive.* It is within this 'technology of power' that he has studied the genealogy of a cluster of institutions which, born of the profound reorganisation of social relations in European societies in the late eighteenth and early nineteenth centuries, have secreted new and strategically connected discourses about and within them; discourses which themselves function as formidable tools of control and power, producing a new realm of objects both as their targets and as instrumentalities.

It is in the context of the development of such a discursive formation that Foucault has seen the pathologising of the female body, in the eighteenth century, as the object of an immense medical attention; the reconstitution of homosexuality as illness in the new medical and psychiatric analyses of the 1870s; the 'discovery' of 'mental illness' in the workings of the asylum; the generation of delinquency in the new apparatus of the prison and the evolution of the new pseudo-discourses of criminology. All these are products of a determinate range of instruments – the hospital, the asylum, the prison, the school, the barracks – exercising a new range of techniques and acting with precision on their newly constituted and individuated subjects. In his studies of the 'birth' of this constellation of institutions in the eighteenth and nineteenth centuries, Foucault opens up a new territory that is neither violence nor ideology, coercion nor consent; that bears directly and physically upon the body – like the camera's gaze – yet is also a knowledge. This knowledge and this mastery constitute what he calls the political technology of the body: a diffuse and multiform instrumentation which cannot be localised in a particular type of institution or State apparatus but is situated at a different level, that of a 'micro-physics' of power, between the great functionings and the bodies themselves, decipherable only in a network of relations in constant tension which go right down into the depths of society.

Power, in this new type of society, has drained deeply into the gestures, actions, discourses and practical knowledge of everyday lives. The body itself is invested by power relations through which it is situated in a certain 'political economy', trained, supervised, tortured if necessary, forced to carry out tasks, to perform ceremonies, to emit signs. Power is exercised in,

*For the concept of 'the technology of power', see Foucault, 1977, (a)

and not just on, the social body because, since the eighteenth century, power has taken on a 'capilliary existence'. The great political upheaval which brought the bourgeoisie to power and established its hegemony across the social order was effected not only in the readjustment of those centralised institutions which constitute the political régime, but in an insistent and insidious modification of the everyday forms of the exercise of power....

'If the economic take-off of the West began with the techniques that made possible the accumulation of capital', Foucault argues, 'it might perhaps be said that the methods for administering the accumulation of men made possible a political take-off in relation to the traditional, ritual, costly, violent forms of power, which soon fell into disuse and were superseded by a subtle, calculated technology of subjection'. [Foucault, 1977a, pp 200-1] What was new in the late eighteenth century was that, by being combined and generalised, the techniques which made up this technology attained a level at which the formation of knowledge and the increase of power regularly reinforced one another in a circular process. It was a process with two movements: an epistemological thaw through a refinement of power relations; and a multiplication of the effects of power through the formation and accumulation of new forms of knowledge.

The development of the police force was integral to this process of change which began in the eighteenth century and effected, in the era of capitalism, a decisive shift from the total power of the monarch to the infinitely small exercise of power necessary to the discipline and productive exploitation of bodies accumulated in large numbers. In order to be effective, this new strategy of power needed an instrument of permanent, exhaustive, omnipresent surveillance, capable of making all visible, as long as it could itself remain invisible. The institution of the police offered just such a means of control which could be present in the very midst of the working population, under the alibi of a criminal threat itself manufactured across a set of new apparatuses ranging from the penitentiary to crime reporting and the crime novel. In England, it was in the latter half of the eighteenth century and the early nineteenth century that pressure grew to replace with a more rigorously organised force the inefficient system of unpaid constables and watchmen which had failed to control crime and disorder in towns swollen by great concentrations of factory workers. The common law conception of a socialised responsibility for keeping the peace dispersed throughout the community was no longer functioning in the urban industrial centres, in the new architecture of life and work, amidst the break-up of old social patterns and demands for new kinds of order regimented to meet the needs of regulation and production....

All kinds of official and semi-official forces grew up in the cities, especially around the ports, canals and navigable rivers where property was at stake. Yet there was still a concerted opposition, and not alone from the radical populace who always saw the police as an 'engine of oppression.' In 1812, the idea of a centralised force was still seen by one commentator as 'a system of tyranny; an organised army of spies and informers, for the destruction of all public liberty, and the disturbance of all private happiness'. [J. P. Smith, quoted in Thompson, 1968, p.89] A parliamentary committee of 1818 saw in Jeremy Bentham's proposals for a Ministry of Police 'a plan which would make every servant of every house a spy on the actions of his master, and all classes of society spies on each other.' [ibid, p.89]... Merchants and industrialists still feared any powers of inspection which might lead to searches of the houses and premises of those suspected of evading regulations. Older vested interests were also threatened by the new pervasive mechanisms of power. Tories feared an overriding of parochial and chartered rights. Whigs feared an increase in the power of central government. In 1822, a Select Committee of the House of Commons under the chairmanship of Sir Robert Peel once more rejected the idea of a police as being inconsistent with political freedom.

Yet it was this same Robert Peel who, as Home Secretary, was largely responsible for setting up the Metropolitan Police Force by Act of Parliament of 1829. Under the Act, three thousand blue-uniformed men, in seventeen divisions under a hierarchy of superintendents, inspectors and sergeants, controlled by a commissioner and ultimately responsible to the Home Secretary, were given jurisdiction over the area of a seven mile radius around Charing Cross. Despite continued agitation for its abolition, the force was bolstered by the appointment of the first special constables in 1831 and systematically extended, first to all urban areas of England and Wales by the Municipal Corporations Act of 1835, and then to the counties and rural areas by act of Parliament in 1856. By this same act of 1856, central government undertook to provide one quarter of the cost of pay and equipment and a regular inspectorate was set up to report on the state of efficiency of the widely dispersed constabularies. In this way, the powers and duties of the constable which derived from the ancient common law of England were subsumed but also transformed in the new police constable who was a member of a disciplined force, subject to strict codes and a hierarchy of inspection and supervision.

The control which such a force could exert was entirely bound up with the real need of capitalist industrial society to protect a wealth — in the form of the means of production — which was no longer in the hands of those who owned it, but of those whose labour set it to work and enabled a profit to be drawn from it. Linked to a series of similarly restructured mechanisms of power, it was the police which installed the new power-knowledge nexus in the very heart of working-class life, extending the emerging techniques of observation-domination beyond the walls of the new disciplinary and reformatory institutions such as prisons and penitentiaries. This special kind of observation which the police brought to bear had to be accumulated somehow. It began, therefore, to be assembled in a growing series of reports and registers. Throughout the eighteenth and nineteenth centuries, an immense police text increasingly covered society by means of a complex documentary organisation. But this documentation differed markedly from the traditional methods of judicial or administrative writing. What was registered in it were forms of conduct, attitudes, possibilities, suspicions: a permanent account of individuals' behaviour.

Now is perhaps the moment to turn to the complicity of photography in this spreading network of power. The early years of the development of the photographic process coincided approximately with the period of the introduction of the police service into this country and for more than a hundred years the two have progressed together....

The value of photographs for the purposes of identification was realised by the police at a very early stage. Though successful portraiture only became possible with the introduction of faster Petzval lenses and more sensitive Daguerreotype processes by 1841, the police employed civilian photographers from the 1840s onwards. The West Midlands Police Museum has a file of twenty-three ambrotypes of Birmingham prisoners taken by an unknown photographer in the 1850s and '60s. The poses are simple and plain but the delicate glass plates are each mounted in an ornamental frame, as if they were destined for the mantelpiece [Fig 1]. Other forces possess similarly early records, though it is most likely that at this time the work was carried out by professional photographers who were not yet members of the police force itself. The great growth of specialised police photographers followed the successful development of Sir Edward Henry's system of identification by means of fingerprints, introduced at New Scotland Yard in 1901. It soon became apparent that the only way to record finger impressions found at the scene of criminal activities was to photograph them and increasing numbers of police photographers were engaged to make best use of the specialised techniques.

Many thousands of identification pictures are now taken each year and the prints filed, together with the prisoner's fingerprints, at the Central Criminal Record Office and at Regional Record Centres. The police in this country have no authority to photograph an accused person who objects but, if necessary, an application for a remand in custody enables the prison governor to take the prisoner's photograph under an authority granted by Section 16 of the Prison Act of 1952. Governors of prisons, remand centres, detention centres and Borstal institutes are themselves required by the Criminal Justice Act of 1948 to register and photograph all persons convicted of crime. Act 17, Section 3, of the Alien Order Act of 1920 also empowered police officers to order the photographing of any alien; though the photographs required were to be full face, with head uncovered. They did not follow the standardised format of full-length, full-face and profile, laid down by the Committee on Crime Detection Report of 1938 which endeavored to improve the quality of prisoners' photographs, going so far as to describe the system of lighting and equipment to be used. What we have in this standardised image is more than a picture of a supposed criminal. It is a portrait of the product of the disciplinary method: the body made object; divided and studied; enclosed in a cellular structure of space whose architecture is the file-index; made docile and forced to yield up its truth; separated and individuated; subjected and made subject. When accumulated, such images amount to a new representation of society.

The use of photography here, as a process which enables accurate records to be made quickly and cheaply, is clearly underpinned by a whole set of assumptions about the reality of the photograph and the real 'in' the photograph which we shall have to examine more closely. For the moment, let us accept that, given this conception of photography, it could be and has been extended to most aspects of police work until, today, almost every photographic process and technique is in use.... The production of photographs for court evidence is now standard practice. Photographs are used to assist in the control of traffic and in the prosecution of traffic offences; to record evidence of bad driving from mobile police patrol cars; to help assess and apportion blame in fatal accident cases before the coroner's court; to provide accurate records of the scenes of crime and of clues found there; to demonstrate the photomicrographic analysis of forensic evidence; to present visual evidence to juries in the court room of wounding, injuries or damage; to record and deter offences against property; to identify thieves and other intruders; to detect forgeries and questionable documents and to elucidate the method employed to produce them; to observe unruly behaviour at football matches and other places of assembly; to survey road junctions and public spaces from overlooking buildings, nominally for the purposes of planning traffic flow but also to observe the movements of crowds and demonstrations; to catalogue the activities of suspected persons who are under observation; to prove adultery or cohabitation in divorce or social security proceedings. The list is not exhaustive.

However, it is not only the police and the prisons who have found photography such a convenient tool for their new strategies of power. If we examine any of the other institutions whose genealogy Foucault traces, we find photography seated calmly within them. From the mid-nineteenth century on, photography had its role to play in the workings of the factory, the hospital, the asylum, the reformatory and the school, as it did in the army, the family and the press, in the Improvement Trust, the Ordnance Survey and the expeditionary force.

In 1856, Dr Hugh Welch Diamond, founder member of the Royal Photographic Society and resident superintendent of the Female Department of the Surrey County Lunatic Asylum, read a paper to the Royal Society 'On the Application of Photography to the Physiognomic and Mental Phenomena of Insanity'. [Diamond in Gilman, 1976] In it, he expounded his theories on 'the peculiar application of photography to the delineation of insanity' and he illustrated his arguments with photographs he had taken, at his own expense, in the Surrey Asylum. Dr Diamond proposed that clinical photography had three important functions in the psychiatric practices of the day. First, it acted as an aid to treatment. Photographic portraits had a value 'in the effect which they produce upon the patient themselves':

> In very many cases they are examined with much pleasure and interest, but more particularly in those which mark the progress and cure of a severe attack of Mental Aberration. [Ibid, p.21]

Secondly, these portraits furnished a permanent record for medical guidance and physiognomic analysis:

> ...the Photographer secures with unerring accuracy the external phenomena of each passion, as the really certain indication of internal derangement, and exhibits to the eye the well-known sympathy which exists between the diseased brain and the organs and features of the body. [Ibid, p.20]...

Central to Diamond's conception of photography as a method of procuring a new kind of knowledge was the idea expressed in the *Lancet* that: 'Photography is so essentially the Art of Truth – and the representative of Truth in Art – that it would seem to be the essential means of reproducing all forms and structures of which science seeks for delineation.' [Lancet, 22 January, 1859, cited in Gilman, 1976, p.5] The links of the chain are truth, knowledge, observation, description, representation, record. The value of the camera was extolled because the optical and chemical processes of photography were taken to designate a scientifically exploited but 'natural' mechanism producing 'natural' images whose truth was guaranteed. Photography presented 'a perfect and faithful record, free altogether from the painful caricaturing which so disfigures almost all the published portraits of the insane as to render them nearly valueless either for purposes of art or of science'. [Diamond, *op. cit.*, p. 24]

It was free, too, from the imprecisions of verbal language:

> ... The Photographer needs in many cases no aid from any language of his own, but prefers to listen, with the picture before him, to the silent but telling language of nature... the picture speaks for itself with the most marked precision and indicates the exact point which has been reached in the scale of unhappiness between the first sensation and its utmost height. [Ibid, p.19]

... What is 'evident' from Diamond photographs, however, is that their naturalness and concision were the products of a complexly coded intertextuality. As in early police photographs, the props and devices were those of a simple studio, the background plain, the poses frontal or near frontal, and attention was directed towards the face and hands of the sitter [Fig. 3].... They drew not only on the conventions of contemporary portraiture but also on the already developed codes of medical and psychiatric illustration found in the line drawings and engravings of works such as J E D Esquirol's *Des Maladies Mentales* of 1838 or the *Physiognomy of Mental Diseases* published in the same year by Sir Alexander Morrison, Diamond's predecessor at the Surrey Asylum. What was remarkable in Diamond's work – it was not unique; it typified a whole tendency in nineteenth century photographic practice – was its constitution at the point where discourses of psychiatry, physiognomy, photographic science and aesthetics coincided and overlapped. But the site where they could work together and on each other was a regulated space: a political space, a space in the new institutional order. Here, the knowledge and truth of which photography became the guardian was inseparable from the power and control which it engendered.

The point was not lost on Dr Diamond. His last argument for clinical photography was that it functioned as a means of rapid identification.

> It is well known that the portraits of those who are congregated in prisons for punishment have often times been of much value in recapturing some who have escaped, or in proving with little expense, and with certainty a previous conviction; and similarly the portraits of the insane who are received into Asylums for protection, give to the eye so clear a representation of their case that on their readmission after temporary absence and cure - I have found the previous portrait of more value in calling to my mind the case and treatment, than any verbal description I may have placed on record. [Ibid, pp. 23-4]

The methods of the new police force are not far away. Commenting on Diamond's paper, T N Brushfield, superintendent of the Chester County Lunatic Asylum, confirmed his view:

> In the case of *criminal* lunatics, it is frequently of great importance that a portrait should be obtained, as many of them being originally of criminal disposition and education, if they do escape from the asylum are doubly dangerous to the community at large, and they may frequently be traced by sending their photographs to the police authorities (into whose hands they are very likely to fall) from some act of depredation they are likely to commit; the photographs would thus cause them to be identified, and secure their safe return to the asylum. [cited in Gilman, 1976, p.9]

Here, in the tentative photographic practice of Dr Diamond and like-minded superintendents of asylums, is the nexus Foucault describes: the very coincidence of an ever more intimate observation and an ever more subtle control; an ever more refined institutional order and an ever more encompassing discourse; an ever more passive subjection and an ever more dominant benevolent gaze....

Such uses of photography were not, however, confined to medicine. In the 1860s, the Stockport Ragged and Industrial School commissioned a local photographer to assemble an album of pictures of each of the teachers and children in the school. [Fig. 2] Similar records were kept in the Greenwich Hospital School. The next decade - the 1870s - saw a great expansion in the use of photographic documentation. The main prisons, such as Wandsworth and Millbank Prisons and Pentonville Penitentiary, set up their own studios employing staff photographers [Fig. 4] Local authorities commissioned photographic surveys of housing and living conditions in working class areas, and private societies, such as the Society for Photographing Relics of Old London, were founded. Children's Homes and Homes for 'Waifs and Strays' also followed the pattern of development, initially employing local portrait photographers then taking a photographer onto their staff. In May 1874,

Thomas John Barnardo opened his first Photographic Department in the 'Home for Destitute Lads' which he had founded at Stepney Causeway in 1871.... Between 1874 and 1905, Thomas Barnes and his successor, Roderick Johnstone, produced 55,000 photographs for Barnardo, mostly systematic records of the children as they entered and left the institution.

The uses of the photographs were familiar by now:

> ...to obtain and retain an exact likeness of each child and enable them, when it is attached to his history, to trace the child's career. [quoted in Lloyd and Wagner, 1974, p.14]
>
> To make the recognition easy of boys and girls guilty of criminal acts, such as theft, burglary or arson, and who may, under false pretences, gain admission to our Homes. Many such instances have occurred in which the possession of these photographs has enabled us to communicate with the police, or with former employers, and thus led to the discovery of offenders. By means of these likenesses children absconding from our Homes are often recovered and brought back, and in not a few instances, juveniles who have been stolen from their parents or guardians or were tempted by evil companions to leave home, and at last, after wandering for a while on the streets, found their way to our Institution, have been recognised by parents or friends and finally restored to their care. [Ibid, p.14]

Chronological reference albums were kept by the photographer, in which the albumen prints were pasted twelve to a page, with the names and dates of the children written under each photograph. Barnardo himself kept smaller versions with three photographs to a page, for his own use and to show visitors, parents and police. Photographs were also mounted on personal history sheets on which were filed printed details of each child's background – sometimes including the child's own statement – statistics of colouring, age, height, and subsequent reports and photographs recording the child's progress. [Figs. 5 and 6]

Since Barnardo's Homes were neither 'voting charities' nor sponsored by any of the churches, their need for funds was always acute. This induced Barnardo to launch an extensive publicity and advertising campaign which exploited the methods of the successful American revivalist churches.... From 1870, Barnardo commissioned 'before-and-after' photographs, purporting to show the children as they arrived at the Home and then, scrubbed and clean, busy in the workshops.... More than eighty such pictures were published. Some appeared in pamphlets telling a story of rescue from the iniquities of a previous life and of a happy life in the Home. Others were pasted onto complimentary cards of the 'once a little vagrant – now a little workman' type which also gave details of the work of the Home on their backs and sold in packs of twenty for five shillings or singly for sixpence. To the theme of observation-domination was added that of advertising and the body as commodity.

The body isolated; the narrow space; the subjection to an unreturnable gaze; the scrutiny of gestures, faces and features; the clarity of illumination and sharpness of focus; the names and number boards; these are the traces of power, reduplicated in numberless images, repeated countless times, whenever the photographer prepared an exposure, in police cell, prison, consultation room, asylum, Home or school. Foucault's metaphor for the new social order which was inscribed in these smallest exchanges is that of the 'Panopticon' – Jeremy Bentham's plan for a model institution in which each space and level would be exposed to the view of another, establishing a perpetual chain of observations which culminated in the central tower, itself open to constant public scrutiny. [see Foucault 1977a, pp 206-9 and 1978, pp 6-19]... Bentham's 'Panopticon' was the culmination and concrete embodiment of a disciplinary technique already elaborated across a range of institutions – barracks, schools, monasteries, reformatories, prisons – in which a temporal-spatial technology, with its enclosed spaces, cellular organisation, minutely graded hierarchical arrangements, and precise divisions of time, was set to work to drill, train, classify and survey bodies in one and the same movement. Foucault took this as a metaphor for that continual process of proliferating local tactics and techniques which operated in society on a micro-level, seeking to procure the maximum effect from the minimum effort and manufacturing docile and utilisable bodies. Yet, by the end of the nineteenth century, the need for this cumbersome architecture had gone. The new will to power, founded on a fateful threefold unity of knowledge, control and utility, could find a new metaphor in the unobtrusive cells of the photographic frame; in its ever more minute division of time and motion; in its ever finer scrutiny of bodies in stringent laboratory conditions....

To reiterate the point, it should be clear that when Foucault examines power he is not just examining a negative force operating through a series of prohibitions. Even where prohibitions can be shown to operate, they do so not only through edicts or laws but in the reality of institutions and practices where they are part of an elaborate economy including all kinds of incitements, manifestations and evaluations – in short, an entire complex outside which prohibitions cannot be understood. We must cease once and for all to describe the effects of power in negative terms – as exclusion, repression, censorship, concealment, eradication. In fact, power produces. It produces reality. It produces domains of objects, institutions of language, rituals of truth.... We might remember, for example, that Marx did not explain the misery of workers, as Proudhon did, as the effect of a concerted theft. He saw that the positive functioning of capitalist production – capitalism's *raison d'être* – was not directed towards starving the workers but that it could not develop without doing so. Marx replaced a negative, moralistic analysis with a positive one: the analysis of production. So Foucault, in examining the 'birth' of the prison, looks for the possible positive effects of punitive mechanisms rather than their repressive effects alone. He sees the development of penal institutions as a political tactic in a more general field of ways of exercising power. Similarly, in studying the genesis of the asylum, he asks; how did the power exerted in insanity produce psychiatry's 'true' discourse? When he turns to sexuality, he is concerned to discover why it has been the central object of examination, surveillance, avowal and transformation into discourse in Christian societies. What, he asks, are the positive mechanisms which, producing sexuality in this or that fashion, result in misery?

Crucial to the development of his thematic has been Foucault's rejection of the idea that knowledge and power are somehow counterposed, antithetical or even separable.... For Foucault, power produces knowledge. Power and knowledge directly imply one another. The exercise of power itself creates and causes to emerge new objects of knowledge and accumulates new bodies of information. Diffused and entrenched, the exercise of power is perpetually creating knowledge and, conversely, knowledge constantly induces effects of power....

Foucault's aim, therefore, is not to write the social history of prohibitions but to trace the political history of the production of 'humanity' as an object of knowledge for a discourse with the status of 'science', the status of 'truth.' As a prerequisite for such a study, he offers us a new set of concepts – a new vocabulary – which must compel us to work over again Gramsci's conception of hegemony and Althusser's conceptions of Ideological State Apparatuses and 'scientific' knowledge. More than this, it must direct our attention to a new and distinct level: that of mechanisms which cannot be reduced to theories, though they overlap them; which cannot be identified with apparatuses or institutions, though they are based on them; and which cannot be derived from moral choices, though they find their justification in morality. These are the modalities according to which power is exercised: the technologies of power.

In analysing these 'technologies', Foucault uncovers a stratum of materials which have so far remained below the threshold of historical visibility. His discoveries have importance both for new and old themes in the history of photography. For example, with the growth of the technology of control and reform, observation and training, a new curiosity arose about the individuals it was intended to transform. It was a curiosity which had been entirely unknown at the beginning of the eighteenth century. In the function of courts at this time, for instance, there had been no need to understand the prisoner or the conditions of the crime. Once guilt had been established, a set of penalties were automatically brought into play that were proportionate and fixed. Yet by the early nineteenth century, in France, Britain and the USA, judges, doctors and criminologists were seeking new techniques to gain a knowledge newly necessary to the administration of power. Prisoners were encouraged to write down their life stories. Dossiers and case histories were compiled. The simple technique of the examination was brought into play, evoking its use on soldiers and children, on the sick and insane.... The emergence of the 'documentary' as evidence of an individual 'case' was tied to this development of the examination and a certain disciplinary method and to that crucial inversion of the political axis of individuation which is integral to surveillance:

> For a long time ordinary individuality - the everyday individuality of everybody - remained below the threshold of description. To be looked at, observed, described in detail, followed from day to day by an uninterrupted writing was a privilege. The chronicle of a man, the account of his life, his historiography, written as he lived out his life formed part of the rituals of his power. The disciplinary methods reversed this relation, lowered the threshold of describable individuality and made of this description a means of control and a method of domination. It is no longer a monument for future memory, but a document for possible use. And this new describability is all the more marked in that the disciplinary framework is a strict one: the child, the patient, the madman, the prisoner, were to become, with increasing ease from the eighteenth century and according to a curve which is that of the mechanisms of discipline, the object of individual descriptions and biographical accounts. This turning of real lives into writing is no longer a procedure of heroisation; it functions as a procedure of objectification and subjection ... [Foucault 1977a, pp 1-2]

It is not only the 'turning of real lives into writing' which is implicated in this process, but also the insatiable appropriations of the camera. Whether it is John Thomson in the streets of London or Thomas Annan in the slums of Glasgow [Figs. 7 and 8]; whether it is Dr Diamond among the female inmates of his asylum in Surrey or Arthur Munby among the trousered pit-girls of Wigan [Fig. 9]: what we see is the extension of a 'procedure of objectification and subjection,' the transmission of power in the synaptic space of the camera's examination.[1]

Whatever the claims of the traditional evaluations of such photographic 'records', whatever the pretensions of the 'humane' and documentary tradition, we must see them now in relation to the 'small' historical problems with which Foucault concerns himself: problems of the entry of the individual into the field of knowledge, of the entry of the individual description, of the cross-examination and the file. It is in what he calls these 'ignoble' archives that Foucault sees the emergence of that modern play over bodies, gestures and behaviour which is the so-called 'science of man' and the constitution of the modern state. [Foucault, 1977a, p.191]

I may have created the depressing impression of an inescapable network of immanent relations of power. Yet, once we have grasped that power is not to be identified with its terminal forms– once we have seen that: 'Power is not an institution, a structure, or a certain force with which certain people are endowed; it is the name given to a complex strategic situation in a given society' [Foucault, 1976, p. 123]– then we can also grasp the possibilities of resistance. It is because power is relational that there is no power without resistance. As soon as there is a power relation, that relation can be modified or deflected within certain determinate conditions and according to a definite strategy...

The form or forms of this resistance– which are so important to social advance yet have been so very little analysed– are bound up, at the level with which we are concerned, with the changed role of intellectuals in the modern technology of power. Analysis of this will show that we are no longer concerned with the intellectual who deals in generalities, prophecies, and legislative edicts, that is, with the 'traditional intellectual' practising writing and claiming a universal consciousness; but with a whole new configuration of 'specific' intellectuals, strategically situated at precise points in specific sectors by their professional conditions of work and their conditions of life. The extreme development of the socio-technical division of labour has produced a multiform ensemble of experts and technicians– including all kinds of photographers– who have direct and localised relations with particular

[1] JOHN THOMSON, Fellow of the Royal Geographical Society, travelled extensively in the Far East, publishing four volumes of *Illustrations of China and its People* (1873-4). With Adolphe Smith he co-authored *Street Life in London* which appeared in monthly instalments from February 1877.

THOMAS ANNAN photographed in and around Glasgow between 1867 and 1877 for the Glasgow City Improvement Trust, publishing *The Old Closes and Streets of Glasgow* in 1868 – the first commissioned work of its kind.

ARTHUR MUNBY recorded details of his encounters with working women from the 1850s on and championed women's right to work at and wear what they wished. He bought and commissioned an extensive collection of photographs of labouring women.

domains of knowledge and particular institutions, who have an intimate familiarity with the specific constraints which hold there, and who are therefore capable of locating and marking the weak points, the openings, the lines of force.

If we could escape our nostalgia for the great universal intellectuals with their visions of the world, we might see our way towards exploiting new strategic possibilities; towards a new kind of political effect based on the specialised knowledge of specific intellectuals and not on a universalising discourse. In the domain of photography, what this implies is not an attempt to devise a single stylistic strategy which will meet all contingencies, but a determination to begin the work of mapping out certain positions within an indeterminate field. [see Tagg, 1979, pp. 70-1] We must pinpoint those strategic kinds of intervention which can both open up different social arenas of action and stretch the institutional order of the practice by deploying or developing new modes of production, distribution and circulation; by exploiting different formats; by evolving different formal solutions; by cutting different trajectories across the ruling codes of pictorial meaning; and by establishing different relationships both with those who are pictured and those who view the pictures. There is no centre to such a strategy; only a multiplicity of local incursions in a constantly shifting ground of tactical actions – specific contests which link up with others in all sorts of ways, which may hold significance for a chain of related struggles, and which are the precondition for any more concerted confrontation.

There is a danger that the particular struggles of photographers and other functional intellectuals may become too dispersed and fragmentary. What gives such sectional actions a wider significance are their precise positions in that network of constraints which produces truth and which, in turn, induces the regular effects of power. That is to say, what is crucial is their special position in the 'political economy' of truth in our society to which Foucault has given the name of 'a régime of truth.' [Foucault, 1977b, pp. 13-14; 1977a, pp. 27-8]

A régime of truth is that circular relation truth has to the systems of power which produce and sustain it, and to the effects of power which it induces and which redirect it. Such a régime has been not only an effect, but a condition of the formation and development of capitalist societies and, to contest it, it is not enough to gesture at some 'truth' somehow emancipated from every system of power. Truth itself is already power, bound to the political, economic and institutional régime which produces it. We must forget the claims of a discredited documentary tradition to fight 'for' 'truth' or 'in favour' of 'truth' and see that the battle is one that should be directed at the rules, operative in our society, according to which 'true' and 'false' representations are separated.

It is a battle waged against those institutions privileged and empowered in our society to produce and transmit 'true' discourse. It is a battle – going beyond the sectoral and professional interests of photography – around the specific effects of power of this truth and the economic and political role it plays...

The territory of the dispute must be clear. You will see that we are thrown back again on that knot of assumptions about the nature of photography which was left to be unravelled in my discussion of police photography. It is the use of the photograph in police work – primarily for its 'value as evidence' – and the insertion of the photograph in legal structures that offer a privileged view of the organisation of the régime of photographic truth in our society and it is to this that I want to turn.

In a manual of police photography written by a former Detective Chief Inspector of Birmingham City Police, we find the following advice. First, on the level of production:

> A good record should of course be properly exposed, processed and printed. It must be correctly focused and sharp throughout, and all vertical lines of the picture must be upright and should not converge in the print.
>
> A photograph should include everything appertaining to its subject, and relevant to its purpose. If this cannot be done with one picture, then others must be taken in order that the whole subject is covered. Photographs of scenes of crime and other aids to evidence are usually examined in conjunction with a detailed plan to scale, showing the scene and enabling a true picture to be obtained.
>
> Photographs made for the purpose of crime detection or for production in any court proceedings should not be retouched, treated or marked in any way. Exaggerated lighting effects must not be used, and deep shadows or burnt-out highlights could reduce the value, as evidence, of an otherwise good record picture.
>
> Photographs should, where possible, be taken from eye level and this applies to traffic-accident photographs where the views of the drivers concerned may be an important factor.
>
> Prints are usually preferred on the 'soft' side, because detail is more important than print brightness.
>
> The police photographer who has in mind these basic requisites of a good record photograph will standardise his procedure and technique in order that the right type of photograph is produced automatically. [Pountney 1971, p.3]

Secondly, on the mode of presentation of the images:

> In producing photographs to court, the police photographer must state on oath the time, day and date he took the photographs, and the fact that he processed the negatives himself. He then produces the negatives to show that they have not been retouched or interfered with in any way, and finally produces prints (usually enlarged from the negatives) which are entered as exhibits with the negatives. [ibid, pp.3-4]

If this cannot be done, an affidavit sworn by the technician who processed the film or even the technician in person will have to be produced to prove the chain of possession....

Confirmation of these basic conditions and procedures comes from the standard British and American work of reference on photographic evidence by S G Ehrlich, a specialist in the preparation of court exhibits, Fellow of the Royal Microscopical Society and member of The American Society of Photographic Scientists and Engineers. Ehrlich is at pains to define the exact requirements of photography as an aid to counsel in civil cases so as to distinguish it from amateur, freelance or photojournalistic practice. But, behind his detailed technical discussion lies the notion that:

> In addition to understanding the scientific principles of physics, optics and chemistry on which photography depends, the good photographer must have the imagination and creative ability to reproduce scenes on films so that they will convey to the viewer the same information and impressions he would have received had he directly observed the scene. [Ehrlich, 1967, p.10]

Later Ehrlich summarises the nature of legal photography thus:

> Legal photographs are made for the purpose of ultimate use in a courtroom, or at least to be exhibited to people who are to be informed or persuaded by them. In making photographs for use in litigation, lawyers and photographers should strive for 'legal quality', a term used here to describe photographs having certain characteristics of objectivity and accuracy.
>
> So far as is possible, photographs should show the matter depicted in a neutral, straightforward way. The photographer should be cautioned against producing dramatic effects; any drama in the picture should emanate from the subject matter alone, and not from affected photographic techniques, such as unusual camera angles, printing variations, cropping and the like. Any such attempt to dramatise photographs may result in their

> exclusion and a consequent suspicion on the part of the jurors that the party offering such photographs cannot be trusted. Therefore, commercial photographers who are not experienced in legal work should be impressed with the importance of a neutral approach when making photographs for courtroom use.
>
> This is not to say that photographers making photographs should dispense with the elements of imagination and artistry, but only that they should strive for accuracy rather than effect. Indeed, advanced techniques,and the use of very specialised and delicate equipment, are often necessary in order to produce photographs that are fair and accurate representations of the matters they depict.
>
> There are courtroom advantages to be gained from using photographs that appear to have been professionally made. Compared with amateur snapshots or home movies, professional photographs have an aura of objectivity and purposefulness, and it is less likely that there will be anything in their appearance to divert the attention of viewers from the matters they depict.
>
> On the other hand, there are instances in which counsel must use photographs of amateurish appearance simply because they are the best, or the only, pictures available. Furthermore, counsel should avoid obtaining photographs that appear too slickly made or too expensive, lest the jurors come to believe that the presentation is being overdone. Legal photographs should be rich in information but not expensive in appearance. [ibid, p.26-7]

These are disarmingly frank texts, with their recurrent themes of sharpness and frontality, exhaustive description and true representation, the outlawing of exaggerated effects and any kind of manipulation, standardised processing and careful presentation, and the expertise and professional status of the photographer. They set these forward, unabashed, as criteria which establish the credentials of the print as a 'good record picture' of 'legal quality' and therefore guarantee its objectivity and accuracy or even that it presents a scene as it would have been viewed if one had been there. They are unshaken in their belief in the photograph as a direct transcription of the real. The falsifications that can occur — cropping, retouching, interference with the negative — are only perversions of this purity of nature....

How are we to explain this configuration of demands and expectations levelled at the photograph? What are we to make of this assertion and qualification of its 'truth'? And how may we bring our explanation closer to our analysis of the field of power relations which constitutes the régime of truth? Recent advances in semiology and the theory of the subject have shown that every text - including the photographic text - is an activity of production of meaning which is carried on within a certain *régime of sense*. It is this régime which gives the productivity of the discourse a certain fixity, dependent on the limits the society in question sets itself, in which the text is produced as natural.

The dominant form of signification in bourgeois society is the *realist* mode, which is fixed and curtailed, which is complicit with the dominant sociolects and repeated across the dominant ideological forms. Realism offers a fixity in which the signifier is treated as if it were identical with a pre-existent signified and in which the reader's role is purely that of consumer. It is this realist mode with which we are confronted when we look at the photograph as evidence. In realism, the process of production of a signified through the action of a signifying chain is not seen. It is the product that is stressed, and production that is repressed. The complex codes or use of language by which realism is constituted appear of no account. All that matters is the illusion; just as in the capitalist market economy, all that matters is the value of the commodity measured against the general medium of exchange — money. Production is entirely elided. [See Barthes, 1975, and Coward and Ellis, 1977, pp.45 - 60]

Realism is a social practice of representation: an overall form of discursive production, a normality which allows a strictly delimited range of variations. It works by the controlled and limited recall of a reservoir of similar 'texts,' by a constant repetition, a constant cross-echoing. By such 'silent quotation,' a relation is established between the realist 'text' and other 'texts' from which it differs and to which it defers. It is this mutuality which summons up the power of the real: a reality of the intertext beyond which there is no-sense. What lies 'behind' the paper or 'behind' the image is not reality – the referent – but reference: a subtle web of discourse through which realism is enmeshed in a complex fabric of notions, representations, images, attitudes, gestures and modes of action which function as everyday know-how, 'practical ideology,' norms within and through which people live their relation to the world. It is by the routes it opens to this complex sphere that the realist text trades with that generally received picture of what may be regarded as 'real' or 'realistic' which is not recognised as such – as a picture – but presents itself as, precisely, the Reality. It is a traffic which brings into circulation not a personal and arbitrary 'association of ideas' but a whole hidden corpus of knowledge, a social knowledge, that is called upon through the mechanism of connotation and which gives the encounter with the régime of sense its solidity.

We are not dealing here with a process of signification which is immutable but one that was, in Nietzsche's term, historically 'incorporated' and which is historically changing. [Nietzsche, 1974 pp. 167-71] Its origins take us back to that same period in which Foucault traced the emergence of a cluster of institutions: the 'disciplinary archipelago.' A crucial part of the attempt of the emergent bourgeoisie to establish its hegemony in the eighteenth and nineteenth centuries was the creation of several institutions of language: in England, for example, the Royal Society with its 'scientific' philosophy of language, as well as the institutions of journalism and literature. [Coward and Ellis, 1977, p.47] It was across such institutions that the realist convention was installed and ceased to be visible as convention, becoming natural – identical with reality. A general evaluation of discourse was established whose absolute value was that of reality itself. The dominant discourse attained this through the creation of an identity between signifier and signified. All other discourses were to be gauged against this measure, according to the varying degrees of 'truth' they contained, so that a strict positionality was established whose reference point was the dominant discourse which appeared to have its point of origin in the Real.

At the same time, this whole process could only operate by placing the consumers – the readers – of the texts in an imaginary position of transcendence in relation to the system, in order that the texts should be intelligible. Just as Marx has shown that recognised, socially fixed positions are necessary for the exchange of commodities which functions through a system of equivalences, so realism fixes the positions of its readers in order that the transaction between signifier and signified may take place. Realism sets its subjects in place at the point of intelligibility of its activity, in a position of observation and synthesis which cannot be questioned by the flux of the text and which cannot be thrown into process by the sliding of signifiers that disestablishes social positionality.

Thus the mechanism of realism has been effected over a multitude of 'texts' – in our case, of photographs and their supporting discourses – which appear diverse and changing but are fixed and dependent on practices of production and reading which seem spontaneous but are determined by forms of behaviour fundamental to capitalist societies: a pattern of instrumentality and consumption which – as in sexuality and economics, the other major forms of exchange by which society reproduces itself – cannot function without a fixed positionality. To intervene in this institution of language is, therefore, to create a disturbance whose effects must necessarily be felt in the other modes of reproduction. What is put at issue are those chains of social meaning which were forged with the irruption of the financial bourgeoisie, whose wealth lay not in the forms of land, title and heredity traditional to feudal and early bourgeois society, but in exchange, the possession of money and the skill in its use. What is at stake in struggle is not only this political economy but what invests it: a universalised mode of representation in which things are individuated, separated and assigned places in an order of equivalence, an 'economy of signs,' a régime of sense...

The documentary mode however... cannot make such an intervention because it is already implicated in the historically developed techniques of observation-domination and because it remains imprisoned within an historical form of the régime of truth and sense. Both these bind it fundamentally to the very order which it has thought to subvert.

References

ALTHUSSER, L 'Ideology and Ideological State Apparatuses (Notes Towards an Investigation),' in *Lenin and Philosophy and other essays,* New Left Books, 1971.

BARTHES, R., *S/Z,* Jonathan Cape, 1975.

COWARD, R., and ELLIS, J. *Language and Materialism. Developments in Semiology and the Theory of the subject*, Routledge and Kegan Paul, 1977.

EHRLICH, S. G., *Photographic Evidence, The Preparation and Use of Photography in Civil and Criminal Cases,* 1967.

FOUCAULT, M., *La Volonté de Savoir,* Paris, 1976.

FOUCAULT, M., 'Power and Sex: An interview with Michel Foucault,' *Telos,* No. 32, summer 1977.

FOUCAULT, M., *Discipline and Punish. The Birth of the Prison,* Allen Lane, 1977 [a].

FOUCAULT, M., 'The Political Function of the Intellectual,' *Radical Philosophy,* No. 17, summer 1977 [b].

FOUCAULT, M., 'Prison Talk: an interview with Michel Foucault,' *Radical Philosophy,* No. 16, spring 1977 [c].

FOUCAULT, M., 'The eye of Power,' *Semiotexte,* vol. 3, no. 2, 1978.

GILMAN, S. L., (ed), *The Face of Madness: Hugh W. Diamond and the Origin of Psychiatric Photography,* New Jersey, 1976.

GRAMSCI, A., 'State and Civil Society' in Hoare, Q., and Nowell-Smith, G., (ed.) *Selections from the Prison Notebooks,* Lawrence and Wishart, 1971.

LLOYD, V., and WAGNER, G., *The Camera and Dr Barnardo,* Hertford, 1974.

NIETZSCHE, F., *The Gay Science,* New York, 1974.

POUNTNEY, H., *Police Photography,* 1971.

TAGG, J., 'A Socialist Perspective on Photographic Practice' in Hill, P., Kelly, A., and Tagg, J., *Three Perspectives on Photography,* 1979.

THOMPSON, E. P., *The Making of the English Working Class,* Penguin, 1968.

Figure 1 ANON. Birmingham Prisoner. Ambrotype, 1860-62. (*West Midlands Police*)

Figure 2 ANON. The Stockport Ragged and Industrial School. Albumen carte-de-visite, c. 1865. (*Stockport Library Local History Department*)

Figure 3 DR. H.W. DIAMOND Inmate of the Surrey Asylum, from album entitled *Portraits of Insanity.* Albumen print, 1852-56. (*Royal Society of Medicine*)

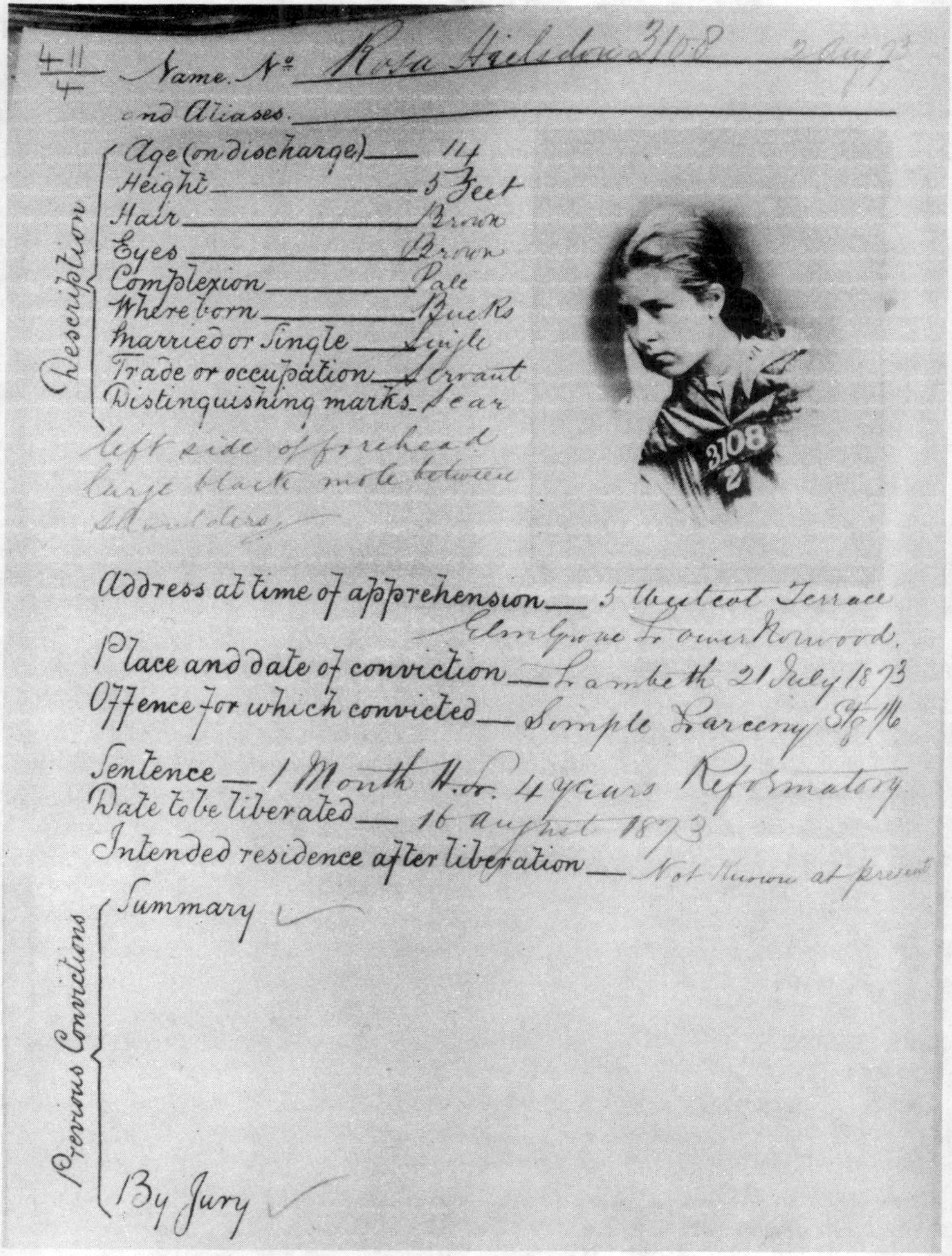

4/11

Name. No. Rosa Heilsdon 3108 2 Aug 73

and Aliases.

Description
- Age (on discharge) — 14
- Height — 5 Feet
- Hair — Brown
- Eyes — Brown
- Complexion — Pale
- Where born — Bucks
- Married or Single — Single
- Trade or occupation — Servant
- Distinguishing marks — Scar left side of forehead large black mole between shoulders

3108
2

Address at time of apprehension — 5 Westcot Terrace Elm Grove Lower Norwood.

Place and date of conviction — Lambeth 21 July 1873

Offence for which convicted — Simple Larceny [illegible]

Sentence — 1 Month H.L. 4 years Reformatory

Date to be liberated — 16 August 1873

Intended residence after liberation — Not known at present

Previous Convictions
- Summary ✓
- By Jury ✓

Figure 4 Wandsworth Prison Records, dated 1873. Photographer unknown. (*Public Record Office*)

Admitted January 5th, 1876.

Aged 16 *Years.*

Height, 4-*ft.* 11-*in.*

Color of { *Hair, Dark Brown.*
Eyes, Brown.

Complexion, Dark.

Marks on body—None.

If Vaccinated—Right Arm.

If ever been in a Reformatory or Industrial School? No.

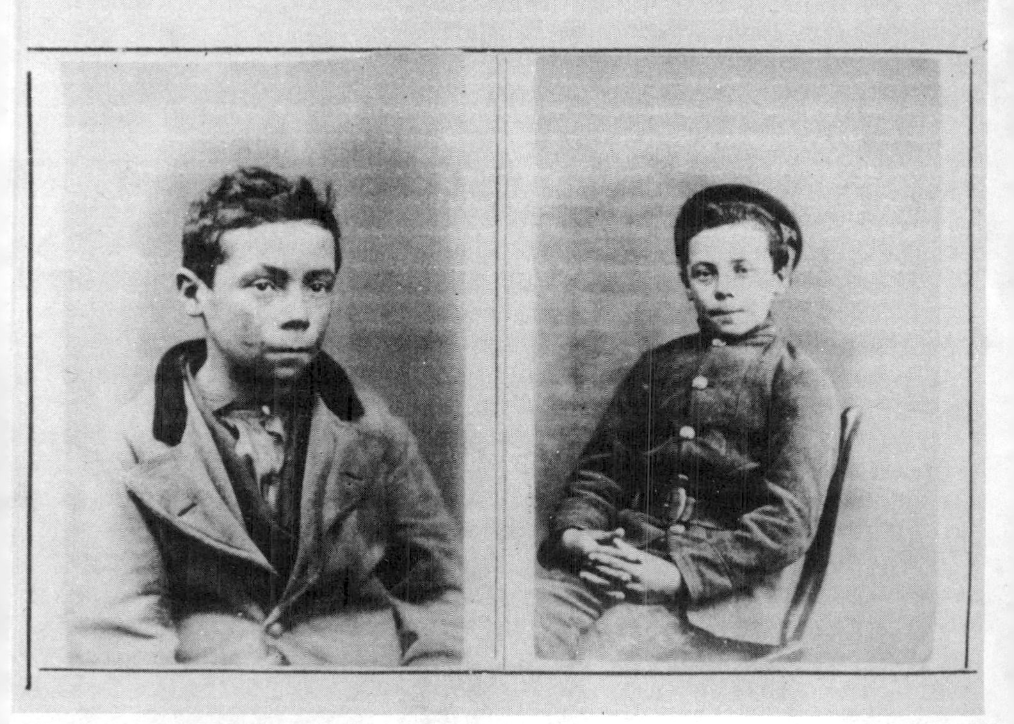

Figure 5 THOMAS BARNES and RODERICK JOHNSTONE. Section of a *Personal History* of a child at Dr Barnardo's Homes. Albumen prints, 1874-83. (*Dr Barnardo's*)

Left Figure 6 THOMAS BARNES and RODERICK JOHNSTONE. Portrait of a child at Dr Barnardo's Homes. Albumen print, 1874-83. (*Dr Barnardo's*)

Opposite Figure 8 THOMAS ANNAN. From *Photographs of Old Closes, Street, &c.* Albumen print, 1868-77. (*Mansell Collection*)

Right Figure 7 'The Crawlers', from *Street Life in London.* Woodburytype, 1877/8. (*Mansell Collection*)

Figure 9 Photograph from A.J. Munby's collection: 'Wigan Pit Brow Girls'. Carte-de-visite by John Cooper of Wigan. (*The Master and Fellows of Trinity College Cambridge*)

Index

Note: because of the frequency of usage of the words 'culture', 'ideology' and 'class' in this collection, they have not been indexed save for those places where they occur in the context of, for example, 'working-class culture', or where a particular author's use of one of these terms is significantly important to be registered, for example, 'Gramsci – concept of ideology'.